Rube Foster in H

Also by Larry Lester

Baseball's First Colored World Series: The 1924 Meeting of the Hilldale Giants and Kansas City Monarchs (McFarland, 2006)

Rube Foster in His Time

On the Field and in the Papers with Black Baseball's Greatest Visionary

Larry Lester

McFarland & Company, Inc., Publishers
Jefferson, North Carolina, and London

Library of Congress Cataloguing-in-Publication Data

Lester, Larry.
Rube Foster in his time : on the field and in the papers
with black baseball's greatest visionary / Larry Lester.
p. cm.
Includes bibliographical references and index.

ISBN 978-0-7864-3927-0
softcover : acid free paper ∞

1. Negro leagues— History.
2. Foster, Rube, 1879–1930.
3. Baseball players— United States— Biography.
4. African American baseball players— Biography.
5. Baseball team owners— United States— Biography.
I. Title.
GV865.F63L47 2012 796.357092—dc23 [B] 2012022245

British Library cataloguing data are available

© 2012 Larry Lester. All rights reserved

No part of this book may be reproduced or transmitted in any form or by any means, electronic or mechanical, including photocopying or recording, or by any information storage and retrieval system, without permission in writing from the publisher.

On the cover: Opie Otterstad (opieart.com), *Rube Foster #1, TBHOF.*
Acrylic on found fence board. 32" × 22". 2004

Manufactured in the United States of America

McFarland & Company, Inc., Publishers
Box 611, Jefferson, North Carolina 28640
www.mcfarlandpub.com

Table of Contents

Acknowledgments

First and foremost I would like to thank Charles Whitehead, author of the 1980 book *A Man and His Diamonds: The Story of the Great Andrew (Rube) Foster*, which laid the foundation for all subsequent research on Foster's journey to achieve equality on the playing field and in mainstream society.

By the time I started this project ten years later, in the early nineties, I shared Mr. Whitehead's passion to examine Mr. Foster's life and answer some previously unanswered questions. Was Rube Foster born in Calvert, or LaGrange, or Winchester, Texas? What was the scope of Foster's mental illness within the medical context of the late twenties? What really prompted the Frank Leland and Rube Foster split? Is there statistical evidence of Rube Foster's pitching greatness? And lastly, does Andrew Foster deserve the title "The Father of Black Baseball" so often bestowed by writers and historians?

These questions and many others could never have been answered without the benefit of several contributors, researchers, editors, and historians. My 15-year journey has resulted in a massive debt to several people. The generosity of Doris Foster, daughter of Rube's only son Mack, was a major contributor in providing vintage photographs, along with essential family genealogy. Genealogists Tim Rives with the National Archives of Kansas City, Missouri, and Bob Bailey from Gainesville, Florida, provided documentation to support her claims.

Thanks to Sherry Williams, executive director of the Bronzeville Historical Society for the informative and personal tour of Chicago to view Rube Foster's stomping grounds.

As research can be a thankless endeavor, I must give a shout out to Dr. James Brunson, III, from DeKalb, Illinois, for his journey through several local Texas libraries in search of information about Foster's early years as a novice pitcher. Notwithstanding personal family setbacks, Brunson's timely discoveries were unprecedented in providing quality and credence to Foster's semi-pro legacy in Texas.

Other researchers include Trey Strecker and Geri Strecker from Ball State University, who documented Foster's pre-teen years as a laborer on Rabb's cotton plantation. Trey and Geri excavated county and state records on visits to the Lone Star State, and they mined information from hundreds of small town newspapers that mentioned Foster.

Gary Ashwill, whose blog (Agate Type) is well-known to researchers of black baseball, was able to find what other Foster biographers could not: the heralded matchup between George "Rube" Waddell and Andrew "Rube" Foster. Ashwill's discovery filled in the last important piece of the puzzle, I'd been working on.

I also owe tremendous thanks to editors Leslie Heaphy from Kent State University (editor of *Black Ball: A Negro Leagues Journal*) and Lisa Feder of Ingleside, Illinois, for their diligence and patience in helping me navigate the English language and its grammar.

Of course, no biographical work can be considered complete without the input of the two walking encyclopedias of black baseball, Dick Clark of Ypsilanti, Michigan, and Wayne Stivers of Plano, Illinois. These statistical and fact-checking gurus provided irrefutable, never-before-published data about Foster.

I am also grateful to the law firm of Brandon Williams and Raphael Morris, LLC, out of St. Louis, Missouri, and their attorney Branden Gregory for his excellent legal brief about the controversial and sometimes symbiotic relationships between Frank Leland, Beauregard Moseley, and Rube Foster.

With great pride, I am particularly appreciative of my daughters, Marisa and Erica Joi, for typing mountainous portions of the raw manuscript in its early stages, while Tiffany Lester Gillam, M.D., offered her medical evaluation of Foster's listed cause of death.

And lastly, a thank you for a man I hold in high esteem for his integrity and commitment to our game, Fay Vincent, baseball commissioner from 1989 to 1992. I thought it would be fitting to have the fans' "Last Commissioner" write the foreword about black baseball's first commissioner.

Overall, the above family of friends provided a guiding light to help me write the comprehensive biography on black baseball's greatest, but still unheralded icon.

Finally, many thanks to the staff at McFarland, who graciously allowed me to miss the March, 2008, deadline several times, as I concentrated on the complexities and challenges of hosting the recent Jerry Malloy Negro League Conferences in Chicago, Pittsburgh, and Birmingham, the biggest and best black baseball conference in America.

Foreword

by Former Commissioner Fay Vincent

This is a remarkable book about a remarkable baseball figure. Rube Foster was the founder of the Negro National League and the first President and Commissioner of black baseball. Finally we have his full story with all the glory and all the tragedy ably and deftly assembled by Larry Lester, perhaps the leading historian of black baseball. With careful research Lester takes the reader through the early days of black baseball, before 1900, when Foster emerges as a powerful, hard-throwing pitcher who quickly gains fame during the rough and tumble days when there was little structure to black baseball and when the games were played on poor fields and with few rewards.

Foster was a big man in many ways. He knew baseball well and had a strong sense of what was necessary to build black baseball. He realized the value of organization and the need for cooperation among the early owners of the emerging black teams. Over the first quarter of the twentieth century he worked diligently to forge a league where none had been thought possible. In the process he fought and struggled, often bitterly and sometimes in court, with those who did not agree with his plans or with his decisions. But in that time, before a sad death from the complications of syphilis, he owned and ran his team, the Chicago American Giants, and stood at the top of black baseball from 1911 until he became seriously ill in 1926. He was a combination, one can say without hyperbole, of such baseball luminaries as Connie Mack, Judge Landis and Christy Mathewson. As a player he was as fine a pitcher as ever played in black baseball, and he surely ranks among the finest baseball executives. But despite acclaim during his life, he has not been treated to the kind of historical regard he has deserved. Larry Lester will have changed all that by giving Foster and his achievements the kind of careful display they clearly deserve.

This book is not hagiography. Much of it is original source material and one can read the contemporary accounts of Foster's activities. Foster is presented to us as a man of his era who was obliged to confront the vicious racism that surrounded everything he tried to achieve. Yet he regularly spoke of the time when the races would play baseball together and he was among the very first to organize games between black teams and even the Chicago Cubs. Not a romantic dreamer, he was well ahead of his time in many ways. Yet this is essentially a sad story, and Foster's victories and his many notable achievements are necessarily set against the times in which he lived. Like many pioneers he suffered and died without seeing the product of his efforts and the best days of his Negro League. One can hardly imagine what he would think today were he to see the impact black players have had on our great game. Without Rube Foster our game today would be very different.

This book is the story of an authentic American baseball icon. One can only hope Rube Foster will finally begin to be recognized for his superb contributions to the great American institution that for so long refused to permit his race to share the field. It is thus a story of shame and redemption. It is the story of our country.

Preface

If there's a book you really want to read, but it hasn't been written yet, then you must write it.—Toni Morrison

There have been more than 120 books in three languages published on the great "Bambino" Babe Ruth. And more than 200 books on American hero Jackie Robinson. These publications range from comic books and children's books, to studious biographies and pictorial histories.

Are all of these publications necessary to tell the story of just one man? Could one book comprehensively capture the essence of these two men's careers, their personal lives and post-career achievements?

Does the plethora of books on Ruth and Robinson encourage more research and more publications, or discourage scholars new to the discipline? Perhaps we will never know the answer, but the unknown provided me with an incentive to write the definitive Rube Foster biography.

My interest was not just in Rube Roster, the pitcher and emblematic mastermind of black ball, but Foster the man. What was behind the man with the smelly pipe, the rolodex memory, and the narcissistic vision? How was his relationship with other, more restrained egos such as those of Frank Leland, C.I. Taylor, Tenny Blount and Ed Bolden, to name a few?

In answering these questions, I examined Foster's letters and editorials, ultimately deciding to embed them within the narrative, often in their entirety. These writings, along with others included here and written about Foster by his contemporaries, are invaluable for what they reveal about his several career incarnations.

This book differs from conventional biography in at least one other important way. The appendices account for roughly a third of its bulk, and a good argument can be made that they contain nearly as much useful information as the main text. Made up of lists, records, court depositions, medical documents, charts, box scores, and other items compiled over the years, they amount to a valuable resource in and of themselves.

There have been other books about the life and career of Foster—Robert Cottrell's *The Best Pitcher in Baseball* perhaps most notable among them—but there continue to be large gaps in our knowledge. My intention, then, has been to provide a one-stop resource for those with a strong interest in Rube Foster, his teams and time, and the very rise of the Negro Leagues. It is hoped that the hybrid nature of the book will—in combining elements of biography, anthology, and reference—encourage further, deeper work on Foster, whose central position in the history of black baseball is or should be beyond question.

Introduction

"Show me a hero, and I will write you a tragedy."— F. Scott Fitzgerald[1]

"When the big game shall have become history there will stalk across the pages of the record a massive figure and its name will be Andrew Foster. A loud voiced man with a smelly pipe who kids his opponents and makes them like it. The dominant power of the commission and of the league.... The master of the show who moves the figures on his checkerboard at will. The smooth-toned counselor of infinite wisdom and sober thought.... The kind who, to suit his purpose, assumes the robes of his jester. Always the center of any crowd, the magnet attracting both the brains and the froth of humanity. Cold in refusals, warm in assent.... Appraising his man the while he dissembles. Known to everybody— knows everybody. That's Rube."— Dr. W. Rollo Wilson[2]

Rube Foster went from son of a preacher man to boll weevil picker[3] to legendary pitcher to entrepreneur to founder of leagues and livelihoods. His vision became a symbol of hope shared by a generation of hopefuls. He was an agent for social change in America.

If you wrap them figuratively in the American flag, boxing promoter Don King and Rube Foster are both symbolic of the American dream: self-made, self-reliant, and self-promoters of the red, white and blue of patriotic hypocrisy. Foster was an early version of King; King combs his hair with electricity, while Foster electrified baseball fans with his stylish and up-tempo play. King smokes Cuban cigars while Rube puffed a malodorous pipe. King, aptly named, rules boxing promotions; while Foster, aptly named, fathered and fostered the grown-up fairy tale of blacks playing big-time sandlot baseball. You either love them or hate them. For both of them, power was and is the ultimate aphrodisiac, and their rule omnipotent. Like King, Foster was flamboyant, braggadocian and egotistical, with a gift for capturing any fan's fancies. "Only in America!" became their mantra.

Foster's American dream started in the segregated South. Like many black youths from this period, Foster had limited educational opportunities. The 1896 Plessy v. Ferguson landmark United States Supreme Court decision had formalized the practice of segregated educational and public accommodation facilities under the doctrine of "separate but equal." The illogical "separate but equal" remained standard dogma in U.S. law until its final repudiation in the Supreme Court decision Brown v. Board of Education of May 17, 1954.

With schools segregated, and funding controlled by white officials, some states were unwilling and/or underfunded to equally finance schools for both white and black students. Oftentimes colleges associated with churches offered the only means of an education for black children.

Since many Southern school districts had shortened terms to accommodate the crop cycle, black students were forced to miss school because they were needed at home or the farm, thus found themselves at a further disadvantage. Pressures from family and landlords and the shortage of facilities for older students forced many out of school by the sixth grade. Often elementary school was the pinnacle of educational achievement for a Southern black youth. A high school or middle school education was simply not offered to rural blacks, due to lack of separated facilities, state funding and de facto shortage of black educators. Southern states usually spent less money on education than their Northern counterparts, and black schools seldom received their equitable share.

With limited educational opportunities for blacks, young Foster's dream of any career athletic opportunities began with the 1897 Austin (Texas) Reds of Tillotson College (now Huston-Tillotson University). The Austin college was an affiliated member of the United Methodist Church where Rube's father, the Reverend Andrew Foster, was presiding elder. After his educational stint, Foster joined the semi-pro Waco (Texas) Yellow Jackets and played two seasons, 1898–99.

By mid-August 1898, the Yellow Jackets had won 19 of 23 games against teams in Arkansas, Oklahoma and Texas. San Antonio's *The Daily Light* reported, "The Yellow Jackets have evidently watched the work of professionals, for at times their playing is quite clever. Some of them are perfect in the art of sacrifice hitting. The base running of some of the men was also good. Their throwing to bases was terrific and unlike others they never complain of sore arms or charley horses. It would appear that a league composed entirely of colored players would prove a success in Texas. The players could be had right at home and at moderate salaries and the novelty would attract the people, which would insure success."[4]

The San Antonio paper also reported after the Yellow Jackets had shut out their local Rosebuds, 8–0, behind Foster's 20 strikeouts, that "Whoever was responsible for the assertion that the Waco colored excursionists who are now in San Antonio came here for the purpose of agitating the labor question certainly has a misconception. A jollier crowd of niggers has not been together in San Antonio since the Nineteenth of June, and it would be a futile effort to search for a grievance committee in this bunch."

Note the "Nineteenth of June" reference to Texas' Juneteenth celebration, dating back to 1865, when the Union soldiers, led by Major General Gordon Granger, landed at Galveston with news that the Civil War had ended and that enslaved blacks were now free. This announcement came two and a half years after President Lincoln's Emancipation Proclamation, which had become official January 1, 1863. Today, it is a celebrated holiday in many American cities.

The Alamo city paper continued, "The colored visitors from Waco are here to enjoy themselves and they are having a big time. They brought a baseball club with them to add to their pleasure. Since their number was so large they prevailed upon the management of the San Antonio & Arkansas Pass railroad to give them excursion rates and with its usual public spiritedness the railroad gave them what they asked for."[5] It was reported that 700 fans attended the first game of the series at Pedro Park. The Rosebuds took the second game on Saturday, 7–6, and lost the state colored championship the next day, 11–3.[6]

According to other newspaper accounts, Foster won 11 games in 11 straight days, giving up no runs, allowing an average of five hits a game. The *Waco Times Herald*, astonished by Foster's feat, wrote, "Andrew Foster had them intoxicated with his playing."[7] The black monthly *Half-Century Magazine* added, "It sounds like a myth, but if it is, the Southern white press wove the myth."[8]

After Richey's Waco Yellow Jackets, Foster matriculated to play for the Palestine (TX) Yellow Jackets (1900) and later Will Snow's Fort Worth (TX) Colts (1901). With the Colts, Foster may have pitched his first no-hitter. On July 21, 1901, in Texas & Pacific Park, several hundred fans witnessed Rube's Colts defeat the Corsicana colored team, 6–0. "Foster has wonderful control of his delivery, and having the utmost confidence in [Andrew] Campbell at the receiving end," reported the Fort Worth paper, which added, "There is simply no limit to his speed. They were both quick and if a batter gets unbalanced, or off his feet because of a ferocious strike, it is to his interest to get right, else another delivery will be made before he can even think."[9] The errorless game was umpired by "Teacake Johnny" from Houston, known for his alertness and powerful voice, along with a huge physical presence to back up his word.

Foster's journey continued toward stardom. Thirteen days later was a bad sign for the Arlingtons of Hot Springs, Arkansas, as Foster pitched his second no-hitter, in a 6–1 win. The Arlingtons scored a run in the eighth on an error by Smith.[10] Game details of strikeouts, walks, etc., were not provided by the local press.

In the spring of 1902, Frank C. Leland, a manager of the Chicago Unions and former Fisk University student (1886), discovered the big, muscular Foster working with Connie Mack's Philadelphia Athletics in Hot Springs. It was reported that Foster had found employment in the local restaurant and spent his spare time pitching to Mack's catchers.[11] Foster was called by the daily Fort Worth paper, "the best colored pitcher in the south."[12] There were several accounts of Union games umpired by future Hall of Famer Cap Anson.

Frank Leland, well known as a clerk in the criminal and circuit courts, a clerk in the board of review, a former deputy sheriff and a member of the Board of County Commissioners of Cook County. Leland would put the first colored team in Chicago's Auburn Park on 79th and Wentworth Avenue (courtesy Christine Loving).

By late July, the best colored pitcher from the south and the Union Giants made a trip to Otsego, Michigan. Foster had been in a pitching slump and neither the team nor the player were contented. The south's best pitcher played first base in a Giant's win over the Otsego club. The press reported, "The coons were too fast for the Otsego aggregation of ball twirlers yesterday as the score of 8 to 2 would indicate. Otsego did some good work and hard hitting, but the exceptional good field work of the colored giants prevented them counting for much."[13] Seizing the opportunity to get a potential gate attraction, the following week, the daily paper reported, "The Otsego team has been strengthened by the adding of another pitcher. His name is Andrew Foster, the strongest twirler from the Colored Columbia Giants."[14] He was joined by teammate David Wyatt a few days later.[15]

Top: The 1902 Chicago Union Giants, top row (left to right), Rube Foster, John W. "Pat" Patterson, William Henry Binga, Harry Hyde, Joe "Kid" Miller and Dangerfield Talbert; bottom row (left to right), Dave Wyatt, Robert Footes, Chappie Johnson and Willis Jones (courtesy Doris Foster).

Bottom: The 1902 Otsego team, after beating Holland, 2–0. Pictured in the middle row are Dave Wyatt and Rube Foster (courtesy Otsego District Library, Otsego, Michigan).

One of Leland's first associations with teams was W.S. Peters' Chicago Union from 1888 to 1900. Top row (left to right), William Joyner, ? Scales, Frank Butler, Frank Leland, Bob Jackson, Richard Shaw, Lou Reynolds; middle row (left to right), George Hopkins, Mike Moore, W.S. Peters, Robert Footes, Doc Buckner; bottom row (left to right), T. Morgan, Harry Hyde, Big Bill Smith, and Will Jones. This caricature comes from the *Chicago Inter-Ocean*, 2 September, 1897.

Wyatt, later one of the framers of the 1920 Negro National League constitution wrote about his experience in Otsego, Michigan.

> Away back in 1902 Rube Foster had just taken out his first papers as a Chicago baseball player. Of course, Rube, like all persons from the South, had to endure the ordeal constantly of hearing the virtues of the North as it concerns the Colored people extolled. We were on the verge of a week's trip throughout the state of Michigan. The boys were highly elated. All came to bat with high sounding praises for the state—"A Negro heaven," "the best state in the Union; they don't know you're Colored." Foster fresh from the supposedly hostile country of Texas, was inclined to look upon this said-to-be attitude towards the Negro with the eye of the skeptic. We crossed the lake and soon arrived at a little town where we were to make our first stand, Otsego, Michigan. Starting on a walk from the depot we had gone but a short distance when we caught sight of a poster which read: "BASEBALL—OTSEGO VS. CHICAGO UNION GIANTS. THE GIANTS ARE GREAT BIG ATHELTIC COONS." Foster at once called the manager's attention to it. John W. Patterson, now a policeman in Battle Creek, Michigan, was road manager, and had been the leading one in praise of the state. He said he had played several years throughout the state and had never heard the appellations usually applied to our boys used. He became indignant and suggested that we cancel the game. We continued our journey, approaching a lawn upon which some small children were player. When they caught sight of us they exclaimed, "Here comes the Niggers." When Foster loomed in view one child smaller than the others said, "Oh, mercy, there's a great big Nigger," whereupon Foster set down this suitcase and went into a spasmodic laugh for about five minutes. Between convulsions he ejaculated, "So this is the Negro paradise? They don't know you're Colored, eh? Why, even the babies know it." It turned out to be a pretty good place after all. Before leaving Foster had come to an agreement with the owners of the club for regular service as a pitcher, also securing for the writer a position as shortstop. We finished out the season in the little burg.[16]

The Otsego team was sponsored by George Edward Bardeen, Sr., owner of the Mac Sim Bar paper mill. Bardeen was known for his benevolent attitude and had great influence in the community, and was financially responsible for the founding of Olivet College. "He was a wealthy man, who loved his small town. For him to recruit a black man, actually two in 1902, I personally believe helped change the minds in our area somewhat on the issue of race relations," said Otsego District Library Director Ryan Wieber.[17]

In the first recorded game found, Foster defeated the Allegan, Michigan, team, 5–2, striking out 11, and even stole a base, while going two-for-four at the plate with a double. The *Allegan Gazette* said, "He is as jolly as a clown, always good natured, perfectly at home in the pitcher's box, and a gentleman on the base ball field. He can throw a ball nearly as fast as one of Uncle Sam's thirteen-inch guns, and works all the curves and shoots known to the art."[18] The Otsego Union paper had a similar assessment of Foster, stating, "Foster, Otsego's new colored pitcher from the Chicago Union Giants, probably the strongest twirler in the country, will be in the box. He is not only a fast pitcher, but is a whole circus by himself, and will give the spectator's double value for their money."[19] The Otsego paper added, "Foster, Otsego's new colored pitcher, is invincible."[20]

However, Otsego catcher Warner had two passed balls in Foster's pitching debut and Warner's inability to handle fast balls would make Foster beatable. Foster and the Otsego club lost to the Kalamazoo team, 2 to 1, as Foster struck out 13, while Warner had two more passed balls. Foster later played right field in a 2–0 win over the Bloomingdales and "threw the fans into consternation by making a home run."[21]

Foster would go on to defeat Greenville, 2 to 1, and lost to Grand Rapids in ten innings, 4 to 3, as catcher Warner added to his total of passed balls. The Otsego club traveled to Holland to play one of the fastest independent teams in the state. Despite more passed balls by Warner, they defeated the Hollands, 2 to 0. "The Holland club went against a proposition Wednesday that it couldn't solve," reported the *Holland News*. "The proposition was Foster, the colored twirler who is doing business for Otsego. He had the Holland boys completely at his mercy and gave them an assortment of shoots, drops and curves that they could not find with a searchlight. The best they could get off him was one hit."[22]

Foster would join the Cuban X-Giants for the 1903 season. His teams would call the Auburn diamond their main home until the summer of 1910 when the park was divided into building lots.[23] Leland's teams would also compete in Chicago's West End Park, Rogers Park, Ogden's Grove, Seneca Park, Tortenson's Park, Artesian Park, Gunther Park and Eclipse Park.

Leland was from Memphis, Tennessee, came to Chicago in 1887 and partnered with Henry Elby, Albert Donegan and W.S. Peters to organize the Union Base Ball Club. For the next three seasons, the team was known as the Chicago Unions, with Leland serving as a part-time outfielder and manager. The new Unions were located at a small park at 76th and Langley Avenue near Grand Crossing (southwest of Lake Shore Drive).

In 1894 the Chicago Unions moved to 37th and Butler Streets, where they played through the 1899 season. That same year, many players from the legendary Page Fence Giants out of Adrian, Michigan, relocated to Chicago and became the Columbia Giants. The Columbia Giants and the Chicago Unions were without an official park for the 1900 season. For the 1902 season, Leland hand-picked a new team from the talents of the two teams, creating the Chicago Union Giants. That year Leland would put the first colored team in Auburn Park. In 1905, he renamed the team the Leland Giants[24] and won 122 games, lost only ten, while compiling a reported remarkable 48-game winning streak. Two years later, in 1907, Leland incorporated the Giants team as the "Leland Giants Base Ball and Amusement Association."

Following an extended illness, Frank Leland died in November of 1914. The well known, 45-year old Republican politician had passed away at his home at 2348 Dearborn Street, of aortic insufficiency, and was buried in Lincoln Cemetery (Lot 9, Section 1) in Blue Island, Illinois. Rube Foster would build on the success originally laid by Frank C. Leland after the turn of the century.

According to the paper, "This club was organized in the early 1880s as a prairie team. Since that time it had made such rapid strides that it stands today as the foremost colored organization of mankind in the world. Many of the players of the Chicago Unions, if given the chance, would hold their own in the major leagues. Last year the team made a wonderful record, winning 100 games and losing 19. This season it look as though it would surpass last year's record. W.S. Peters controls the entire stock of the club and is the home manager."

1st Inning.
The Early Pro Days, 1903–1906

Leland's discovery was reported to have pitched a shutout in his first game with the Giants, but had very little success on the mound thereafter. After spending only three-quarters of the 1902 season with Leland's Union Giants, Foster joined the Cuban X-Giants in late June of 1903. The X-Giants were a Philadelphia–based club owned by E.B. Lamar, Jr.

The New York *Evening World* announced Lamar's acquisition as the "greatest twirler he ever saw. He has been pitching with wonderful success in the West during the last two years. He is a southpaw, and has the best record of strikeouts of any colored pitcher in the country. Lamar will use Foster in the box against the crack Hoboken team at the St. George Cricket Grounds in Hoboken on Sunday."[1]

Lamar's team was reported to weigh an average of 185 pounds, "the heaviest lot of ball players ever seen on the diamond." A Trenton (NJ) paper reported "Foster, who weighs 230 pounds, is said to have more speed than any living pitcher."[2] According to a *N.Y. Sun* article,

> The Cuban X-Giants Baseball Club as it stands to-day is the strongest combination of colored ball players ever gotten together in this country. The line up is as follows: Pitchers, Dan McCullen [McClellan], James Robinson, Ed Wilson, and Harry Buckner; catchers, Robert Jordan and William Smith; first base, Ray Wilson; second base, Charles Grant; third base, William [Bill] Monroe; short stop, Grant [Home Run] Johnson; left field, [Big Bill] Smith or [Robert] Jordan; centre field, William Jackson; right field, a pitcher. In the list are three new players, Johnson, Grant and Buckner. Charles Grant is not only a good hitter but a fine fielder. He played part of last season with the Baltimore American League Club. Buckner has the reputation of being the best colored pitcher in the West to-day. All clubs desiring games with the Giants this season should address E.B. Lamar, Jr., 766 East 175th Street, New York city.[3]

Lamar enticed Foster with a significant raise: $40 a month [$964 in 2010], plus 15 cents for each meal to join the best team in the land. Legend has it that Foster developed a nasty screwball from his unique submarine delivery while with Lamar's club.

Originally known for overpowering batters, Foster would usually employ brawn over brains. However, as an X-Giant, a proud, but unseasoned Foster lost his first game, 13–0, to a semi-pro Hoboken, New Jersey team, who got 14 hits while baserunners took advantage of his huge windmill wind-up. Overall, the season proved to be a humbling experience, developing Foster into an audacious competitor. As Lamar explained, "That taught Rube a lesson. From then on he made a study of the game and every chance he got he would go out to the big league parks and watch the big leaguers in action."

Until now there had been no bragging rights for the "Colored professional baseball champion" title, as the Cuban X-Giants and the Philadelphia Giants often claimed the mythical title. After two years of challenges, bragging and counter-agreements, the com-

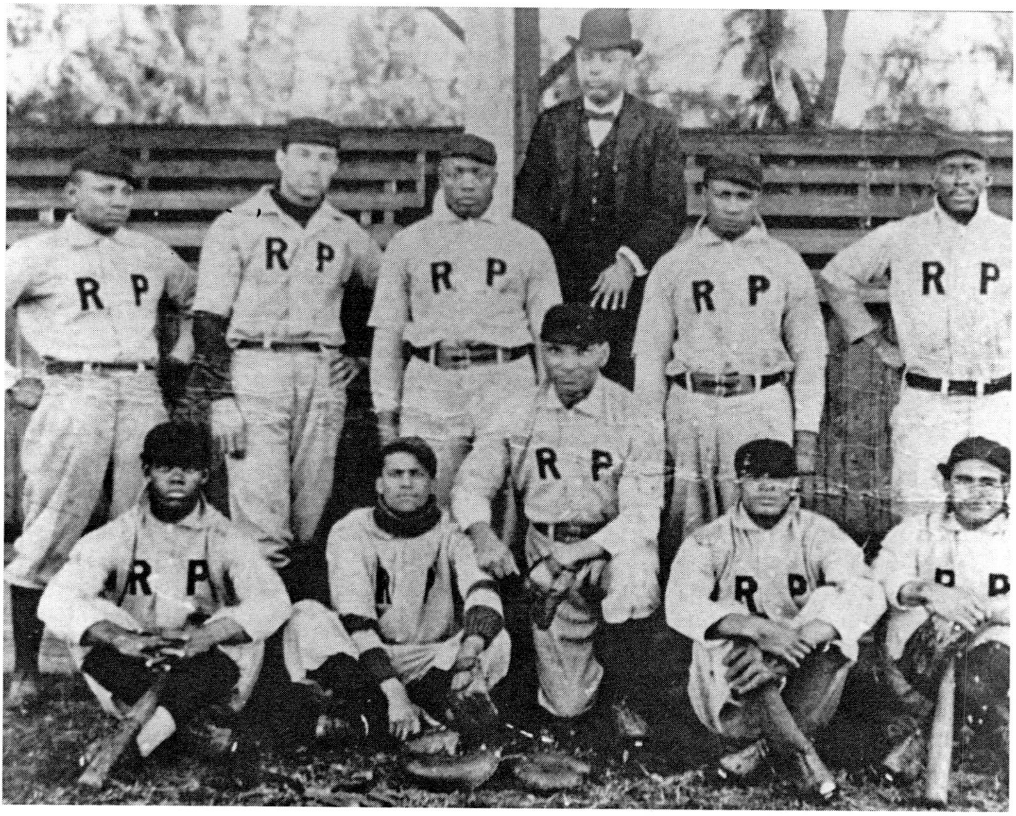

Above: In 1903, Foster headed east to play for the Cuban-X Giants based in New York. The team posted a 51–4 won-lost record and Foster pitched them to four victories against the Philadelphia Giants to claim the unofficial "Colored Championship of the World." The nomadic Foster switched over to the Philadelphia team for the next three seasons. Here Foster appears in the nondescript Philadelphia uniform (courtesy Chicago Historical Society).

Opposite, top: While pitching for the Philadelphia Giants in 1905, Foster beat his former team, the Cuban X-Giants, twice in the championship series. He struck out 18 batters in one game, easily exceeding the major league record of 15. The 1905 Giants, from left to right (top row), Grant Johnson, Rube Foster, Emmett Bowman, Walter Schlichter, Sol White, Pete Booker and Charlie Grant; (bottom row) Dan McClellan, Pete Hill, Tom Washington, Mike Moore and Bill Monroe (NoirTech Research).

Bottom: During the winter months many players went south to play for teams such as the Royal Poinciana of Palm Beach, Florida. The players of this 1904/05 squad were: top row (left to right) Dan McClellan, unknown, Rube Foster, H. Smith (suit), Mike Moore and Grant Johnson; bottom row (left to right) Pete Hill, Bill Monroe, Sol White, Big Bill Smith, and Charlie Grant (courtesy Jay Sanford).

batants decided to play a ten-game series, as Foster entered the central stage of his baseball career.

The 1903 series matched a confident Philadelphia team composed of some of black baseball's hardest throwers and best hitters: Robert Footes (c), Harry Buckner (rf), William Binga (3b), John Patterson (lf), John Nelson (1b) and William Evans (cf). Behind the pitching of William Bell and Clarence "Kid" Carter, and managed by the distinguished King Solomon White from Wilberforce University (1886–1890), the Philly team reportedly won 89 games while losing 37. White's team also had the solid double-play combination of Bill Monroe (ss) and Frank Grant (2b).

One paper boasted of Monroe in a game against Ingersol-Sergeant, from Easton, PA. "Because of high winds, several errors were made," the press claimed, "Grant, at second, played a star game, while the inimitable [Bill] Monroe was, as usual, all over the field, and kept the crowd amused with his witty sayings and whimsicalities. The Giants won 11–6, with Grant and Monroe combining for seven of the 15 hits.[4]

Arguable Monroe was Foster's best middle infielder. The comical "Monie" would tell opposing batters to "sit down" on any ball hit to him, they knew that he was going to throw them out. One Jersey paper claimed, "Monroe, the greatest shortstop outside of the major league and funniest coacher on the side lines since the days of Arlie Latham [clown prince of the old St. Louis Browns], is in charge of the [Brooklyn] Royals [Giants] and this is sufficient guarantee of the caliber of this teammates. Monroe is very popular with the fans here, for aside from his remarkable qualities as a ball player, Monroe keeps everyone amused."[5]

On the other hand, Grant earned the dubious distinction of being called the "Black Dunlap," in comparison to the National League's Fred "Sure Shot" Dunlap, the premier second sacker of the white leagues. Although *Sporting Life* declared Grant to be the "best all-round player that Buffalo [1886–1888] ever had," the International League imposed a ban against hiring black players, forcing future Hall of Famer Grant to eventually seek employment with the all-black Big Gorhams of Ansonia, Connecticut, before the century rollover.

A Sunday Denver paper reported, "Grant, the colored second baseman of the Buffalos [sic] is the only Negro playing professionally with any club in the different associations. He is a fine tosser, all the same, and hasn't many superiors among players either white or black. I think he gets $600 per year [$14,400 in 2010] for his services, while if he had a white skin, he could easily demand $2,000 [$48,000 in 2010]."[6]

The *Daily News* added, "Grant is very popular in Buffalo, and for that reason the management is forced to hold him, although the players of the club are said to feel keenly having to play with a colored man. In the east Grant goes with the other members of the club, stops at the same hotels, eats at the same table and possibly occupies the same room. While in Rochester he is registered at the Galt house, but is roomed with the colored help and takes his meals with them."[7]

Despite having a quality team that included a future Hall of Famer like Grant, Sol White's team would have to face the highly regarded X-Giants with Clarence Williams (c), Robert Jordan (1b), James Robinson, Ed (utility) and Clarence Ray Wilson (utility), John Hill (3b), William Jackson (lf), Andrew Payne (cf), William Smith (rf), Walter Ball (p) and Grant "Home Run" Johnson (ss).[8]

Jorge S. Figueredo, in his book *Who's Who in Cuban Baseball* (p. 353), says Johnson played five seasons in Cuba, 1907, 1908, 1908/09, 1910/11 and 1912. Career–wise, in 156 games, he got 175 hits in 549 at bats, with 11 doubles, eight triples and four home runs, for an overall .319 batting average. He twice led the leagues in hits and became the first American, in 1912, to win a Cuban winter league batting title, with a .410 average.

According to historian and author Ray Nemec, Grant Johnson got his nickname in 1894, when he blasted 60 home runs for the Findlay (Ohio) Sluggers. He may have been the first player, black or white, to reach that magical number. An early prototype of Ernie Banks, Johnson was a tall, rangy, right-handed, power-hitting shortstop.

Grant "Home Run" Johnson with Findlay in 1894. When Sol White published his classic book in 1907, he picked Rube Foster to write a section on the science of pitching. Of equal importance was his selection of Grant "Home Run" Johnson to write his formula for successful hitting, entitled: "Art and Science of Hitting" (courtesy Hancock Historical Museum, Findlay, Ohio).

The X-Giants would also add Danny McClellan, who threw the first recorded perfect game by a black pitcher, against the Penn Park Athletic Club of York, Pennsylvania, champions of the Tri-State League, on July 17, 1903. Included was the straight-haired, high cheek-boned, cafe au lait-complexioned second baseman Charlie Grant, whom John McGraw tried to sneak into the lineup of his 1901 Baltimore Orioles as "Chief Tokohama."[9] This cluster of outstanding players also included diamond delight Rube Foster.

"The Cuban X-Giants had an infield that was so airtight that you couldn't get a pea through it. There were Wilson, first base; Grant, second base; Hill, third base; and Home Run Johnson, shortstop," claimed Frank Miller, former X-Giant. Miller added, "Why those fellows covered so much territory that there really wasn't any need for an outfield, especially behind the pitching of Rube Foster and McClellan. Not only did they field well, but all of them hit the ball, particularly Johnson, whose powerful slugging gave him his nickname."[10]

The classic confrontation was originally scheduled for ten games but later shorten to a seven-game series. The first game was won by Foster, 4–2, beating William Bell. Riding the glory of his perfect game over the Penn Park Athletic Club back on July 17th, McClellan pitched both games of the New York doubleheader, winning the first game, 8–1, and losing the second game, 5–2, to William Bell. With the X-Giants leading the series at 2–1, Foster captured the third win with a 3–1 victory over Kid Carter. With two days' rest, McClellan sought revenge, but Kid Carter, who had pitched the day before, threw a five-hit shutout for a 3–0 Philly victory. Three days later Foster returned, beating William Bell and Kid Carter, 12–3. The seventh and final game was played seven days later with Foster defeating

Kid Carter with a three-hit shutout, 2–0. The Cuban X-Giants won five out of seven games in the intra-city series, with Foster earning four complete game victories. McClellan was credited with a fifth X-Giant victory, while William Bell and Kid Carter each won a game for Philadelphia. The X-Giants attack was led by first sacker Bob Jordan with a .371 average and a .429 slugging percentage. That included 13 for 35 with two doubles and five RBIs. The X-Giants' premier player, Grant "Home Run" Johnson, had a dismal showing, with a .235 batting average and three fielding errors, but did knock in eight runs.

The Cuban X-Giants, without any native Islanders, laid claim to the first Colored Championship. Meanwhile the Philadelphia Giants' best hitter was shortstop Sol White, hitting .321. Overall, the Phillies batted .146 as a team, with Frank Grant (.207) and Diamond Bill Monroe (.273) the only other regulars to bat over .200 in the series.

Foster pitching totals for the seven-game series: Games Started — 4, Complete Games— 4, Shutouts—1, Innings Pitched — 36, Hits allowed —19, Strikeouts— 20, Walks— 5, Hit Batters—1, Runs— 6, Earned Runs 3, ERA 0.75.

Foster batting totals for the seven-game series: Games— 5, At Bats— 21, Runs— 3, Hits— 6, Doubles—1, Triples—1, RBI — 3, Average — .286, and Slugging Percentage — .429.

According to several sources, Foster's superb performance in the series prompted John McGraw to hire Foster to teach Christy Mathewson and Joe "Iron Man" McGinnity how to finesse pitch and the art of throwing a screwball. Until 1903, "Mathewson's" won-lost record was 33 wins and 37 losses. With Foster's coaching, over the next three years, Mathewson won 30, 33 and 31 games, while leading the league in strikeouts every season. Old man McGinnity won 31 games in 1903, and added 35 wins the next season. In 1904, McGraw's New York club won the National League pennant with a 106–47 record, as his M&M aces won more than 60 percent of their games.

Sol White was also impressed with the Foster mystique, enticing Rube to join his Philly team in 1904. Along the way Foster influenced many of his teammates to join White's Philadelphia Giants, booked by businessmen Walter Schlichter and Nat Strong. That year the Philly Giants won 95 and lost 41 games (.699) that year, with Foster pitching his third no-hitter on July 7 against the Mt. Carmel Athletic Association in Philadelphia. His fourth no-hitter came against the Trenton (NJ) YMCA team as he struck out 17 men in a 1–0 squeaker. Once again they played the X-Giants for the city championship — but this time with Foster in their dugout.

The press favored the Cuban X-Giants to win the series. They had won 86 and lost only 26. Their 86 wins included 15 shutouts, and conversely they were only shut out once. Plus the X-men were riding an 18-game winning streak, equaling the record set by the New York Giants.

The favorites looked poised to win as their chances increased when Foster took ill just days before the series. After a pleading from manager King White, Foster agreed to travel with the team to Atlantic City for the heated contest. The Cubans, still upset with Foster for jumping to the rival Philadelphia team, were looking forward to avenging Foster's exodus.

The Cuban fellows suggested that Foster was faking his illness and did not want to face the quickness of Walter Ball, better known as the "Georgia Rabbit." Earlier, in 1899, Ball had won 25 games in 28 appearances for North Dakota's champion Grand Forks team. More recently, on September 11, Ball had defeated Leland's Union Giants, 6–1, giving up five hits in Auburn Park. The local paper reported, "A tall dark gentleman who was on the slab for the Cubans had a few too many whippoorwills and dynamiters up his sleeve, and with the able assistance of a catcher [Clarence Williams] whose specialty was fouls, he effectually put it on the local championship aspirants."[11] The paper added that the entire game was played in the rain with half the crowd consisting of white fans. They claimed the play of the Cubans was "excellent" and Ball's team made a "good impression."

Realizing the challenge in facing the formidable Ball, Foster yielded to the pressure and decided to play. Before 4,000 fans at Atlantic City's Inlet Park, he won the first game, 8–4. He pitched a seven-hitter, walked five and blazed the Cubans with 18 strikeouts, beating Ball and reliever Dan "No-hit" McClellan. The Philadelphia newspapers hailed Foster's striking performance, reporting breakage of the major league record of 15 strikeouts set by Fred Glade of the St. Louis Browns on June 19, 1904, against the New York Highlanders.

In 1886, Frank Grant, perhaps the greatest black second baseman of the nineteenth century, was described by the *Buffalo Express* as a "Spaniard." That year he hit a team-high .316 (.441 Slugging) for the Meriden Silvermen in the Eastern League. When the Meriden club folded, Grant joined Buffalo of the higher-class International Association and hit even stronger at .346 (.530)— overall the third best in the league (NoirTech Research).

After the Philly victory, the odds switched to 3 to 2 in favor of Foster's club. Behind Buckner's six-hitter, the X-Giants won the second game, 3–1. In the rubber game, with only two days' rest, Foster won again, 4–2, allowing only two hits and striking out six. He defeated former teammate Danny McClellan for the second time in the series. In this series John Patterson led the Cubans attack with a .364 batting average, a homer and five stolen bases; while the competitive Foster led the Philadelphia assault, batting an even .400, with one triple and a stolen base.

Foster's pitching totals for the series: Games Started — 2, Complete games— 2, Innings Pitched—18, Hits Allowed—10, Strikeouts— 24, Walks— 6, Earned Runs— 5, ERA— 2.50.

Amid protests, the All-Cubans club had split the four games against the Philadelphia Giants and wanted their shot at the championship. It was the one-game winner-take-all, to be played on September 27 at the Philadelphia A's Columbia Park. The proceeds of the game would go to a building fund for the Douglass Hospital in Chicago. Before a crowd of 1,200 fans, the Philly club won handily, 13 to 3. Rube Foster clinched the victory with 14 strikeouts, yielding five hits. Offensively, Foster added a double and a single, and drove in two runs in Giants' 13-hit attack. Their star outfielder, Pete Hill went four-for-four, beating out three infield hits. Sol White declared, "Both players and spectators were worked to the highest pitch of excitement. Never in the annuals of colored baseball did two nines fight for supremacy as these teams fought."[12]

Following the game, Philly owner H. Walter Schlichter issued the challenge to all Eastern teams:

> The Philadelphia Giants having won the world's championship in colored baseball do hereby challenge the winner of the Tri-State League championship for a game or a series of games for $500 a side, the winner to take all the gate receipts as well as the wager. The Philadelphia Giants have a better percentage than the Tri-State leaders, and I am sure that is a better team than any of the above-named organization. The fact that the Giants are colored can cut no ice with the Tri-Staters, because all of them have played colored teams this year. If the manager of the winning team desires to make some money, let him communicate with me, and I will be "Johnny-on-the-Spot" with the loot.[13]

The Giants split the first two games with the All-Philadelphia Independents as Foster won the first game. The Giants had to salvage the title game without Foster, as he was summoned home to Calvert, Texas, because of the serious illness of his older sister, Christina. Despite Foster's absence, the Giants clinched the final game to claim the Philadelphia championship.

Meanwhile, in Chicago, the Cubans Giants were defeating the Leland Giants (aka Union Giants) 6–1, in what was called the Colored World Series by the *Chicago Tribune*. The paper's headline read "Chicago's watermelon patch deserted by exodus to Auburn Park, where rival dark horses of baseballdom battle for championship." The paper reported the streets were practically deserted as Auburn Park was hosting the Leland Giants of Chicago for the "colored championship of the world." Although the entire game was played under raindrops, there was a big crowd on hand, half of which were white patrons. The *Tribune* considered the play on the field as "excellent" and the visiting team made a good impression.[14] Awkwardly, the white daily newspapers boasted of the stellar play on the field.

Having the most attractive team in Chicago was not without its critics. In May of 1905, in an unsigned editorial called the "Sporting Comment," the paper blasted the Leland club

In 1905, Leland created one of Chicago's trademark teams, the Leland Giants. The roster included (1) Dell Matthews, (2) George Taylor, (3) Leland, (4) Dave Wyatt, (5) Bruce Petway, (6) Charles Joe Green, (7) Walter Ball, (8) Andrew Campbell, (9) Dangerfield Talbert, (10) William Horn and (11) James Smith (courtesy Dick Clark).

for making excuses to play doubleheaders. The editorial said, "The attempt to foist such attraction here in Chicago by the semi-professional managers is a cheap-john, catch-penny idea that is a disgrace to sport. All baseball on Sunday is opposed by many worthy people, but their ideas are not shared by a majority. If the toleration of it, however, is abused as the Leland Giants are abusing it the Sunday observers will be justified in stepping in and stopping the nuisance. There is no excuse for 'double headers' among the amateurs and semi-professionals."[15]

Heavyweight boxing champion Jack Johnson was known for his flamboyance outside of the ring and taunting in the ring (NoirTech Research).

Little did the cynics know that fan interests in this all-black squad would increase dramatically over the next few years.

The apex of Foster's career came in 1905. As a seasonal warm-up contest they played Johnson's Pets, coached by future heavyweight champion Jack Johnson. The Pets went down to defeat, 13–4, with first baseman Johnson getting two singles and scoring a run. In the field he made one error and was credited with eight putouts. The local press reported, "Johnson was the shining light for the colored fans to gaze at and [Bill] Monroe's antics with the big fellow kept the brethren in a continuous uproar of laughter from the start to finish. Johnson does not make as good a ball player as he does a pugilist, but at that he covered first in fairly good style. At batting, however, he had his troubles."[16]

Years later, in 1913, Johnson would solicit Foster's help to escape charges resulting from the Mann Act, which forbade the transportation of women across state lines for immoral and illicit purposes. Judge George Carpenter had fined Johnson $1,000 and sentenced him to a year of incarceration in Joliet Penitentiary for transporting his future white wife, Lucille Cameron, across state lines for immoral purposes. Unknown to Foster, Johnson disguised himself as Andrew, joining the team enroute to Hamilton, Ontario, where he purchased tickets on the steamer *Corinthia* bound for Paris, France.

Foster and Johnson were tall, heavy, dark-complexioned and bald-headed. Playing on the assumption that law officials thought that all black people look alike, Johnson escaped on a train from Chicago's Englewood Station, avoiding charges for the next seven years.[17]

The Giants had a tremendous start following the Jack Johnson contest, winning 18 of their first 20 games. They were led by Bill Monroe's .440 average and ten stolen bases, and Grant "Home Run" Johnson's .405 batting average, while Pete Hill was off to an uncharacteristic slow start with only a .311 average. According to Dave Malarcher, future American Giants' manager, "Pete Hill was the greatest hitter there ever was. Oh yes, better than Oscar

Charleston. Charleston was the greatest all-round ball player, but as a hitter, Pete Hill was the greatest hitter."[18]

Good team hitting was contagious as pitcher Rube turned into hitter Rube. In 86 recorded games in 1905, Foster slapped 114 hits, with 22 doubles, four triples and three homers on his way to a seasonal .289 average. In the 28 recorded pitching appearances, he produced an incredible 1.39 ERA, striking out a "reported" 115 batters in 271⅔ innings, with four shutout victories, in compiling a 24–4 won-lost record. He led the Giants to a record of 134 wins, against 21 losses, with three ties, while enjoying a winning streak of 18 games. An incredible winning percentage of .865 marked their most productive season in team history.

It has been often reported that this was the season that Andrew became "Rube." In an interview with Frederick North Shorey of the *Freeman* after a Giants victory over the white All-Stars, Foster responded to how he acquired his nickname:

> In 1905, I won 51 out of 55 games I pitched for that season, and that was doing pretty well. We played the New York Giants, the Philadelphia Athletics, the Nationals, the Brooklyns, the teams of the New England and the Tri-State leagues, and cleaned 'em all up. It was when we beat the Athletics, with Rube Waddell pitching, that they gave me the name of the colored Rube Waddell.[19]

The quote from Foster has led many biographers to believe his historic meeting against Rube Waddell and the Philadelphia A's came in 1905. However, in print, on several occasions, Foster was called "Rube" before 1905, leading to specification that Foster and Waddell may have dueled earlier. In tracing the timeline backward for references to Foster we stop in the late summer of 1903.

Pete Hill was a four-tool player. He could run, hit, throw and field. Hill's consistent hitting became a speed bump in the lineup for any pitcher. His only deficiency was a lack of power. "Pete Hill was the greatest hitter there ever was. Oh yes, better than Oscar Charleston. Charleston was the greatest all-round ball player, but as a hitter, Pete Hill was the greatest hitter"—Dave Malarcher (NoirTech Research).

In the night edition of New York's *Evening World*, on June 26, 1903, a headline read "New Pitcher to Oppose Hobokens." The paper reported, "Manager Ed Lamar, of the Cuban X Giants, the colored team of ball-tossers, has just signed a colored pitcher for his team who, he claims, is the greatest twirler he ever saw. His name is Foster and he has been pitching with wonderful success in the West during the last two years. He is a southpaw, and has the best record of strike-outs of any colored pitcher in the country. Lamar will use Foster in the box against the crack Hoboken team at the St. George Cricket Grounds in Hoboken on Sunday." The description of Foster as left-handed is mistaken, but the reference is unquestionably to Rube. The next day, the paper reported that Foster would face Lindeman, who "will do the box work for the Jerseyman. The Hobokens have beaten the Cuban X-Giants in the last four games they have played them." With Foster joining pitching aces James Robinson and Danny McClellan, they were poised to face the best talent around New York.

Foster was now with the X-Giants and George Edward "Rube" Waddell in his second year with the Philadelphia A's. Waddell at the time was only weeks away from a five-day suspension, imposed in July by American League president Ban Johnson, for running into the stands to confront known gambler Maurice Blau. Earlier, in June, Waddell married his second of three wives, May Wynne Skinner, who more than once had George jailed for non-support. That season he struck out a record 302 batters, compiling a 21–16 won-lost record and an ERA of 2.44. This would be his second of four consecutive seasons with 20 or more wins. His 302 strikeouts were 115 more than runner-up Wild Bill Donovan, and his performance the following season, 1904, was no less impressive, as he amassed 349 strikeouts, 110 more than runner-up Jack Chesbro. The 26-year-old Waddell was known for missing scheduled starts, leaving the dugout in the middle of games, and his battles with alcohol addiction. He was also often portrayed by the media as a bad-tempered teammate. Despite his shortcomings, however, Rube Waddell was considered the game's top southpaw for the period.

In leading up to the historic contest against Rube Foster, Waddell pitched on Monday, July 27, in Philadelphia, against the Washington Senators. He pitched a five-hit shutout, walking seven and striking out six for a 3–0 win. Three days later, on Thursday, Waddell pitched six innings against the Senators, yielding five runs, as his A's rallied for three runs in the seventh and eighth innings for a 6–5 win.

The following Saturday, Waddell's Athletics traveled to New York to face Jack Chesbro and the Highlanders on the grounds of Washington Heights. Both hurlers worked hard and went the distance, with future Hall of Famer Chesbro coming out on top. Happy Jack gave up one walk and struck out five men, while Waddell struck out 13 men and walked six in a 3–2 lost. Overall, Waddell had pitched 23 innings since Monday, with a welcome day off as New York's blue laws prohibited diamond play on the Sabbath.

But Nat Strong, manager of the Murray Hills, a midtown Manhattan semi-pro team, recruited Waddell to pitch against Lamar's Cuban X-Giants win on blue Sunday. The classic duel at Olympia Field between Foster and Waddell saw the X-Giants win, 6–3, with both pitchers going the distance. A tired, rubber-armed Waddell, listed in the August 3 *New York Sun* as "Wilson" in the line score gave up 11 hits while Foster yielded seven. Both pitchers worked without their regular catchers; Waddell threw to O'Neill and Foster to Big Bill Smith, normally an outfielder for the X-Giants.

It is unknown whether Foster pitched on significantly more rest than Waddell, who without rest and pitching to an unfamiliar catcher provider an obscure footnote to the brilliant career. By losing he had gifted Andrew Foster with his moniker. Without missing his start in the three-day rotation. Waddell was back on the mound for the A's two days later, on Tuesday, against the future American League champion Boston Red Sox. He would lose to 21-game winner Big Bill Dinneen, 3–0, on four hits. Charles Dryden, known for his humorous writings, on August 5 wrote about the unsanctioned game against Foster for the *Pittsburg[h] Press*, in an article titled "Rube Waddell Afraid to Give His Arm a Rest."

> We deem it worthwhile to announce that Mr. Waddell is still taking splendid care of himself and framing up a scheme to win the next game he pitches. The actor man has been unlucky of late, but he predicts that a change will soon come. Rather than have his wonderful arm go stale by resting on the Holy Sabbath, the strenuous Mr. Waddell pitched an exhibition game on that day and lost it.
>
> The Cuban X-Giants whacked the "Reuben" about a dozen [actually 11] times, and he struck out 12 of the Africans. Because his catcher [O'Neil] had no life insurance. Mr. Waddell was obliged to

cut out his curve ball. The catcher couldn't stand the pace, and the coons bumped the speedy straight ones.

The Giant pitcher [Foster] hit our southpaw in the head, but as the people seemed to like it, Waddell didn't mind. "Rube" [Waddell] played with the Murray Hill team and hit the hottest foul tip on record. The ball whizzed into the stand and struck a man on the side. He had in his pocket a box of matches that blew up and became ignited. The coat was ruined and the gentleman was pretty well done on one side before they got his extinguished. Some queer freaks have been recorded in the history of baseball, but this one takes the bun. "Rube" not only saves people from the flames, but he sets them on fire as well. Nothing like it![20]

Going forward to 1905, did Foster win more than 92 percent of his games as he told Shorey? In 35 games found, Foster won 28 and lost 4 for an equally impressive 87.5 percent. We may never know if he won 23 more games with no additional losses to match the 51 out of 55 majority decisions reported. Always the entertainer by either mouth or mound duty, he was a notoriously slow practitioner on the dirty knoll. Foster was described in a 1905 *Philadelphia Item* article as having "...an aggravating way of taking his time. He is a man of huge frame. His arms are like those of a windmill. He would swing them like the pendulum of a clock, looking the while, about the diamond. Suddenly he would twist up like a Missouri grasshopper about to make a spring and the ball would shoot from the pitcher's box. Time and again he struck out his man."

On August 22, 1905, Foster pitched his fifth no-hitter, this one against the Camden (NJ) club. He struck out five and walked three batters, facing only 30 batters. By October the *Philadelphia Item* reported that the Giants have a "remarkable" 132–21–3 won-lost-tie record, while noting that nine of the losses were by one run. The trio of Foster, Danny McClellan and Scotty Bowman were unbeatable. Soon after the *Philadelphia Telegraph* wrote, "If Andrew Foster had not been born with a dark skin, the great pitcher would wear an American or National League uniform. Rube Waddell, Cy Young, [Christy] Mathewson, [Joe] McGinnity and others are great twirlers in the big leagues and their praises have been sung from Maine to Texas. Foster has never been equaled in a pitcher's box. Out of 49 games pitched his season he has won 45. Aside from the twirling ability, he is heavy hitter and a fine fielder and ranks among the foremost of the country." The *Indianapolis Freeman* echoed the sentiment, adding "Andrew Foster deserves every word of praise ever said of him. He is undoubtedly among the very best pitchers that America affords." Meanwhile, the *Harrisburg Telegraph* noted his flirtation for a six no-hitter. "Foster is the giant who has many pitchers beaten [by] a mile. He proved his ability yesterday when he held Harrisburg down to one hit, and that bingo was looked upon as rather doubtful. Bonner was credited with having one hit, but many who witnessed the game thought it was a no-hit contest."[21]

The original Rube was considered by Connie Mack the greatest lefthander he ever saw, saying, "What pitcher had the best combination of speed and a curve ball? My goodness, I think that's quite simple. His name is Rube Waddell." Waddell, known for his strikeout prowess, led the American League in strikeouts six years in a row. In 1908, as a member of the St. Louis Browns, he whiffed 16 Philadelphia A's in a game.

Moreover, the *Chicago Height Star* reported "Rube Foster, who plays with the Leland Giants, is considered as great a pitcher as Rube Waddell. He is a southpaw with a Waddell physique and assortment of curves, and would be a star in fast company if it wasn't for the shade of his complexion. Foster is of such a dusky hue that no manager has ever tried to ring him in."[22]

The dusky one and the Philadelphia Giants closed out the season with a championship series against the Brooklyn Royal Giants. John W. Connor, owner of the Brooklyn Royal

Café, agreed to meet the Philly club in Atlantic City, New Jersey, for a three-game series at Inlet Park. In the opener Scotty Bowman for the Philly Giants shut out Bill Merritt and the Royal Giants, 2–0. Rube Foster won the second game, 7–6, followed by Dan McClellan, who picked up the third win, 7–2, for the sweep.

The 1906 season had Foster start with the Quaker Giants, where he pitched 3⅔ innings for the club on April Fool's Day. He gave up eight runs, four of them earned, striking out three and walking four, to take the loss.

Ten days later he was back with the Philadelphia Giants, playing right field when the local paper reported that "Rube Foster, last year's phenomenal pitcher for the Philadelphia Giants, the colored champions of the world, who this season has played with the Philadelphia Quaker Giants, a New York organization this morning joined his old team in Altoona, [PA] and will be found on the firing line for the locals the rest of the season. Foster's record shows but four defeats in the fifty-five games he pitched last year."[23]

This edition of the Philadelphia Giants' key performers now included John Henry "Pop" Lloyd, Pete Hill, who later hit safely in 116 consecutive games in 1911,[24] Charlie Grant at second, and battery mates Bruce Petway and Danny McClellan. The press reported that McClellan won 44 straight games, leading the club to 108 victories in 145 games (.745) with six ties. Based on box scores found, the Giants won 44 games against 14 losses (.759), and three ties.

In September, Foster's team would play the Cuban X-Giants for the International League championship and Freihofer Cup. Roughly 16,000 fans witnessed a Philly Giants win by 3–2 at the Athletics Park. Foster pitched brilliantly, scattering ten hits, striking out nine and getting out of two bases loaded jams.[25]

After the 1906 season, officials of prominent black clubs met at the Lions Club at 87 Fleet Street in Brooklyn, New York, to entertain thoughts of an organized league. The new league was christened the National Association of Colored Base Ball Clubs of the United States and Cuba. H. Walter Schlichter (Philadelphia Giants) was elected president; J.W. Connor (Brooklyn Royal Giants) was elected vice-president; and J.M. Bright (Cuban Giants) treasurer, and with Manual Campos (Cuban Stars), and E.B. Lamar, Jr. (Cuban X-Giants) composed the Board of Trustees. Bookie Nat Strong, who fielded many semi-pro white teams, was elected secretary. The league was made up of the following teams: Philadelphia Giants, Cuban X-Giants, Cuban Giants, Brooklyn Royal Giants, Cuban Stars.

Manager Grant Johnson of the Royal Giants claimed an organization was necessary by the financial results of last season, when every owner of a colored ball club in the East lost money due to the exorbitant salaries paid to players and the keen competition among the various clubs.

The idea was to provide colored baseball with a solid business foundation and to prevent jumping from one club to another on the slightest pretext, as done in previous seasons. It was intended to protect the managers from unscrupulous and unreliable managers of independent clubs who engaged the colored clubs and unceremoniously canceled the date at the last moment if so inclined. The full text of the agreement read:

> The National Agreement for the government of professional colored base ball, entered into this day, October 22, 1906, between the Philadelphia Giants Base Ball and Athletic Association, Inc., of Philadelphia, PA, the Cuban X Giants Base Ball Club of New York, the Royal Giants Base Ball Club of Brooklyn, NY, the Cuban Giants Base Ball Club of New York and the Cuban Stars Base Ball Club of Havana, Cuba.
>
> This agreement made and entered into by and between the Philadelphia Giants Base Ball and

Top: **1906 Philadelphia Giants advertised themselves as the "World Champions," and perhaps they were. The press reported they won 108 games of the 145 played (.777) with six ties. Top row (from left to right), William Henry Binga, unknown, Sol White, Rube Foster and Nate Harris; bottom row (left to right), Danny McClellan, Pete Hill, Pete Booker, Willis Jones, Emmett Bowman, unknown (courtesy Dick Clark).**

Bottom: **The Philadelphia Giants smirk in their double-breasted studio uniforms. Top row (left to right) H. Smith, Mike Moore, Emmett Bowman, Sol White, Tom Washington and Dan McClellan; (middle row) Grant Johnson, Charlie Grant, Walter Schlichter, Rube Foster and Pete Hill; (bottom row) Bill Monroe and Pete Booker. Jones did not appear in any games that year (courtesy Dick Clark).**

Athletic Association, Inc., of Philadelphia, PA, the Cuban X Giants Base Ball Club of New York, the Royal Giants Base Ball Club of Brooklyn, NY, the Cuban Giants Base Ball Club of New York and the Cuban Stars Base Ball Club of Havana, Cuba, known as the National Association of Colored Base Ball Clubs of the United States and Cuba, shall be styled like the National Agreement and shall have for its objects:

(1) Perpetuation of colored base ball, in keeping with the national pastime of America by surrounding it with such safeguards as will warrant absolute public confidence in its integrity and methods, and by maintaining a high standard of skill and sportsmanship in its players.

(2) Protection of the property rights of those engaged in colored baseball as a business without sacrificing the spirit of competition in the conduct of the clubs.

(3) Promotion of the welfare of ball players as a class by developing and perfecting them in their profession and enabling them to secure adequate compensation for expertness.

Article 1.

Section 1: This agreement shall be indissoluble except by the unanimous vote of the parties to it, and if any of said parties withdraws from it or violates any of its fundamental principals the party so withdrawing or offending shall be treated as the enemies of colored baseball.

Article 2.

Section 1: Each party to this agreement retains the right to conduct its affairs and governs its players according to its constitution and by laws.

Section 2: The annual meeting shall be held at a place designated by the president on the third Monday in October in each year.

Article 3.

Section 1: Each member shall have one vote on all questions that may come before any meeting which may be held and such meetings may be called at the request of one or more members of the parties of this agreement.

Section 2: A secretary shall be elected yearly. The secretary's salary shall be ________ and his duties shall consist of keeping accurate minutes of the proceedings of this organization and giving every possible aid in securing engagements for the parties in this agreement.

Section 3: Whenever two or more clubs cannot amicably arrange differences over a player the case shall be presented to the disinterested members of this agreement and the decision made by a majority vote, but should it be impossible to reach an agreement and the decision made by a majority vote, but should it be impossible to reach an agreement or the decision not satisfactory to those involved the question in dispute be submitted with all evident in writing to the President of the National Commission, of white ball players whose decision shall be considered final and binding.[26]

Royal Giants manager, Grant "Home Run" Johnson hailed the event as an opportunity for credibility, saying. "The association was modeled on the lines of the National and the American League white clubs and the purpose was for the perpetuation of colored baseball by surrounding it with such safeguards as will warrant absolute public confidence in its integrity and methods and maintaining a high standard of skill and sportsmanship in its players."

Despite the formalities, the league failed to materialize for unknown reasons.

Instead the Freihofer Bakeries organized a colored league and invited the Cuban X-Giants, New York Cuban Giants, Brooklyn Royal Giants and the road warrior Cuban Stars to join. Printed on each loaf of bread was a coupon good for one admission.[27]

Founded in 1884 by Charles Freihofer, son of German immigrants, the bakery did not extend an invitation to the defending champion Philadelphia Giants. The outlawed team retaliated by taking Bruce Petway and Nate Harris from the X-Giants. By July 4, Lamar's X-Giants were in last place and dropped out of league competition. The Philly club replaced the X-Giants and took their dismal record before going on to win the pennant.

2nd Inning. A New Beginning: The Leland Giants, 1907–1909

Indianapolis Freeman, 16 November 1907

Growing Interest Taken In Proposed League

Baseball Enthusiastics All Over the Country Will Take Stock

Increasing interest is being felt more and more each day so far as the organizing of a National Colored Baseball League is concerned. Letters of inquiry continue to pour into this office in added numbers with each mail and everyone of them are of an encouraging nature. One correspondent states that "the league will be the proper thing, simply for the reason that it will give everyone an opportunity to see the National Game played in its best form. We will have the pleasure of enjoying good ball playing with the air of freedom that the white man does in his park. But, best of all, it will do all towards keeping a standard among our ball clubs and individuals. When we visit a ball game we will know that it will be worth seeing for the teams playing belong to the National League, which indicates professional playing." The formation of a league will do much toward separating the "scrub" from the professional players so as to insure fast ball playing. Also it will give the good player a chance to work up to good salaries.

All this is well and good, but the most important thing is yet to come. Arrangements must be made for railroad rates; salaries must be figured on; ball grounds have to be secured — that is suitable ones for the lady fan — and a hundred other things which will take a deal of brains, money and time. That is why it will be, indeed, necessary for those interested to get together by the 18 of December or January 1, at Indianapolis or Chicago. Already Mr. Frank C. Leland, Rube Foster, Ran Butler, Elwood C. Knox, J. D. Howard and others have signed their names to an agreement to meet at either date at either place mentioned which ever date or city shall best meet the approval of the majority interested.

The editor of sporting news of this paper desires that everyone send in their view concerning the league, when and where it shall meet and how it should be constructed.

However, 1906 would be Foster's last year with White's Philly Giants. As a lasting tribute he gave Sol White his secret for success with an essay on "How to Pitch" for his classic publication *History of Colored Base Ball.*

History of Colored Base Ball, 1907, editor Solomon White

How to Pitch
by Andrew Foster

It has been clearly demonstrated in the history of the national game of base ball that all positions need men that can play their respective positions and play them well. But it matters not how strong the infield or outfield may be, or how fast a team is on the bases, the main strength of all base ball nines lies in their pitchers. It does seem strange that a team composed of star players of today are weak without some first-class pitchers. It is common occurrence to hear or read the report of a game of ball where the headlines read, "He pitched great ball, but his support was bad," or "they never hit behind him," or "he was wild and ineffective." Sometimes the pitchers get great credit, especially when he has had support. There is always sympathy expressed for him, showing plainly the responsibility resting on his shoulders.

Any pitcher who expects to pitch regularly or play professional ball should first learn the essentials of making a pitcher.

Some people consider a young pitcher with terrific speed and a variety of curves a wonder, but the experienced base ball "fan" will watch his work for some time before they class him with the star twirlers. I have seen young pitchers at times pitch wonderful ball when receiving extraordinary support, but they never stop to think that it matters not how much speed or how fast their balls break, or how they fool the batter, that the batter is daily figuring on him and it is only a matter of time before they will solve his delivery. Being used to fooling batters, some pitchers, when they get hit, become worried and they will say "they don't break right for me today." Everything may work wrong for awhile and people will begin to lose confidence in him, especially if he is a youngster in fast company.

So many pitchers ruin their chances by not being in condition. Condition is the main essential to pitching. Some pitchers are better in warm weather than in cold weather. A pitcher should never fully let out until his arm becomes warm and limbered up. I have lost games by not being warmed up; but what is a game, to a pitcher's arm.

[Author's note: Ironically, the lack of conditioning would contribute to Foster's ineffectiveness in later years.]

I have a theory of pitching that has helped me considerably. A pitcher should have control of every ball he pitches. But it matters not how good a pitcher is, he will become wild at times and can't get them over. Do not become disheartened at that, don't slacken your speed to get a ball over the plate, but teach yourself to master the weakness. Some pitchers when they have three balls and two strikes on the batter, often bring the ball straight over the plate and as the batter is always looking for it that way he will possibly "break up the game" for you.

I used a curve ball mostly when in the hole. In the first place, the batter is not looking for it, and secondly they will hit a curve quicker as it may come over the plate, and if not, they are liable to be fooled. Most pitchers in the independent teams use a fast ball close to the batter which the batter can easily see will be on the in-corner of the plate and they get their eye on it very easy.

A pitcher should learn to field his position. Always try to get a ball in a position to throw it.

The real test comes when you are pitching with men on bases. Do not worry. Try to appear jolly and unconcerned. I have smiled often with the bases full with two strikes and three balls on the batter. This seems to unnerve them. In other instances, where the batter appears anxious to hit waste a little time on him, and when you think he realizes his position and everybody yelling for him to hit it out, waste a few balls and try his nerve; the majority of times you will win out by drawing him into hitting at a wide one.

I often sit on the bench and watch the opposing teams' batting practice to see how they swing at the ball and I gain a great deal by it. Try everything you can on a batter, and if he hits, don't become discouraged. Batters often have a day on and will hit any kind of ball, no matter where you put it.

The three great principles of pitching are good control, when to pitch certain balls, and where to pitch them. The longer you are in the game, the more you should gain by experience. Where inexperience will lose many games, nerve and experience will bring you out victor.

If at first you don't succeed, try again.

Later, in a 1915 *Chicago Defender* interview with writer George E. Mason, Foster revealed his reasons for leaving the club. He shared that after the 1906 season, Schlichter initiated some new administrative changes, offering lower salaries for some players and a meal allowance ceiling of two meals at 15 cents a day. Management also insisted that the players provide their own uniforms and be paid every 30 days. Instead of bi-weekly, Foster thought these new arrangements were unacceptable, considering the large crowds he had witnessed. And Foster knew out to draw a crowd. In February, he pitched a shutout for the Fort Worth Colts, defeating a colored team from Dallas, 9–0. The winners took the purse of $400 before a sell-out crowd.[1] It was then that Foster developed the great qualities that made him equally successful as a manager and a pitcher. He called several of the players of the Philadelphia Giants together and told them, while his contract or salary had not been reduced, he did not think they were being treated fairly, and they were going to starve trying to better themselves. He added he would guarantee their salaries offered by the Philly management, and place a team in Chicago, or if necessary they could all starve together.

The result of the clubhouse meeting was the reorganized Leland Giants. In 1907, Foster rejoined forces with Leland's Giants as a manager, bringing James Booker, Dangerfield Talbert, Nate Harris, Andrew "Jap" Payne, George Wright and Mike Moore over from the Philadelphia Giants. "We feel safe to say that there is no better semi-professional club in the world than the Leland Giants," reported the *Englewood (IL) Times*, "but they all get streaks and when they do they play like a lot of haymakers from Reubenville. For instance, even Rube Foster, who knows ball as well as he does his bible and some better, gave some of the most insane suggestions that a sane man could give."[2]

However, Foster found potential revenue less than satisfactory. Normally a club's big payday, the July 4 doubleheader, commanded only $150. Foster asked Leland permission to negotiate a new contract, while asking for 40 percent ownership. Foster was successful in securing a long-term pledge for 50 percent of the gate receipts, resulting in a $500 firecracker of a payday. The Giants became one of the biggest attractions in Chicago, as the paltry pennies paid became a thing of the past. Together with Walter Ball, Sam Strothers and Bobby Winston, the 1907 Leland Giants, skippered by Foster, won 86 games in 112 contests (.768), shutting out their opponents 13 times.[3] The wins on the field resulted in the Leland association increasing its capital stock to $100,000 from $25,000.

That season, Foster was praised by the *Englewood Times*; "Foster's pitching is too much for any of the semi-pros, and only for his color, he would be a $10,000 beauty in the big leagues."[4]

The following season, 1908, after joining the Chicago City League, the Giants won 92 of 128 games (.719), with 18 shutouts. The majority of the games were played against the Logan Squares, the Gunthers, the West Ends, Anson's Colts, and the Milwaukee White Sox, members of the metropolitan league.[5]

It is believed Foster pitched his sixth no-hitter that year, defeating the South Chicagos and Homer Hillebrand, 1–0. "Lefty" Hillebrand, from Princeton, had pitched for the Pittsburgh Pirates for three seasons (1905–06, 1908). According to press accounts, "Reuben shoved the pigskin across the plate with such terrific speed, that the southsiders showed actual terror. The southsiders came with all kinds of noise-making devices, from the automobile 'honk' down to the street urchin's squeak. Four thousands five hundred witnessed the last game and enthusiasm was at an even higher pitch than when [Joe] Gans[6] made his last fight. Rube Foster is now to baseball what Gans is to prizefighting, but the main feature that characterizes this battle of pitchers from the one of the fighters upon Labor Day is the fact that the white boy did not claim a broken wrist, neither did he quit when the Lelands landed the solar plexus blow in the sixth round, which really brought home the bacon. It was only one little score, but it looked as large as the Masonic Temple to the visitors because Foster had struck his gait and was striking them out so often that they kept up a regular procession [of] 'beatin' back to the bench."[7]

Defeating all-white squads was challenging as black clubs would also have to beat the home town umpire. One example came during a Chicago City League game against the Gunthers at Gunther Park, as the superior team struggled for a level playing field. With one of the Giants on third base, the catcher threw the ball over the head of the third baseman. The American Giant started for home and the pitcher ran over and tripped him. The third baseman retrieved the ball and put him out.

Foster immediately protested to the umpire and asked the Gunther manager for his support, but was denied. Foster called his men off the field and then decided to play the game out, winning 5–0. "All we have to beat is the umpire," claimed Foster.[8]

As the season ended Foster's Giants faced Mike "Turkey" Donlin's All-Stars, called by the *Chicago Examiner* "the best semi-professional team in the country." Donlin had vacated the New York Giants in 1906 after batting .356 and leading the National League with 124 runs scored. From 1908–1911 his career on grass was occasionally interrupted with the one-act play, "Stealing Home," as a vaudeville entertainer. Later in 1915, he appeared in a film about his life, "Right Off the Bat."[9]

Donlin's team was composed of many major leaguers who played under fictitious names to avoid the wrath of the National Commission. Besides Donlin, the All-Stars included future 1910 American League home run king, Jake Stahl (later player-manager of the Boston Red Sox and manager of the Washington Senators), pitcher Ed Hughes and five-time walk king, Tully "Topsy" Hartsel. Other All-Stars included Jimmy Callahan and Jimmy Ryan, a lifetime .306 hitter, whose major league career had ended four years earlier.

With more hype than a heavyweight championship fight, on August 27, the teams took the field for the first of six games. Foster took the opener, holding the All-Stars to three hits, winning 3–1. He struck out five and walked one. At bat, he singled and scored a run.

In the first game of the series, Foster was pitching a shutout through nine innings when the All-Stars loaded the bases after two were out. With the winning run on second base and the tying run on third base. Up to bat came the Philadelphia A's lead-off hitter, 5'5" Topsy Hartsel. Known for his cleverness, Foster sought to dig his way out of the hole with the tough left-hander at the plate.

Down in the count, 2–1, catcher James Booker and Foster held a conference halfway between the pitcher's mound and home plate. As they walked back to their positions, Booker yelled to Foster, "Take your time, big boy, and walk him because he'll break up the game." Foster stared down at Booker, and gave him a sign. Booker nodded and moved to one side, behind Hartsel, as if to take the first pitch-out of an intentional walk. When Foster fired his pitch, however, Booker glided back behind the plate, just in time to catch strike two!

Booker went back towards the pitcher's mound and in words loud enough to allow Hartsel to hear, he shouted at Foster, "What'd I tell you to do? I signaled for a ball and you chucked over a strike. Do you want him to break up the ball game?"

Seldom one to overplay his strategy, Foster decided to embellish his deception with a bit of acting. He summoned Booker to the mound once again. The fans started pounding their feet on the stadium's wooden plank boards and booing loudly. Hartsel complained to the umpire and asked him to hinder Booker and Foster from stalling. "Make him pitch the ball!" shouted the first base coach, "Don't let him stall, he's scared!" came the cry from the third base coach.

"All right, big fellar," said the umpire. "Quit your stalling and play ball or I'll call the game." Booker and Foster nodded to each other and resumed their positions. Foster rubbed up the ball, fastened his big-eyed gaze on Hartsel and commanded, "Take your foot off the plate!" So realistic were his words and actions, Hartsel looked down to see if his foot was actually on the plate — and Foster without any arm motion rammed strike three into Booker's mitt. "Y'er out!" yelled the ump. The Leland Giants won the game, 3 to 1, as Foster grinned boastfully and strutted off the field.

In the remaining games of the series, the Donlin All-Stars found the Foster crew to be tough, losing four out of six games to the Giants. Foster beat the stuffing out of Turkey's all-stars, pitching four complete game victories.

After the series was tied one game apiece, Shorey of the *Indianapolis Freeman* wrote, "Rube Foster is the pitcher of the Leland Giants, and he has all the speed of a [Amos] Rusie, the tricks of a [Hoss] Radbourne, and the heady coolness and deliberation of a Cy Young. What does that make of him? Why, the greatest baseball pitcher in the country; that is what the best ball players of white persuasion that have gone up against him say. But his color has kept him out of the big leagues, and that is why the Leland Giants, the Philadelphia Giants, and other colored teams for the last ten years have had the advantage of a pitcher who otherwise would be a priceless boon to the struggling White Sox or the ambitious Highlanders just now."[10]

When Shorey asked Foster what type of stuff he used to defeat the major league all-stars, he modestly replied, "I don't rely on any kind of ball, and I don't use any kind of system. I just kind of size up the batter and give them what I think he can't hit. Sometimes it's a curve, sometimes it's a straight ball, but I can most always tell, sort of by instinct, what's coming off behind me. Five or six years ago, I think, I'd have been a first-class pitcher, but I found then I'd got as far as I could go and that there was no hope of getting into the big leagues, so I kind of let myself go. I was playing with the Philadelphia Giants then."[11]

At the game, Foster's pitching style was admired by the Chicago White Sox players in attendance, as Charles Dryden wrote, "Most of the White Sox were present to get a line on the much touted Foster. The world beaters agreed that Rube had no style and no motion, but that his execution was fearful. He just grabs the ball in one hand and slams it, sometimes when the batsman is not looking."[12]

Overall, the most descriptive visual of the famed hurler was written by Shorey in his *A Historical Account of a Great Game of Ball.* "In appearance he is almost the typical stage darkie—husky, black as coal, with a halting stride, a head sunk between his shoulders, and without any ostensible neck. When he enters the box [pitcher's mound] he takes a calm survey of the field to see that his men are in place, sizes up the batter, and suddenly, before the batter realizes what has happened, the ball is over the plate for one strike. This is the most frequent of Rube's tricks, and he has plenty of them. He has the faculty of whipping the ball across the plate with or without the preliminary winding up [windup], which is the most painful performance of so many pitchers, and he can do it underhand, with a side-wheel motion [side-arm], overhand, or apparently snap it with his wrist. And when he is in a tight place he seemingly can pitch so that the ball will be batted to a certain place."[13]

With all due respect to Pan-Africanist W.E.B. DuBois, the dean of Negro intellectuals,[14] Shorey added the ultimate compliment, writing "if it were in the power of the colored people to honor him politically or to raise him to the station to which they believe he is entitled, Booker T. Washington would have to be content with second place."[15] Washington had become quite popular with white Americans in 1900 with the publication of his book, *Up From Slavery,* which expressed a non-vindictive attitude toward racism and slavery. The following year, 1901, Mr. Washington would become the first African American to prompt the question "Guess who is coming to dinner?" when he dined at the White House with President Theodore Roosevelt.[16]

Charles Dryden of the *Daily Tribune* added this comment about the Foster and the game: "There was no color line drawn anywhere. Why, Mr. Foster even saved the white umpire [Connolly] from the profane grasp of two enraged African athletes [Jap Payne and Nate Harris] and brought peace into the arena. [Payne had slid into first base] As a common leveler the national pastime has Booker T. Washington, and the 15th amendment, beaten eight furlongs flat. Nothing to it."[17]

Furthermore, Dryden wrote, "While Payne and Harris squabbled with the ump near first base Mr. Foster hastened to extend first aid to the imperiled. Passing between the two athletes from behind, Mr. Foster placed on the stomach of each a hand like a steam shovel and moved them to the rear. He then spoke softly to Mr. Connolly, using the first two fingers of the right hand for gestures, and the war cloud drifted away. When it comes to pitching at white folks and bossing men of his own color Mr. Foster is supreme."[18]

Also in Dryden's article, "Leland Giants Drub All-Stars: Mr. Foster is the Whole Melon," wrote that "A large, dark cloud, that looked like Rube Foster, some pitcher, obscured the All Stars yesterday in Mr. Comiskey's yard. The constellation under James John Callahan, the demon semi-pro'er, did not even twinkle. The Stars flashed just once in a black and tan combat that ended 3 to 1 in favor of the Leland Giants." Dryden added, "He is a student of the dry school of pitching, much esteemed by the unbleached Americans of South State Street. Rube's obsolete delivery parched the Stars with three hits, and the one run was a gift at the massive hands of Mr. Foster himself." With roughly 5,000 fans in attendance, with some placing bets, Dryden continued, "and in consequence the darktown followers of the esteemed Foster are picking up quite a bit of crap money."[19]

Forty years before Jackie Robinson crossed the color line, crap money came from more than 30,000, mostly white fans, who witnessed the Foster mastery of the All-Stars. Sportswriter David Wyatt of the *Freeman* in his article *Booker T. Washington or the Fifteenth Amendment*[20] wrote,

> There was no color line drawn anywhere; our white brethren outnumbered us by a few hundred and all bumped elbows in the grand stand, the box seats and bleachers; women and men alike, all whetted freely with one another on the possible outcome of the series, the effect it would have upon the future of the Negro in baseball, the merits of the different players, etc. All through the games you could hear nothing but praises for the colored boys. "Rube" Foster coming in for the lion's share, owing to his winning four games or all that he pitched. All the baseball critics in the city were out to look the Lelands over, many under the impression that they were overrated. The most interested of the number was Mr. Comiskey, owner of the White Sox, upon whose grounds three games were played. After witnessing the first game the White Sox boss said if it were possible he would have annexed the signature of at least three of the boys to contracts, and he was so enthused over the fast, snappy work of the Lelands that he had his world's champions to lay over one day in Chicago to watch the boys play.
>
> "Outgeneral the Whites": The colored boys demonstrated clearly that they were not a bunch of overgrown corn-fed athletes, despite appearances and many who thought they would see a gang of "piano movers" instead of ball players were greatly surprised, because the colored boys played so fast, pulled of so many tricks and outwitted the All-Stars to such an extent that their friends were compelled to express their sympathy in an open manner.
>
> The Lelands won the series, also the people of Chicago, because they have played to the largest crowds that have ever been seen on semi-professional parks. The two Sunday games since the big series, was the largest attendance ever shown at Auburn Park, reaching the 6,000 mark the first Sunday, and the boys have packed all the other parks where they have played, clear to the limit. Besides wining the All-Star series, they jumped right in Sunday, September 1 and beat the Normals, 2 to 0. This team won the pennant in the Park Owners' Association having a record of one game lost this season. Now satisfied they beat the River Forest team, which was accorded the title of champions of the traveling teams in the Inter-City Association, score 2 to 0. No all you can hear in baseball is the Lelands, wherever baseball is discussed, and its universal here. The colored boys come in for much praise. All we need is the courage; we have the talent and their ability is well known.[21]

Foster closed out the season as a hired gun for the St. Paul Colored Gophers. He defeated an all-star team of players from the cities of Minneapolis, Milwaukee and St. Paul, 5 to 3, on a two-hitter, striking out ten men. Wyatt wrote, "Rube was there with the strong arm and the way he shoveled the sphere across the plate was worth going miles to see. Rube made ten of the leaguers fan the air, and the rest went 'dippy' watching the operation."[22]

Following the 1907 season Foster sailed off to the island of Cuba. Playing for the Fe club, he won nine games against six losses in 16 starts. His 15 complete games remain an all-time high in Cuban Winter League history.

In 1908, the Leland Giants christened a ball park in an all-white neighborhood near 69th and Green Street as the Leland Giants Base Ball Park (a.k.a. Normal Park), advertising locally:

> Upon the success of the Leland Giants this year depends on the Negro's continuance as a factor in the baseball arena. This Park is the only Park in the city operated and controlled by Negroes. This should be sufficient for every Negro to attend the games at this Park.[23]

The park seated 3,000 grandstand patrons, with 400 box seats and 1,000 bleacher seats. It was unquestionably the finest park ever in the Midwest under black ownership. Along with a fine park, the *Indianapolis Freeman* on July 25 added that the Giants were "the best organized semi-pro team in the world today" with players "of high moral character and not the ball players of years ago." With the team's financial capital of $100,000 as a result of a successful 1907 season, the newspaper advertised the sale of Leland Giants stock:

> Leland Giants Base-Ball and Amusement Assn. Now Organizing — Capital Stock, $100,000.
>
> The Stock-Holders of the Leland Giants Base-Ball Association, has concluded to dissolve that Association in order to give room for the former, with its increased Capital for the purpose of buying a Permanent Home for The Leland Giants Base-Ball Club and Establishing for All The People, The Only First Class, Up-To-Date Amusement Park, With Its Theater (Light Opera), Figure Eight, Shoot the Chutes, Miniature Rides, Electric Theater, Dance Pavilion, Roller Skating, Hurley Burley, Double Swing, Boating, Auto Riding, and all the latest fun making devices and laugh producing concessions, together with a First Class Summer Hotel, large enough to accommodate 1000 guests, at its present location, 79th and Wentworth Ave., twenty (20) minutes ride on the Electric Cars to the Loop District in Chicago.
>
> The Public is Base-Ball mad, and amusement Crazy. Stocks have doubled in value in a single season. Millions can be made by those Who Take Stock in This New Enterprise.
>
> Are You In Favor Of The Race Owning And Operating This Immense And Well Paying Plant, Where More Than 1,000 Persons Will Be Employed, between May and October of each year, where you can come without fear and Enjoy The Life and Freedom of a Citizen unmolested or annoyed? The Answer can only be effectively given by subscribing for Stock in this Corporation. It has been made purposely low so that all Loyal Members of the Race can have a Share and Interest in this Twentieth Century Enterprise. Think of it, Shares Only Ten (10.00) Dollars Each. You Squander More than this amount Any Holiday around Amusement Parks and Public Places, where you are not wanted and never welcome. Come! buy and build one of your own by filling out the attached Coupon and mail with Ten Dollars to the Leland Giants Base-Ball and Amusement Association. Do it today so that we may commence to build.
>
> Leland Giants Base Ball & Amusement Assn., Mr. Beauregard F. Moseley; Treas., 6258 Halsted Street, Chicago, Ill.
>
> All payments on Stock Accounts must be made to the order of B.F. Moseley, Treasurer, 6258 Halsted Street, Chicago, Illinois. All Stock-holders are entitled to preference as employees and should inform the Treasurer with their final remittance of their intentions to apply for employment. For further information, address Leland Giants Base-Ball and Amusement Assn., 6258 Halsted St., Chicago, Ill.[24]

Going into the Memorial Day weekend, Foster had won six consecutive games. "Decoration Day put no stop to the winning streak of the Leland Giants. They went over to the Riverviews in the morning and when they had finished with them they piled up three to the good, while the Riverviews had a fat goose egg," wrote the *Englewood Times*. It added, "In the afternoon they took 13 innings to down the Logan Squares, each getting one in the fourth, and finally the black men got tired of fooling [around] and piled up three in the thirteenth, winning 4 to 1. Rube Foster pitched the morning game and Norman the afternoon. On Sunday Foster pitched again and the Marquettes got in the solar plexus 14 to 3. A remarkable feature was that Rube Foster has pitched 46 innings and not a single run was made off him until Sunday.[25]

In July, the biggest series of the year was played when the Philadelphia Giants visited Logan Square Park for a seven-game series to decide the colored champions of America. Foster had offered a winner-take-all purse of $2,500.[26] Leland's team took the first game, 6–4, Scotty Bowman outpitching Danny McClellan. Foster played first base and helped turn two double plays.

In the second game, the Philadelphia club evened up matters by defeating the Lelands, 5–4, over 11 innings. Leland's Buster Garrison gave up 13 hits as Bugs Hayman pitched a four-hitter, both pitchers going the distance. Game three saw Leland score the winning run in the ninth, as Walter Ball brought home the win over southpaw Fisher.

In game four, Foster took the mound against Dan McClellan. McClellan was bombed for seven hits and eight runs in four innings, as Foster pitched a complete game, allowing five hits and one run in the 11–1 Leland victory. According to Foster's scrapbook, in 12 previous encounters with McClellan, he was undefeated.[27] Foster returned to the mound four days later and received a whipping by the Philadelphia Giants, as Pop Lloyd got four of the team's 12 hits, resulting in an 8–2 loss for the Chicago club.

With the series favoring Chicago, three games to two, the Philly Giants won game six by a score of 7–4. The *Chicago Daily Tribune* boasted of the fielding by shortstop Pop Lloyd. "Lloyd was a whale at fielding and batting, grabbing off nine chances, everyone of them hard, besides batting in two tallies and scoring three times himself."[28] The seventh and deciding game was never played, for reasons unreported.

Overall, Foster pitched 18 innings and gave up 17 hits and nine runs. He struck out seven batters and walked four. Future Hall of Famers Pete Hill and Pop Lloyd hit for averages of .308 and .379 with slugging percentages of .500 and .448, respectively, to lead their teams.

Later in August, Foster rejoined the Gophers for one game against the Hibbing Colts, a seasoned squad from Minnesota's Iron Range. The team was composed of ex-professional players but provided little competition for Foster's wit as he no-hit the Colts for the seventh jewel of his career.

Earlier in the season, after a game on Memorial Day, "A remarkable feature was that Rube Foster has pitched 46 innings and not a single run was made off him until Sunday," in 4–1 win for Leland's club.[29] The local Chicago white paper cried, "If Professor Rube Foster of the Leland Giants were a pronounced blond, he would be in one of the big leagues drawing a salary of his own prescribing."[30]

The sporting editor for the *Detroit Free Press* described Foster this way in 1908:

> Several of them would be in the big leagues, were it not for their color, and notably among these players is "Rube" Foster, who is considered among the best pitchers in the world, barring nobody. He has worked against the leading batters of both leagues and they have found his offerings as vivid a proposition as anything in the hurling line to ever cut loose. He played all over the United States several times; also invaded the Island of Cuba. He managed a Cuban Club, the Cuban Nationals. He is the best known Colored man in the world today.[31]

It was reported that the Leland club did not lose a game in the Chicago City League.[32] Overall the team won 53, losing four games, beating the Cuban Giants of New York five straight games, and the All Havanas of Cuba in 11 out of 13 games played.

Before heading to Cuba following the 1908 season, a Temple, Texas, lady named Sarah Watts married Rube Foster on October 29. Foster joined the Havana Reds and won eight games, losing five. He compiled nine complete games in 15 starts, en route to winning eight of 13 decisions.

The following year, 1909, the Leland Giants joined the competitive integrated Chicago City League. Foster's first city league game of the season on May 6 was an 8–1 win over Cap Anson's Colts. He pitched a complete game, striking out nine and adding a triple in three plate appearances. The *Englewood Times* claimed, "The Leland Giants walked all over the Anson Colts Sunday at the latter's grounds. Rube Foster doing the pitching act, and he could scarcely do enough to get warmed up as Anson's orphans were such easy meat, the big fellow felt sorry for them and only defeated them 8 to 1 when it might just as well been 80 to 1 if the dark boys had have wanted the spring exercise."[33] The *Indianapolis Freeman* reported, "Foster is without doubt the most popular ball player in the country."[34]

Pop Lloyd's rolling-stone career spanned four decades, making the eternally youthful Lloyd a father-figure to many a protégé. Homestead Grays owner Cum Posey once said, "Lloyd is the Jekyll and Hyde of baseball — a fierce competitor on the field, but a gentle, considerate man off the field" (NoirTech Research).

Of course, Foster didn't win every game. On May 31, 1909, before 20,000 fans, he suffered perhaps the most humiliating defeat of his career against the West Ends at their park. Big Bill Gatewood had started the game for the Leland Giants, and had a 5–2 lead going in to the ninth inning, when he tired and loaded the bases. Without warming up Foster took the hill to face the opposing pitcher Jack Vance. On Rube's only pitch of the game, Vance launched a grand slammer for a 6–5 win, denting his armored immortality. The *Freeman* claimed, "Reports have it that the 1000's of citizens saw the ball pass over the city, going in the direction of Detroit. However the ball has not been seen or heard of since."[35]

Although enjoying another fine season, Foster suffered another setback on July 12th, against the Cuban Stars in Chicago's Gunther Park. Playing first base that day, Foster had doubled in a run and then scored from second on Wright's single, sliding in to home plate and injuring the leg. The *Chicago Tribune* reported, "Foster, largely depended upon to lead the colored team [to] the Chicago league pennant, left the field unaided, but a rough examination in the clubhouse indicated that a small bone in his left leg was broken, and it may be late in August before the heavyweight will be back on the mound."[36] Leland won the game, 13–6.

So far in 18 starts, Foster had completed 15 games, losing only three. His 15 victories included six shutouts and five one-run games. His ERA was less than a run. Foster was such a dominating force that season that after one commanding victory the *Indianapolis Freeman's* headlines simply stated: "FOSTER PITCHED, THAT'S ALL" with no box score printed.[37]

Despite the mid-season loss of Foster, the Giants won the city league championship and challenged the second-place Chicago Cubs of the National League to a three-game series at Gunther Park. The Cubs had won 104 games that year, finishing 6½ games behind the Pittsburgh Pirates, winners of 110 games. With a league championship in 1906, and World Series titles in 1907 and 1908, the Cubs were led by their ace Mordecai "Three Finger" Brown, a future Hall of Famer.

As a youth, Brownie lost parts of two fingers on his right hand in a feed cutter. He overcame his handicap, using it to his advantage in developing one of the nastiest curve balls the game had seen, posting 20-plus wins from 1906 to 1911. The team also featured baseball most celebrated double-play combination, Tinkers-to-Evers-to-Chance. But the Cubs' "Peerless Leader" Frank Chance, reportedly injured in the White Sox series, decided not to play and scrappy second-sacker Johnny Evers traveled home to upstate New York (Troy) to be with his wife Helen and their new baby boy.[38] Meanwhile, the Giants strengthened their team with two players, Bobby Marshall and Felix Wallace, from the Colored Gophers out of St. Paul, Minnesota, at $50 per game. Wallace was captain of the Gophers and was called "one of the brainiest and clever infielders ever produced in the Negro ranks."[39] Marshall was

After his baseball career, Robert Wall "Rube" Marshall, at the age of 40, played nine games as an end for the 1920 National Football League (NFL) Rock Island Independents, and three games for the 1925 Duluth (MN) Kelleys (NFL). He is the only former Negro Leaguer in the Football College Hall of Fame (NoirTech Research).

an All-American end and punter for the University of Minnesota Gophers football team.

The bitterly played series started with the Cubs' "Three Finger" Brown, who led the National League with 27 wins (he also had a 1.31 ERA) that season to face off against the formidable Walter Ball. The *Daily News* noted that "Walter Ball is pitching the best ball of his career and at present is the mainstay of the leaders of the Chicago Baseball League."[40] The Cubs won, 4–1, on three unearned runs, with Brown going the distance, striking out seven and walking one. The Giants' only run was the product of a Ball hit, steal of second, sacrifice and a "Three Finger" error.

An otherwise fine pitching performance by Ball was hampered by six Giants errors, two by the newly recruited Bobby Marshall. Failing to get a hit, he was benched the final two games. The popular Gopher was admired for his hitting and fielding around the first base bag. The *Hibbing Daily Tribune* reported that "He is tall, rangey (sic) fellow and spears the ball with one hand when they come high."[41] The *Twin City Star* noted the first baseman for his long "reach, fielding ability, and fearlessness," for "nothing but a locomotive" could hurt him in a collision near the bag.[42] The *Minneapolis Tribune* also admired his "wonderful fielding stunts around first base."[43] Also popular off the field, Marshall was called "the Idol of the Gridiron, the Star of the Diamond, the Pet of the Lady Fans."[44] Earlier in the year against Foster's Leland Giants, he hit a mammoth center field home run off of Walter Ball for a 10–9, extra inning win. The Colored Gophers took three of five games from the Foster–less Leland club, and laid claim to the unofficial "Champions of Colored Baseball" title.

Perhaps the most exciting play of the Cubs-Giants contest occurred in the eighth inning with Giants center fielder Joe Green on third base. In a pick-off attempt by Cubs catcher Pat Moran, Green slid back into the bag but was blocked by Harry Steinfeldt, breaking his leg, as the ball sailed into left field. Green struggled to his feet and proceeded to hop wildly on one leg toward home plate. The Cubs' left fielder Sheckard's relay nipped Green at the plate, as he collapsed in pain and was carried off the field on a stretcher.[45]

Down one game, the Giants enticed Foster to pitch the next game — his first since July 12 when he fractured his leg. The one-legged hurler was beating the Cubs' Ed Reulbach (19–10, 1.78 ERA) and reliever big Orvie Overall (20–11, 1.42 ERA) with a 5–2 lead going into the ninth inning.

A disgusted manager Frank Chance had already left the ball park in the sixth inning, after two Cubbies were caught off of first base by baseball's oldest trick.[46] With a runner on first base, the Giants' first baseman, Strothers, faked throws back to the pitcher, only to tag out the surprised Cubbies when they inched off the bag.

With a three-run lead in the ninth inning the masterful Foster, perhaps suffering from the lack of conditioning, gave up singles to Moran, Overall and utility man Heinie Zimmerman. With the bases loaded, Foster gave up his first walk of the game to Jimmy Sheckard, forcing in a run. Rightfielder Frank Schulte forced Overall at the plate on a hot grounder to the hot corner and Dick Wallace. The next batter, Del Howard, singled off the right field fence, driving in two runs to tie the score, moving Schulte to third.

With "Wildfire" Schulte on third base, Foster habitually threw over to third, allowing Dougherty time to warm up. The *Chicago Daily Tribune* described Foster's efforts as "about as fast as a hippopotamus would run on skis."[47]

A weakened Foster called time-out to summon his ace to finish the game. The Cubs players stormed the field claiming Foster was stalling for extra time. Surprisingly, as Umpire Meyer was breaking up the huddle on the mound, "Wildfire" dashed home from third base with the deciding run, giving the Chicago Cubs a 6–5 win. Foster protested that time had been called, but the Cubs' contested tally stood.

Satirical writer Ring Lardner also questioned the allowance in the *Chicago Tribune*: "Then came Foster's interview with Dougherty and the fans getting on the field, the argument with Meyer who claimed he did not hear Foster call time and Schulte going home with the winning run unmolested."

Lardner added, "Even the rabid Cubs fans agreed that it was a 'dirty steal' but added 'what can you do about it?'

Lardner continued, "The chances are that the game would have been protested if there had been anyone with whom a protest could have been lodged. Captain Foster asserted that he was not stalling at all, but merely asking Dougherty to take his pitching job away from him. Furthermore, he wanted to know how one Cub could be allowed to steal home when three or four others were standing on the diamond in conversation. There was no answer to this query since Meyer had made his ruling and the athletes had left the field."[48]

In the final game the Cubs recalled Three-Finger Brown, and could only beg three hits against southpaw Pat "the Black Marquard" Dougherty, who came from the Sprudels of West Baden, Indiana. Veteran player Bingo DeMoss of the Giants recalled, "I remembered the time we played the Chicago Cubs in 1909 and Pat tied into Brown in a pitching duel. In the first inning Pat faced Heinie Zimmerman, Jimmy Sheckard and Frank Schulte. He struck them out, in succession, on nine pitches."[49]

Ring Lardner, in his column "Brown Snuffs the Last Chance of Colored Team to Boast of Victory," agreed. "Pat Dougherty, left handed pitcher, fooled the Cubs almost as much as Brownie fooled the Giants. The first three men to face the dark left hander were called out on nine strikes and most of the Leland rooters were disappointed because he didn't keep on fanning people as fast as they faced him."[50]

In the bottom half of the inning, the Giants struck quickly when third sacker Wallace singled up the middle and Harris sacrificed him to second. Up to bat came a pitcher's worst nightmare — Pete Hill — a combination of Wade Boggs, Tony Oliva and Tony Gwynn all rolled into one. Hill was a lefty who sprayed line drives everywhere. Foster called him a "money" hitter.

With runners in scoring position Hill fouled off one pitch and missed another one, then watched a third strike pass a few inches above the ground for a called third strike. Ring Lardner said the pitch: "would have cut off his toes if he had not hopped out the way."[51] The questionable call seemed to take the steam out of the Foster team, eventually losing, 1–0. Bingo DeMoss added, "In the second (inning) though, Joe Tinker caught one for a double and scored on a fly ball by Brown. That one run was the ball game although we out hit the Cubs 4 to 3."[52] The Giants' left fielder, Andrew "Jap" Payne, known for his defensive abilities, failed to make the radar throw home, allowing Tinker to sneak in the winning run.

The Cubs swept the three-game series, claiming bragging rights for the city championship. Frank "Fay" Young, *Chicago Defender* sportswriter, stated, "The Giants lost all three games by one run as fans made fun at the way officials deliberately favored the Cubs just enough to assure victory."[53]

Despite many valiant attempts in subsequent years, Foster was unable to schedule a rematch with Frank Chance's Chicago Cubs. After the series an astonished Chance called Foster "the most finished product I've ever seen in the pitcher's box."[54]

Despite the Giants' loss, Foster was still the toast of the baseball world, as Howard A. Phelps, a sportswriter for *Half-Century Magazine*, boasted: "Foster harbors no envy. He beats the best of Colored teams and then coaches them as to their mistakes. He had never had his head swollen and is the same good natured, unassuming man, whom I marveled at years ago, when as a boy one afternoon, I saw him laughingly retire to his seat after striking out the last 16 men to face him in a game at the A.B.C. Baseball Park in Indianapolis. Still I wonder at him, not so much as a player now but more for this gentlemanly bearing and conduct." Phelps added, "Foster leaves a record that will stand for generations to come. He won more games than any pitcher who ever pitched. He was a student of the finer points of pitching; at home under any condition; the coolest man under pressure that ever stepped on a field."[55]

The 1909 *Spalding's Chicago Base Ball Guide* reported,

> This success was attained in spite of the loss of three of their star players during the schedule though broken legs, Bobby Winston and Joe Green, both left-fielders, and "Rube" Foster, the big pitching star, all being put out of the team through mishaps on the ball field. Winston and Foster were injured early in the July. In spite of the loss of the big players the team kept up its winning streak and won a majority of its games from all of the other clubs in the circuit. Walter Ball's pitching and the heavy hitting of Joe Green, Pete Hill, Mike Moore and George [sic, Sam] Strothers proved the main factors in the success of the colored club.

For the season the '09 Guide revealed the Giants' batting average for the 40 games at .273 with a slugging percentage of .327, tops in the league. Completely dominating, they led the league in runs scored, hits, total bases and stolen bases. Individually, Joe Green finished third for the batting title with a .330 average, behind the Logans' Jimmy Callahan's .362 and the West Ends' Bobby Lynch's .342. Pitching statistics were not published.

1909 Batting Statistics

Giant	G	AB	R	H	TB	SB	Avg	Slug
Mike Moore	40	136	24	43	61	5	.316	.448
Pete Hill	37	140	21	45	60	15	.321	.429
Sam Strothers	8	22	0	8	9	1	.364	.409
Joe Green	24	100	18	33	39	7	.330	.390
Rube Foster	11	39	7	10	14	1	.256	.359
Bill Gatewood	5	14	2	5	5	2	.357	.357
Walter Ball	25	80	13	19	27	3	.238	.338
George Wright	40	150	16	44	47	3	.293	.313
Danger Talbert	39	139	22	34	43	9	.245	.309
Jap Payne	37	140	17	39	39	9	.279	.279
Nate Harris	39	149	30	38	41	17	.255	.275
Pat Dougherty	13	37	3	7	10	1	.189	.270
Pete Booker	37	138	19	31	34	6	.225	.246
Bobby Winston	12	50	10	12	12	11	.240	.240
William Norman	6	17	0	3	4	0	.176	.235
Chappie Johnson	10	30	3	5	6	2	.167	.200
Totals	**40**	**1381**	**205**	**376**	**451**	**92**	**.273**	**.327**

The highlight over many seasons was raising funds for Provident Hospital which provided services at a time when most hospitals in Chicago would not treat African Americans. The hospital was founded by Dr. Daniel Hale Williams, an African-American cardiologist, credited with performing the first successful open heart surgery, without the patient dying from infection, in 1893.

The benefit game played on August 5 would be the first visit by the Cuban Stars to the White Sox Park at 39th and Wentworth Avenues. Regardless of the game's outcome, 4,000 estimated fans attended, including Mrs. Booker T. Washington. Heavyweight champion Jack Johnson umpired the game.[56]

3rd Inning. Legalities and Realities: Now There Are Two Lelands in Town? 1909–1910

Black Chicagoans were completely excluded from white-owned commercial amusements— skating rinks, dance halls and amusement parks. Invariably they were banned from America's favorite pastime — baseball. During the prewar years, Foster and other prominent blacks made repeated attempts to counter discrimination by organizing black baseball clubs and other recreational enterprises. Attorneys Robert R. Jackson and Beauregard F. Moseley promoted the first successful baseball team on the South Side — the Leland Giants. Officially known as The Leland Giants Baseball and Amusement Association, they held raffles, sold fish and chicken dinners, and baked goods to raise funds for an "all-colored" park at 69th and Halsted. The association also operated a dance hall at the popular Chateau de la Plaisance, a roller rink, food and drink club with vocal and band entertainment at 5318–26 South State Street.

> THE CHATEAU GARDENS. The Leland Giants Base Ball & Amusement Association added another feature to their already splendid list of attractions at their Chateau De La Plaisance established 5318–26 State Street, when, on last Saturday they opened after a months [sic] cessation to the largest crowd that was ever entertained in the City by means of our people. The Garden is a perfect dream with a double decked Parisian Gallery overlooking it from the South, a dance pavilion that will accommodate fifty couples, a band stand and stage with a solid up-right façade for moving pictures and illustrated songs, a health Merry Go-Round, swings and 200 tables and easy chairs opening by means of stairways, upon this gallery and Garden is the finest Roller Skating Rink in the west, with a separated Rink for beginners, above and connected with the inner galleries is a fine café presided over by that master of epicureans, C.D. Rice late of the Pekin Inn, Armant's Orchestra entertains with music from 7 to 11:45 each evening, Jerry Mills late of the Pekin [Theater][1] has charge of the vocalist and show department with Madam Lena Bryant the sweet singer and Lorain Board the renown baritone as leading characters; everything from soda to venison was served and every lady was happy, no discriminations, no boisterous or bad mannered people present and those who wish to patronize an institution meritorious and worthily will make a mistake if they don't visit the Chateau at least one evening a week. Tonight and tomorrow night there will be a special skate and dance program and a complete change in pictures and songs. Visit it tonight and be the guest of the only live Negro organization in the City.[2]

The Chateau was often advertised as "The only amusement park and pavilion owned and controlled by Negroes in the world," and "The only summer resort of its kind in the world."[3] Thought to be newsworthy, it was reported that Rube Foster's new bride, Sarah, "would take her first lessons on Rollers next Tuesday afternoon at the Chateau Rink."[4]

At the close of another profitable and winning season, Foster took exception to Leland for not fully sharing the gate receipts with his players. Facing financial challenges, Leland dissolved the corporation and sold his interest to an investment company owned by Chicago attorney Beauregard Moseley. Moseley retained Foster as captain and team manager of the newly formed organization.

Meanwhile, Leland re-incorporated the remnants of the original team, calling them

The 1908 version of the Leland Giants sporting a unique motif. Top row, left to right, Pete Hill, Jap Payne, George Wright, Walter Ball, Pete Booker, Bill Gatewood and Rube Foster. Bottom , left to right, Dangerfield Talbert, Mike Moore, Frank Leland, Bobby Winston, Sam Strothers and Nate Harris. That winter, Pete Hill, as a member of the Havana Reds, led the 45-game Cuban League season in runs scored (53), triples (5) and hits (60). The future Hall of Famer finished with a .343 batting average (NoirTech Research).

"Leland's Chicago Giants," creating a promotional quandary with the "Leland Giants" name now owned by attorney Moseley. This feud resulted in Leland's resignation and subsequent legal battle over naming rights.

A motion was rendered stating, "It is HEREFORE ORDERED, that hereafter, NO PERSON OR PERSONS ACTING FOR THE DEFENDANTS, SHALL IN ANY WISE USE THE NAME LELAND GIANTS' AS THE NAME OF THE DEFENDANT CLUB OR FEATURING THE NAME LELAND' IN CONNECTION THEREWITH, etc."[5]

Complete court filings and depositions can be found in Appendix I. The summation and legal briefing from attorney Branden Gregory of Williams & Morris, LLC follows.[6]

LELAND GIANTS BASE BALL & AMUSEMENT ASSOCIATION
V.
FRANK LELAND'S CHICAGO GIANTS BASE BALL CLUB, A CORP.; FRANK C. LELAND, MAJOR R.R. JACKSON, A.H. GARRETT, NATHAN HARRIS, AND CHICAGO CITY LEAGUE, A CORP.

Plaintiff Representative: Melville & McGavin

Defendant Representative: E.H. Morris

Procedural History: On 3/19/1910, Plaintiff entered Complaint against Defendant. On 4/8/1910, Plaintiff requested a temporary writ of injunction. On 4/12/10, Plaintiff entered an amended complaint against Defendant. Defendant entered answer to amended Complaint. On 4/20/1910, J. Baldwin prohibited Defendant from using name "Leland Giants," but allowed Defendant to advertise that Frank C. Leland is manager of Defendant's club. On 9/22/11, J. Walker entered a final judgment.

Issue(s): Whether or not Defendant can use the name "Leland" in connection with their baseball club known as "Frank Leland's Chicago Giants Base Ball Club."

Facts: Plaintiff alleged since 1905 Defendant, Frank C. Leland, owned and operated a baseball team which began playing baseball in Chicago under the name and title of the "Leland Giants." Plaintiff further alleged the team became indebted to A.G. Spalding Brothers (for uniforms and baseball supplies) resulting in financial problems. In the early spring of 1907, Leland sought the assistance of Beauregard F. Moseley (Treasurer and Secretary of Chicago, Cook County, Illinois) to help him keep the team in existence. Moseley allegedly suggested that Leland incorporate the team and issue capital stock to fund his team's operations.

On April 13, 1907, Leland Giants Base Ball Association was formed and incorporated. Stock was issued in the amount of $500 — which was filed in the Recorder's Office on June 3, 1907 (Doc. # 4045555; Book 9600; Pg. 362). The charter was also filed in Cook County on June 3rd (Doc. # 4045555; Book 156 of Corporation Records; Pg. 353). The incorporation was allegedly organized by Willis V. Jefferson, Frank C. Leland, and Beauregard F. Moseley.

The team began operating and advertising under the name "Leland Giants, The Championed Colored Base Ball Team of the World" throughout Chicago and Illinois. All contracts with reference to the team were known and referred to by the words "Leland Giants." The team played exhibition games throughout the summer and fall of 1907 without losing a single series— earning a record of 103 wins (32 shutouts) and 1 loss. The team became known as the "Leland Giants" throughout the country and were titled "The World Champions" under the "Leland Giants" name.

The demise of the original Leland Giants in 1909 signaled an end to an era in Chicago baseball. Frank Leland dissolved the organization, selling his interest to Chicago attorney Beauregard Moseley. Moseley retained Foster as captain and team manager of the new Leland Giants. Leland reincorporated and presented a new team called Leland's Chicago Giants Baseball Club. Now there were two teams in Chicago using the name of "Leland" (courtesy of Christine Loving).

In the fall of 1907, stockholders thought the capital stock in Leland Giants Base Ball Association was unvalued (worth $2,500) and wanted an increase in the capital stock. By vote of the stockholders, the Board of Directors was authorized to pay off all debts and sell all of the team's assets to the Leland Giants Baseball & Amusement Association (LGBAA). On December 4, 1907 a bill of sale was executed and all rights, privileges, powers, franchises, patents, royalties, grants, immunities and all property, real, personal and mixed, agreements, all debts, and the name and good will of the "Leland Giants" was sold to the LGBAA (Doc. # 413328; Book 8424; Pg. 597). LGBAA then issued $55,000 worth of stock to stockholders on March 6, 1908 — which was filed on March 17, 1908 (Doc. # 4173234; Book 143; Pg. 129). Stock issuance was organized by Frank C. Leland, John H. Bolden, Willis V. Jefferson, Andrew Foster, and Beauregard F. Moseley. For the year of 1908, the elected officers were: Frank C. Leland, President & Booking Agent; R.R. Jackson, 1st Vice President; Willis V. Jefferson, 2nd Vice President; Beauregard F. Moseley, Secretary & Treasurer; John H. Bolden, Rink Manager; and Andrew Foster, Manager & Captain.

Plaintiff claimed that under the name and style of the "Leland Giants," the LGBAA participated and won the pennant in the Chicago Base Ball League, and played exhibition games throughout the country. As a result of their reputation and success, they were able to play a series of games against the Chicago Cubs, a National League Club. As LGBAA, Plaintiff claimed it had invested money under the "Leland Giants" name. Expenses included stationery, uniforms with the "Leland Giants" name, and more than $1,000 in advertising costs under the "Leland Giants" name. LGBAA claimed they generated annual profits of more than $30,000 under the "Leland Giants" title.

On September 20, 1909, Frank C. Leland was fired as the Booking Agent for promoting another baseball club that competed with LGBAA. Allegedly, Andrew Foster replaced him and made arrangements with various teams throughout the country and within the city of Chicago to play exhibition games in 1910. After being terminated, Plaintiff claimed Frank C. Leland began to manage a team named "Frank Leland's Chicago Giants," and allegedly began using the name "Leland Giants." Plaintiff further asserted Frank C. Leland and the Chicago Base Ball League were going to release a baseball schedule depicting "Frank Leland's Chicago Giants" as Plaintiff's "Leland Giants." Plaintiff also claimed Defendant was advertising under the "Leland Giants" name; contacting owners of baseball teams, clubs, and parks to arrange games to play in 1910 under the "Leland Giants" name; and allegedly signed discharged players from the LGBAA's 1909 team to induce others into believing Defendant's team was Plaintiff's "Leland Giants."

LGBAA feared a decrease in their team's popularity, low gate sales, decreased attendance, and lower profits as a result of Defendant's actions, and sought an injunction to prevent Defendant from using the name "Leland Giants." Defendant claimed it incorporated the name "The Frank Leland's Chicago Base Ball Club" on November 2, 1909 and began playing against other clubs in 1910. Defendant denied Plaintiff's allegations that it intended to use the name "Leland Giants." Defendant claimed it advertised itself and sought to be known as the "Chicago Giants Base Ball Club," or the "Chicago Giants." However, Defendant stated Frank C. Leland had successfully managed for over 13 years (1896–1909) and it desired the public to know that its baseball club was under the management of Frank Leland because of his reputation as a baseball club manager.

Holding: J. Walker ruled in favor of Plaintiff. Held Defendant or any person, firm or corporation acting for the Defendant or the Defendants for themselves, is prohibited from using the name "Leland" in connection with the baseball club known as "Frank Leland's Chicago Giants Base Ball Club." Defendant was also ordered to pay costs related to lawsuit.

Concurring/Dissenting Opinions: N/A

Indianapolis Freeman, 2 October 1909

Frank C. Leland Resigns
Withdraws His Connection with the famous Leland Giants

Special to the *Freeman*

Chicago, Ill.- Frank Leland, manager of the Leland Giants and for several years the owner of the club, resigned from it last week and incorporated a new team, which he will enter the local circuit next year under the name of Leland's Chicago Giants. Up to this year Leland owned the club alone, but the team was sold to a stock company and for several months the former manager has had but little say in the management of the team. "Rube" Foster being the active head. Leland formed the club several years ago when he split up partnership with W. S. Peters, who owned the Chicago Union Giants with Leland. Leland will endeavor to get a franchise in the Chicago League next year.

Mr. Leland writes us the following in regard to his resignations as a president and a member of the board of directors of the Leland Giants Baseball Club:

Sporting Editor of the *Freeman*:

Sire — Since writing you I have resigned as a member of the board of directors and the presidency of the baseball team known as the Leland Giants, only to take a similar position in a new corporation known as Leland's Chicago Giants Baseball Club, or in short " Chicago Giants" and I have already opened offices at 5318–24 State Street, and my first official business was to sign for the new big colored team the famous boy wonder, Wm. Lindsey, who pitched against the Leland Giants at Kansas City, striking out sixteen men, allowing the Lelands only one hit. In leaving my associates in the Leland Giants I go wishing them nothing but success, but as everyone knows in baseball there are nothing but rivalry, and as I have worked very hard for my former associates success and every follower of the nations pastime knows that they have had nothing but success under my reign, I am going to put forth my strongest effort make in my new team the "Chicago Giants" the world's greatest baseball club. I tour the whole country and pick nothing but the best players we can have for the Chicago Giants. It will in all probability be the highest salaried colored baseball club in the world. The players report at New Orleans, LA, March 15, and there put in two weeks of hard practice, then start a tour of the Southern cities making such places as Birmingham, Mobile, Memphis, Chattanooga and other cities in route home to Chicago by May when we shall start our Northern campaign and in all probability as a member of the Chicago League.

Just before closing I would like to comment on Mr. James Smith and his baseball article last week. In one particular remark when he claimed Walter Ball as being the greatest colored pitcher during the past season, I heartily indorse it and can frankly say Walter Ball's brilliant work as a pitcher and fielder practically responsible for the Lelands winning the Chicago League pennant. Thanking you for the space and time that I have taken to announce the coming of my new big team, the Chicago Giants.

I am yours truly,
Frank C. Leland

Walter Ball, a native of Detroit, began his baseball career in 1893 with the St. Paul (MN) club, later playing with Grand Forks (ND) in the Red River Valley League, where he pitched in 28 games and won 25 for the 1899 North Dakota championship. Ball bounced around with some other North Dakota teams and was named captain of York (ND) the second half of the season. Quite the honor for the sole colored stud on the team for the times.

As a drawing card, in 1902 Ball joined St. Cloud (MN) where he received lots of press and praise. He was their staff ace and played second base when not on the mound. He batted either clean-up or fifth in the lineup, giving evidence of a good bat. The *St. Cloud (MN) Journal-Press* (June 5, 1902) reported after one victory, "Ball is what we have been looking for. He is not only a first class pitcher but plays the game in all of its stages. His initiative work in the ninth was the salvation of the game. Ball has won a happy home in St. Cloud." Ball also played center field for the St. Cloud club. The local press (July 3, 1902) claimed, "Ball's fielding was a feature of the game. He made a dash, for a high fly, covering a long distance and got the ball on the dead run."

Walter Ball, or the "Georgia Rabbit," would join his first all-colored team, the 1903 Chicago Union Giants. With the quickness of a wild hare, Ball only played one season for Leland's Union Giants before jumping to the 1904 Cuban X-Giants under E.B. Lamar. Ball then started the 1905 season with the Brooklyn Royal Giants, only to finish the second half back with the X-Giants. At the start of the 1906 season, Ball was with the Quaker Giants out of New York. When the team disbanded in July, he re-joined the X-Giants but finished the season with the Leland Giants. A new season, 1907, meant a new team for Ball. He organized and managed the St. Paul Colored Gophers for Reid and Hirshfield. After the Fourth of July, Ball went back to the Leland Giants.

In 1908, he was with the Minneapolis Keystones before Leland got his release to rejoin his Giants in mid–June, and he stayed through 1909. That year, he pitched in 25 games and lost only one, helping the Leland Giants win the City League championship.

As the Foster-Leland feud split the team apart, Ball remained with Leland's new team, the Chicago Giants. Later, his career including stints with the St. Louis Giants, Schenectady Mohawk Giants, New York Lincoln Stars, and other Chicago–based teams before retiring in 1924 at the age of 46.

Notwithstanding the Giants' success, the combination of two domineering leaders, Leland and Foster, caused fiction as Leland dissolved the partnership in September of 1909, and selling his interest in the Leland Giants Baseball Club and Amusement Association to an investment company, owned by Chicago attorney Beauregard Moseley. Moseley retained Foster as captain and team manager. At the same time, Leland re-incorporated a new team, officially naming them the Leland's Chicago Giants Baseball Club. Leland had formed the original Leland club in 1905 when he and W.S. Peters broke up the Chicago Union Giants. Now, there were two teams in Chicago using the name of "Leland."

In an effort to retain his birth right, Frank Leland filed a suit against the Moseley Corporation in March of 1910 for $100,000 in copyright damages. The following month, lawyer

Moseley won an injunction to block Leland's use of the name "Leland Giants," forcing Leland to name his re-organized club the "Chicago Giants" without the "Leland" antecedent.

The aftermath of the legal ruling resulted in the Chicago Giants retaining the services of Nate Harris (2b), captain, Charley Green (rf), Bobby Winston (lf), Harry Moore (cf), George Wright (ss), Bill Pettus (c), Walter Ball (p), Billy Norman (p) and Dangerfield Talbert as utility infielder. They brought over Bob Marshall (1b), Felix Wallace (2b), George "Chappie" Johnson (c, 1b), "Candy Jim" Taylor (3b), and pitcher Johnny "Steel Arm" Taylor from the St. Paul Colored Gophers. Plus a Texan from the San Antonio Broncos called "Cyclone," later known as future Hall of Famer Smokey Joe Williams.

Nationally known, sometimes the box scores from the period listed Joseph Williams as "C. Joe" [short for Cyclone Joe] in the Broncos lineup. It would take marginal efforts by historians to connect the dots and resolve this naming mystery.

Walter "Georgia Rabbit" Ball played on the integrated 1902 St. Cloud team of Minnesota. He was their staff ace and played second base when not on the mound. The Georgia Rabbit was called "a first class pitcher" by the local press. The next season Ball would join his first all-colored team, the Chicago Union Giants (NoirTech Research).

Meanwhile, Moseley and Foster retained the nucleus of the championship club and barnstormed across the Midwest, capitalizing on the recognizable Leland Giants name. The spinoff from Frank Leland allowed Foster to sign Jimmy Booker (1b), Grant Johnson (2b), Wes Pryor (3b), Pete Hill (cf), Andrew Payne (rf), and battery mates Sam Strothers (c) and Pat Dougherty (p). Foster enriched the roster by adding Pop Lloyd and a superb signal caller named Bruce Petway from the Philadelphia Giants. The lean Petway was renowned for throwing out "the Georgia Peach," Ty Cobb, trying to steal twice in a game in Cuba (in 1910)[7] and was known as one of the first catchers to run down the base line to back up the first baseman on an infielder's throw. In addition, right-handed fastball pitcher Frank "Ant" Wickware joined the team. An outstanding but unheralded pitcher, Wickware would later beat 36-game winner Walter "Big Train" Johnson before 6,000 fans in Syracuse, NY, on October 5, 1913, 1–0.[8]

Without a season-ending championship series to determine the best black ball club in America, many teams boasted of being number one in the land. James H. Smith, former shortstop of the original Leland Giants, voiced his opinion, in a letter to *The (Indianapolis) Freeman*, in the winter of 1909:

There seems to be quite a little discussion hereabout concerning who is and who is not the colored baseball champion. I have played on all of the colored teams of note, with the exception of the Philadelphia Giants. I was captain of the Leland Giants of Chicago the first year (1905) they changed their name from the Chicago Union Giants, winning a record forty-eight consecutive victories. I was also on the famous Algona Brownies, the Chicago Unions, Cuban X-Giants and captain of the St. Paul Colored Gophers. In 1904, as a member of the Cuban X-Giants, we won the title.

The following year we were to play the Philadelphia Giants in an eleven game series, but after they won two out of three games, they claimed the championship. The Giants have held the title ever since. The Leland Giants have never been the champions, as they have never played or beaten a team for it.

Last season (1908) they played the Philadelphia Giants a series of six games and split three games each. This season (1909), they played the St. Paul Colored Gophers for the advertised, "World's Colored Championship." The Gophers won three out of five games. Since that series, the Leland have lost to the Philadelphia Giants and the Kansas City (Kansas) Giants. My contention is that the Philadelphia Giants are still the champion team until beaten.

Smith's letter stirred the competitive spirits of black teams laying claim to the title of World's Colored Champions. Back in August, the St. Paul Colored Gophers, with ace "Steel Arm" Johnny Boyce Taylor, defeated the Leland Giants (without the injured Foster) three out of five games in St. Paul, Minnesota. Taylor had coached baseball at Biddle University [later renamed Johnson C. Smith University] in Charlotte, North Carolina, and M. and I. College [now Rust College] in Holly Springs, Mississippi. "Steel Arm" had won 37 and lost six games that season, splitting time between the Birmingham Giants and the Gophers. Taylor, known for his assortment of curves, claimed he never used tobacco or indulged in any beverages stronger than soda water or lemonade. The Colored Gophers had a record of 305 wins against 54 defeats with six ties over a three-year period. In 1907 they reported winning 37 straight games.

Another claimant, the 1909 Kansas City (Kansas) Giants, with their ace Bill Lindsey, had defeated the Leland team (again without Foster) two out of three games in September, in Kansas City. In one game, Lindsey struck out 16 and allowed only one hit. The Kansas Giants' record of 128–19, along with 54 consecutive wins the previous year, reinforced their claim. Other challenges came from the French Lick (Indiana) Plutos (126–20), Brooklyn Royal Giants and Louisville Cubs.

Attempting to end the debate, Foster issued a statement, in the Spring of 1910, to *The (Indianapolis) Freeman* with the ultimate challenge to all pretenders and contenders:

Rube Foster's Leland Giants challenges any ball club in the world for a series of games to decide the championship, for a side bet of $500 to $3,000, or for 75 per cent to the winner and 25 per cent to the loser, or for all the gate receipts. The Leland Giants will play on the above terms any place in the United States. I offer this inducement to all the so-called champions. We are open to play any place or any club. If our challenge is not accepted this year, we will claim the undisputed right to the championship of the world.

For fifty cents and a free cup of ice water, fans watched the re-organized 1910 Leland Giants win 35 games in a row, before losing in July to the Chicago Gunthers, 3–1, with Foster yielding nine hits.[9] The *Daily Tribune's* headline proudly boasted, "Lelands Defeated At Last: Gunthers Break Winning Streak of Colored Players"[10]

Never without confidence, in August attorney Moseley issued another worldly challenge:

We Challenge the World. The Leland Giants offer a chance for the Chicago Giants, Cubs or any team that thinks it can play ball. WEEP FOR MORE TEAMS TO DEFEAT. To the public in general

Attorney Moseley's Leland Giants of 1910. Top row (left to right), Bruce Petway, Pop Lloyd, Pete Hill, Pat Dougherty, Bill Lindsey, Frank Wickware, Rube Foster; Bottom row (left to right), Grant Johnson, Pete Booker, Jap Payne, Sam Strothers, Pete Duncan and Wes Pryor (courtesy Dick Clark).

> and to any manager, owner or representative of a first class baseball club in particular, greeting: In order to put at rest all doubt as to what baseball club is the champion of the world, the Leland Giants will being a tour of the world Octobers 1st, 1910. Before leaving Chicago they will meet all comers for $1,000 a side and gate receipts for three or more games. If this challenge is not accepted on or before September 15th, 1910, the Leland Giants will be heralded as the champions of America.[11]

In the end, the "chocolates," as they were often labeled by the white press, claimed the unofficial title as the "World Colored Champions" by winning 123 games and losing only six. Their astonishing record included 21 shutout victories. While intimidating, the popular team, with mega-stars like Pop Lloyd, Pete Hill, Grant "Home Run" Johnson, Bruce Petway and Frank Wickware, routinely outdrew their major league cross-town rivals, the Chicago Cubs and White Sox. In later years, Foster often claimed this was his greatest team. Manager John McGraw of N.Y. Giants fame, with whom Foster often traded logistics, bragged, "If I had a bucket of whitewash that wouldn't wash off, you wouldn't have five players left tomorrow."

In this record-setting year, 1910 (based on box scores found) Foster won 18 games and lost two, with four shutouts and a 1.23 ERA. However, the staff ace was the new addition, Frank Wickware, who won 20 games in 21 starts, against no losses, boasting an ERA of 1.66. That season, Wickware pitched a no-hitter against the Chicago Athletics, striking out 14 victims, walking two, with only one ball leaving the infield.[12] The trio of aces was completed by Pat Dougherty winning 16 of 17 decisions.

Frank Leland's 1910 Chicago Giants Baseball Club, top row (left to right), Candy Jim Taylor, Bobby Winston, Frank Leland, Charles Green, Dangerfield Talbert; middle row (left to right), Walter Ball, Nate Harris, Mike Moore; bottom row (left to right), Chappie Johnson, Bill Pettus, Cyclone Joe Williams, and Dick Wallace (courtesy Todd Peterson).

Indianapolis Freeman, 13 November 1909

Come, Fans, Rally Around the Flag!
By Andrew Foster

It has been often discussed, all over the entire country, which was the world's champion colored baseball club. After so many writers have given their views—some from a prejudiced standpoint, others from their limited experience—to all fair minded fans I will, by request, give the real facts and let you be the judge.

In 1903, I joined the Cuban Giants at New York, and played seven games, Cuban Giants of New York vs. Philadelphia Giants of Philadelphia, Pa., for the colored championship of the world. I defeated the Philadelphia Giants, under the management of Sol White, four straight games, without a defeat. The Philadelphia Giants were composed of such players as [John "Pat"] Patterson, [Harry] Buckner, [William] Binga, Frank Grant, Sol White, [William] Bell, [Charles "Kid"] Carter, [Robert] Footes and [John] Nelson. Winning the world's championship so easily from the Philadelphia Giants, in 1904 found me with them [the next year].

We again played for the championship, and only three games were played. I succeeded in winning two games out of the three. The Philadelphia Giants then claimed the world's championship and since that time the Royal Giants of Brooklyn have defeated the Philadelphia Giants.

Now, who is the champion colored baseball team of the world?

The Philadelphia Giants played the Leland Giants six games in 1908, breaking even—three games apiece. The Philadelphia Giants refused to play the tie off, and returned East satisfied and tickled to death to break even. Now, I have never heard of any championship of the world being played for in three games, and in 1904, after playing three games, the Philadelphia Giants, winning two, claimed the championship, and would book no other contests with the Cuban Giants, and in the series of seven games in 1903, the Cuban Giants defeated the Philadelphia Giants five out of seven games for the championship, and the following year the Philadelphia Giants, after winning two out of three games, quit and claimed the championship of the world.

But as no team, East or West, ever defeated the Cuban Giants of New York for the title in a series of seven games, I am convinced that the Cuban Giants disbanded as champions of the world, and when the Royals defeated the Philadelphia Giants, there was no title involved, and the Royals could not be counted or figured in as world's champions, and there is really no club in the country that is world's colored champions.

The St. Paul Colored Gophers recently claimed the title of world's champions by defeating the Lelands three out of five games in St. Paul, Minn. These were only exhibition contests, and no man who ever saw the Gophers play would think of classing them as world's colored champions, or would think the playing ability of the other clubs was very weak. No doubt they need advertising. Had you asked me who and where is the best colored ball team in the world? I could answer you with a smile, and as a fact: the Leland Giants are head and shoulders above all the teams in all departments of the game.

For three years, when the team was intact, no team ever won a series of games from them, and before [Bobby] Winston and Foster broke their legs and were no longer in the lineup. The Lelands lost two games out of Chicago in three seasons, none out of Illinois, and beat all comers.

The Philadelphia Giants played the Lelands in 1908. The first four games the Lelands won three out four. Then [George] Wright, the shortstop, and [Nate] Harris, second baseman of the club, were out of the lineup for the rest of the series, and the Philadelphia Giants evened up the series— the only team to do even that well. The Leland left Chicago with their full strength, April 6, 1909, playing in eight States, meeting all comers, winning every game.

We then met the Cuban Stars of Cuba, with our lineup again intact. We won eleven out of sixteen games from them, the only team in the United States to defeat them in a series, and also broke the winning streak of their crack pitcher, [Jose] Mendez — the only club in the United States to defeat him.

The series with the Cubans started the bad luck of the Lelands, in which Foster and Winston broke their legs, and neither have been of any service to the club since, and it was this much crippled club that had never lost a game out of Illinois who were at one time this past season without a pitcher, and also for three weeks, five of the regular team's men were on the hospital list and unable to play — it was then that the club began to meet reverses and let teams that would not be a card in Chicago defeat them, and each time each of the clubs had their lineup intact.

These are facts no one can dispute and while I have played on the same clubs with all the players that constitute the big clubs, having defeated them all at one time or another. I believe I am more competent to tell which is really the best club.

The Leland Giants are known far and wide. They have received more recognition from the press, having raised the standard higher than all the other colored teams together.

Three years ago, when I brought the now Leland Giants to Chicago, Mr. Frank C. Leland then owned the club. He made me a proposition to come to Chicago and manage the Lelands. Finally I consented to come. I released his entire club and brought my team all from the East. Baseball was never so popular as it is now. But unless the men who control the clubs get together and quit trying to put each other out of business, the ball player can no longer speak of his profession with pride, for it won't take it long to get back where it was before the Leland Giants come to Chicago in 1907.

Too much credit cannot be given the Lelands for winning the City League pennant. Being crippled, and playing under difficulties all the time proved of what caliber there were. And, still crippled, they played the Chicago Cubs, twice world champions, to a standstill — much harder than the American League champions played them.

In playing the Chicago National League club the Lelands accomplished what no other colored club in the country ever accomplished. Their gentlemanly way and good ball playing gained so much prestige that public sentiment forced the Cubs to meet the Lelands.

The Lelands will no doubt be out of the City League next year, and the Chicago Giants installed under Frank Leland. I go out on my own accord. I could not tear down the reputation of the club I sacrificed so much to make, under such circumstances. I only hope the new club will maintain in every respect the reputation and of all succeed in winning the pennant.

We have done all we could, have won all the honor we could, in the league, and have for the first in history a real pennant flag, and will fly it on our new grounds on the South Side in 1910. Those who are true and appreciate my efforts for three years will come and rally around the flag.

Yours respectfully,
Andrew Rube Foster
Manager Original Leland Giants

In the winter of 1909, the Leland Giants withdrew from the City League, along with the Gunthers, and joined the Park Owners Association (POA). Besides the Gunthers and the Giants, the POA consisted of the Roseland Eclipse, Meyers' Cubs, Senacas, Felix Colts, Specials, Koster Colts, all park-owning clubs, together with DeKalb, Joliet, Chicago Heights, Whiting Mutuals, The Shamrocks, All Chicagos, Chicago Grays, Nippersinks, Tom Moores, and the Webers as traveling teams.

Indianapolis Freeman 15 January 1910

Leland Giants to make Great Southern Tour
Rube Foster will lead Chicago Baseball Team on 9,072 mile tour.

One of the longest base ball trips ever arranged for a club composed of Negro players was began last Tuesday by the original Leland Giants, winners of the Chicago League championship of 1909. Sixteen [the correct number was 12] of the leading players in America, with Manager Rube Foster in charge, departed for Palm Beach, Florida. The trip will consume nearly five months' time, as the team will not return until May 14, when it will open the season with the Gunthers at W.C. Niesen's park.[13]

The trip was arranged by Manager Rube Foster and he writes that it is for the purpose of getting his club in shape to win the championship of Chicago a second time. Preliminary training will be done at Palm Beach, Florida. They will remain there until March 18.

Foster has scheduled games to be played in Texas, Louisiana, Florida, Mississippi, Missouri, Tennessee, and Georgia. In his journey through these different states the team will play 45 games in 24 towns. With the group of star players Foster has signed for the season of 1910 he expects to "bring home the bacon" in every contest. According to Foster's estimate the club will travel 9,072 miles before it returns.

For this trip Rube Foster has signed practically the entire Leland Giant team which won the Chicago League championship last season. The only men he will not have are Walter Ball [pitcher], Robert Winston [left fielder], and Harry Moore [centerfielder].

These [men] have decided to cast their lots with Frank Leland, who has organized the Chicago Leland Giant Club, which will run in opposition to the team to be handled by Foster, probably at Normal Park this coming summer. Foster has signed three pitchers to assist him on the trip. They are Pat Dougherty, [Frank] Wickware, known as the "Kansas Cyclone" and [?] Shanks, the leading twirler of the Texas "colored'" league. His infield will be made up of [Pete] Booker, [Nate] Harris, [George] Wright, and [Pop] Lloyd and [Puggey] Hutchinson. Pete Hill, the hard-hitting center fielder, will hold his regular position, Payne will be in right field and Duncan of the Philadelphia Giants in left, Foster also has succeeded in signing catcher Petway, star backstop, to fill Booker's place. Struthers also will assist behind the bat.

Foster has been training at Marlin Springs since November and he expects to have the best season of his career next year. His ankle, which he fractured in a game against the Cuban Giants at Gunther Park, has healed. While there he hopes to complete arrangements for a series of games for the Negro championship of the world, which probably will be played in the East and in Chicago. Foster is seeking to win this title also. Teams from Philadelphia, Brooklyn, Kansas City, Cleveland and New York will be involved in this championship test.

Author's mileage log of Leland's 1910 southern tour.

January 4	Chicago to Palm Beach, FL (training camp)	220 miles to
March 18	Ormond, Florida (1st game)	100 miles to
March 21, 22, 23	Jacksonville, FL	150 miles to
March 24	Savannah, GA	175 miles to
March 25	Macon, GA	250 miles to
March 26, 27, 28	Birmingham, AL	700 miles to
March 30	Chicago, IL	550 miles to
April 3, 4, 5	Memphis, TN	100 miles to
April 6, 7, 8	Jackson, TN	275 miles to
April 9, 10	Chattanooga, TN	400 miles to
April 11, 12	Jackson, MS	200 miles to
April 15, 16, 17	New Orleans, LA	350 miles to
April 18, 19, 20, 21	Houston TX	75 miles to
April 22, 23	Brenham, TX	175 miles to
April 24, 25, 26	San Antonio, TX	85 miles to
April 27	Austin, TX	100 miles to

April 28, 29	Waco, TX	35 miles to
April 30	Temple, TX	215 miles to
May 1	Sabina, TX	325 miles to
May 2, 3, 4	Fort Worth, TX	35 miles to
May 5, 6, 7	Dallas, TX	210 miles to
May 8, 9, 10	Oklahoma City, OK	350 miles to
May 11	Kansas City, MO	530 miles to
May 14	Chicago League Opening Day	

Roughly 100 years later, a calculated total of approximately 7,000 miles on modern highways (according to 2007 mileage charts) gives evidence that Foster's estimated trek of 9,072 miles in 1910 to be fairly accurate.

After a week of training the Giants, the *Palm Beach Daily News* reported,

> At the first game of baseball for the season, there was a large attendance and everyone who was present had an enjoyable time, though the score of 4 to 1, in favor of the Leland Giants team may have created a sad feeling for the enthusiastic fans who wished to see the Royal Giants carry off the victory. Nevertheless, all were satisfied with the good and exciting game. A great deal of life and snap was [sic] thrown into the game by the humorous catching in which George Johnson engaged. Johnson was first baseman for the Leland Giants, Al Robinson was first baseman for the Royal Giants and was equally as good. There was no lack of musical accompaniment and the brass band was most generous in its contribution of one lively selection after another. Rube Foster, the Colored Champion Ball Pitcher of the World, added grace and dignity to his title as he struck out 4 men and gave the Royal Giants only 3 hits, while the Leland Giants got 4 runs and 11 hits off of Earle, pitcher for the Royal Giants. They play again next Wednesday.[14]

As the Leland club trained down south, upgrades to the new stadium were in the process. "The repairing, painting and addition now being done on the Leland Giants' new ball park, 69th and Halsted Streets, by Secretary and Treasurer B.F. Moseley, when completed will make it the prettiest and most comfortable park in the city. There will be over 3,000 grand stand seats and nearly 400 box seats, and about 1,600 bleacher seats, making a seating capacity of 5,000. This Park can be reached by any South Side service line on Cottage Grove, State, Wentworth, Halsted, Centre, Ashland, and Western or the South Side 'L,' making it the most accessible Park in the city."[15] In mid–April, the paper reported, "The Leland Giants' new Park is about complete and is the prettiest thing in town."[16]

As scheduled, Foster's club did open the season in Chicago at the Gunthers on May 14 and 15. On Sunday, May 22, the Leland Giants played their first home game in the refurbished Normal Park on 69th and Halsted. It was reported that between 4,000 and 5,000 fans passed through the turnstiles as the Giants defeated the Gunthers 5 to 1.[17]

With financial limitations and the lack of quality facilities, it was uncommon for most black clubs to train during the off-season or have such an extensive spring training regiment, such as Foster's Giants, as they were often economically bounded to a few local warm-up exhibition games before Opening Day.

By June, the local paper reported that the Leland Giants had won 33 straight games.[18]

Indianapolis Freeman, 16 April 1910

Success of the Negro as a Ball Player
By Andrew Rube Foster

Manager and Captain of the Famous Chicago Leland Giants, World's Colored Champions, Pennant Winners of Chicago Baseball League, Season of 1909.

Great strides have been made by Negro baseball players in the past few years, and if he continues to receive the encouragement and hearty support of his own Kinsmen in a business way, the distance between him and the designated as wonderful success will be materially lessened. I don't mean to say that Negro players at this time or in the past have been successful, but I must admit that he has been quite backward when we look around and note the number of leagues that have been formed and are succeeding. We are aware of the fact that the plans and franchises of clubs and leagues are not owned or controlled by the players. The players are a part of the business and are looked upon as the most active and valuable assets of clubs and leagues as without the players there could be no league and without the leagues the players would be worthy of but a small amount of consideration. Therefore, we can readily see that one cannot be successful without the other. Baseball is a business just as much so as banking or manufacturing; and in order to be successful either, one must follow the rules, and principles that have long ago been laid down by men who can spell success a half a dozen different ways.

Began Wrong

The Negro started wrong, and after doing so he been the victim of all kinds of bad advice and has been an innocent participant in numerous wild schemes for prompting the game. In short, I will say that the business end of the game is sadly in need of repairs, and has failed to keep up with the pace of success, that the players have set.

To speak of the success of the Negro as a ball player, practically fighting single-handed with nothing but his health and strength to back him up, is a subject which requires— no delicate handling, and I do not think that anyone other than a score-worn warrior, who has been in the thickness of the many fights for success, can possibly make a statement which will pass the keen eyes of the critics of the game with anything like a chance to make believe that the Negro ball player has been successful.

Advanced in Many Ways

From a playing standpoint the Negro has been successful in various ways. A few years ago the colored player was being used as an attraction, solely through the comedy or fun that his peculiar acts upon the diamond brought out; his baseball ability was a secondary consideration, and he was looked upon in disfavor unless he had a half dozen men in the line-up with a vocabulary of witty sayings and comical antics. The players some years ago would write for a job; and it was only necessary for the promoter to say "yes" and the player would catch the first freight train headed in that direction, usually landing with no mention whatever as to contract, salary, etc. Such is not the case at present. The colored player has in the past few years advanced from the Knight of the Rod [and Reel], and his playing ability has reached such a stage of development that promoters make it their special duty to see that the physical condition of all players intended for a team is safe guarded in the best possible way.

[Author's note: Fishing was a very popular recreational sport in 1910.]

Training trips for colored clubs a few years back would have been looked upon as a joke, but at present such trips are a certainty, and are considered a necessity, considering the class of teams that are demanded by the public and the many requests that are coming in for an opportunity to see the representative stars among our race. The people who support the game have advanced far beyond the circus idea in baseball. So when a team takes the field and the fans soon make the fact known that they are there to see baseball, an exhibition of the national pastime and not a fancy comedy. The colored player recognizes this fact and he began at once to show a heated interest in the fine points of the game.

He has studied the game and has experimented with it from all angles until now we have players who are classed with the best in the land. This fact might be disputed upon the ground that we have had no chance to show it. But, nevertheless, such an honor has been given unto the colored lads by some of the best judges of baseball players in the country. Quite often you hear the remark: "Too bad he is a colored man," or "If so and so was only a white man he would be in the big leagues."

These [comments] together with many other complimentary praises have been hurled at our boys, and such remarks have not come in the nature of a jolly. But on the other hand they have appeared in print over the signature of men whose opinions are worth something and whose ideas are being studied, and are receiving consideration of thousands of lovers of the game. This shows that the Negro in a measure has been wholly successful as a player.

Up to the High Standard

Physically, mechanically or mentally speaking, the colored player has no superior. We have players at this time who can safely be classed with the highest types; and considering our resources for training and traveling in the business, I doubt if any of the big league stars could maintain the high playing standard and preserve their physical makeup to the extent that the colored player has, when you consider that he is compelled to ride in ill ventilated cars and make long jumps and is forced to put up with all sorts of inferior hotel accommodations, usually exhibiting on diamonds that are likened onto the proverbial corn fields. In spite of this handicap, he usually shows up in a condition fit to give battle to the best in the land. It is the honest opinion of many baseball men that were the Negro surrounded by the same financial resources of his white neighbor, that he would far outclass the latter.

There is nothing, mechanically speaking, which applies to the great baseball player of the country. But what the colored player has added to this repertoire and has practiced, studied and developed the same to such an extent that he has been given credit for adding many noted improvements to certain styles of play, which are in vogue at present.

Considering the fact the Negro has no league, it might appear that he does not study baseball. His doing does not receive anything like definite consideration, by the leading baseball journals of the country. But I want to say right here that such ideas are mistaken ones. I doubt if any race playing the game studies it more closely than the colored man. He is constantly upon the alert for something new, and if such does not appear, he sets to work trying to improve upon the old ones. It is a well known fact that when his studies upon a play are ended he has polished the same to such an extent that no rough spots are discernable. There is not a play in the game today that is foreign to the Negro player, and many plays which are receiving two column write-ups in the daily papers are being pulled off regularly by the colored boys. These are not receiving a great amount of attention because the best we can do is to mingle with the semi-pros; and the supposition is that all such class of teams are only copying after the big fellows.

Successful Artists

The Negro in the past few years has advanced from the barnyard class of teams up to aggregations that many big league managers would be glad to annex to their string.

Aside from being endowed through Nature with a grand physique, the Negro has developed to the highest point all in the way of art that should accompany the same. We have pitchers who can well be classed as artists from the fact that they have accomplished everything that has made the white player the talk of the country. I believe that our pitchers have brought more renown to our race than any other particular position named in connection with baseball. The pitcher is the most important personage upon a ball team. That is when the game is in progress. All eyes and attention are centered upon him and the deportment of his associates to a great extent depends materially upon his actions. If he is in the proper condition and is going good, it has a bearing upon the men behind him, which means much in the way of success. But if the reverse circumstances are true, it invariably has an effect upon his teammates, which often results in a rank failure of the whole team.

It is my honest opinion that our pitchers are the real students of the game; they are constantly studying and designing ways to deceive the other fellow. He is upon the aggressive at all times, and my opinion is that to be aggressive in baseball it brings into action more brain work than to be in a defensive position. The great studies the pitchers have made in the way of making the batter powerless before their deliveries show that such is true and we now have the whole country trying to devise some plan by which the effectiveness of the pitcher may be lessened. Now, considering the fact quite a few of our pitchers have shown enough in the way of merit as to be classed with the best in the country, it must mean that the player of color is a success. Following close behind our pitchers come our catchers.

The man behind the bat, to a certain extent is looked upon for being responsible for the great effectiveness of the pitcher. Playing this position, we have players, were they white, they could name their own salaries. It is the opinion of many that the great studying of his position by the pitcher is putting catching fast into the class known as a lost art. This is alarmingly true, not only among colored players, but also in the big leagues.

I doubt if there are over a half dozen top notch catchers in the whole country. Still in the list of what few we have there are men who can safely be classed in the best class. These latter facts tend to throw much light upon the success of the Negro player from the fact that our best representative players are shining in positions which are considered the head and brains of all clubs. We have players who are good as basemen and outfielders. We also have a few who are great batsmen, but how they would stand if working regular against the highest type of pitching is a question that time only can settle.

Should Organize

In my opinion the time is now at hand when the formation of colored leagues should receive much consideration. In fact, I believe it is absolutely necessary. We have now been in the game for a score of years, and we are no closer related to our white neighbor than when we first started; in fact, we are farther apart as he is going ahead, forming leagues in every little hamlet; and the forming of leagues produces a barrier which we cannot surmount, try as we will, unless we come to understand the heading of.

Organized Baseball

What we need is the proper financial backing and encouragement. The business end of the game has lagged along to such an extent that we now find ourselves in a dangerous predicament. We have a country full of colored ball players, well developed as to playing; but the places for giving employment to them are being promoted with such an eel-like pace, and the majority are founded upon such an uncertain business principle, that is having a tendency to throw a dense cloud over the Negro as a promoter of baseball. The players have through all sorts of adverse conditions, been able to bring our race to the notice of thousands who are interested in the game. Now will our business men and friends of the profession make an effort to help us to reach the coveted goal of complete success, or will they stand by and see us fall? Which shall it be?

I am sincerely yours,
Andrew Rube Foster
Mgr., Leland Giants B. B. C.

To kick off the 1910 season, the Leland Giants ran this weekly ad:

Play Ball
As it was never played.
Is what we are doing every Saturday,
Sunday and Holidays at our new park.
69th and Halsted Sts.
To the MOST SELECT AUDIENCES in
The city.
Games with the best talent procurable.
Come and visit our park and see RUBE FOSTER,
The world's greatest pitcher, assisted by
WICKWARE and DAUGHERTY
The SEASON'S SENSATION; Petway and
Booker, THE STARS; Hill and Payne, Prior,
Hutchinson, Lloyd and Home Run Johnson.
CELEBRITIES who CAN ONLY BE SEEN
ON OUR DIAMOND.
Game called at 3:30 P.M.

Grand Opening of Parks
May 15th
BOX SEATS reserved by mail or phone:
If order is accompanied with cash, 50c per seat.
Special attention to ladies and children.
Ice water served free.
Take any South Side surface car to 69th Street
And transfer to park or Normal Park car,
Englewood Branch South Side "L."
6221 S. Halsted St. Phone Went. 215.[19]

By 1910 the Leland Giants were the talk of the Midwest as they played before the largest crowds of any club in the league. The *Freeman* reported 102 wins against only four defeats, including 21 shutouts and one tie.[20] The paper also reported that the Giants were "the first and only colored Ball Club in the Union to become Champions in a white league."[21] Not satisfied with being champions of Chicago, attorney Beauregard Moseley issued a challenge to the world with a $1,000 side bet and all the gate receipts for three or more games. He noted if this challenge was not accepted on or before September 15, his Leland Giants would also be heralded as "champions of America."[22] There were no takers.

In 1910, the Giants would play some games at South Side Park III or Schorling Park at 39th and Wentworth. Recently rebuilt following a fire in 1909, the wooden structure would survive another 30 years, before becoming a dog-racing track in 1933, forcing the American Giants to play their home games in Indianapolis in Perry Stadium. However, wagers on dog racing were never legalized in Illinois, allowing new team owner Robert "King" Cole to regain control of the property.[23]

Schorling Park was located in the Armour Square district, basically a working-class white ethnic neighborhood. Built in 1891, it was home to the Chicago Wanderers cricket team, and hosted various other sporting events. Charles Comiskey leased and renovated the park for his White Sox in 1900 and at times the field was called South Side Park, White Sox Park, or 39th Street Grounds. It seated roughly 4,500 folks and cost an estimated $15,000 to rebuild.[24] A pitcher's park with distances of 350 and 360 feet down the lines and 450 feet to dead center, it was home run stingy. In later years it became the site of Colored World Series games in 1924, 1926 and 1927.

On December 23, 1940, a fire started in the west end bleachers, eventually burning the wooden structure to the ground on Christmas day. The estimated damage according to league president and team owner Horace G. Hall was $8,000.[25] Attempted efforts to repair the fire damage were abandoned in the spring of 1941. In 1947, the public housing Wentworth Garden Apartments were built on the site.

The 1910 season also saw a reappearance of Jack Johnson, fresh from the controversial "Fight of the Century" where he defeated James J. Jefferies before 22,000 fans in Reno, Nevada, on firecracker day. When Jefferies quit in the 15th round, after hitting the canvas twice, it caused race riots around the country, as America's "great white hope" had failed to answer the crowd's chants, to "kill that nigger."[26] The ringside band played the cakewalk syncopated "All Coons Look Alike to Me" by the late Ernest Hogan, an African American dancer, musician, and comedian.

In August the third annual Monster Ball game, a benefit for the Provident Hospital, was played in Comiskey Park between the Leland Giants and the Gunthers. The press advertised "Don't be surprised, if the umpire happens to be Jack Johnson."[27] Johnson had umpired the benefit game in 1909. Equally popular and hated, "for more than thirteen years, Jack Johnson was the most famous, and the most notorious African-American on Earth."[28]

A week earlier, the Leland Giants had promoted a game against the Cuban Stars, "Jack Johnson at Ball Game. Sunday is Jack Johnson Day at the Leland Giants Park, 69th and Halsted Street and the management, in addition to having the promise of the World's champion to be present in person will present to every lady entering the grandstand a souvenir of the great fighter. This is in keeping with the progressive spirit characterizing the Leland Giants Baseball and Amusement Association."[29] The Giants defeated the Stars, 5–2.

What kind of baseball player was Jack Johnson? Columnist Walter H. Eckersall of the *Chicago Daily Tribune* visited Johnson's training camp before the Jeffries fight and found Johnson running about eight miles a day, chopping wood, tossing the medicine ball around and playing a little baseball with his trainers in a vacant lot near his South Side home. Eckersall reported, "Jack knows baseball as well as pugilism. He stood up to the plate and looked the pitcher over with the eye of a major leaguer. When he swung on a fast one the ball traveled a long distance. His position on the field is first base and he is a fielder of no mean ability. Although he admitted he did not like to take chances by catching swift, thrown balls, his actions in playing the bag were enough to demonstrate that he knows the game. Whenever he was in doubt of catching a thrown ball he stopped it with the pad, for he asserted he does not want any broken fingers." Eckerall added, "For a big man Johnson runs the bases pretty fast. On his long hits he tore around the sacks and made the circuit several times during the game. His wind was good and after the game he did not show many signs of fatigue from the strenuous day's work."[30]

Following a banner year, the Lelands traveled to Havana and played before 8,000 fans to open a 16-game series. The Kansas Cyclone, Bill Lindsey, won the opener, 5–4 over Habana. The remaining 15 games had the following results.

W — Leland 7, Habana 4	WP — Lindsey, LP — Pereda
L — Leland 2, Almendares 5	WP — Pedroso, LP — Wickware
W — Leland 7, Almendares 0	**WP—Foster**, LP — Munoz
W — Leland 0, Almendares 1	WP — Mendez, LP — Dougherty
L — Leland 1, Almendares 3	WP — Pedroso, LP — Lindsey
W — Leland 4, Habana 1	WP — Wickware, LP — Mederos
L — Leland 2, Almendares 5	WP — Mendez, **LP—Foster**
W — Leland 3, Habana 2	WP — Dougherty, LP — Gonzalez
W — Leland 6, Habana 2	WP — Lindsey, LP — Pedroso
W — Leland 7, Almendares 6	**WP—Foster**, LP — Mendez
T — Leland 1, Almendares 1	10 inning tie.
W — Leland 11, Habana 7	WP — Wickware, LP — Mederos
W — Leland 6, Habana 1	**WP—Foster**, LP — Gonzalez
L — Leland 0, Almendares 1	WP — Munoz, LP — Lindsey
L — Leland 4, Almendares 5	WP — Mendez, LP — Dougherty

Like Jose Mendez, Foster won three of four outings, as his Giants won nine of 16 games with one tie. Pop Lloyd led the Giants attack, hitting .400 in 11 games.

Lloyd, Pete Hill, Grant Johnson and Bruce Petway remained on the island to play with the Habana Reds against the incoming Detroit Tigers with Ty Cobb in tow. The Tigers would play both the united Havana Reds/Leland Giants and the Almendares Blues in an 11–games series, and win seven games, to reverse their embarrassing loss of 1909. Three of their four loses came against the Habana/Leland team.

The *Chicago Daily News* reported: "It's the Cuban's turn today as Cuban ace Jose Mendez shuts out the Tigers, 3–0. On a steal attempt, Ty Cobb is thrown out three times by Bruce Petway, who played last year for the Chicago Leland Giants. On his last attempt, Cobb argued that the bag was three inches too far. When measured, Cobb was proven correct, but he was still out stealing."[31] Cobb, the current American League stolen base champion, with 76 thefts, was thrown out six times in six attempts.[32] A frustrated Cobb cut short the tour and returned to the U.S. The Tigers ended their Cuban swing at 7–4, with a tie. This was a reversal of 1909's 4–8 record, when they played the Cuban teams without Cobb and Crawford. The champion Philadelphia A's also played in Havana at the same time, finishing with a 4–6 record. The 23-year-old star was without a theft when he shipped out. However, Cobb did hit .368 (7 for 19 in five games), while his Tigers did little to tame Pop Lloyd (.500), Grant "Home Run" Johnson (.412) or Bruce Petway (.389).

Game Summaries

W — Detroit 10, Habana\Leland 2	WP — Ed Summers, LP — Pareda
W — Detroit 3, Almendares 0	WP — George Mullin, **LP—Jose Mendez**
L — Detroit 2, Habana\Leland 3	WP — Lico Mederos, LP — Ed Summers
L — Detroit 1, Almendares 2	WP — Lico Pedroso, LP — Ed Willett
L — Detroit 1, Habana\Leland 2	WP — Luis Gonzalez, LP — Geo. Mullin
T — Detroit 2, Almendares 2	Tie Ed Summers vs. **Jose Mendez**
W — Detroit 4, Habana\Leland 2	WP — Ed Willett, LP — Pareda

W — Detroit 4, Almendares 0 WP — Geo. Mullin, LP — Jose Munoz
L — Detroit 0, Habana\Leland 2 WP — Luis Gonzalez, LP — Ed Willett
W — Detroit 3, Almendares 2 WP — Ed Summer, LP — E. Pedroso
W — Detroit 12, Habana\Leland 4 WP — Geo. Mullin, LP — Lico Mederos
W — Detroit 6, Almendares 3 WP — Ed Summers, **LP—Jose Mendez**

After the first eight games, the American team had a slim 4–3 edge in victories, giving the fans stateside some concern. The *New York Times* stated, "The success of the Cubans against the Americans in Havana is something of a mystery to the Tigers. The players can advance any number of reasons for their inability to outclass the Cubans. The one best argument is the peculiar effect the climate has on the American ball tossers." The paper continued, "On the other hand, the Cuban players are in their element in this climate. A two-hour workout or a grueling extra-inning game scarcely gets up perspiration while the Americans are in a lather before their preliminary practice is over."[33]

Despite the heat, the Tigers prevailed. In the series, three games were shutouts, four games were decided by one run, one game was tied, and three contests went into extra innings. Quite an exciting series, with crowds estimated at 8,000.

The Cuban pitchers had targeted the much heralded "Georgia Peach," every time he came to bat, as Havana fans appealed for pitchers to strike out the mighty Cobb.

Cobb paid his respect and got off to a great start by hitting a home run in his first plate appearance and added two more hits later in the game. Only on his final appearance in the last game against Jose Mendez, did Cobb strike out. The great hitter took healthy swings on three pitches as the crowd went wild. On the street that evening all the fans could be heard saying, "Did you see Ty Cobb punch out?"[34]

The close of the 1910 season saw another attempt at creating an all-black league when Attorney B. F. Moseley announced his 17-step plan, "Tentative Plan National Negro Baseball League of America."

- First I would suggest that the league of Colored baseball players be named the National Negro Baseball League of America,
- 2nd, President-Treasurer,
- 3rd, that it be composed of 10 Clubs,
- 4th, that each Club pay in $10.00 by March 1, 1911,
- 5th, winners of games 50 per cent, losers 30 per cent, grounds 20 per cent of gate receipts,
- 6th certificate from both managers to Treasurer for transportation in case proceeds in any series of games is less than expenses and cost of transportation to next town where scheduled games are to be played and the same charged to and retained from the Club's share by the Manager of the Club next played with, where the percentage of debtor Clubs share exceeds the expenses and cost of transportation to be the next point where scheduled game is to be played and forwarded to the Treasurer,
- 7th, that the sum of $1,000 be the maximum amount to be retained in the Treasury,
- 8th, that any Club not clearing with Treasurer in 30 days be assessed the amount of its indebtness and if not paid in 10 days to be suspended,
- 9th umpires be employed of competent men, half of whom shall be Colored,
- 10th, 15, 25c, 35c, and 50c be charged for admission for boys and adults, as follows, boys 15c, adults bleachers 25c, Grand Stand 35c and Box seats 50c,
- 11th, players salaries to be classified A.B.C. and shall in no case exceed 80 per cent of the earnings of the club to which they belong except in cases of Clubs now under contract with players for year 1911,
- 12th, that a list of all players signed and under contract be recorded by the Club owners with the Secretary and the same shall not be tampered with by other Clubs, Managers or owners unless released by the Club first obtaining contract,
- 13th, that no expelled players be permitted to play in the League until re-installed by the Association,

- 14th that all grievances be made to the Association officers in writing by the aggrieved party and the party complained against promptly notified 10 days before any action is taken,
- 15th, that umpires receive a salary of $5.00 per game and to be paid from the gross receipts by the home Club,
- 16th, that the President receive a salary based upon a percentage of the moneys handled,
- 17th, that a meeting of all interested parties be called by Elwood C. Knox, of the *Freeman* on or before the 15th of December next 1910, and definitive plans made.

These are my suggestions and if they appeal to you I would be pleased to have you assist me in getting it before the Public, and especially those interested in the game of baseball by writing me.
Respectfully yours, B.F. Moseley, 6221 South Halsted St, Phone Wentworth 215.[35]

Later in November, a banquet was held to honor Rube Foster and his successful Leland Giants. Moseley took the opportunity to tell the well-wishers of his efforts to start a new league. In attendance were M.J. Fitzpatrick (an umpire), Professor William Emanuel, Julius F. Taylor, editor of the *Broad Ax*, Colonel J.H. Johnson of the Eighth Regiment, and Cary B. Lewis, among others. Lewis had moved to the city six months earlier as a news correspondent to the *Indianapolis Freeman*. This month he was made managing editor of the *Chicago Chronicle*, and eventually would play a prominent role in developing a viable constitution for the Negro National League in 1920.

A declaration to start the league was presented and signed.

Whereas, the undersigned having been and still are interested in the National Pastime, Baseball, and

Whereas, the Professional Negro Ball player is compelled under present conditions to live and die a Semi Pro there being no other field open to him, thus compelling veteran players to be classed and pitted with amateurs, and

Whereas, the Capital invested in the Semi Pro Parks and players can be utilized for the active formation and operation of a Negro National Baseball League, THEREFORE BE IT RESOLVED, that the undersigned and such other persons who may be interested in the formation of such a League meet at the Chateau De La Plaisance, 5324 State street, Chicago, Illinois, Wednesday, December 28th, 1910 at 12 M. Noon, in National conference for the purpose of organizing, securing Park franchises, creating a circuit and appointing a schedule committee, etc.

RESOLVE that the tentative plan heretofore issued by Beauregard F. Moseley, be the nucleus or basis upon which the organization shall be formed. This 30th day of November, 1910. Signed

Beauregard F. Moseley, representing Leland Giants of Chicago, Illinois.
Frank Colombo, representing New Orleans BIB. Club of New Orleans, La.
Ralph Clemmons, representing Dixie Park Baseball Club of Mobile, Ala.
S.R. Gibbs, representing Fall City Stars of Louisville, Ky.
S.M. Cohen, representing Cohen Baseball Club of New Orleans, La.[36]

The new League selected Beauregard F. Moseley as its temporary chairman, and Felix H. Payne of Kansas City, Kansas, as temporary Secretary. The eight towns to be ports of call of the Colored Association, were Chicago, Louisville, New Orleans, Mobile, St. Louis, Kansas City, Mo., Kansas City, Kansas, and Columbus, Ohio.

Under the suggested plans of the League it would incorporate in Illinois, with $2,500 capital, each Club paying $300.00 for its franchise. Other resolutions that went through were to have at least half of the umpires Colored men and pay them $5.00 a game; to establish a black list of players who may jump a reserve list to be agreed upon by the Clubs at the next meeting; to limit the League to one franchise in each city.

Outside representatives present at the meeting when lawyer Moseley called it to order were Tobe Smith and Payne of Kansas City, Kansas, and Frank Walker, of New Orleans, Louisiana. Other Clubs were represented by proxies, held by local colored fans. The league elected an executive committee to wind up all details and accept applications from cities desiring to get in the League, which would meet in New Orleans sometime during Mardi Gras week, not later than February 15th. The committee consisted of Moseley, Payne, and Walker. It did not appear Rube Foster was part of the creative team. The proposed National Colored League of Professional Base Ball Clubs failed to emerge as perhaps transportation costs were outside team budgets.[37]

4th Inning. Strive to Survive: The American Giants, 1911–1914

After the 1910 season, Foster's baseball career had a change of menu — less pitching, more managing. The second course of Foster's career between 1911 and 1920 instilled a lasting impression on the baseball landscape, as the American Giants marched onto the scene. Moseley emphatically advised in the *Broad Ax* newspaper on January 21, 1911, that black people:

> ...are already forced out of the game from a national standpoint ... presages the day when there will be no opportunities for colored ball players, except when the Negro comes to his own rescue by organizing and patronizing the game successfully, which would of itself force recognition from minor white leagues to play us and share in the receipts.

Moseley's statement of cause was clearly an expression of Booker T. Washington's doctrine of self-help, described in his Atlanta Compromise speech, with Moseley adding "...let those who would serve the Race and assist it in holding its back up ... organize an effort to secure ... the best club of ball players possible."

Soon after that year, Foster joined forces with John M. Schorling, a white tavern owner and confidant of Charles A. Comiskey, White Sox owner. In 1910 Comiskey's White Sox had moved into their new stadium on July 1, leaving behind Old Roman's Park (a.k.a. South Side II) on 35th and Wentworth.

Comiskey ordered the stands torn down and the lumber sold in an effort to keep out the competition.[1] In the interim, Schorling obtained the lease and rebuilt the structure at 39th and Wentworth.

In May, the *Tribune* announced "Dedication of a new ball park on Sunday, 'Home of Colored Team'— Spaldings and the colored American Giants to Play on Site of Sox Old Grounds."[2] The park became the home of black baseball's finest team, as the White Sox moved to newly built Comiskey Park, four blocks away. Foster put "THE GREATEST AGGREGATION OF COLORED BASEBALL PLAYERS IN THE WORLD" on their letterhead stationery to promote this fact (see page 65). The Giants normally played semi-pro teams for a guarantee of $60, rain or shine, with fifty percent of the gross receipts guaranteed if their ace, Rube Foster would pitch.

On August 29 of 1911, the American Giants met the Cuban Stars in Atlantic City, NJ. It was a match-up of two future Hall of Famers, Rube Foster and Jose Mendez. The showdown of this game lived up to its billing as Mendez and the islanders defeated the American Giants, 1–0. Playing Foster–style baseball, when Hernandez tripled in the eighth inning, Mendez executed a bunt down the first base line for the perfect suicide squeeze play to score the winning run. The menacing Mendez struck out six, walked one and gave up four hits in victory, while Foster struck out four, walked two and yielded five hits in defeat.

Indianapolis Freeman, 16 December 1911

Trouble in Colored Base Ball
By Andrew (Rube) Foster
Manager American Giants Baseball Club, Chicago, Ill.

Petty jealousy over prosperity seems to be the factor that has sounded the death knell of Negro baseball, starting back as far as 1905, when the trouble began to brew throughout the East. The organization of the National Association of Colored Baseball Clubs in the East met with disfavor with Western promoters, and it failed to get the support of the latter section of the country. This brought about a guerilla campaign in baseball, which resulted in the majority of the star players landing in Chicago.

The organization of the Leland Giants, of which I was manager in 1907, was the signal for prosperity and that season saw it at its height. The financial success of this club and association aroused such an amount of enthusiasm and interest in the game that it at once brought forth enmity upon all sides, and strange to say, the greater portion was right within the ranks of the association itself. Who should receive the big end of credit for the great work of prosperity and in whose hand should the destiny of the game fall, and who should be Czar of the baseball universe, soon turned out to be the main topic for discussion. The destinies of the game appeared to be already in good hands and operated upon a more business like plan than had ever before or since been inaugurated. The downfall of colored baseball in Chicago and throughout the South lies at the feet of Frank C. Leland, who is a mere accident in baseball. Trouble began to brew in the organization when he tried to become manager. The men who invested their money in the club thought it advisable to keep me as manager, as I had accomplished in one year what he failed to do in a lifetime. His low, dirty, undermining tactics against me, and his ambition to exterminate me from baseball, dug a grave for him in baseball, and he is now a detriment to the game.

A few seekers after notoriety, who were endowed with more ambition than brains, began to lay secret plans to overthrow (namely, Chicago Giants) the ruling powers and thereby corral the spotlight position. The insurgents mustered up quite a following and the result was that Chicago became a regular hotbed of guerilla campaign in baseball. As the old fellows say, “We just can’t stand prosperity,” was never more fully demonstrated. Chicago soon became the scene of two big clubs struggling for superiority and popular favor, with a lot of influential backers of the insurgent type upon one side, against the practical baseball men on the other side. The rebellious immediately declared war and prepared to go to the last ditch in the fight, while the other side was equally as firm. Therefore, what was considered an enterprising business venture panned out to be speculation of the wildcat kind of a financial struggle of the survival of the fittest.

During the crusade my club was torn asunder. I retained only a few of the men who had made Chicago such a financial success to Negro players and owners. The same men, Leland and Mayor Jackson, who were associated in business with me for three years, persuaded our players, by offering fancy salaries to jump. Having baseball at heart, I tried to reason with them, telling them they would soon have their players jumping them, and if they wanted them to respect their contracts they ought not to teach and persuade them to jump or break my contract.

But to no avail. I started out and got a new club that have proven by their work to be the best colored club ever gotten together, the only club capable of measuring arms with the big league clubs. I challenged them (Chicago Giants) and they turned a deaf ear to us, saying they intended to put me out of business in Chicago. They not only refused to play us, but wrote all over the country to other managers, telling them they could not play them if they played me, and also told all the white clubs around Chicago. We went right along, defeating everybody and our enviable reputation opened the eyes of the baseball world, and in the season of 1911 signed a contract to manage the American Giants, occupying the franchise they had played under in the Chicago Baseball League for J. M. Schorling.

This was the blow that killed father. They made all overtures to me, and, while I had a chance to crush them, I had a better way to reap my revenge. Soon inflated stories of dividends derived from semi-pro ball began to circulate and parks sprang up, and Chicago found itself congested with the semi-pro game. It required but a short period to discover that there were too many clubs and parks, and business began to fall away, and soon some of the largest semi-pro parks in Chicago nailed up their gates, leaving only four parks in the city out of twenty. There are only two parks on the North Side, one of the West Side and one on the South Side. Our park, on the South Side, is the finest semi-pro park in the world, reaching by every street car in Chicago, right in the city.

The notoriety seekers were too busy in the war of extermination to listen to sensible entreaties, and in their haste of planning strategic movies against their colored brothers, they forgot to keep up with the whites and their movements. Just how much their life and the strength of their fighting depended

PLAY BALL

Genteel, Scientific and Gentlemanly Ball Playing By

LELAND GIANTS

Every Sunday at their Park

69th and Halsted Street

"Upon the success of the Leland Giants this year depends the Negro's continuance as a factor in the baseball arena. Their Park is the only Park in the city operated and controled by Negroes. This should be sufficient for every Negro to attend the games at this Park."

"Genteel, Scientific and Gentlemanly Ball Played" was the promotional theme by the Leland Giants (*Chicago Defender* 20 May 1911).

upon the other race they failed to compute. Soon they were put in touch with the fact that the semi-pro game was on its last legs, and the destinies of the Negro were in the hands of a few whites. Then a wild scramble ensured for popular favor of the white man and a commanding foothold at his table. The South Side of the city dwindled down to where there was but one park, and this was the abandoned White Sox grounds. J. M. Schorling, who had furnished a home for a decade for Negro clubs, secured this ground, built a palatial plant and selected yours truly as the best available personage to organize and head a club.

This last move put the insurgent element to their wits' end, and they finally decided upon peace. This panned out to be a hoax, pure and simple, as it was soon discovered that the hand which carried the olive [branch] also concealed a dirk. Soon the hammer and anvil chorus began and a search of the baseball house, from garret to basement, began, and every little thread was fully unraveled in hopes that it would lead to a vulnerable point of attack.

Not satisfied, the manager, and players became objects of attack; players were persuaded to leave; others were knocked, and organized gangs, friends of the insurgents, led unmerciful attacks against the club and its methods. The team seemed to waiver under the strain, and when a point was reached where it was thought that disruption had set in, a series of games were arranged. Supremacy in baseball was the watchword, but extermination was the aim, and to the latter end not a stone was left unturned in its accomplishment.

We decisively won 11 out of 15 games before the largest crowds ever at a semi-pro game. Convinced of the superiority of my club, every cheap, mean, low trick was resorted to for the purpose of not only discrediting my club, but to hamper and ruin the prestige of the owner of the plant, if possible.

My club came out victorious in the struggle, and who stands the cost? Negro baseball.

PLAY BALL

As only the celebrated Athletes

Leland Giants

Can play it at their Park

69th and Halsted Sts.

The only Park in the city owned and operated by our People every Sunday, Saturday and Holiday

Opening Game Sunday, April 23rd

LELAND GIANTS VS. MUTUALS

Box seats 50c reserved by phone 215 Wentworth
Grand Stand 35c, Bleachers 25c, Boys 15c

B. F. MOSELEY, Secretary and Treasurer
6221 Halsted Street

For a half dollar, fans could see the best black team in Chicago playing in the only park owned and operated by local African Americans (*Chicago Defender* 14 April 1911).

It is nothing short of a crime in the face of the vast amount of prosperity with which the game is now surrounded, to see the Negro an object of pity and poverty, all due to his own folly. It would seem that if such men as [former] President [Theodore] Roosevelt and [future Secretary of State William J.] Bryan should lend their aid to the great game it would give it a monstrous impetus.

Therefore, when some of the so-called leaders of our race take a hand, and the game retrogrades to the lowest ebb or level, it is high time that we bury our faces in shame. Four flushers and notoriety seekers in baseball should be relegated to the discard and their places should be filled with men with rich, red blood running through their veins. The old-time methods and ideas, which bring nothing but disruption and discord, should be forgotten, and the twentieth century policies, the methods that bring success, should be inaugurated.

The wild, reckless scramble under the guise of baseball is keeping us down, and we will always be the underdog until we can successfully employ the methods that have brought success to the great powers that be in baseball of the present era — organization.

We have had enough good men associated financially with clubs to insure success, but the same spirit that has existed in Chicago exists there — one man trying to "do" the other. With clubs in St. Louis, Kansas City, Louisville, Indianapolis, Chicago and Detroit, operated by businessmen, in an organization, it would be the best thing yet in baseball.

There is enough capital in the club owners to put up parks, and let the league own Indianapolis and Louisville. Then we could all reap the benefit. It will pay.

We make the same jumps without a league and it is a certainty we could with a league, and we would

THE CLUB IS COMPOSED OF THE FOLLOWING PLAYERS
ANDREW (RUBE) FOSTER
THE GREAT COLORED MANAGER AND PITCHER
LEE WADE
WM. LINDSAY
CHAS. DAUGHERTY
HORACE JENKINS } P
BRUCE PETWAY
JAS. BOOKER } C
JESSE BARBER, 1ST
WM. MONROE, 2ND
WM. FRANCIS, 3RD
J. H. LLOYD, S. S.
EDW. GANS, L. F.
J. P. HILL, C. F.
FRANK DUNCAN, R. F.

American Giants Base Ball Club
ANDREW (RUBE) FOSTER, CLUB MANAGER
THE GREATEST AGGREGATION OF COLORED BASE BALL PLAYERS IN THE WORLD
Park Located at 39th St. and Wentworth Ave.
(WHITE SOX OLD GROUNDS)
FINEST SEMI-PRO. PARK IN THE U. S.
OWNED AND OPERATED BY
JOHN M. SCHORLING, OFFICE, 403 WEST 79TH STREET

Chicago 6/26/15 191

Mr. J.V.Brasfield, Mgr,

Henry Greys-B.B.Club,

Dear Sir:-

Your letter confirming the date there-wednesday-July 14-also accepting the terms-of a gaurantee of Sixty Dollars-(Same to be paid in case of rain, or no game) received, replying to it-beg to say, I will try and not play in the Immediate vicinity of Henry-before playing there--but am trying to fill out a week, around there, so as to make it pay-hence the terms to you--send me a list of some of the good places around, also the days that they play---I will pitch the game there for you, providing I am not sick-or disabled--The terms are with option of Fifty percent of the gross receipts-- Respectfully Yours-

Andrew Foster

A rare letter from Andrew Foster confirming dates and terms of upcoming contests with a semi-pro team (courtesy Doug Averitt).

receive better patronage, also a standing in baseball, and the winner in our league could force, by public sentiment, the same as Jack Johnson forced [Jim] Jeffries, the winners in the white league to meet us for the championship.

I am for no wildcat schemes. But I know this to be the best way, and when I say I know, those who know me know I am not guessing. I am willing to co-operate with all in doing anything to uplift Negro baseball.

Several iron-man pitching performances occurred in the 1912 season. On June 16, 1912, Cannonball Dick Redding of the Lincoln Giants struck out 24 All-Leaguers at Olympic Field in New York. Redding gave up three hits in picking up the 6–0 win. All three batters had two strikes on them before singling. Redding's 24 K's, over nine innings, beat any record by either professional or semi-professional pitchers at the time. At the time, the professional record was 19 by Charlie Sweeney of the Providence Grays back in the 1880's

Later in the year, on August 4, Redding pitched a perfect game against the Cherokee Indians at Olympic Field to capture a 1–0 victory. The box score reveals he struck out 14 batters, and yielded no walks. The Giants did not commit an error and did not turn any double plays, therefore Redding pitched a perfect game.

In an August doubleheader played at Olympic Field between the Brooklyn Royal Giants and the Lincoln Giants, Frank Wickware for Brooklyn and Redding for Lincoln faced off in both games. Wickware won the opener, 3–2, with Redding winning the second game, 3–0.

COMISKEY PARK
35th and Shields Ave.
THURSDAY, AUG. 22nd

CHAMPION
Jack Johnson's
FIELD DAY

2 WRESTLING MATCHES
ILLA VINCENT—The Cuban Wonder vs.
HALY BEEN—The Invincible Turk
MONTY CUTLER, Johnson's Sparring Partner, vs.
JOE LEVY, England's Pride

Running, Jumping, Feats of Strength, Etc., Etc.

BALL GAME
"RUBE" FOSTER'S AMERICAN GIANTS vs.
NIESEN'S ALL STAR GUNTHERS

The Famous 8th Regiment Military Band

Benefit PROVIDENT HOSPITAL
N. B.—In case of rain postponed until next day

Seats on sale at the hospital a week in advance.
Get them early and avoid the rush.

Jack Johnson's Field Day featuring a marching band, wrestling matches, along with some track and field events (*Chicago Defender* 10 August 1912).

Later that year on October 27, Smokey Joe Williams shut out the New York Giants, 6–0. Williams struck out nine, walked none and gave up four hits to shut out John McGraw's National League champs who had finished the season with a 103–48 won-lost record for the pennant before losing the World Series to the Boston Red Sox, 4–3–1.

A couple of days later, Joe Williams shut out Chase's All-Stars, really the New York Highlanders, 6–0, giving up four hits. The Highlanders would become the Yankees next season, had finished fifth in the American League with a 50–102 record.

Foster had plenty of company for the "Pitcher of the Year" award. One newspaper, the *Fort Wayne Sentinel*, questioned Foster's effectiveness as he crept into his mid-thirties, with an article entitled, "Rube Foster One of the Marvels of Game but Color Hurt him" claiming,

> Without a doubt Rube Foster is the greatest ebony skinned ball player in the game. The "Black Mathewson" just about hits the nail head. Not that "Big Six" and "Rube" are constructed on the same physical lines, far from it. "Matty" is an athlete, while Foster bears a resemblance to a barrel. He is the heaviest human that ever played ball for money, with the possible exception of Cap Anson — and "Anse" had considerable longitude on Foster.
>
> At one time Foster "had everything" in speed and curves, but Father Time has robbed him of some of his stuff leaving him with the finest assortment of baseball tricks in the game.
>
> Rube and his team, the American Giants have cleaned up about everything in the amateur and semi-pro line, and but for their complexion would continue the process among the big fellows.

> Foster winters in Cuba, where he is popular. For craftiness he has no ball player equal, although figures prove the Cuban [Jose] Mendez is a better hurler. Still every time they meet "Rube" downs the island star.
>
> If some Westinghouse-Edison-Marconi [Guglielmo of radio telegraph fame] would "shake a leg" and invent something to change the complexion of Mistah Foster's underwear, we would see him in the majors.[3]

The Giants traveled west to Los Angeles in mid–October in preparation to play in the four-team winter league, starting on November 1. After a workout on October 17, writer Harry A. Williams gave his equally unkind scouting report of the black Big Train Johnson in his "Hits & Runs" column:

> Last night I had my first glimpse of Rube Foster, the Walter Johnson of the colored race. Rube called around to announce that his team, the American Giants, will play a double-header at Doyle's Sunday afternoon against the All-Natives and Harris & Franks. Rube weighs something like a million pounds, and measures about seven feet across the shoulders. Any white weakling who will stand up to the plate with him pitching deserves a medal for bravery.[4]

Two weeks later, Williams wrote "Negro Ball Stars Shine" with the sub-captions like: Rube Foster's Dark Players Look the Part, and White Men Must Play to Beat the Brunettes.

> Hear [sic] he comes. This warning from Bruce Petway, a tall, saddle-colored individual and there were unmistakable signs of action among the American Giants. A mammoth figure had just emerged from the clubhouse and was streaming ponderously across the outfield toward the home plate. It was "Rube" Foster boss of the Giants and the Walter Johnson of the colored race. "Rube" had tarried uptown to allow a "picture man" to take a shot at him, and his men had beat him to the daily team practice at Jack Doyle's eminent domain. As a rule it takes some stretch of the imagination to liken a human being to a battleship, but if "Rube" Foster, ploughing up toward the home plate, a calabash pipe in this mouth and said mouth emitting as much smoke as an ocean liner, did not bear a close resemblance to the biggest dreadnought afloat then I am "seeing things."
>
> Rube was decked out in a brand new uniform of robin's egg blue. Just why "Rube" selected this delicate tint is best known to himself. Probably he figured that it would accentuate this brunette beauty. If that was his object he succeeded beyond all expectation. Thus esthetically garbed, "Rube" loomed up like the only and original "cinder."

Williams could not contain his roast of the dapper Giants. "As usual, there was quite a delegation of darktown sports on hand to claim relationship of past acquaintance with 'Rube.' One of these finally ventured out near the plate. He was the sportiest of the sports. He was decked in an ecru-colored (shade grayish-pale yellow or a light grayish-yellowish brown) suit and his flaming red cravat (tie or bow-tie) served as the background for a 'rock' of questionable authenticity." Harry Williams could not avoid best infielder on the team, Bill Munroe, as "a little bow-legged chap with a burnt sienna complexion."[5]

Ten days later, writer Williams pounced on Foster again, pinch-hitting for the losing Giants against the Tuft-Lyons team, 5–1, as his headline read, "All Look Alike to Leverenz, Who Is Invincible."

Williams wrote, "Rube Foster fanned in a pinch! Rube, of the mightiest athletes that ever emanated from the colored race, a human mastodon [pre-historic elephant], who has made a specialty of shattering dollar and a quarter balls, succumbed on strikes while 1,000 of his countrymen showed the whites of their eyes in pained surprise. Lawdy, can you imagine it?" Williams added, "Well, to abbreviate a long story, Rube fanned. He fanned furiously. He fanned with all the fervor of his ample being. Each time he swung the whole world swayed and 1,000 of his compatriots gasped in astonishment. Those who have never seen 1,000 compatriots gasp in astonishment have no adequate idea of the scene. All of Rube's friends are the best kind of gaspers, and for them to gasp in concert was quite a treat."[6]

However, Foster wasn't the only black pitcher to be characterized in a negative light. The *San Diego Union* paper of November 18, 1912, appeared to enjoy descriptive imagery of ball players.

Outside of John Donaldson, Cannonball Dick Redding may be the best pitcher from black baseball not in the National Baseball Hall of Fame. Redding is credited with two no-hitters (1912 and 1920) and pitched two games on the same day on four occasions, winning seven of eight games (NoirTech Research).

"In the seventh a Mistah Gatewood, commonly known as 'Dixie' as slow as proverbial molasses, with the windup of a windmill and a swing which resembled a picnic ground affair, took the mound for the Giants. He didn't have much, outside a glove and a smile, but he kept the locals from further scoring."

Gatewood was often tortoise-like on the mound, as he needed time to moisten or scratch up a baseball. In a 1921 game, as a member of the Detroit Stars with Bruce Petway catching, the Cuban Stars protested to the umpire that the ball was doing "funny things." The umpire examined he ball and found a nick and tossed it out of play.

A short time later more complaints were registered and another examination of the pellet revealed another nick. The Cubans demanded that Gatewood be searched. The pat down revealed a half a dozen bottle caps in Gate's hip pocket.

Busted and now angry, Gatewood started off batters with knock-down pitches and eventually struck out 10 and walked two batters en route to a no-hitter.[7]

A 44-year-old Gatewood would throw another no-hitter in 1926 against the Birmingham Black Barons as a member of the Albany (GA) Giants.[8]

San Diego Union continued with its yellow journalism, noting, "Hamilton struck out seven of them, but true to their advance notices the 'shines' hit 'em a mile and lots times also, and ran bases like ghost had scared them."[9]

"Foster coming out of retirement?" asked the *San Diego Union.*

"Goodbye, Mistah Foster! Bullfrog Foster they called him. It was a traffic departure, 5 to 3. After seven and a half innings, with the score 3 to 1 for the Gold Dust team yesterday, Rube Foster weakened for a moment, lost the game to the Bears, lost the series and the place at the top of the Winter League column.

"RUBE" FOSTER, BLACK MATHEWSON OF NATIONAL GAME, A GREAT BALL PLAYER, DESPITE HIS RESEMBLANCE TO A BARR'L

The local Fort Wayne paper claimed, "Without a doubt Rube Foster is the greatest ebony skinned ball player in the game. The 'Black Mathewson' just about hits the nail head. Not that 'Big Six' and 'Rube' are constructed on the same physical lines, far from it. 'Matty' is an athlete, while Foster bears a resemblance to a barrel" (*Fort Wayne Sentinel* 1 October 1912).

"One small moment only Rube weakened. Yes, it was not the psychological moment—rather, it was in the eighth inning. It was a most sensational fish, most extraordinary finish—and the chap who afterward remarked that it was the crowd that won was not far wrong, but he wasn't right. It was this way: Two walks, two singles and a slashing triple by Baerwald after two were out did it. Four men crossed the rubber and the game was over."[10]

On Christmas day, *San Diego Union* reported, "Headed by 'Rube' Foster, the American Giants arrived here last night from Los Angeles. The colored outfit has plenty of good gloves with them this trip. It also brought along a barrel labeled confidence. This collection of bunny hoofs is large enough to give one to each Son of Ham who will caper about the Athletic Park this afternoon when the invaders will hook up with the Bears in the first game of a five-cornered series."

The paper added, "All of the good luck charms know to the hoodoo doctors will not be enough to swing victory to the dark side of the house, according to the way the Bears were dealing out the 'dope' last night."[11]

"'Guess I'll pitch tomorrow,' said 'Rube' yesterday. "I'm weighing 267 pounds now and I need the work to rid of some of this surplus meat."[12] With a closing comment about Foster's tour in California, "This season Rube Foster, he of the dusky color and extreme avoirdupois brought out from Chicago a mighty slick squad of colored baseball artists known as the American Giants. And right here it should be written that these aforesaid

RUBE FOSTER IS TEARFUL AS HE BIDS VICTORIOUS BEARS ADIEU

The San Diego paper continued its assault on Foster's team, writing, "All of the good luck charms known to the hoodoo doctors will not be enough to swing victory to the dark side of the house, according to the way the Bears were dealing out the 'dope' last night" (*San Diego Union* 18 November 1912).

Giants played ball of high caliber of quality that could be compared with the work of major league teams."[13]

Indianapolis Freeman, 28 December 1912

"Rube Foster's Review on Baseball"

Reviewing the past season in baseball, we find the American Giants again leading as usual all the big colored clubs. Some of the clubs' playing strength has equaled the strength of the Giants, but lacked the pilot at the head to bring results. At the beginning of the past season the outlook for a prosperous season at Chicago was not at all encouraging, but the management of the American Giants, through his efforts and the co-operation of the loyal fans, saw Chicago in its most prosperous season, and better ball played, better clubs and larger attendance than any previous season.

For the first time in history Chicago saw weekday games played and supported them better than any place in the country. The coming season bids fair to eclipse anything attempted before, and from the list of good clubs to be booked, the Chicago fans have a treat in store for them. During the past season the American Giants defeated every club who battled with them in a series of games, excepting the Cuban Stars, who broke even. In 132 games played, the American Giants won 112 games. Flushed with their wonderful success and record, the American Giants, whose motto is to surpass anything attempted by other clubs journeyed to the Pacific coast, where they hold a franchise in the California Winter

League. Their great playing, which characterized their work in the East, has been more brilliant on the coast, and they have forged to the top in the league race.

Their team plays have opened the eyes of all the big leaguers on the coast including such stars as [Chief] Meyers, catcher for the New York Giants; [Earl] Hamilton, pitcher for the St. Louis Browns; [Tom "Pete"] Daley of the Athletics; [Ewart Gladstone "Dixie"] Walker of Washington; [Fred] Snodgrass of New York [Giants], [Rube] Ellis of St. Louis [Cardinals]; [Tom] Downey of Cincinnati; [Fred] Carisch and [Ivy] Olson of Cleveland; [Drummond] Brown of Boston [Braves]. [Walt] Leverenz of St. Louis; [Wade "Red"] Killifer of Minneapolis, and all Class AA players. Not a semi-pro player is on the payroll of either club.

[Toots] Schultz of Philadelphia [Phillies]; [Irv] Higginbotham of Cards; [Bruce] Hitt of Vernon, [Walt] Slagle of Minneapolis; and [?] Plegler of Indianapolis are some of the crack pitchers the Giants have made taste the sting of defeat. The Giants leave California the 15th of March, playing at San Francisco, Oakland, Sacramento, Portland, Oregon, Salt Lake City, and by the way of Texas, to Oklahoma, Kansas City, Missouri, Davenport, Iowa, and opening in Chicago, April 20, 1913.

On October 12, 1913, the American Giants played their 200th game of the season, defeating the Logan Squares, 9–3, on their home grounds. This achievement included games played in the Pacific Coast Winter League. This was perhaps the first time in baseball history that any team, pro or semi-pro, had appeared in 200 contests in a single year. The *Chicago Defender* reported, "Rube Foster's popularity as a ball twirler seems to be on the increase, at the Sunday ball games especially. They standing room sign is a regular feature."[14]

Harry Williams of the *San Diego Union* wrote that "Rube weighs something like a million pounds, and measures about seven feet across the shoulders. Any white weakling who will stand up to the plate with him pitching deserves a medal for bravery" (*San Diego Union* 7 December 1912).

Back on June 8, 1913, Coogan's Smart Set from Paterson, New Jersey, blew into the Windy City with a hot 21-game winning streak. In the first game, the sizzling Smart Set was cooled off by a Lou "Dicta" Johnson no-hitter, losing 9–0. Johnson struck out seven and gave up four walks, while his fellow Giants committed three errors. The following day, on Monday, Coogan's team jumped into the flames of another no-hitter, losing 8–0, stifled by the sly Pat Dougherty. The third game of the series made it a goose egg trifecta, 5–0—this time a curve ball specialist, lefty Bill Gatewood. Three games, three shutouts!

In the fourth and final game, the Smart Set managed to score a run, but lost again, 4–1, to Bill Lindsey and crew. Lindsey struck out 12 and walked five. Overall, the Smart Set scored one run in four games and suffered back-to-back no-hitters, ending their winning streak.

The big event of the year was the

much awaited series with the Lincoln Giants from the Big Apple. Foster's team was a heavy favorite after the destruction of the Smart Set. On Sunday July 27, between eight and ten thousand fans jammed into Schorling's Park. Every automobile and taxicab available on the Chicago's South Side was in operation. Marching bands and women dressed in the latest fashions were the sight of the day.

While Big Bill Gatewood was participating in a four-team winter league, one local writer claimed, "Mistah Gatewood, commonly known as 'Dixie,' is as slow as proverbial molasses, with the windup of a windmill and a swing which resembled a picnic ground affair" (courtesy Chicago Historical Society).

The New York team had some of the finest players around. Leading off was Spot Poles, followed by Jude Gans, Pop Lloyd and Lou Santop. The Lincoln lineup included a speedy catcher named Bruce Petway leading off, along with the notorious Pete Hill, Jess Barbour and Billy Pierce. Meanwhile, Foster picked up first baseman Ben Taylor and pitcher Steel Arm Johnny Taylor from the West Baden Sprudels for the series. The Taylor brothers joined Candy Jim, already a mainstay at the hot corner.

The first game featured Lincolnite "Cyclone" Joe Williams against Bill "Kansas Cyclone" Lindsey. Williams pitched a shutout on six hits, winning 8–0. In the sixth inning, batting in the seventh slot, he hit a three-run homer off the Bull Durham tobacco sign to pick up a $25 bonus. The next day, the American Giants, with Bill Gatewood on the mound, were defeated again, 3 to 1, on a seven-hitter by Lee Wade. Their single run was unearned, avoiding back-to-back shutouts.

Down two games, the Chicago American Giants pounced on Homer Bartlett for four runs in the first two innings. Chicago built a 7 to 2 lead going into the ninth inning before the Lincoln club rallied for four runs. Chicago had scored the marginal run on a double-steal of home and third base in the ninth inning. Sam Crawford pitched a complete game for Chicago, yielding 12 hits, walked four and struck out two for the 7–6 win. Foster's traditional aggressive style of play proved successful once again.

Cyclone Joe Williams was back on the mound for game four. He had pitched one inning in yesterday's loss, yielding one earned run. Although he was given a four-run cushion, courtesy of American Giants pitcher Dicta Johnson, in the first inning, Williams's third mound appearance proved fatal. Big Bill Gatewood relieved Johnson and gave up one more run over the next eight innings, as Williams was smoked for 15 hits and nine runs. The tired flame thrower had only one strikeout. Chicago won 9–5.

The series was now tied at two games each. The teams split the next four games, Chicago winning games five and six, and the Lincoln club games seven and eight. Joe Williams had won game eight back on August 2 and was back on the mound seven days later for the ninth contest. This time, Cyclone picked up his third series win, outpitching the Kansas Cyclone, Bill Lindsey, Gatewood and Steel Arm Johnny Taylor, 11–6.

The Lincoln squad also won the first game of a doubleheader three days later, 3–2, with Lee Wade picking up the victory. In the second game, the Lincoln Giants lost Pop Lloyd when Jess Barbour spiked him on a play at second in the opening inning. Lloyd was carried off the field on a stretcher to Provident Hospital, where doctors found a severed artery. Pop was out for the series. Based on available box scores, Lloyd, Lincoln's clean-up hitter, batted roughly .300 with one extra-base hit.

The despondent Lincolnites went down to defeat 3–0. After 11 games, the series tally had Lincoln with six wins and Chicago with five. The road-weary Lincoln team, behind Jude Gans' pitching, defeated Chicago and Bill Gatewood, 4–1. With the Lincoln Giants winning seven out of 12 games they were crowned the unofficial Colored Champions of the World.

After three weeks in Chicago, the Lincoln team returned immediately to New York. Considering the magnitude of the series that featured four future Hall of Famers, the local press provided poor coverage of the event. The *Chicago Defender* provided the following explanation on August 9, before game nine, under the headline "There's a Reason."

> We have had a number of inquiries as to why we have not given more publicity to the world's series between the Lincoln Giants of New York City and the American Giants of Chicago. The games warranted lengthy write-ups and this and other race papers would have been glad to have done so could they have afforded it. The management of the park, strange to say, does not deem it necessary to advertise or spend any money with the colored papers, though they are making their money from the race. Our papers have been exceptionally friendly and generous when they were struggling for recognition and playing to hands full of people. Now the heyday of their success is here and those who stood by them in time of need should come in for a share of the success. Managers of teams in other cities advertise in their local papers. Why not the American Giants?
>
> We are glad to say as we go to press that Mr. Foster called over our ad man and had him estimate on an ad of seven columns. When he was through he said, "I'll take that space." If you look on the sporting sheet you will see a big ad.

After a bitter defeat by the Eastern team, Foster sought solace with an editorial to the *Indianapolis Freeman* newspaper. He took the defeat hard, but turned the setback into a positive promotional note for colored baseball.

Indianapolis Freeman, 20 December 1913

"What the Greatest Pitcher of His Time Thinks of the Baseball Situation"

The past season among the big colored clubs has created more interest among the fans than any previous season, both in attendance and enthusiasm. Incidentally, the past season's success has caused more unrest and uncertainly among the men who own and control the density of future clubs. Baseball, growing more popular every day, and the fans learning more of the game each day, are demanding first-class clubs and first-class attractions. This has made the men who control the clubs doubly anxious to please the fans, regardless of the cost. Often times they have paid the prices for players who would come up to the demand of the fans. Then, after a series of games, the owner would find that the players were costing him more money than his share of receipts and have been compelled to promise prices and salaries that, in many instances, they could not afford to pay. Notably, among these, were the St. Louis Giants, Chicago Giants, Mohawk Giants and the Smart Set of Paterson, N. J. The consequences were that they either had to disband their clubs or play on the co-operative plan.

During the past the past season we have played all the big clubs and each club was far superior to the same lineup they used a year ago, all playing a magnificent game of ball. The clubs we had easily defeated a year before were either beating us or carrying games out into extra innings for decision. The Lincoln Giants, of New York, the class of the East, defeating all comers from major league ball clubs down to semi-pros, and recognized as the eastern champions, and the Americans, of Chicago to decide the supremacy of the two big clubs, which proved to be the big colored baseball event of the year. It created the greatest interest yet in a series of games between colored ball clubs, in attendance, playing ability and deportment, and drawing the largest crowds ever recorded by colored clubs. Never were two clubs more evenly matched and so desperately determined to win than these two clubs. The advancement of colored players was never more clearly shown than in the makeup of these two clubs.

It was the first series of games played for the championship of the world by the two recognized leading clubs since 1904, when the Philadelphia Giants of Philadelphia, Pa., wrested the championship from the Cuban Ex–Giants of New York. Only four players of these two famous clubs were identified with the event of the year: Grant Johnson, then captain of the Cuban Ex–Giants, now manager of the Lincoln Giants; Pete Hill, outfielder of the Philadelphia Giants, now captain of the American Giants; Bill Monroe, shortstop of the Philadelphia Giants, now second baseman of the American Giants, and the writer, who was pitcher for the Philadelphia Giants and is now manager of the American Giants.

Up to 1904 and on top to 1913, the event of the Philadelphia Giants and the Ex–Giants was the biggest event among the colored clubs and drew immense crowds and the players and fans thought it would never be equaled again, nor that the talent to draw on from the younger generation of the players would be able to put up such brilliant ball playing as was put up by the contesting clubs for the colored championship of the world.

The Cuban Ex–Giants of 1904 was composed of [Robert] Jordan, first base; [Pat] Patterson, second base; Grant Johnson, captain and shortstop; James Smith, third base; W. [William] Jackson, left field; Harry Moore, center field; Danny McClellan, pitcher and right fielder; Clarence Williams and W. Smith, catchers; [Walter] Ball, [Harry] Buckner, [James] Robinson and McClellan, pitchers. The Philadelphia Giants had Chappy Johnson and [Robert] Footes, catchers; Sol White, first base; Johnny Grant, second base; Monroe, shortstop; J. [John] Hill, third base; [Jap] Payne, left field; [Pete] Hill center field; [William] Bell, pitcher and right field; Foster, [Kid] Carter, [William] Horn and Bell, pitchers. But the big event of 1913 saw an array of talent developed into baseball players that were superior to the combination of stars of 1904.

There were stars introduced among the younger generation of players that the big leagues of today cannot surpass. Such stars as [Bruce] Petway, heralded as the greatest living catcher; [Pop] Lloyd, the most wonderful shortstop of the age; [Bill] Francis, [Jude] Gans, Leroy Grant, [Doc] Wiley, [Lou] Santop, [Spot] Poles, [Fred] Hutchinson, B. [Ben] Taylor, [Jesse] Barbour, [Frank] Duncan, Hill, Monroe, Monroe, Williams, Gatewood, Lindsey, [Pat] Dougherty, [Dibo] Johnson, [Bill] Pierce and [Frank] Wickware, an array of talent equal to the best, and whose services no minor league could hold. These are only some of the few great colored players developed in the past ten years.

The attendance at one of these games was more than for the entire series of 1904, and the interest was far greater. Then the center of attraction was centered in the eastern clubs. The past big series was an eastern club pitted against the cracks of the West, and I am one who takes his hat off to the victorious Lincoln Giants. Their great playing and wonderful defense was never surpassed, if equaled, on any diamond. The writer has been much criticized after the loss of such an important series of games, concerning the judgment used in defending the title with the easterners, and that his ambition for records by playing his ball club every winter had caused his players to go stale and broke down a winning combination of the best club that ever represented the West.

In defense of which I will say no man can go on winning forever, and especially be successful, without encouragement from the fans of the city he represents. Although the writer deeply regrets the loss of championship to easterners, he believes that with the proper encouragement from the fans of the city we could repeat [as champions] what has often times been demonstrated, that in his career as a manager and a player, still had his first series of games to lose. He had often times done for the colored fans what all his predecessors had said was impossible.

First, he was instrumental in placing colored baseball players in the confidence of the public. Was the first to pay the players promptly every penny on the first and fifteenth of the month and no one ever heard that any player who has played under his direction has ever had to wait for his money.

He was the first to ride the players throughout the country, South, East, North and West in private Pullman cars; the first that ever took a northern club throughout the South; the first and only one to win a city league pennant three years for Chicago; the first to give and see that the fans had a first-class park within walking distance of the home, which is the finest semi-pro park in the world, and eclipsed only by the big league parks; a place where the fans could go and feel at home, and to me it was the fulfillment of a great ambition to know that I had secured for my people a park and a club that was a credit to any city; not a park that was discarded or run down and remodeled, but built new from the ground up, solely for the accommodation of our fans and I thought that pride alone would influence any race person to cheer me up; and not for any just reason on earth, but simply because I had achieved so much for Chicago and colored baseball, to put obstacles in my way and try to tear me down.

It was with much pride I enjoyed your loyal patronage, and it was a real joy to me to see you watch our boys and note the difference in appearance of our club and visiting clubs, and knew you could truthfully say no ball club, in the major minor leagues, were better equipped than our boys. I was doing this because I loved your pride and wanted your encouragement. It was a sad blow to my men and me on returning to Chicago the past April at the welcome received from the wonderful record of your boys who represented your city. A record not equaled nor approached nor soon to be surpassed by any ball club in the world.

We bade you goodbye on October 19th, and for six months and twenty-three days added to our list of victories the California Winter League pennant [December, 1913], a league composed of and all Class AA players; traveled 11,833 miles and added honor upon honor to your city and more especially our race; won 94 out of 104 games, defeating Pacific Coast League clubs and Union Association League clubs decisively, and each were the champions of their respective leagues.

This wonderful feat was all accomplished on foreign grounds, and that in it, I thought, would give you an added inspiration to pull still harder for our future success, and not to rejoice at our downfall and root so hard against us. Strange to say, it was the opposite, receiving more appreciation every place than at home. Daily reports were flashed all over the country of our wonderful success, and at home the fans allowed so much fame thousands of miles away from home, eclipsing any record yet set up by any bail club, to come home without the slightest demonstration or their appreciation of such wonderful success. But when the Lincolns returned East, victorious, they received a welcome, were met at the station with a brass band, paraded over the city, wined and dined as champions, the same as we gave Jack Johnson when he returned victorious from Reno, and they had not accomplished one-tenth of the success that the American Giants had accomplished for the American Giants and clubs handled by the writer have traveled further and introduced the game in more places where colored players have in combined.

During the series, a reporter from the *Daily News*, asked: "Rube, why do your people root so hard against you? They should give you all the encouragement, for even I do not relish the thought of the championship going to the East." I cheerfully replied, "We have won so much that they think we cannot be beaten and their sympathy is only with the visitors as an encouragement. They do not believe they can win." But deep down in my heart I knew and felt different, so the next day, he sent me the following, entitled "Fleeting Glory":

> "You who find fault when a fumble is made, you who are noted because you complain, always deploring the way they play, list to this unsympathetic refrain. Be optimistic and don't count the cost, cheer them no matter how poorly they play; if they have won a game, if they have lost, theirs is a glory that lasts but a day. Why mourn and groan when the pitcher is bad, when he can't put them right over the pan, costs you but little to make him feel glad, help him by praising whenever you can. Boost for each one of them, cheer them along. Be with the team, though one-sided the fray. Be a good loser and warble a song. Theirs is a glory that lasts but a day. You who are always on edge to explode, willing at all times to holler and jeer, adding your burden of scorn to the load, hark to this roundelay weighted with cheer. Smile when the milling is brutally poor, doesn't help any to groan in dismay when luck is against them, but just grin and endure. Theirs is a glory that lasts but a day. Ponder the good things they have done for the cause; heroes today and tomorrow they are gone. Therefore, get in with your mile of applause. Think of that monster, Old Age, coming on, never emblazoned on history's page. Name, fame and splendor will soon pass away, so let this thought your attention engage, theirs is a glory that lasts but one day."

Future

The future of colored baseball, it can be safely stated, will not last long, unless it becomes organized. Organization is its only hope. With the proper organization, patterned after the men who have made baseball a success, we will, in three years, be rated as other leagues are rated, and it would perpetuate colored baseball, so great would be the results in the above length of time. We have the players, and it could not be a failure, as the same territory is traveled now by all the clubs, with no organization or money. If such is true, then why wouldn't the league be a success?

It would give us a rating and standing in the daily papers which would create an interest and we could then let the best clubs in our organization play for the world's championship with other clubs, champions of their leagues. Public sentiment would compel them to do it. Every little city, where they can draw $100 gate receipts per day, among the whites, has a league, leaving no city where any money can be made outside of an organization. The organizations have a schedule and no open dates. Hence, the visiting colored clubs can get no engagements where every hamlet and village of the United States has a team, and our people have improved on such progressive ideas, that it has left us to solve our own salvation and future. With baseball more popular and recognized as the national sport and an American game, it would be a crime for the Negro who has such an abundance of talent in such a progressive age, to sit idly by and see his race forever doomed to America's greatest and foremost sport.

There are no banks or real investments that pay the dividends a ball club will earn on the money invested. Comiskey built a ballpark costing $750,000, besides the help, salaries of the officers and players, to play 74 games out of 365 days, barring rain. It can be seen at a glance that when a park at such a cost can be kept idle three-fourths of the time and a man get rich in ten years, the enormous profit there must be in baseball. The players have, through adverse conditions, been able to bring our race to the notice of thousands who are interested in the game in many cities throughout the great Northwest.

I was asked on several occasions: "Where did the colored men learn to play ball?" They went out of curiosity to see them, little dreaming that they were by any means going to see a contest worthy of the name of baseball. To see our men daily defeat the best of their city representation composed of some of the most widely-known players of the age, seven regular members being regulars in the past world's series. These people stood for hours and hours, clamoring for a chance to see a game, and paying enormous prices. If unsuccessful in gaining admission, they were satisfied to remain to get a glance at the players who had achieved so much fame in their different leagues as to be picked to play in a contest for the championship of the world, representing the two best clubs of their race. Is it little wonder they were dumfounded?

They never knew or had never seen their pictures in the paper. They had never read their reports. They had never heard of men paying princely salaries too their men to train and teach them how play ball, and to see the pride of their nation humbled by men of an inferior race — it is to be marveled at, but such was true.

When the American Giants set up a record of playing 202 games in a year with 13 men, losing 42 games and winning much praise on the Pacific Coast from both press and fans, and herald as the greatest club in the world. They thought we had all the colored players who could play. And you can imagine their surprise when the Associated Press handling all of our games, flashed our defeat to the Lincoln Giants to all parts of the country. It not only brought the whites to their senses, but made them realize that the American white man has not a patent on baseball, or if he has, it is sadly in need of improvement. While in Frisco, the sporting editor of the *San Francisco Chronicle*, the best paper in California, who is one of the expert writers, said of the American Giants: "The colored players here, representing the American Giants, would be stars in the big league. We hate to say how good this ball club really is."

These few words mean more than any three columns he would write and you can imagine these thoughts and the thousands of readers of his papers when it was in all parts of the United States, that the Lincoln Giants, another colored club, had wrested the championship from the American Giants. I have often thought and wondered what and how great a ball club they think the Lincoln Giants must be.

There is only one hope for the future of colored baseball. It lies in the formation of an organization for the welfare of all and not for an individual, and can only be successful on the same basis as a big league is formed.

Let us hope that the beating of the American Giants received at the hands of the Lincoln Giants is a blessing in disguise. Now, will our businessmen and friends of the profession make an effort to reach the coveted goal of complete success, or will they stand by and see us fall? Which shall it be?

Chicago Daily Tribune, 21 December 1913

Success of Negro on Diamond Told by Rube Foster
Colored Manager Points out Great Strides Made by Players of His Race.
Advance Under Handicaps.
Leading Teams now Include Men Who Rank with the Stars of Organized Baseball.
Lack of League Halts Progress

Tribune note: Andrew "Rube" Foster, author of the subjoined article on the progress of the Negro in baseball, is a pioneer among colored baseball managers. He has acted as pitcher and manager successively of the Leland Giants, Chicago Giants and American Giants. His teams always have been well behaved on the field. This article is reproduced as actually written by Foster, without editorial rewriting or revamping.

Author's Note: This article was originally published on April 16, 1910, in the *Indianapolis Freeman* paper. Although similar to the original, some additional commentary is provided by Foster.

By Andrew "Rube" Foster

Manager American Giants

Great Strides have been made by the Negro ball player in the last few years and if he continues to receive hearty support and encouragement from his own race in a business way the distance between him and the point designated as wonderful success will be materially lessened.

I don't mean to say that the Negro player ever has been successful. But I must admit he has been quite backward when I look around and note the number of leagues that have been formed and are successful.

We are aware that the plans and franchises of leagues do not belong to the players, nor are they owned or controlled by them. The players are a part of the business and are looked upon as the most active and valuable assets of clubs and leagues. Without the players there could be no leagues. And without the leagues the players would be worthy of only a small amount of consideration. Therefore, it can readily be seen that one cannot be successful without the other.

Says Negro Started Wrong

The Negro started wrong. After doing so he has been the victim of all kinds of bad advice and has been an innocent participant in numerous wild schemes for promoting the game. To speak of the success of the Negro as a ball player, practically fighting single handed, with nothing but his health and strength to back him up, is a subject which requires no delicate handling.

I do not think anyone who has watched the progress of the Negro on the diamond can doubt that the colored player has advanced considerably.

From a playing standpoint the Negro has been successful in various ways. A few years ago he was used as an attraction, merely for the laughs drawn by his peculiar acts upon the diamond. His baseball ability was a secondary consideration. A Negro team was looked upon with disfavor unless it had a half-dozen men in the lineup with a repertoire of witty sayings and comical antics.

Travel by Freight Trains

The player some years ago would write for a job, and it was only necessary for the promoter to say yes, and the player would catch the first freight train headed that way, usually landing with no mention whatever of salary or contract. Such is not the case now. The colored player in the last few years had advanced from the knight of the road and his playing ability has reached such a stage of development that promoters make it their special duty to see that the physical condition of all players intended for a team is safeguarded in the best possible way.

Training trips for colored clubs a few years ago would have been looked upon as a joke, but at present such trips are made and are regarded as a necessity because of the class of baseball demanded by the public, and the many requests received for an opportunity to see the representative stars among our race. The people who support the game have advanced far beyond the circus idea in baseball. So when a team takes the field the fans soon make the fact known that they are there to see baseball as an exhibition of national pastime and not a farce comedy.

Player Meet the Demand

The colored player was one of the first to recognize the fact and he began to show an interest in the fine points of the game. He has studied the game and has experimented with it from all angles until now we have players who are classed with the best in the land. This fact might be disputed upon the grounds that we have had no chance to show it, but nevertheless such an honor has been given the colored lads by some of the best managers and judges of baseball players in the country.

Quite often now you hear the remark, "Too bad he is a colored man," or "If so and so only were white he would be in the big leagues." These, together with many other complimentary remarks, have been made regarding our boys and have not come in the nature of a "jolly." In fact, such things have appeared in print over the signatures of men whose opinions are worth something and whose ideas are being studied, and are receiving the consideration of thousands of fans. This shows the Negro, in a measure, has been successful as a player.

Hardships of Colored Teams

Physically, mechanically, and mentally the colored player has no superior. We have players at this time who can safely be classed with the highest types. With our limited resources for training and traveling I doubt if any of the big league stars could maintain their high playing standard and preserve their physical makeup to the extent the colored player has, especially when you consider that the Negro is compelled to ride in poorly ventilated cars and make long jumps, is forced to put up with all sorts of inferior hotel accommodations, besides exhibiting as a rule on diamonds that are like unto the proverbial cornfields.

In spite of these handicaps, he usually shows up in a condition fit to give battle to the best in the land. It is the honest opinion of many baseball men that if the Negro had the financial resources of his white brother he would far outclass the latter.

Mechanically there is nothing which applies to the great white players of the country the entered player has not added to his repertoire. The Negro has practiced, studied and developed to such an extent that he has been given credit for adding many noted improvements to certain styles in vogue at present.

Pitchers in the Limelight

I believe our pitchers have brought more renown to our race than the players at any other position. The pitcher is the most important personage upon a ball club. All attention is centered upon him, and the deportment of his associates to a great extent, depends materially upon his actions. If he is in the proper condition and is going good, it has a bearing upon the men behind him, which means much in the way of success. But if the reverse is true it invariably has a bad effort on his teammates and often results in the rout of the club.

Following close behind our pitchers come our catchers. The man behind the bat is looked upon as being responsible for the great effectiveness of the pitcher to a certain extent. We have catchers who, were they white, could name their own salaries. It is the opinion of many that the advance of the pitcher is fast making catching a lost art. This is alarmingly true, not only among colored players, but also in the big leagues. I doubt if there are six topnotch catchers in the whole country. Among these few we have men who can safely be classed with the best. Our best representative players are shining in positions which are considered most difficult in baseball.

Stars in Every Position

We have players who are good basemen and outfielders. We also have a few who are great batsmen, but how they would stand if working regularly against the best pitching is a question. All this is backed up by proofs. For instance, thousands and thousands of readers of *The [Chicago Daily] Tribune* have never known that the greatest stars of the big leagues have been pitted against some of the crack colored players and have been found wanting.

I have seen [Bruce] Petway, our catcher, turn back the great Eddie Collins of the Athletics, and on several occasions Collins was chased out between second and first. I have seen Petway sit on his rear the great Georgian, Ty Cobb, when Ty was trying to pilfer bases, and so successfully that the daily papers were headed "Petway Has Ty Cobb's Goat." I have seen our players defeat the New York Giants, New York Americans, Philadelphia Nationals, and Brooklyn Nationals. While four of our players were in the regular lineup of the Cuban club that team humbled the Athletics, champions of the world, who had just defeated the Cubs. The Cubans won eight out of twelve games with [Chief] Bender, [Gettysburg Eddie] Plank, and [Jack] Coombs pitching for the Macks [Connie Mack]. The papers said that Lloyd, shortstop, was even superior to Jack Barry. And that was no comparison between [Ira] Thomas or [Jack] Lapp and Petway.

Home Run off Joss

Once, with the score 2 to 0 in favor of Addie Joss, now deceased, and with three men on bases and two out, I saw [John Henry "Pop"] Lloyd hit the longest home ever seen in Cuba, winning the game.

Only this fall, before the World's Series between the Giants and Athletics, Walter Johnson, voted as the greatest and most valuable pitcher in the American League, lost a shutout duel to [Frank] Wickware, one of the colored cracks. These facts along justify me in saying the Negro has been quite successful as a ball player.

Thousands of big league patrons have never seen colored players play nor read anything about them. Last winter we were playing in the California Winter League, in which were such stars as Chief Meyers, [Tillie] Shafer, and [Fred] Snodgrass of the New York Giants; Hop Meyers, Boston Nationals; [Joe] Schultz of the Philadelphia Nationals; [Fred] Carisch and [Ivy] Olson of Cleveland [Naps], [Tom] Daley of the [Philadelphia] Athletics, [Rube] Ellis of the St. Louis Nationals, [Walt] Leverenz and [Earl] Hamilton of the St. Louis Americans, and the others at least class AA men. Playing on a 60–40 winner and loser basis, we found them easy pickings and easily won the pennant.[15] We defeated Coast League clubs, Northwestern League clubs, and Union Association clubs, in each instance the champion team of each league. We lost only thirteen out of 104 games.

[Author's note: According to the *Grand Folks Herald*, "The American Giants baseball team, under the management of Rube Foster, won the pennant of the winter league in California. The Giants won 18 games and lost seven. San Diego finished second, Tufts-Lyons third, and McCormick's fourth. Foster kept up his winning streak and won all but one of the games he pitched. Lindsey and Wickwire [Wickware] also twirled good ball. The Giants will now go to San Diego, where they have arranged to play 15 games with an all-star aggregation."[16]]

Negro League Needed

These facts show to what extent Negro players have succeeded. And we have no managers or high priced men to train and teach us the finer points of the game. Upon such acknowledged proof no one could doubt the great possibilities of the colored player were conditions for him the same as for his white brother.

In my opinion the time has come when the formation of colored leagues should receive consideration. In fact, I regard it as absolutely necessary. We have been in the game a score of years and we are no closer related to our white neighbor than when we started. In fact, we are farther apart. He is going ahead, forming leagues in every little hamlet and village, and the forming of leagues produces a barrier which we cannot surmount, try as we will, unless we come to understand the meaning of organized baseball.

What we need is proper financial backing and encouragement, then we could form an eight club circuit, superior in playing strength to either the American Association, International League, or Pacific Coast League.

In 1914, Nat Strong brought his Brooklyn Royal Giants to town. The series would be featured as the "Colored Championship of the World." But Strong's players were mere weaklings against Foster's men. The Chicago pitchers shut out the Brooklyn stars, 3–0 and 7–0. They swept the four-game series with two more victories over their Royal aces, William "Dizzy" Dismukes and Franklin "Doc" Sykes.

As Foster temporarily reclaimed the colored championship of the world, he suffered some personal setbacks. While standing in front of the Northwestern Railroad Station, a pickpocket lifted $600 from Foster.[17] The team had just arrived in the city from Gary, Indiana, and Foster was waiting to board a street car back to the city when one of the thieves touched him and ran; his two accomplices blocked Rube's pursuit of the thief.

A few weeks later, one of the pitching staff's mainstays since 1911, Bill Lindsey passed away. Foster recalled, "I have lost a great ball player, a fine gentleman and a noble friend."

Wanting a larger piece of the baseball pie, Foster sought to build a team in Louisville, Kentucky, to capture the delights of Southern fans. He combined the Mohawk Giants from New York with the White Sox of Louisville to form the Louisville Giants. With solid teams

1914 Chicago American Giants. Top row (left to right), Lee Wade, Jesse Barbour, Rube Foster, Hamp Gillard, Pop Lloyd, and Jude Gans; bottom row (left to right), Chappie Johnson, Pete Hill, Bill Francis, Bill Monroe, Horace Jenkins, Jack Watts, Pete Booker and Frank "Pete" Duncan. Foster reported that his team won 108 of 124 contests (NoirTech Research).

in Chicago and Louisville and C.I. Taylor's strong Indianapolis team, the ambition of a league started to materialize. Unfortunately, the Louisville team never came together as the South was not ready for colored baseball.

Seattle Post-Intelligencer, 5 April 1914

Rube Thinks Black Men Will Play in Big Leagues
"And They'll Cut Some Ice, Too," says Famous Leader of American Giants—
Tells of Colored League Plans.
By Royal Brougham

Before another baseball season rolls around colored ball players, a score of whom are equal in ability to the brightest stars in the big league teams, will be holding down jobs in organized baseball.

This is the statement of Rube Foster, who travels around the country in a special car with a bunch of ball players that has beaten the strongest major league teams. He believes that the time when a player can be kept out of baseball because of his color is past. Rube is manager of the American Giants, colored, which team is now touring the Northwest.

"The Feds are going to force it," says Foster.

With five men on this team that baseball experts have proclaimed as good as any big leaguer of the present day, Foster believes that the new league has made players, good players, scarce, and that soon the colored ranks will be invaded, and the best talent picked to fill the breach. He thinks that the magnates will overcome the prejudice which has kept the black man out of baseball, and that the bars will be let down, because there is no other way out of it.

Taking on Cubans

"They're taking in Cubans now, you notice," Rube says, "and they'll let us in soon. Remember last year when there was so much fuss was raised because the Cubans were trimming the major league team? Well, listen." Rube showed a row of even white teeth, and his 262 pounds of flesh shook in a chuckle. "There were more Negroes on the team than there were Cubans."

"And when they let the black men in," he added, "just watch how many present-day stars lose their positions."

Foster tells how organized baseball planned to form a colored league with teams in the towns which the Federals were playing, to take the crowd. It was last year, before the new organization had cut so much ice in baseball, that several big fellows got together and decided to put the league on a basis the same as a big league. The players were to have the same privileges and be governed by the national body. The black teams draw enormous crowds in the East, Foster says, and the idea would have been a good one if it had been carried out. But last fall, when things slowed up in the new league, and it was not thought that anything could be feared from the Feds, the magnates gave up the plan.

We Wouldn't.

"A few months later, Foster grinned, "when Gilmour and the rest of the live wires began to shout, I received a message from one of the party which mentioned the colored league last year. He was very anxious to go through with the thing, then. But we—and 'we' seems about to control things in colored baseball—"had our schedule arranged for this tour, and it was too late. I would not consider the thing. But at that, I would not be surprised if the league is organized next year."

Foster is positive that he has the greatest player in the world in [John Henry "Pop"] Lloyd, the 200-pound shortstop.

"If you don't believe it, wait until he gets into the big leagues—then watch the [Jack] Barrys, the [Honus] Wagners and the [Joe] Tinkers sweat to keep their jobs."

Chicago Daily Tribune, 19 September 1914

Foster Anxious To Tackle Jinx
American Giants' Manager Issues Challenge to Chicago Feds
Points to 1914 Record
by Handy Andy

Rube Foster, manager of the American Giants, has a solution for the desire of the Chicago Federal league baseball team to engage in a post-season struggle.

Anticipating the refusal of the White Sox and Cub managements to admit the jinx to their annual argument for the city championship, and of the American and National League champions to admit a mysterious stranger to the world's series, Rube Foster suggests a series between his Negro champions and Tinker's team for the championship of the north and south sides.

Manager Foster's Challenge

Manager Foster's challenge is modified in the following communication addressed to the sporting editor of *The Tribune*.

"On behalf of the American Giants baseball club, and through the solicitation of hundreds of fans and letters requesting a series of games between the Chicago Federal league baseball club and the American Giants, we challenge them for a series of seven games to decide the championship between the north and south sides. We will play them on any reasonable winner and loser basis.

"We read in *The Tribune* the challenge of the Federal League to organized ball, and they cited the great American sport, that the national game of baseball belonged to the people and that a series of games between the winners of organized ball and the Federal League winners would only be fair to the baseball public who support the ball.

Anxious to Show Skill

"Granting this argument to be true, if the Federal League believes in true sportsmanship, as they would have the public believe, we would welcome a chance to show to the thousands of baseball fans and the public our ability in contesting with them for the championship.

"In playing the American Giants the Federal League will not establish a precedent for such managers as Frank Chance, John McGraw and Connie Mack have played colored ball clubs.

"The record of American Giants with thirteen men is 108 winning games out of 124, from champions of Pacific Coast League clubs, champions of Northwestern League, champions of Union Association League, involving traveling over 15,000 miles during the season. Such as achievement is worthy of consideration, and having defeated all comers for championship honors, we do hereby challenge the Chicago Federal League for a series of games for the championship."

A. Rube Foster
Manager American Giants Baseball Club

The *Janesville* (WI) *Daily Gazette* (August 11, 1914), *Duluth News Tribune* (September 19, 1914) and the *Syracuse Herald* (September 29, 1914) reported that Foster had won 23 straight games against the Northwestern-Pacific League teams that included Portland and Spokane. They wrote, "Rube Foster, the Christy Mathewson of colored baseball stars, has pitched 23 games for the American Giants, a colored semi-professional team and won them all, according to the team's official record ... [which] included games played up to July 30. In the 23 games Rube average one base on balls per game. He modestly admits that he'll never see the underside of 40 again."[18]

Foster strengthened his team during the "Great Migration" or the "Field-to-Factory Movement" of 1915 when thousands of black men and women left the South in hopes of a better and freer life in the industrial centers of the North. The movement allowed Foster to add slugger Hurley McNair (Marshall, TX) and southpaw sinker baller Dick Whitworth (St. Louis, MO). With the transition of black folks coming North, baseball fans would finally see the best of the West meet the beast of the East. Billed as the "World's Colored Championship," the Foster's Giants of the Midwest would face off against the Lincoln Stars from New York. The Harlem based team showcased the finest catalog of players with Cooperstown credentials. Besides having Hall of Famer "Pop" Lloyd, they featured Jude Gans, a star third baseman, and Bill Pettus at first, who in 1906 had gathered 15 hits in 18 at-bats during a series in Las Vegas, Nevada.

In the leadoff spot was the left-handed and fleet-footed Spot Poles. Future Sergeant Spottswood Poles served his country in France as a member of the "Men of Bronze," the 369th Infantry of the 93rd Division. The "Hell Fighters," as they were called by the Germans, were the first American unit to reach the Rhine, spending 191 days in the trenches and never losing a foot of ground. After the Armistice was signed, Poles was awarded five battle stars and a Purple Heart.

The Stars also included home run hammer Louis Santop and an impressive pitching staff of Lee Wade, "Doc" Sykes and "Cannonball" Dick Redding. Redding had won 20 straight games, some against major league clubs, before losing to Dizzy Dismukes and the ABC's, 2–1, the last week of July. Former teammate Frank Forbes said, "Dick Redding was like Walter Johnson, nothing but speed." Like Johnson, Redding developed a curve ball later in his career along with a pre–Paige hesitation or hiccup delivery motion.

Meanwhile the Giants would send in Wickware and future Sergeant Major Whitworth to do battle on the mound. The pitching staff was supported by the dainty, but powerful leadoff hitter Hurley McNair, and streak hitter Pete Hill. Dependable Hill was described as "Captain Pete Hill seldom strikes out and when in center you can close your eyes when a ball comes his way and say the man is out. Hill leading in the batting percentage with [Pop] Lloyd a point below."[19] The much celebrated series began on a good note. The Knights of Pythian Band entertain the crowd, while Oscar DePriest, the first alderman of color for Chicago, threw out the first ball.

The first two games of the series were split, by identical 11–3 scores, the first victory going to Wickware of Chicago, and Redding of Lincoln picking up the win in the second game. The third contest was a close one, won by Tom Johnson for Chicago, 2–1.

In the fourth matchup, Foster was up to old tricks again. In the last half of the ninth, down by one run, Lincoln manager Sol White pulled Frank Harvey and inserted the Cannonball to close the game. Not accustomed to relieving, a usually calm Redding walked McNair, and the next batter, Bill Francis, slapped a single to right field, with McNair going to third. Hill then bounced to second baseman Kindle, who fired home, catching McNair trying to swipe the tying run. Jess Barbour then hit a rope to Pop Lloyd, who dug it out of the dirt, forcing Hill at second and holding Francis at third. Next up was Bill Parks, who had doubled in two runs earlier in the game, as the crowd became frenzied. After taking a strike and fouling off several pitches, Parks singled up the middle, scoring Francis and tying the game.

With two down, Barbour on third and the score tied, clean-up hitter Horace Jenkins came to bat. Foster called time for no apparent reason. Umpire Fitzpatrick was having little success in calming down the Chicago crowd, as Foster shouted instructions to Jenkins, meanwhile harassing Redding. The calm Redding ignored Foster's taunts, but third baseman Sam Mongin returned the verbal assaults. Redding ignored the distraction as he got two quick strikes on Jenkins. Redding wasted a high hard one, as Mongin and Foster continued to exchange chatter. With Barbour high on his toes, ready to go, Jenkins hit the next pitch, an inning-ending grounder, down the line to Mongin. Barbour dodged the grounder as Mongin fielded the ball cleanly, but hurriedly threw wide to first base, allowing the winning run to score. Foster had failed to distract Redding, but succeeded in harassing Mongin and winning another close one.

Playing all the games in Chicago did not seem to bother the Lincoln Giants as iron man Redding came back the next day and shut out Foster's team, 13–0, on a seven-hitter. Not to be outdone, Foster decided to make his only series appearance. Unimpressed, the Eastern fellows banged up Foster for ten singles and 11 runs, winning 11–4 and tying the series at three all.

The seventh and eighth games featured outstanding performances by Frank Wickware. In the first game, he pitched 12 innings, scattering nine hits for a 2–1 victory over Doc Sykes. In the second game of the doubleheader, he pitched nine innings and gave up only six hits, but lost 1–0 to Tom Harvey. With the Series tied a four games apiece, Lincoln proceeded to win the ninth game, 6–2, and Chicago triumphed in the tenth game, 9–4. The tie-breaking eleventh game was played as the second half of the doubleheader on August 12 to decide the Series winner. In the fourth inning, with Lincoln ahead by one run, the game was called because of darkness.

The series ended in a tie, with Redding winning three out of four games and batting .385 for the Stars and Wickware winning two for the Giants. Horace Jenkins led the Giants attack with a .351 average, while Pop Lloyd, batting in the third slot, belted out a .390 average.

Obviously impressed with the New York players, Foster enticed Jude Gans and Lloyd to join his club. In a press release he announced:

> I have engaged Mr. John Lloyd, captain of the New York Lincoln Stars, to play with the American Giants. The fans realized that he is the greatest shortstop in the business and I am convinced that I cannot do without him. The fans of Chicago deserve the best that is on the market and I am determined to have the best. Mr. Lloyd will report for the August 29 game and will play the rest of the season, 1916 and 1917. I hope to have the best men that can be obtainable and with these men will journey to California, where we hope to return with the pennant. We will go also to Honolulu and upon our return will play all western teams. We will make the longest trip ever made by a colored team.

The Giants later added other Southern players like Oscar Charleston, Louis Santop, "Bingo" DeMoss, Bruce Petway and pitchers "Cannonball" Dick Redding and "Smokey" Joe Williams (41–3 record in 1914), and a Cuban youngster named Cristobal Torriente. He was a powerful left-handed pull hitter, notorious for swinging at pitches out of the strike zone. The magnificent seven comprised one of the most talented bunch of stars assembled that decade.

On September 17, just before the profitable post-season competition, Uncle Sugar drafted defensive first baseman Leroy Grant and shortstop Bobby Williams (a Dillard University graduate), Redding, Whitworth, Johnson, Petway, and Dixon for duty with the 93rd Division in Paris, France.

5th Inning. Family Feud: The ABC's and the American Giants, 1915–1916

Chicago Defender, July 31, 1915

Fight Ends A.B.C. Game
American Giants in Fierce Riot at Hoosier City

Umpire Hits Pete Hill with Gun in 7th Inning in Battle Royal against the Indianapolis A.B.C.'s — Wickware Pitches Great Game and Leads Up to 8th

Other Players Hurt in Melee

Team Plays at Federal Park and is Witnessed by 3,500 Fans — Taylor Brothers Planned to Win, While "Rube" Determined He Would Not be Cheated — In Dispute Game is Forfeited.

(Special to the *Chicago Defender*)

Indianapolis, Ind., July 23 — There came near being a riot at the baseball game last Sunday between the American Giants of Chicago, Ill., and the A.B.C.'s of this city. There were 3,500 lusty fans out to witness what was expected to be the battle royal of the season. Each team had blood in its eyes. The Taylor Brothers bragged that they were going to take the first game in the series because "Rube" Foster and his team had won the best three out of five at Chicago a few weeks ago.

The game was called and Wickware was put on the mound for the Giants. He pitched a steady, conscientious game. "Wick" was in splendid form. It was remarked by many of the old fans that he was never in finer condition. His opponent was hurling some great ball. It was a pitcher's battle. The game went smooth up to the seventh inning. The score was 3 to 2 in favor of the Giants. "Rube" sat on the bench directing his team. In the seventh he sent Whitworth to the mound, then Gatewood. Things looked dangerous for the "old Roman" and dust began blowing around the diamond; it looked cloudy. The two teams came to home plate, an argument ensued. Both teams grabbed bats, the umpire and Pete Hill had an argument and the umpire jerks out a gun and hits "Pete" over the nose. It was reported that his nose was broken. Several other players were hurt in the melee. The umpire forfeited the game to the A.B.C.'s.

Hundreds of people were betting on the Giants and when the game was forfeited, fans who were betting had scraps. The scene on the diamond was a disgrace. The game was played at the white Federal Park. No more will these teams play at this park. There was too great a contrast between the gentlemanly playing of the Federal teams and the riot scenes enacted Sunday. Such games mean that baseball in this city will be reduced to a low ebb and respectable people will not patronize them. It was a bloody chapter. Another one will kill Afro-American ball playing.

Chicago Defender, 31 July 1915

Rube Foster's Signed Statement of the Giants — A.B.C. Mixup
By Andrew Rube Foster

Indianapolis Freeman, 7 August 1915

Rube Foster's Explanation
To the Base Ball Public of the United States

After much persuasion, and careful consideration I have consented to give to the baseball public, an account of the disgraceful series of games that were played last week at Indianapolis between the American

Giants and the ABC's of Indianapolis, the most disgraceful scenes yet to be seen in public, with the possible exception of the daily riots at West Baden by C.I. Taylor, now stool pigeon of the present ABC's baseball club.

The game played at Indianapolis, Sunday, July 18, and was forfeited to the Indianapolis club, which created the most disgraceful climax to a great game happened in this way—in the eighth inning the American Giants made one run, when the Indianapolis club started their last half of the eighth inning, the bases were full, and no one out—the game was interrupted at this point by a wind storm, and as the ground had not been sprinkled, the dust blew at such a rate, the umpire called time, as it was impossible to see the outfielders. During this time, the management of the Indianapolis club got a hose and began to sprinkle the grounds and did sprinkle the grounds between third base and second base. The umpire said to me that he was not going to be shown up in allowing the manager of the ABC's to bring a hose on the grounds. I told him that it was all right so far as I was concerned, only they would have to sprinkle between first and second base and he told me that it was up to me to see that it was done.

Before they had completed sprinkling between third and second, it began to rain, and Bowser, the owner of the club, told the umpire to make us play ball. I appealed to the umpire, and told him to make them sprinkle that ground between first and second base, as it was impossible to see the right fielder. He was told again to make us play ball. I pleaded to him, explaining that he should be more considerate, reasoning with him, that even if the rain did fall, so as to not continue the game, where it could be sprinkled between first and second base. The score at the end of the seventh inning stood two to two and the rain would have no results on the game as it were impossible for the Indianapolis club to lose by it—also impossible for us to win—and that every condition pointed to a victory for the ABC's with the bases full, and none out.

It was against the rules and fair play to try and force us to play under such a handicap, with it raining, and the air full of dust. He told me that it made no difference, he was not going to have the game delayed any longer. (Remember it was not at our suggestion that time was called.) He was told either make us play or forfeit with him, pleading to him that there were so much money at stake on the result of the game, how fair it would be to all to permit the weather to calm and if the grounds were not in condition to play—in 30 minutes—he could, as the rules require—call the game back to even innings and the results would be a draw.

He was again told by the owner to make us play, and getting angry, called four balls on the batter and forced in the tying run and then forfeited the game to the Indianapolis club. It came so suddenly and unexpected, I stood at the home plate dumbfounded, and anyone familiar with professional ball would have done as I did and Pete Hill, captain of the club ran over to see what the umpire had done, and his haste was so mistaken by the followers of the ABC's that the players and fans rushed on the field and started a riot, yet no one was hit or hurt. The disgrace of the entire trouble was with Officer Fleming, who drew his pistol on one of our players. Yet the results of the game was not what the management of the Indianapolis club wanted so much, and I will prove it later on in this statement, and I will leave it to you to judge just who was responsible for this disgrace.

Granting that we had deliberately forfeited a game—this is not a crime, and has often been done by the greatest managers in baseball, and it certainly did not warrant the abuse that we received at Indianapolis. All that saw the game will agree that all during the game I did not for once in action or words, question the decisions even at the home plate, when he told me that the game was forfeited, made no demonstration, either by acts or words, but started directly to our bench—and to my surprise, turned and saw the most disgraceful scene I have ever witnessed; officers, who were supposed to protect you, and who the manager signed a contract to give the American Giants police protection, saw these officers of peace and protection, draw guns and threaten to shoot those they came to protect.

Where there is Crime, There is a Reason

On Monday, July 18, I received the most complete humiliation, both for my ball club and myself. It was the beginning of the third inning. We had scored two runs; the ABC's were at bat. I started out to the coaches box and a police sergeant came upon the field and called me back, calling me the dirtiest names I had ever had said to me, first asking me who were it that started the argument at Sunday's game. I said I did not know, and he said to me: "You black son-of-a-b..., if you open your mouth, I will blow your brains out." He stood there for at least five minutes abusing me, and Bauchman, who I sent to the third base line to coach, in going to the coacher's box, found the base out of line. He took his foot and pushed the base in line. C.I. Taylor, the manager, saw him, rushed from the bench, pushed him aside and called the police, and the officers came out and began beating him over the head. The people yelled shame, and asked us to not play. All of this happened and there had not been a kick of any kind during the game — between the umpire or the players, nor was the game in progress. It was the dirtiest work that I or anyone else had ever seen on a ball field. It was a crime, and there is no one responsible for it but the owner — Bowser — and the ingrate — Taylor.

A policeman cannot come upon a ball field unless asked to do so by the umpire, only in the case of a fight, or trouble, unless requested by the owner or manager. In this case there was neither an argument, fight or had there been a shadow of unpleasantness, then, or during the game. There can be but one answer to fit. The owner — Bowser — being in with the police, and a bondsman, had instructed them to do so, for no officer could, or would go on the ball field, and begin to beat up players, unless they had resisted arrest, for some deed committed, unless they had been told to do so. If we had been at fault, in any way, as sore as they were, it does seem reasonable why we were not arrested — yet no one was arrested.

You may ask why I refer to Taylor as the Ingrate. It is because I have found him to be one of the lowest kind. I have known of him to be beaten upon the playing fields time and time again, by his players, and by others, and his low tactics ruined baseball at West Baden, yet I did not think he were of the type that I have at last found him to be. I had wondered why his brothers— Jim and Ben — refused to play for him, and I had to furnish them money, and guaranteed their pay to get them to come to Indianapolis. All during the winter and they showed their appreciation. Jim hit an umpire here while with the ABC's yet was not clubbed or beaten up. C.I. has acted disgraceful at Chicago, still he has never been beaten up. All the Eastern attractions, they played last year and this year were furnished transportation by me, and sometimes I had to go to New York, and leave my club to get them, and only the day before we played there we sent $594.50 to the Lincoln Stars, so as to play there.

Some have said I were unfriendly to Indianapolis, still the above is the way I have shown it, and at the present time, players, the manager of the ABC's in fact all the colored players are indebted to me for favors, when they were not playing, and could not get assistance from any other source, and it was done at times when traveling with the owner of the clubs. We have been fortunate enough to not have to call on any of them for assistance, but have lent financial help to all the colored clubs that have traveled here, and at times in the winter, have sent financial help to their players. My efforts has always been to try and help, and not tear down, and advance colored ball, as well as players, and I hope the lovers of right, and fair play, will — as in the past — judge me by what they know and not what they hear.

The incident was more painful to me than to any that saw or read it; it was the complete humiliation of a life's effort to advance and promote baseball among our people and I can forgive the many hard words that may have been said, knowing that they had been said before you had a chance to learn the facts, and you can rest assured that I have not up until the present, and would not in the future, do one single thing to hurt baseball, or stoop low enough to permit, or stand to see any ball club, or players treated as the American Giants were at Indianapolis— whether they were right or wrong — and even now would not permit the public, players, or police to come on our grounds, and beat, abuse, or humiliate the Indianapolis ball club. Hoping this explanation will meet with your approval,

I am yours for the Good of Colored Baseball.

Andrew (Rube) Foster,

Manager American Giants Baseball Club.

Indianapolis Freeman, 14 August 1915

C. I. Taylor Standing Up For His Baseball Integrity

Rube Foster Careless in His Speech
— Could be convicted for Libel —
Jealous of the A.B.C.'s Manager

Mr. R. S. Abbott, L.L.D., Chicago, Ill.:

Dear Sir — I note in the issue of your paper of July 24, 1914, under scare headlines: "American Giants in Fierce Riot at Hoosier City." And a sub headline, that "Pete Hill's nose was broken by umpire with gun and other players were hurt in the melee." All this appeared as Special in your publication. Then in your issue of the week of July 31st appears in bold type, on front page: "Rube Foster's Signed Statement of A. B. C. Trouble."

It is not my purpose to deny the allegations as they appeared in your paper, for it is only necessary for the people of Chicago, many of whom who see Pete Hill every day, to just ask him if he was assaulted by the umpire with a gun or they may look into his face and see that he did not get his nose broken, nor any of the other players were injured in the "melee." Neither is it my intention to deny the many

The 1915 Indianapolis ABC's. Top row (left to right), Russell Powell, Ben Taylor, Dick Redding, Bingo DeMoss, Morty Clark, and Dan Kennard; middle row (left to right), Oscar Charleston, Dicta Johnson, C.I. Taylor, Jimmie Lyons, and Todd Allen; bottom row (left to right), George Shively and James Jeffries (NoirTech Research).

malicious and libelous statements as appeared in the "Signed Statement" of the self-styled "Greatest Manager" the game has produced.

But it is my desire to show, through the columns of your paper, a few facts concerning the incident, and the work that I have spent many years trying to help get accomplished. And in this way it may be that some of the venomous and libelous statements that appeared in your paper about me, may be offset, in that they are as untrue as the statement that Pete Hill got his nose broken with the gun. I am sure, too, that you will publish what I have to say in bold type, since I am not going to malign anybody, or try to destroy the usefulness and life's effort of any individual. On the other hand, I am going to tell the truth; whatever I may say will be uncontradictory, and will be of much more benefit to the readers of any good newspaper than the malicious and libelous stuff that came out in glaring headlines the past two weeks.

In regard to the trouble at Indianapolis on the 18th and 19th of last month, let me state that Pete Hill did not get his nose broken nor did any other of the American Giants, except Bauchman, get the weight of anybody's hand on them. And the case of Bauchman occurred on Monday, twenty-four hours after the great and "bloody riot." I must admit right here that I did not approve of the striking of Bauchman by the officer nor the abuse the manager of the American Giants was subjected to by the police sergeant.

Although I have been maliciously and libelously styled a "stool pigeon" and all the other things which a poisoned mind could think to call me, it is true, nevertheless that I am not a stool-pigeon, or in any way, except to do as I did at Federal park, Indianapolis, on Sunday, July 18th, act in the capacity, insofar as I was able, to keep someone from being carted away to the police station.

It is also true that manager of the American Giants has laid himself liable for a libel suit in the Federal courts for such a libelous and slanderous letter as he has put his signature to, unless he can prove every single charge. If he will take the time to consult his lawyers he will find that he would have to prove beyond doubt that I am a "stool-pigeon," and an ingrate, that he has found me to be "low down and dirty," that I had been "beaten up" on many occasions by my own players and others, on the ball field, and that even my "own brothers would not play with me," and that I "ruined" baseball at West Baden, Ind.

Now permit me to say to the readers of your paper and to the baseball public of the United States, that each and all of the above charges are absolutely false, and must convict the author of them as maliciously putting forth every effort, whether it be fair or unfair, to shift his own misdoings to the shoulders of another. As wise as he seems to be, it is interesting to note that he would lay himself liable to accountability before a United States court for such matter as he has his name signed to. There is a limit to what one person may say, through the newspapers, concerning the character of others.

He says he has helped the ballplayers in the United States, by lending them money during the off-seasons for many years past: well, if he keeps up just such tactics in the way of false representations as the case at issue, he will have the privilege of paying out some of his wealth in a libel suit.

It might not be amiss just at this time to request of the readers of your paper, and especially those of Chicago, to ask Pete Hill, if, during the game Sunday, July 18th, did pitcher [Frank] Wickware, right in the middle of the game, deliberately take a ball that was in play and throw it to centerfield to Hill and he (Hill) took the ball and threw it out of the back side of the park (the ball has not been found yet), and while you are asking, don't forget to ask the writer of that malicious and libelous article if he, last year, in our park, took a brand new ball and deliberately cut it on his spikes till it had to be thrown out of the game?

Also ask him if those balls cost anything, and if that is clean sport. It need not be mentioned in this connection that the author of that libelous letter has had to, more than once, smuggle one or more of his men from more than one city in this country for just such tactics, and worse, that caused the trouble down here last month. It is true also that I caught hold of Bauchman and pushed him away from third base, but we still believe even Bauchman can and will tell the truth; ask him if it is not absolutely true that he was spiking and stabbing third base, instead, as is claimed, he was trying to put it back in line. I don't for a moment contend that I was right in going to him and pushing him right away from the base, neither was he right in spiking it as he was, but readers, remember that sometimes, "forbearance ceases to be a virtue." I have been handed many hot deals on different occasions, and sometimes we get tired and resort to other methods.

As regards the police sergeant abusing the manager of the American Giants, I feel it very keenly, but I knew nothing more of it than the people of Chicago knew, and they were many miles away. I am not a "stool-pigeon" and neither am I chief police of Indianapolis, or in any way connected with the police department, and therefore plead lack of responsibility for their misdoings.

The other malicious and libelous statements of that venomous letter do not need and are not worth referring to and I shall take the balance of my time writing of the things that are of much more vitality to the baseball public of the United States than the little incident which occurred here. In fact, it amounted to such a little that the white press did not even make mention of it. And I am sure that it is a very rare case when the white press in any part of the country don't make capital out of any Negro riots. If it had been as it appeared in the columns of your paper, it would not have had the privilege of breaking the news to the baseball public of the United States, for the reason, the *Associated Press* dispatches would have carried it to every nook and corner of this country while your paper was setting up its type.

The thing that hurt Foster most was that he legitimately lost four straight games down here.

In the past five years, I have written many letters, mostly individual, some public, on the organization of the Negro league, and I have met with all sorts of opposition from sources which would be a great surprise to the baseball public of the United States.

Baseball is in its infancy among colored people and with the nourishment of organization, it will grow to be a giant organization such as the entire race will be proud of, and hundreds of our young men who are athletically inclined and desire an education, can become members of professional ball clubs during the summer months and through college on their own account, for the day of our young college men getting enough out of hotel waiting seems to be a thing of the past.

I write many letters to Mr. Andrew Rube Foster every winter and every summer, making suggestions as to how and when the time is ripe for the launching of the Negro baseball league.

Just this year, during the months of April and May, I have written him nearly one pound of typewritten matter as to the organization of the league. And he has agreed that I am right in every statement that I have made in all this matter. I have told him that he is the rightful man to begin the work. I have told him that he is the rightful leader of us in the organization of the league; I have told him that I only wanted to act as a lieutenant in helping him accomplish the thing that has been uppermost in my mind, and his, too, I suppose, for these many years. I made a proposition to him last fall that for him and me to travel together, in all the cities which we believed would be interested in the organization of the league, and that I would pay my own expenses and he could do the same. We could go and get the colored business men of each city together, discuss the organization of the league with them, form a local association, in each city and then, about during the holiday, 1914, call a meeting at some city, say Chicago, and have a representative or a couple of representatives from each local association attend the meeting for the meeting for the purpose of forming a permanent organization, by electing a president. (I even suggested that he would be the best man for president, and mentioned in the meantime that most likely he would rather not have that position for the reason that he might rather be a contender in the league race as manager of his club), and by fixing salary limit and doing many other things that come up at such meetings.

One year, he gave as an excuse for not making effort to organize, the birth of the Federal League[1] and its wide publicity, stating that it would likely be short-lived and there would be many parks idle that we might be able to get for the colored teams (which was pretty good figuring). Then last fall I kept the malls hot after him about making the effort this year and he said what we needed most was good ball clubs, and managers, which are all true but he never did state how to get the good ball clubs. But let me state to the baseball public of the United States that the way to get good clubs and managers of clubs is an equalization of strength and putting a stop to players jumping from one club to another after they have agreed to play with a club. And that can only be done by organization. The formation of a league is the only remedy.

Just at this stage of this article it might be in order to give the public an excerpt of a couple of letters written to Mr. Foster, May 5th and 17th, 1915, respectively. Remember, readers, when these letters were written, fully two and one-half months before the "great" trouble between the American Giants and the A. B. C. Baseball club, there was no idea in my mind that it would ever become necessary to make the same public, and I would not do so now except that it seems to be the purpose of Mr. Foster to destroy, by false accusations and misrepresentations, a life's effort.

He seems to have in view the desire to make the baseball public of the United States believe that he is the only man in the whole country who is trying to build, while all others of us are tearing down. No one will deny that he has done a great deal for baseball, but he has not worked single-handed. There are others of us who have done a great share in getting colored baseball up to the high standard it is, although we have not got the wide publicity he has. It must be kept in mind, too, that some of us have not sought publicity in the matter, either. We have done what we could for the good of colored baseball, for the good of the game, and not for self-aggrandizement.

Here are the letters:

Indianapolis Freeman, 5 May 1915

The Foster-Taylor Correspondence

Mr. Foster:

Dear Sir — Both your letters to hand. I have noted very carefully what you have to say in regard to the proposition that I have made you concerning the league. As I said in the letters, I do not care to be put in the light of the public at all; as I think the leadership rightly belongs to you. All I have said was in the way of suggestions to you, with the hope that you would see that the other managers of us can do anything without the aid of others of us are willing to follow. You are aware of the fact that none of us do anything without the aid of others of us. In other words, the thing that I am making effort to do is get all of us together; all of us to thinking in one channel as nearly as that is possible. And unless that can be done there will be little success for the formation of a league on the tentative plan or on a permanent plan.

What we all have got to see ultimately is, that there can be no real success for us individually except we are successful as a whole. And again we cannot succeed as a whole except we recognize someone of us as a leader, but in recognizing one of us as a leader will not mean that each of us will not have a perfect right to our ideas of things, even if our ideas do not suit the leaders' ideas, or rather, if they are out of harmony with his ideas. The thing needed most is a high regard for everyone's rights and then how to the line in bringing about perfect accord in our midst.

It is just as you say, we need ball clubs, but you say nothing as to how to get the ball clubs; when they are continually raided on by higher salaries to the men under verbal contract to play with the teams that they are already on. An equalization of strength is what is needed and that can only be brought about by the plan that I have mentioned, and to which you agree. I am writing in this strain because I think I see in your letter a luke-warmness that spells defeat for the movement. It must have your co-operation if it is to amount to anything. I am discussing things very frankly to you, but at the same time, with no intention of bringing about a controversy. It is nothing new for me to put you in the position as a leader. I have been with you at all times and all matters pertaining to the future welfare of the game among us. I admit, we have had our differences, but I am sure you are too manly to think that I ought to do otherwise than have my own idea of things. In other words, I am trying now to act as a lieutenant in this matter of getting hinged around you, all the other managers so that if you have any scruples in approaching any of them, the job will be put on me and not you. And after this has been accomplished you could go ahead with the organization.

It is just as you admit most anything is better than the plan we are now working on. Then why not make a strenuous effort to put another plan on foot? The one on which we are working now without doubt had its day and is in great need of relegation to the scrap heap.

As you say, this poor year in baseball may serve to bring the players back to their senses, but I can say two things for the ball players, viz: they have not done anything that the white players would not do under like circumstances and further, they have not done what we as managers have not caused them to do. The only difference is, that some of us have felt their misdoings much more keenly than others of us.

I have always occupied the smallest place among the managers, but years ago I began preaching against the habit of players jumping from one club to another. I knew eventually it would arrive at the point it now is. And if some radical change is not made, our future in the game is sure to be disastrous. It seems to me that everybody has gotten together, in organization, except the colored baseball clubs. There are all sorts of organizations among our people and it is surprising that colored baseball has made the progress it has and yet is unorganized.

I would not care to issue any call unless it had the stamp of your approval on it. It would not amount to very much. I cannot see any success in anything that I might put on foot alone, but I think I can see much in what we might inaugurate together and in harmony; believing that our undertaking is for the good of one and all.

Sincerely yours,
C. I. Taylor

Indianapolis Freeman, 17 May 1915

Mr. Andrews R. Foster
3242 Vernon Avenue,
Chicago, Ill.:

Dear Sir — Your reply to my letter is now before me. Just as I have stated to you on many occasions before, there is entirely too much of the "Great" I am among colored people in baseball for any of us to amount to what we might. You will find that it is not to the best interests of you nor anybody else to threaten to wipe somebody off the map in baseball every time somebody happens to ask to have the privilege of having something to say and do with affairs that concern them as well as yourself. I note very carefully, that almost every letter you write me, provided we are differing on some matter, that you offer a threat to have me banned forever from baseball. Now, it looks very reasonable to me that if you can forever wipe me from the baseball map that it would not be good business to do so, for many reasons. First, it must be conceded by you and all fair-minded people, that I always have a fairly good ball club. And that being a fact, it I have sense enough to operate a ball club, any fair-minded man would not object to me having my own idea of things and having the manhood and courage to let my ideas be known.

I am speaking to you frankly, but cautiously, for the reason that I am not willing to be drawn in to a controversy with you nor anyone else. On the other hand, it is my purpose to have as good ball club as I can get together, and with the aid of anyone who will be fair enough to help me, provided I am worthy of help, to make the best of the opportunities that may present themselves to me. At the same time, it is also my purpose to lay no stone in anyone's way who may be striving to the same end. I believe, it is their God–given right. I have no chip on my shoulder, it matters not what you may say or think. And I fully realize that you nor any of us will have the success that awaits us if you or any of us adhere to the principles as laid down in your letter.

Lastly, I will say that I would be very sorry if you would put anything in my way to keep me from making an honest living. It is unfortunate that these acrimonious wrangles couldn't be buried for all time. This time could be spent too much better advantage in trying to get the colored league organized.

Yours,

C. I. Taylor

Let me say, finally, to the baseball public of the United States that the above are excerpts of letters I have written Mr. Andrew Rube Foster this year. And I fully believe that those of you who saw and read that malicious and libelous letter denouncing me as a "stool-pigeon," and an " ingrate" and other venomous appellations, will draw your own conclusions as to their truthfulness.

Let me further state that I have for many years fought every evil that has menaced the national sport. The truth will ultimately be known.

Yours for clean sport,

C. I. Taylor

Manager A.B.C.'s. Indianapolis, Ind.

At the end of the season the American Giants sought some claim to legitimacy and challenged the Chicago Whales of the Federal League.

The *Chicago Defender* added its say in the challenge;

Rube Foster Challenges Tinker's Feds

Will Play Games for Charity — No Answer Received — Will Postpone Trip for Series— is Tinker Scared?

Rube Foster, the greatest baseball manager on earth has challenged the Chicago Federal League, winners of the pennant race in their league. Rube wants to play the Chi-Feds [better known as the Chicago Whales in 1915] in order to prove to them that he has a much superior team. Manager Tinker, up to the time we go to press, had scheduled several games with the local semi-pros, but has failed to answer Rube's challenge. Yet he and [lunchroom owner Charles] Weeghman want to butt in on the Worlds Series with organized ball. They holler they are not getting fair play. How about the [American] Giants? Are they getting fair play? Not by a darn sight. It is simply a matter of color prejudice with them.

Rube goes so far as to offer to play them a series of games and the proceeds going to charity on a winner and loser basis— that is, for white and colored institutions. Manager Tinker is scared. The Giants will leave for the West Saturday unless answer is forthcoming.[2]

The Chicago Whales had won 86 games against 66 loses, with outstanding seasons from two veteran pitchers: George McConnell (age 37), who lead the league with 25 wins against 10 losses, and Mordecai Brown (age 38), 17–8. "Three-finger" Brown, then with the Cubs, had beaten the American Giants twice in 1909, and a rematch would have been a welcome setting for the vengeful Foster.

Instead, Foster took his team westward, making pit stops in Omaha and Denver, before engaging the competition in the California Winter League (CWL). They had not appeared on the west coast since the 1912–13 season. With some of the best players in the land — Pete Hill, Frank Duncan, Pop Lloyd, Jude Gans, Bruce Petway, Dizzy Dismukes, Cyclone Joe Williams and Frank Wickware — they were stacked with talent. Wickware was the ace of the staff, as he had four complete games in seven appearances. He was credited with six of the team's nine wins against one loss. Their biggest competition came from the San Diego Pantages, who had bombed Joe Williams in the opener with 14 hits and seven runs, in a 7–4 loss.[3] However, Wickware was awesome, pitching a one-hitter over the Cline-Cline team for a 4–0 victory. He would have had a no-hitter over the Pantages but Lloyd and Hill failed to communicate on a Texas Leaguer by Dick Bayless in the ninth inning. Hill and Lloyd each had two hits in the 4–0 win.[4] In January of 1916, they captured the CWL title with a 3–2 victory over the Pantages.

Coming into the 1916 season with the added swagger of beating the best in the west, the *Chicago Defender* bragged that "the Giants would make the Chicago White Sox look like a bunch of bush leaguers."[5] C.I. Taylor's Indianapolis ABC's challenged the Giants for

Top: 1916 Chicago American Giants. Top row (left to right), Bill Gatewood, Jess Barbour, Leroy Grant, Pop Lloyd and Jude Gans; bottom row (left to right), Bill Francis, Dick Whitworth, Pete Hill, Rube Foster, Bruce Petway, unknown, and unknown (courtesy Tim Cammett of Diamond Images).

Bottom: Robbery! In a scheduled 12-game series to decide the World Colored Champions, game eight ignited a volatile relationship between Foster and Taylor when, coaching at first base, Foster refused to remove his fielder's glove. Foster countered the protest saying there was no rule against it. With the ABC's leading 1–0, the umpire ruled the game a forfeit victory for Taylor's men. After winning the next two games, the ABC's claimed the title, while the Giants pointed out the series did not go the full 12 games. Taylor and Foster continued their battle in the press (*Indianapolis Freeman* 25 November 1916).

In 1914, C.I. Taylor purchased a 50 percent interest in the ABC's from Thomas A. Bowser, a white bail bondsman with political connections. A native of Anderson, South Carolina, the Spanish-American War veteran served with the all-black Tenth United States Cavalry Regiment, in the Philippines. After the war, Taylor attended Clark College where he recruited the nucleus for his Birmingham Giants team in 1904 (NoirTech Research).

the "world's colored championship." It was the best of 12 games. Chicago took three of first four games played in Chicago, (August 27 through August 31) with the fifth game called after ten innings, tied 3–3, on account of darkness. The second series of seven games was scheduled for Indianapolis in late October. The American Giants took the opener, 5–3 with the second game of the evening called after three and a half innings due to darkness. Game number eight ignited the volatile relationship between Taylor and Foster to another level. With the ABC's leading 1–0, Foster, coaching from the first base box, put a glove on, to the dismay of Indy's first baseman, Ben Taylor. The umpire demanded Foster remove the glove, and Foster countered that there was no rule against wearing the equipment. As each man lobbied his point of contention, the umpire ruled a forfeit victory for the Taylor lads. The

Pictured are E.C. Knox, managing editor of the *Indianapolis Freeman*, Rube Foster (American Giants), J.D. Howard, owner of the *Indianapolis Ledger*, and C.I. Taylor, manager of the Indy ABC's. Knox and Howard were interested in the contest for supremacy in colored baseball, while Foster and Taylor wanted bragging rights. According to the *Freeman* (11 November 1916), the photo was taken a few minutes before the umpires called "play ball" for game six of 12, on October 22 (NoirTech Research).

ABC's took the next two games, 8–2 and 12–8, and staked their claim to the title of world colored champions. The *Chicago Defender* challenged the judgment as, of the nine games played, each team won four and another was a contested forfeit in favor of the ABC's. Foster is his letter below pointed out that the series did not go the full 12 games and therefore no champion could be declared.

Chicago Defender, 18 November 1916

Rube Foster Speaks

Flays Methods and Umpiring in Indianapolis; Concerning Recent Series

Owing to the many letters received at this office, asking who were champions, the A.B.C.'s or the American Giants, at my request Mr. Foster has covered the article, telling why he withdrew his team, and as you read you will see that the *Defender* was right when it said the series stands four won each, it being the only paper that did say so.—Sports Editor.

The questions of whether the A.B.C's are champions has been put to me hundreds of times both here and while at Indianapolis and my answer is No. Based on the facts, and contract covering the series, made between Taylor and myself, the agreement called for a series of twelve games. For the A.B.C.'s to win or the American Giants to win, each would have to win seven games—there was no stipulation that the winner of the majority of the games would be the Champions, but twelve games played to a decision, the winner of the seven out of twelve games to be champions. Just why such would have been published, especially as Taylor knew the conditions of play, is not only an injustice to baseball, the fans of Indianapolis, but the American Giants as well. This will be the conclusively proved by Taylor's statement in the *[Indianapolis] Ledger* of September 11, 1916.

Taylor's Statement to the Public

C.I. Taylor replies to scathing attack of Chicago sport writer—A.B.C. leader tell his side in a calm and dispassionate review of the whole Chicago series—the peerless local manager puts his case squarely into the hands of the impartial baseball public.

Note again the *Defender* knows full well the American Giants and A.B.C's have twelve games to play for the colored championship, and that only five of the games have been played—American Giants two games ahead of the Indianapolis club for the colored championship with eight full games to be played to complete the championship series. We fail to see any reason for the Sport Sheet of any reputable newspaper to carry headlines declaring either club World's Championships, when there is a stipulated agreement that twelve games are to be played for the championship (colored title) and only four of the games have been played to a decision, yet the *Defender* in Glaring Headlines, "American Giants Again World's Champions," if the two clubs are engaged in a twelve game series for the title and one club should win three of the first four games played, we fail to see why they should be declared "World's Champions" by any well informed sports writer, for with eight full games to play, the club which is two games behind has at least a chance to catch up and even win the series. The *Defender* says itself that twelve games are to be played for it to declare our comprehension. There is yet some virtue in the truth. We believe that the people are as anxious for facts now as in days past.

In spite of the statement that the American Giants are again "World's Champions," the A.B.C's of Indianapolis have eight more games to play with that club for that title before the people of this country will rightfully knew whom the champions really are. Cheap notoriety doesn't make for permanent success.

Signed,
C.I. Taylor

I am not going far enough to say that the *Freeman* and *Ledger* are not reputable newspapers, or that the sport writers of these papers are not reliable, as probably they have wrote as they have been informed by the A.B.C. management whose honesty to them is unquestioned, and as they are the mouthpiece of the baseball fans, they have the opportunity to explain to their readers just why after writing the statement of Taylors' with eight games to be played also acknowledged by him as an agreement with me, also in this statement they were hoodwinked to write the A.B.C.'s champions after out of the twelve games to be played for the title, with only nine played to a decision, the A.B.C's winning five, American Giants winning four, leaving three full games unplayed, they called the A.B.C.'s champions.

I repeatedly told the editors of both the *Freeman* and the *Ledger* after Thursday's game was played and it was announced that the next games would be played in a double header Sunday, that it was impossible for either club to win, even if one should win both games, as if we or the A.B.C.'s won both games we would have won only six games out of twelve, and to be the winner of the championship would have to win seven games. The argument might be advanced that we had ample time to play all of the games, but in drawing up the agreement of the series Taylor was allowed to name the playing dates there, and they would be acceptable to me, for the seven games to be played there (Indianapolis) and he named the dates as follows, and so advertised on posters all over Indianapolis, "Double Header Sunday, Oct. 22, continuing Monday, Tuesday, and Wednesday; Double Header Sunday, Oct. 29." It rained on Wednesday and we played the game scheduled for that date the following day. I admit that Taylor wanted to play the other date, but as I had lived up to the agreement, to play as contracted and with no stipulations for postponements in our agreements, it was a matter left entirely up to me, and my refusal was perfectly correct. On Saturday night before the last games scheduled we were discussing the probable winner the following day, and was asked by the editors of the *Freeman* and the *Ledger* if the American Giants won would they be champions, and I told them under the agreement with Taylor it would be impossible, and Knox said, I had better call Taylor up and see as things are not as they have been represented to me. Knox, calling Taylor up, asked him if the A.B.C.'s won tomorrow would they be champion, and he told him beyond a doubt, "Yes." This was only the invisible hand that was weaving the unfair spirit of the fans, but had made me refuse to play other than contracted.

Series should be American Giants Four, A.B.C.'s Four.

The Tuesday's game that was forfeited to the A.B.C.'s would never in a thousand years been award to the A.B.C.'s under the rules of baseball. It would have been thrown out and ordered to be played over again. It was so raw and uncalled for; I had taken the club from the field and even yet feel justified in so doing, admitting that I regard taking a club off the field one of the gravest crimes in baseball, and would not under any conditions, regardless of the decision, where it was a question of judgment of the umpires, covering the things that the rules emphatically state, there is no protest.

But my banishment from the game was not a point of judgment on the part of the umpire, but one of the humiliation and against the rules of the duty of an umpire, laid down in the book of rules. All that saw the games played between the two clubs will admit that every close play during the series went to the A.B.C.'s and not once during the series was their protesting of such a nature as to even the cautioned during our stay at Indianapolis and we accepted for granted, it was the judgment of the umpire, so mild our actions.

In the third game I went down on the first base line to coach, after the close of an inning, picked up the glove at first and put it on my hands. Ben Taylor told the umpire to make me take it off. He asked me to take it off. At first I thought he was joking, but he said, either take off the glove or get off the coacher's line. I asked him if it was against the rules. He said he did not know and I said, then "We will appeal to the umpire-in-chief." Appealing to him, I related what the umpire had said to me and said, "Taylor wants the glove removed, and you will have to take it off." I told him I was playing by the playing rules and not Taylor's rules. He said that I would have to take it off or leave the line—holding up the game. I then took the ball club off the field, and it was done in a manner as quiet as anything could have been done, without the least demonstration. Can you imagine a club contesting for a title subjected to such unfairness? It was so raw, and the intentions were so evident that I refused to play, only as contracted; in so doing I knew it was impossible to lose the Championships but my actions were more than vindicated the following Sunday when at the opening of the first scheduled game I took my position at first base, as in the game forfeited picked up the glove, and again put it on my hand as before. Taylor again objected, but the umpire-in-chief, Mr. Geisel, chief of the American Association Umpires told me I was in every way obeying the rules and he was an umpire that knew the rules from A to Z.

Foster continued his rebuttal the following week.

Chicago Defender, 25 November 1916.

Rube Foster Speaks

Where there is crime there is always a reason. My reasons in taking the ball club from the field was prompted by the seeming prejudice handed to me at Indianapolis, and on each occasion it was done, with no play of the game involved; when there last year the police hit one of my men on the field and an officer came and not only insulted me, but offered to shoot me if I opened my mouth during the game. I had not, or any of the players, questioned the decisions of the umpire; nor was the game in process; the sides were changing and I had just started to the coacher's box and when the umpire asked me off the line this season for going to the coacher's box, putting on a glove, the first thing that came into my mind was the incident a year ago, hence the results. I not only did that this year, but would at any time, provided the offense was the same and prompted by the same motives as on both occasions at Indianapolis.

There are times when patience ceases to be a virtue and this was one of the occasions with me as there was no chance as the rules give you to play the game under protest and if the ruling of the umpires was wrong the officials of the league throw the game out and order it played over.

First Know That You Are Right Then Proceed.

The umpire knew that I had no chance to have a hearing on a protest and went outside of the playing rules to humiliate me and rather than stand for such I took my club off the field, as in any other place but Indianapolis I would have passed the incident as nothing and immediately have obeyed the umpire. It is true that Taylor used four umpires on Sundays there, but it does not mean that all four were competent or that they were there for the right thing; yet he had one that was competent behind the plate, and he did umpire satisfactorily. This umpire would NOT go out of the rules to banish a man, and tell you that it was NOT against the rules. Taylor was banished from the game at Chicago for violating the rules, in arguing with the umpire concerning some play of the game, which was perfectly right, and under the rules. I was banished from the game, not for arguing about a play or anything pertaining to the game, but simply because I picked up a glove on the coacher's line, the coacher's box. Mine was in keeping with the rules. Taylor's was in disobedience of the rules.

Mr. Taylor said in his signed statement that the A.B.C.'s of Indianapolis had eight more game to play with the American Giants for the title before the people of this country would rightly know who the Champions really are, but on the back of that he plays five of the eight games and tells you that his team is World's Champions. Disregarding the agreement (written) that the series was played under, forgetting the statement he made through the press. Admitting this to be true, he is content on having hoodwinked the fans into the belief that he has accomplished their greatest desire, a statement not only false, but an evidence of just how much an honest man he is and regards his word, his respect of a written contract, his value of his own signed statement to the press, and how ignorant he classes the fans.

I agree with him that the cheap notoriety as stated by him does not make for permanent success, and I presume he knew what was coming when he made that statement. It does not seem that if the A.B.C.'s are as represented by Taylor, admitted to by me, a wonderful club, that they are never asked to return after a foreign engagement, and the American Giants are not only asked, but received with open arms.

This has been the fundamental principle of many successes, and I want to correct the statement that appeared in the *Ledger* that I was so egotistic and felt so cocksure of winning the series that I purchased the belts for all the players and had the Champions engraved on them. But it is true that we have such belts and did wear them to Indianapolis, but they were presented to the American Giants by Mr. E.R. Litzinger (white) of Chicago as the winner of the Lincoln Stars championship series, which we won and was advertised as such, and not a present from me. That was just an unfair as the big headlines that came out with five games to be played, saying, "A.B.C.'s Win Series."

I don't wish anyone to think this article is prompted by any desire to reflect upon the players, managements or the public but facts are facts and while it may disappoint some the baseball public is entitled to the real truth as requested by the editors of the *Defender* for the baseball fans of the Race and I will not be party to any false representations.

I really admire the A.B.C.'s as a baseball cub and would not wish to direct a better ball club. They are undoubtedly a wonderful ball club and their great spirit being handicapped not only by injuries, three games behind and rout a club of experienced players as the players on the American Giants, is marvelous; their great playing was second to the wonderful spirit shown, so powerful that it swept us off our feet, especially as we figured that they were out of the running. It was the greatest show of courage that I have ever seen and was a revelation to me. Such spirit should be rewarded with the efforts sought, but under the agreement the games were played under, they are just where they started at.

I have been the recipient of many honors in baseball the past twenty-two years have received many demonstrations from fans of all races, have tasted the joy from wonderful achievements, and have drank from the cup of glory that comes with victory, but in all my life I have never felt so happy as at the close of the last game, when the fans of both races rushed on the diamond and asked to shake my hand. I felt even greater in defeat than I was ever made to feel in victory, and it made a lasting impression on me, and I would not return that feeling for all the honors I have received on the diamond.

Respectfully yours,

A. Rube Foster.

Chicago Defender, 6 October 1917

A Manager Is Up Against — Just a Few Plain Facts

Dear Sir:

I have read Howard's scathing denunciation and humiliating charges broadcast to the world under the heading: "A.B.C's Get First Ledger Roast." In one of the latter paragraphs of the "Roast" will be found this statement: "It certainly would be interesting information for the Colored fans of this city to know just why no effort was made to give them a better run in the series just played with McGill's Indians."

Since the *Ledger* in its first "roast" and I will add, its first opportunity to "roast" has left down the gap in the foregoing paragraph giving us the privilege of setting forth the facts as to just why no "effort" was made to strengthen the club for the games with the Indians. The paragraph referred to is our apology for this explanation, taking for granted the *Ledger* is magnanimous enough to publish the explanation the fans ought to have. Upon first reading, and knowing, as I do, that not one effort was made by the *Ledger* to obtain the facts before going to the public with its "Roast," it sounded ridiculous and a joke; and to the average baseball fan it will give the impression that the *Ledger* had carefully investigated and knew for a truth that no "effort" had been made to have the club in the best possible condition.

Let us set forth the facts and see if any effort was made to make a real showing against the Indians or did we sit idly by and make no preparation to give the fans a run for their money as charged by the *Ledger.*

Roster of Players

In order that the fans may see for themselves we give below a roster of players and the positions they have played this year in our efforts to maintain a high class ball club:

[Dizzy] Dismukes, pitcher, left of his own accord; [Lem] McDougal, pitcher, three months on trial, failed to make good; [James] Jefferies, pitcher, center field, right field and left hand; [Dicta] Johnson, pitcher, sore arm, off form all year; [Bill] Gatewood, pitcher and first base; [Russell] Powell, catcher, second and first base, injured at Muncie, August 12th; [Jack] Watts, catcher, left club in early part of year; [Dave] Malarcher, catcher, pitcher, second baseball, right field and third base; B. [Ben] Taylor, first and second, suffered with pneumonia, having poor year; [Frank] Warfield, second base, shortstop, sprained ankle half the summer; [Morten] Clark, shortstop, right field and third base, trouble with eyes, had poor year; J. [Candy Jim] Taylor, third and second suffered with charley horse and bad ankle all year; [Al] Cobb, catcher, rib broken in St. Louis September 15th; [Oscar] Charleston, center field, pitcher, first base and right field, injured August 19th in double header against American Giants; [George] Shively, left field, insubordination, left club of own accord; [Charles] Blackwell, left field and right field, suffering with charley horse; [Thomas] Lynch, center field and right field; [Jimmie] Lyons, left field and center field, suffering with charley horse; [Chippy] Britton, pitcher; [John] Landers, pitcher; [Stringbean] Williams, pitcher, had great year, held up the club.

In other words we have used twenty one (21) players who have played forty-two (42) different positions, in our efforts to keep the club in the running. And this is not all; in our efforts to bolster the club we made a trip to New York, Philadelphia and Atlantic City. We tried to hire "Cyclone" Joe Williams, offering him two hundred dollars per month, which, he admitted, was far in excess of the salary he was receiving. We made flattering offers to Spotswood Poles, the Lincoln Giants' left fielder. We tried to secure Kimbro, third baseman of the same; we negotiated with [Louis] Santop and [Bill] Gatewood, both catchers of the Brooklyn Royals [Giants], and tried to bolster our pitching staff with Dan Johnson of the Bacharachs of Atlantic City, offering each and all of these player's salaries far in excess of what they were drawing. Many of the fans are familiar with the above facts.

Other Facts

We sent Powell to West Baden, Ind., to be treated by a specialist. We had an x-ray picture made of his shoulder in our efforts to get him back in the game.

The *Ledger*'s Roast

But the *Ledger*'s "roast" or charge is that nothing was done to bolster the club for the games with the Indians. Well, let us see: In the first place if it were possible to throw a great ball club together in a few hours not only would we have been thoroughly prepared to meet the Indians, but we would have copped the world's Colored Championship this year.

Roast Hasty

The *Ledger* "first roast" was hasty and made without investigation and without regard to the facts which we will show. As before stated, it is impossible to throw a great ball club together in a few minutes as the *Ledger* would have it appear, but it takes time, patience, energy, money, much experience, and last, but not least, it takes men. We have used 21 men in our efforts to give to the fans a great ball club; we have spent thousands of dollars, many sleepless nights, and many hard days of rigid practice and much diplomacy. We have been untiring in our efforts to satisfy and gratify a sport-loving public.

And then, to be charged with carelessness and afraid to spend a few pennies to bolster my club wherever it was weak without first knowing the truth is far less than I could expect from the *Ledger.*

The Fans' Support

The *Ledger* says that the fans alone are responsible for the A.B.C.'s getting the privilege of playing the post-season games. We take that to mean that we have done nothing; we take that to show that our four years of hard work in bringing about a new era in baseball has been nothing and if anything has been done it was done by the people. It leaves us to wonder who made the *Ledger*, the people or the editor-owner? We fully believe he would want some of the credit for its success laid to his own untiring efforts.

We further believe that if on any occasion he had done his best to give the people the best possible service and for some cause over which he had no control had failed, he would not feel the people should withdraw their support from this paper till at least the facts were known; neither would he feel that that the people ought to withdraw their support from the *Ledger* because it might fail to measure up to the standard of the *Indianapolis Star* or *News.*

The *Ledger* further says it would have been far better not to have played the games. This is only another one of the many absurd statements contained in the "roast." Mr. McGill said to me early in August that if his club won the flag he would likely play my club a post-season series. I said all right. They clinched the flag September 17th and Mr. McGill wired me at Kansas City, September 18th, that the games were on and there was nothing for me to do but play the games.

Wired Foster for Help.

The *Ledger* says no effort was made to bolster the club, but as soon as the series with the Indians was assured I sent the following wire to Rube Foster, which explains itself:

Telegram
Mr. Andrew R. Foster
3242 Vernon Avenue
Chicago, Ill.

The Indianapolis Association team won pennant. We play them Saturday, Sunday. My club short entirely to pieces. Powell out of games since August 12th. [Al] Cobb sustained broken rib last Saturday in St. Louis. [Candy Jim] J. Taylor has charley horse. [Oscar] Charleston has sprained ankle and all the men more or less injured. Must have [Bingo] DeMoss and [catchers Tubby] Dixon or [Bruce] Petway. Answer here quick.

C.I. Taylor

Foster replied immediately and explained that he had just completed arrangements for an important series of games at Beloit and other places in Wisconsin and would not return to Chicago till late Saturday night or early Sunday morning and therefore could not give the desired aid.

We must concede that his games were as important to him as ours were to us.

One week before knowing definitely that we were going to play the Indians I made further overtures to [Louis] Santop of New York City and [Yank] Deas of Atlantic City, but could secure the services of neither. At the same time I was trying hard to get my own men in condition. I secured the services of a trainer at Kansas City and paid his fare all the way to Indianapolis for the purpose of working on my men who were injured so as to get them in fair shape for the games.

I still have this man in my employ. No other Colored ball club ever employed a trainer. No other Colored ball club ever played the pennant winners of a major-minor league club. No other Colored man ever built up such a baseball club as the A.B.C.'s in so short a period of time. There is no agency in the city of Indianapolis which has done more or brought more prestige and advertising to Indianapolis than the A.B.C.B.B. club, and then to think because we made a poor showing in the recent series of games, a leading journal, which stands for the uplift of the Race, would be the first to suggest that the support of the people should be withdrawn is more than even a prejudiced mind could conceive.

Arraignments of Williams

The most unjust attack and severe arraignment that ever came to my notice since I have been in the game was that of the Ledger against pitcher Williams. Mind you, no effort has been made to know the probable cause of Williams' wildness in the Sunday's contest. This same Williams, who is the recipient of such a severe and unjust attack by the *Ledger*, has been the mainstay of the A.B.C. club since joining us. And has won 85 percent of his games.

Censure Players

I often find it necessary to censure ball players, but I have not one word of criticism for Williams because of his showing against the Indians. His great effort to win the game single-handed provided his downfall. He knew the weakened and crippled condition of his club — he knew that he, Malarcher and B. Taylor were the only men on the club who were not more or less incapacitated.

He knew that a Colored ball club was for the first time pitted against the pennant winners of a major organization and that the burden of proof was up to him almost entirely because of his many crippled teammates. It was a supreme occasion and Williams made as game an effort as I ever saw. I can only say that I hope to land him for my 1918 club.

Warmed Up Well

Powell did the receiving while Williams warmed up for the game and he reported to me afterward that Williams had more on the ball than he had ever seen him have, though he was a trifle wild, due, he thought, to the fact he had so much. Powell's prediction was that if he could get it over the Indians were beaten already. It was a case of having "too much" which is not unusual on great occasions.

The Figures

The game in figures do not tell a sad tale at all. They show that we outhit the champions; they show that J. Kirks, whom the Indians imported from the Louisville club, made four of the Indians' seven hits. They show that the crippled A.B.C's made two errors, while the champions made one. They show twelve Indians left on bases and eight A.B.C.'s. They show four hits off Williams; three of Johnson and none off the champion twirler.

In our crippled condition we played a better game in many departments of the game than did the champions. Williams' inability to locate the plate would naturally make the club look bad, but figures do not lie.

We did our best and if the *Ledger* says we must go, all right.

C.I. Taylor
Manager-Owner A.B.C.'s
Indianapolis, Ind.

6th Inning. The Pitfalls of Black Baseball, 1917–1919

When the Chicago American Giants played at Kuebler's Park (home of the St. Louis Giants) on North Broadway in 1917, a 12-year bat boy named Normal "Tweed" Webb served as batboy. Webb recalls those glorious eight games of history:

> It was a great thrill.... I made a quarter per game.... Rube was a heck of a manager. Firm! I mean he was a business man. A tremendous disciplinarian. You had to hustle for him all the time. He didn't even want you to eat peanuts on the bench. Rube would permit, cigars and pipes—but never light a cigarette. You better not even hold one in your hand. He was something else.
>
> Webb added, "But Rube was respected by the all his players. They honored him. Son of a Methodist preacher. He was the greatest entity in baseball. A truly outstanding athlete. Foster was the most brilliant figure the great national sport has ever produced. He should have entered the Hall of Fame before Satchel Paige. He should have been the first man in the Hall of Fame. Rube was the greatest."[1]

Webb was nationally known as a major resource of documented records about the Negro Leagues, and was the official scorer for St. Louis Stars' home games from 1922 to 1929. As the first African American selected to the Greater St. Louis Amateur Baseball Hall of Fame as a writer for the *St. Louis Argus*, he campaigned annually for the inclusion of Negro leaguers in the National Baseball Hall of Fame. Webb's mantra was "I've Seen Them All." His all-time all-star team included Biz Mackey and Josh Gibson at catcher, Ben Taylor (1b), Bingo DeMoss (2b), Dave Malarcher (3b), Pop Lloyd (ss), Outfielders Mule Suttles, Cool Papa Bell, Oscar Charleston and pitchers Smokey Joe Williams, Satchel Paige and John Donaldson. In 1998, the Society for American Baseball Research's Negro Leagues Committee established the Tweed Webb Lifetime Achievement Award given annually at the Jerry Malloy Negro League conference.

Another St. Louis resident, James Bell concurred: "Mr. Foster tried to get black ballplayers into the major leagues before some of us were born. He is the father of black baseball and was one of the best pitchers in baseball. He should have been the first black to go in (the Hall of Fame).[2]

Webster McDonald, a fine submariner who pitched for the Chicago American Giants in two World Series in 1926 and 1927, agreed with Webb in his assessment of a great leader.

> There was no question about who was the boss. Rube was strict. You did it his way or you didn't play at all. When you were pitching, he called everything. I mean everything, what to pitch, where to pitch it, and even what motion to use. The catcher would give signs, but it didn't mean nothing. Your natural tendency was to resist so much authority, but you had no choice. Besides, he was right most of the time.
>
> Our catcher, Jim Brown, got into it with Rube once. Brown was kind of an ornery guy anyway. He came out to the mound to give me hell about a pitch I'd thrown. I told him Rube had called it. Well, Brown complained about Rube in a real loud voice. After the inning was over, Rube told Jim to go into the clubhouse and take his uniform off. Rube followed him in and locked the door. Brown was a big strong guy, but Rube just whipped him. Boy, was Rube tough![3]

By now, Foster was legendary. A 21-year-old Mohawk Indian named Chief Turner sought to capitalize on the Foster image. The 163-pound Turner fought as a middleweight boxer under the name of "Young Rube Foster," winning some impressive victories with his jab and run style. He was often compared to champion Stanley Ketchel, the premier middleweight of the period, but never quite made the grade.

After World War I, Foster teamed up with a white fellow, John Schorling, a tavern owner. With Schorling's finances and Foster's ingenuity, the salt and pepper combination organized one of the greatest dynasty teams in modern baseball history—the Chicago American Giants.

Foster made certain the newly formed American Giants had the ambience of the finest teams. Foster would dress his team in the latest uniform styles as they traveled in the finest Pullman coaches. The American Giants were known to have as many as five different sets of uniforms. Dave Malarcher, third sacker for the Giants, in an interview with sportswriter John Holway, boasted: "The American Giants came down to New Orleans in 1915 to play against the Eagles, the semipro team I played with. I never saw such a well-equipped ball club in my life! I was astounded. Every day they came out in a different set of beautiful uniforms, all kinds of bats and balls, all the best kinds of equipment."[4]

Foster's new team generated excitement never seen before in American ball parks. Fans came to see Foster give signals with puffs of smoke from his ever-present corncob pipe. His managerial successor, Dave Malarcher, claimed,

"Rube often signaled his players by his pipe, my shifting it in his mouth, puffing it, taking it out with either hand, pointing with it, tapping it out, loading it—you name it—he had signals that never were stolen. He did the same with shifts of his head or his looks."[5]

Even the coolest of players, "Cool Papa" Bell, thought Foster was a little chilly, "That Rube always seemed so casual. You'd think you had picked off his signs and then the next day they would be completely different. He was a brilliant man."[6]

Former pitcher Wee Willie Powell, who played for Rube in the mid–20s, remembered the savvy soul: "When Rube would sit there on the bench in his street clothes, fans always thought he was giving signals with his smoking pipe. Sometimes he would, sometimes he wouldn't. To confuse the opposition, he made other players think that was what he was doing. While they'd be watching Rube, somebody else on the bench was giving the real signals. Foster was the smartest baseball man I ever knew."[7]

Foster exploited the game rules to every advantage known to the national pastime. He introduced the hit-and-run play, bunt-and-run, drag bunting, the double steals, the suicide squeeze play and tilting of the base lines for bunt control.

Every Giants player was required to learn the art of bunting, including the sluggers. Each player eventually learned to become a switch-hitter. At one time, as many as seven switch-hitters were in the line-up. Against tough pitchers, they learned how to consistently foul off pitches, eventually earning a free pass to first base. It was not uncommon for a Foster team to score a run without getting a hit. "There were teams like the Kansas City Monarchs, the Detroit Stars who would club you to death.... Well, the Giants ... they starve you death.... Trying to score a run off of them was like trying to make change for a penny." said Ted "Double Duty" Radcliffe. Double Duty added, "Shucks, playing Rube's team was like watching a talkie (movie) without popcorn ... boring."[8]

Frank "Fay" Young, a Chicago sportswriter, once described a Foster team executing a play:

> A man was on second and one out, the shortstop had gone over to cover second and the minute he moved, Foster gave a signal with his pipe to the batter and the base runner. Bobby Williams who was on second was off with the pitch and with a good start he rounded third just as Jim Brown dragged a slow one towards first and went out on a sacrifice. Before the first baseman had time to think, Williams was three-fourths of the way home and won the game with a slide under the catcher who took the throw.

Foster's whole heart and soul was wrapped up in the game. He moved his fielders for every batter. He moved his infield back and forth at will, brought them up on the grass like they were set of mechanical players and sent them back at the proper time. He also taught his players to hit to left or right field when ordered. His players behaved like soldiers in boot camp."

But Foster strategy was not confined to the fielders. Former pitcher Webster McDonald recalls:

> Now, in black baseball, the teams didn't have a lot of pitching depth. If you could get into the other guy's bullpen, you usually win the game. In fact, I think the lack of pitching depth was the only real difference between our teams and major league teams.
>
> Anyway, when we went up against a veteran pitcher who couldn't be rattled, Rube's strategy was to wear him down. He was very definite about hitting only good pitches, and sometimes the batters weren't allowed to swing until they had two strikes. We also bunted to both sides of the mound to make the other pitcher work even more. I've even seen Rube give the opposing pitcher an intentional pass just so he would have to run the bases. By the seventh inning, the American Giants were usually ready to move in for the kill.[9]

Frank Young recalled another Foster maneuver:

> In a 20-inning game against the Bacharach Giants in 1922, their manager Pop Lloyd yanked outfielder Frank Duncan in the tenth inning after Duncan had opened the frame with a scorching single. Raminez, a speedy outfielder, was put on first to run for him. "There goes the ball game," said Rube, knocking ashes out of his trusty pipe. "That Cuban can't throw like Duncan." Raminez was forced at second on the next play and then Treadwell hit into a double play.
>
> In the last half of the twentieth inning, Torriente walked and was sacrificed to second by Bobby Williams. The next batter, Dave Malarcher turned to Foster for orders. "Hit it to right field," Foster signaled. Dave waited for his pitch and dumped it into short right in front of Raminez. Torriente who had broke with the pitch, rounded third at full throttle and dashed for home, beating the weak throw by two feet—winning the game one to nothing.

Rube had turned Lloyd's strategic move into an advantage for his team.

Traditionally, the Foster game was a flambé of speed. The players beat out drag bunts for singles, stretched singles into doubles and stole bases at every opportunity. Speed and quickness, gambling and risk were trademarks of the Foster game. His team ran the bases with a swiftness and boldness absent from the white man's game. They scratched, scuffled, hustled and intimidated teams with their daring, innovative style of play. Foster's younger brother Willie told sports historian Charles Whitehead about Rube's style of play:

"We played what you would call 'Inside Baseball.' Inside baseball is bunting, and dragging and you noticed it didn't come into existence in the major leagues until the blacks started in. You will find more bunting and stealing right now than in any other time in baseball history."[10]

Dave Malarcher added, "We had seven men in the lineup who could run a hundred yards in around 10 seconds. All speed, and with Rube directing it, it was something. Rube telling us what to do—push it here, hit by the first baseman, hit over there. He directed your play all the time."

"I've seen Foster have his club bunt seven straight innings and then beat you," claimed Birmingham pitcher Harry Salmon.[11]

AMERICAN GIANTS BALL PARK
39TH ST. AND WENTWORTH AVE.

SUNDAY, OCTOBER 21, 1917, 2:30 P. M.

FINAL GAME! FINAL GAME!

AMERICAN GIANTS vs.

BIG LEAGUE ALL STARS

Seats on Sale at Box Office Thursday, Friday and Saturday Afternoons
BUY SEATS EARLY. BOXES RESERVED BY PHONE. YARDS 6630

The American Giants closed out the 1917 season with a 9–3 victory over an All-Star lineup of talent that included Cincinnati Reds, Chicago Cubs and several minor league players. The *Defender* claimed, "But all this array of talent failed to bring across the bacon and lots of pale faces went home with empty pocket books" (*Chicago Defender* 21 October 1917).

James Bell of the St. Louis Stars didn't care much for Foster's tactics: "Don't get me wrong, I think Foster was the greatest man in black baseball, and he was a very good to me, but I didn't approve of some of his methods.

"Before a home game, Foster would freeze the balls that were going to be pitched against the opposition. One of those big strong guys would come up and really connect. The ball would take off and then die like it had lead in it.

"He would also wet down the infield so much that it seemed like the middle of a rainstorm. Bunts would roll dead about 10 feet from home plate. He also built little ridges along the baselines. You could hardly see them, but they kept bunts from going foul."

Bell adds, "His favorite play was the steal and bunt. The runner on first would take off and the batter would bunt the ball so the third baseman had to field it. If he threw to first, the lead runner just kept going to third. If he held the ball, it was runners on first and second. It was a beautiful play and Foster's team made it work over and over again. To make it work, his guys had to be able to really place their bunts. They used to practice for hours bunting the ball into areas Rube would mark off with chalk.

As it was, I tried to use his tricks against him. I chopped the ball, bunted, dragged, and all that stuff. It sure frustrated him when I used his methods."[12]

Critics of Foster labeled this brand of ball as "tricky" baseball, only to shamelessly incorporate his techniques later. His "train the brain" stylish play was later adopted by the major leagues, as evidence by the 1934 St. Louis Gashouse Gang with scrappy "Pepper" Martin, "Ducky" Medwick, and the crazed "Dizzy" Dean. Some of Foster's influences were seen in the late fifties with the "Go-Go" Chicago White Sox with their high octane running game led by Luis Aparicio and MVP second baseman Nellie Fox. In the early sixties, the weak-hitting L.A. Dodgers with their potent pitching staff of Koufax, Drysdale and Osteen, and tactical road warrior Maury Wills, emphasized the Foster philosophy, by stealing more than 100 bases one season.

Later Foster's influence was conspicuously present in the "small ball" concept employed by the Kansas City Royals and the St. Louis Cardinals, under the management of Whitey Herzog from 1975 to 1990. In many ways, Herzog played blackball, Herzog's Royals stole 811 bases from 1976 to 1979, averaging more than 200 steals per season. They led the majors in 1978 (with 206 steals) and 1979 (207). Not only were the Royals the king of thefts, they won the American League West three times and finished second once, in the four full seasons under Herzog.

Some say Foster influenced the style of play performed in Japan. Today, Japanese players place heavy emphasis on the one-run-at-a-time philosophy. The sacrifice bunt, hit-and-run, squeeze plays and steals are a big part of their overall strategy. Invariably, Foster's special blend of "inside baseball" techniques appealed to the big league appetite of sports fans worldwide.

By 1918, many Major league and Negro League elite players were drafted to serve their country, crippling the overall quality of talent across the board.

After another successful season, 77 wins and 27 losses (.740), the American Giants scheduled a game against Kenosha in late October. It was an all-star team of major leaguers with Jim "Hippo" Vaughn scheduled to take the mound. Chicago Cub Vaughn had just led the National League in wins with 22, ERA at 1.74, strikeouts with 148, games started at 33 and eight shutouts. Perhaps the best pitcher in the league, this was his fourth season as a 20-game winner. Vaughn had picked up one of two victories in the World Series loss to the Boston Red Sox and Babe Ruth. Vaughn lost the opening game of the series, 1–0, with Ruth on the mound for the crimson sox, but came back in Game five for a 3–0 shutout.

If Foster's Giants defeated Vaughn and the Kenosha team, it would cement their claim as one of the greatest teams in the land. The time had come for black baseball to get its due. However, fate was not so kind. The health department issued a decree preventing congregation of people because of the influenza epidemic, forcing the closure of Schorling Park and shutting down the baseball season.[13] The pandemic Spanish Flu that broke out in the spring had infected 50,000 people in Chicago by October.[14]

With the setback news at hand, the *Defender* somewhat softened the disappointment with kinds words that Foster was a "genius" and "without doubt one of the greatest leaders in baseball, and if he had 25 men, as the big leagues do, all trained with experience before they come to him, there is no league pennant he would not have a monopoly on."[15]

The 1918 season appears to be Foster's last year as an active player. He had appeared in only one game as pitcher and one game at first base for the Pop Lloyd All-Stars. To celebrate his final field appearances, "Rube ate a whole five-pound steak and drank a gallon of ice team, [and] then ate half a watermelon."[16]

Rube Foster's pitching record from 1902 to 1917 was impeccable. It included at least seven no-hitters and more than 190 verifiable wins against fewer than 60 losses. Any pitcher would be satisfied with winning three-fourths of his games. Foster is the only Hall of Fame pitcher with a winning percentage over .700, with his closest competitor, Whitey Ford, at .690. Foster amassed double-digit strikeouts in 19 games (17 twice) and threw 45 shutouts in 259 starts.

Unlike most newspapers of the period, the *Philadelphia Item* reported earned runs, and with the *Chicago Defender* and others papers providing similar stats via game descriptions, an exceptional Earned Run Average of 1.82 has been calculated, matching Ed Walsh's record low career Major League ERA. Meanwhile, a runs scored per nine innings average of 2.80 shows incredible ability to keep his team in the game. Also note his WHIP rating, that shows how many base runners a pitcher allows on base per inning, is less than one at .903. Overall, Rube Foster was not only a great manager and league organizer, but a phenomenal pitcher.

See Appendix C for a game-by-game account of Rube Foster's batting and pitching career.

As Foster made his exit from the field to the clubhouse, he wrote this dissertation on the trials and tribulations of baseball in a four-part series.

Chicago Defender, 26 November 1919

Pitfalls of Baseball, Part I

Reconstruction in every line of business has taxed the patience of the world. Coming along as a side issue, we are facing in the coming season reconstruction in baseball, with the big Colored clubs. It is of vital interest to their many followers and will rock the foundation of many well-laid plans for the future, with it the breaking off of relations as to eastern clubs and western clubs meeting each other. This may prove a good idea, and as developments appear on the scene of action it will be left for fandom to judge.

Radicalism versus Conservatism

There is an element in baseball that does the game no good. They are bent on destroying what little has been accomplished, as the tactics they are practicing cannot be based on past accomplishments. For instance, there is not a Colored Club that the owners of that club can show a profit of $1,000 per season for their time, trouble, money or investment (with one exception). Those who have weathered the storm over such length of time have operated at a loss. How long they will stand to lose is questionable. If they do not stand longer this time than their previous efforts were, next season will be the end. Ball players are worth no more to anyone than a fair exchange in earnings of the clubs. The attendance must warrant big increases. At present, there is not a Colored player in the business that knows of ten games they will play next season. They have never known, nor will they until they are organized.

Operating Expenses Are High

Baseball has developed into a one day a week schedule for clubs. The weekdays do not pay. This is cushioned by the high cost of living. Our people cannot lay off from their work even with the added attendance such profits are eaten up by the extra high cost of materials, parks and everything connected with baseball. A fair example of operating expenses is the present American Giants Park admitted to be the finest, large and best equipped park in the United States, enjoying the largest patronage ever given a club of color, when idle costs $945 a week; when operated three days a week, $1,346. When you pay a visiting club out of money taken in, to just break even, the attendance must be double. Should you catch three rainy Sundays during the season, it is operated at a loss.

My way of reasoning the present controversy over the situation is easily explained — that if the present high price for players can be made, that either the owners have made money and do not give the players their just salaries, or that they are willing to dig down deeper than ever to accomplish their aim. Conner of New York City had a club, even advancing the figures that the others were paying, he drew as well, the prices were the same, yet in a few years he had to give it up, saying that it was a losing proposition. Strong of New York City took hold of the club; he could not make ends meet; he also gave it up. Schlichter broke himself. Lamar, with no salaries, had to give it up. Several tried it at Atlantic City. The same results. If they could not make ends meet at the salaries that existed at that time, which were at the figures now offered, $1,000 more, railroad, hotel, all necessary expenses have been almost doubled, everything advanced but the prices, and a small increase in attendance no greater (with present expense), comes a few resurrected dreamers saying that they can pay over $2,200 and operating expenses with a club and make money. They may, but conditions will have to change wonderfully, and they will all do the same as in years previous. Have they made money and kept it, refusing to pay the men, or have they patented a new discovery? Just wait.

Chicago Defender, 13 December 1919

Pitfalls of Baseball, Part II

Baseball as it exists at present among our people needs a very strong leader, and this leader to be successful must have able lieutenants, all of who have the confidence of the public. Only in this way can we be assured of success. Experimenting with the game from every angle, I am more convinced than ever that something firm must be done, and done quickly.

I have paid salaries longer than anyone connected with the game, and one would draw the conclusion that Foster has not paid salaries in proportion to the worth of the players. This propaganda has been instituted by eastern men and several players. The owners knew different, but the players have been

American Giants' Baseball Park

39TH ST. AND WENTWORTH AVE.

TAYLOR'S A. B. C.'S

OF INDIANAPOLIS

WITH JOHN DONALDSON PITCHING

SUNDAY, JUNE 9. GAME CALLED AT 3 O'CLOCK

Box Office Open Saturday Afternoon. Get Tickets Early

Top: **It is believed this photograph is of the 1916 Chicago American Giants. From left to right, Pete Hill, unknown, unknown, Leroy Grant, Jude Gans, Bruce Petway, Foster, Jess Barbour, unknown, unknown, Pop Lloyd, unknown and unknown (courtesy Jennifer Koos and Stuart Thompson).**

Bottom: **The strikeout artist John Donaldson returns to the Windy City with C.I. Taylor's ABC's. Approximately 14,000 saw Dick Whitworth defeat the great John Donaldson, 5–2 (*Chicago Defender* 8 June 1918).**

victims of such propaganda. I will frankly admit that all who played for me have done so at their own figures, and they have in the majority been overpaid, and no Colored baseball club has ever approached the salaries have been paid to men who are not worth any more, if ability is the standard that one must draw monthly stipend on.

Past Salaries of Leading Clubs

In 1902 there was a salaried Colored club in the business that paid $700 a month [$16,800 in 2010]. The Cuban X-Giants, then the co-operative concern, part salary, part co-plan. This club was composed of [Clarence] Williams, [Big Bill] Smith, [T.] Wilson, [Sol] White, [William] Jackson, [Oscar] Jackson, [Dan] McClellan, Rube Foster, [James] Robinson and [Ed] Wilson. We played every day. The Philadelphia Giants, that reached the supremacy in salaries in 1903, had [Pete] Booker, [Sol] White, [Charlie] Grant, [Grant] Home Run Johnson, [Diamond Bill] Monroe, [Pete] Hill, [Danny] McClellan, Rube Foster, [Emmett] Bowman and C. Johnson, admitted to be the best club ever in the East. We drew $850 per month. This club finally had to disband, as we could not even get the money for such high prices; yet we played every day. Then came the Lincoln Giants. This club cost only $225 per week. At this enormous figure they wrecked the other clubs as they could also had to disband, and the men sued for their money and judgment here in Chicago.

But before this high-priced club came into existence the Leland Giants, under my direction, was the only straight salaried club in existence. This club cost $250 per week. Chicago fans doubt even yet if that club has been equaled, after which in 1910 Chicago has the reputation of having the greatest club of all time. [Pete] Booker, [Tim] Strothers, [Grant] "Home Run" Johnson, [John Henry] Lloyd, [Wes] Pryor, [Frank "Pete"] Duncan, [Jap] Payne, [Fred] Hutchinson, [Frank] Wickware, [Bill] Lindsey, [Pat] Dougherty and Rube Foster won 126 games, lost 3 in the United States and 6 games in Cuba, passed through New York and won 22 straight games, and yet this wonderful ball club lost $2,100 on the season. The salary of this club was less than $300 per week. At the present rate each Colored club is costing more than any of these clubs, and you know there is no comparison as to ability and deportment. This club was wrecked by the Lincolns, who paid $325 [$7,800 in 2010] per week, and the Lincolns, as stated before, went broke.

Present Salaries

The American Giants have never paid since they were organized less than $1,500 monthly. This figure has been gradually raised until the past season it ran into $450 weekly. Adding the extra cost of $575 for extra players during the season, it was the highest priced club ever at Chicago, and the poorest in ability. The salaries for the coming season will not exceed $2,000 per month. We are going to pay that for players. This amount has not been equaled in the east, nor will they be able to surpass this amount on past performances and records. If they do they can afford it.

Future Salaries

The smallest salary paid to the American Giants and Detroit equals the salary of any post office carrier, clerk or city school teacher in the United States. They have to put in about twenty hours per month for this, have all the time they want, sleep all day, yet they are underpaid. They are receiving more than the government, railroad companies pay their employed. These firms have billions, and from a little institution that can barely exist they are entitled to more. They love to see you dig, and have many that fall for such. When the time comes that I must pay more for anything than that thing can earn, you can take it from me that Foster is going to leave that thing where it is. Strong Leadership must come quickly.

The 1918 season was Foster's last year as an active player. He appeared in only one game as pitcher on August 4th and one game at first base for the Pop Lloyd All-Stars (NoirTech Research).

If we are to advance with the present reconstruction we must do so under leadership that has been tried and proved able to meet any demand made upon it. There is no one that would follow capable leadership quicker than I. The great harm that confronts us is that we tear down instead of building up. For anything to be successful we must do it as a whole.

Present-day promoters are blind to many facts. They do not realize that to have the best ball club in the world and no one able to compete with it will lose more money on the season than those that are evenly matched. The majority do not know a ball player when they see one. They have paid big prices for many lemons, thinking that if the man was a success with Foster we will work wonders with him. They forget that I have been a player, whose intellect and brains of the game have drawn more comment from leading baseball critics than all that I am a student of the game. They do not know, as I do, that there are not five players, nor three owners among the clubs who know the playing rules.

Chicago Defender, 20 December 1919

Pitfalls of Baseball, Part III

Baseball as it exists at present among our owners is a disgrace to the name of good, honest sportsmanship. It is no conducted that to be a success you have to turn your back on many things that happen in dealing with a club owner that in legitimate business you would frown on and cast it aside. The present unrest among many followers of the clubs would not exist if the owners of the different clubs would for once put aside the success of someone else and put their business dealings on a fellow man in the face, the public, and smile with a clear conscience.

1919 Chicago American Giants. Top row (left to right), Bingo DeMoss, Leroy Grant, Dave Brown, Rube Foster, Oscar Charleston and Richard Whitworth; middle row (left to right), Dave Malarcher, Bobby Williams, unknown, and John Reese; bottom row (left to right) unknown, Jimmie Lyons, Bill Francis, unknown, and Bill Hall (NoirTech Research).

Owners Wreck Their Chances

I have seen every ball club for the past fifteen years wrecked by different owners. The first came in 1906, when the Philadelphia Giants were the best club in the East. They packed the parks in New York. The owner of the Philadelphia giants could get but $100 for a game. His highest was $150. We drew far better than the present Lincoln Giants are drawing in the same parks. Our owner wanted more. The results were that before they would pay more they jumped, wrecking our club. This has been practiced all along. The progress of the clubs was curtailed and baseball was at its lowest up to 1910. I took the Leland Giants to New York. Our wonderful showing there resurrected the game. The first thing they did was to offer more money, wrecking the club. The same conditions were in operation in the West between the different owners. It was common practice to steal a man advertised to play with one club and disappoint the fans where this particular star was to show. They lost confidence in the manager and said he was fooling the public. When the manager was not at fault these disappointments happened wherever Colored club were. The coming season will see it as its worst. It is a pity, set it is the construction that different owners speculate on success. My resourcefulness in rebuilding ball clubs has stood useful to me in the days to come. I have nothing to fear.

Based on Past Achievements

What is needed is a foundation that we can build on, something that we can merit the wonderful attendance and pride our followers have in us. This can be done jointly between players and managers (owners). The players have much to be appreciative for, as they have found many lambs in their careers, men who have paid them until they could not, and when the time came, regardless as to the sacrifice the man had made, they looked for the lamb that was fat, ready to eat and put on the table. There is no denying the fact that Conner, Jackson, Schlichter, McMahon, Leland, Major Jackson, L.B. Anderson, Taylor, Lamar, Tobe Smith and about twenty-five others lost in their venture with baseball, bad management, offering more than they could earn, and the competition of the goose that was in waking to be killed. Taylor spent fifteen years with nothing but ambition. Finally his long wait was crowned with success at the making of another man. The press notices that he got made him believe that the time had come when he should appear as the lord of lords. He was given and allowed to have his way. He is running a billiard parlor and will be there until resurrected. He will not let a few successful seasons paralyze he has had was made by the writer. The money made at the beginning and his sudden retirement was the result of not or the hand that tided him along.

Chicago Defender, 27 December 1919

Pitfalls of Baseball, Part IV

The men who are entering baseball have not made their money in baseball. They must have some business ability to make money, and I am in hopes that the mistakes of the past will prove of great value to their future effort, abolishing the practice of allowing a man to take care of man all winter, advance money and bury his relatives for him. When the time comes for the players to report to the various clubs, offer the man an increase in salary. Naturally the player will accept, if he does not pay the money back advanced to the man, and the publicity that he sues all winter given the man. When the season opens he falls to appear. The fans do not know the reason the player did not report, many saying he would not pay the man anything. Here is the owner's biggest fault. When the player gets money from him he again jumps. Then the owner writes and tells you, "Don't play against so and so; he owes me money." This is the owner's biggest fault. They don't realize that when you teach a man to be dishonest they are teaching him something that he is sure to experiment on you with. This has brought more hard feelings and revenge of the clubs able to give an eye for an eye, a tooth for a tooth, than anything else. This kind of revenge has made players think that the owners were making money, by the big boast in salary, when the owner is doing for revenge. Several players have said to me, "How can he pay so much and you cannot?" The answer to all of them is easy—they have failed, quit, and many owe players. I have never quit, ran a club longer than any five, and met each obligation. Why, I am immune to such ethics, only I sometimes give an eye for an eye, but I wait until I know the dear lamb can no longer strike back.

Honest Men Connected With Baseball

I do not believe a single man that has been in the game has not had the best intentions, meant well. The actions of certain players disheartened them. Among these were J.W. Conner, who as a man I personally admire. He is very ambitious, wanting nothing but the best. He should not be lost to baseball. His only failure has been was that he was not steered right. Baron and I are personal friends. They mean well. Major Jackson, Anderson and Leland (deceased) were fine men. Everything that they did was from their heart. They were honest and their dealings above suspicion. Still they realized that the way things were conducted there was no future. C. L. was an able lieutenant; has many good qualities; he is full of fire and needs only patience. Ollie Jackson was a game man, he had plenty of money; he spent it on his club; had no management. His players had no discipline. He said, "I don't know what to do; I have made nothing out of baseball; dropped a few thousand. I would not care, but the players don't appreciate it. I am going to pay them off."

It is historic for years that Colored people will not stand for organizations outside the church and secret societies. They are so afraid to die, they support the church; so afraid when sick, they will suffer. They support such institutions. Outside of these they have proven they cannot agree, all of which is very regrettable; still it is true. There is no sane reason that we could not as a people have things among us and pattern after the ways others have wrote success in history. It can be done if we would only stop to consider what is best. Nothing is impossible if all parties are allowed to air their differences.

Organized Effort Our Only Salvation

I am going to make the effort, willing to let bygones be bygones; arrange to have all the owners in the West to meet the owners in the East, either at Chicago or New York; pick an arbitration board from experienced men of business, and from this agreement draw a working agreement for all of us to abide by, the signers to such an agreement to deposit $500 in good faith that they will live up to such an agreement.

It is not a proposition to exchange players. Each club will be allowed to retain their players, but cement a partnership in working for the organized good of baseball. Conducted in the same identical plan as both big leagues and all minor leagues, even the semi-pro leagues, the outcome would be the East would be the same as National Leagues, the winner of the majority of games in the East to meet the western winners in a real world's championship. This will pave the way for such champion team eventually to play the winner among the whites. This is more than possible. Only in uniform strength is the permanent success. I invite all owners to write for information on this proposition. It is open to all.

Chicago Defender, 27 December 1919

Pitfalls of Baseball, Part V

In again taking up this subject I am going to touch on the disadvantage clubs have had to encounter to keep the game in front of the people. Some have had good intentions, meant well many times hoping against hope that some unforeseen miracle would happen to enlighten them on their way; that unforeseen hand has not appeared. When it does come you will find that few Colored men will be interested in the clubs.

When you can the list of the past and present owners of Colored clubs, you will find among them, men who are not due any success, with a few exceptions. To be successful in anything, one must pattern after systems and methods of men who have made success in the same line of business. This you cannot put into the heads of those that want to promote the game. A practice among the various club owners has been to take men from different clubs, many times after they have drawn money from the club they are leaving. It has gotten so bad managers do not trust players, nor do the players truth the managers. It's folly for one to teach a player to jump and not pay the manager he leaves and expect that same player to be honest with him. When someone persuades that same man to leave him, disgusted, he will wire you, "If you play such a club, I will not play you." This stopped it for a while, but each club adopted the habit of taking each other's men until they have so complicated things they do not play each other.

Organized Baseball Great Pitchers

In organized baseball each club secures men from different clubs. It must be an arrangement between the club owners that a player is the property of the club who retains his services until released. There is no ball club in the country that can secure his services. Even the big leagues do not tamper with different clubs' players. With all the money invested in their clubs, they have deemed it necessary to form some agreement to work by protecting each other's rights. Yet our club owners laugh at such protection and have year after year done just the opposite.

Player Do Not Want Organization

I have talked with several players and they asked me, did I not think organization would hurt their chances as to salaries. When the club owners get together they will play what they please; we do not want organizations. I said if you ever expect to really make any money out of baseball it will be done through organization. There are several players playing ball that get more to play one season than the salary list of any three Colored clubs at the present time. They play under organization. Has it hurt them? Do you realize that if protection was given men there would be money put into baseball, parks would be built, that it would offer inducement to players do try and develop, knowing there was some future attached to their professional.

Assets of Our Clubs

The time has passed when you can camouflage the public. The public has been wised up to many things. Now it's up to the men who want to continue to give the people something besides bunk. There are not four Colored clubs North that could not go out of the business today and lose nothing but the uniforms they had last season; yet they will parade around and tell you they own a ball club. Clubs like the A.B.C's, Detroit, Kansas City, Royal Giants and Cuban Stars have never had a dime invested beyond their uniforms and advance money. It is natural for them, with the expense of only salaries, to be in a position to do much damage to the clubs that are burdened with heavy overhead expense. Admitting that the clubs are important to the success of both parties, one would not expect the club with the heavy expense to compete with the clubs with apparently no expense; yet they must do more and have.

Ball Parks Necessary

It is very necessary that we have parks to play in. Without them there would be no incentive for one to chose baseball as a profession. Yet these parks must not be burdened too heavy as when they go baseball North will pass along as the building restrictions are much and real estate so high that you could not expect Colored owners to promote such an expensive plant just to be given employment to a professional when it must boat a loss. Yet you cannot get the men to come together and try and cement some plans for the betterment of the game.

Organization Is Sure to Come

We cannot get along without organization. Neither will we have a sufficient parks to play in to warrant playing greater salaries than we are at present unless we organize. There are thousands of dollars ready for such an organization. The money will naturally come from the whites. The game will be supported better than the American Association, whose salary limit is $5,000 per month. Then will come the cry that it's a shame that all this money goes into the hands of the whites. Yet we will be the ones at fault. They can easily triple the present salaries and make money as they will systematize it, build sufficient parks and give employment to many hundred Colored players. There is no hope to even maintain the standard that we have reached. Rentals of all parks have gone up. At any minute the leases of present parks can be terminated. Many Colored men with money have begged to get into the game, but they want it patterned after the way leagues are conducted.

Last Attempt to Get Owners Together

This will be the last time I will ever try and interest Colored club owners to get together on some working basis, I have so often been refused the necessary capital, not desiring to give to others the chance of monopolizing Colored baseball, but they are not going to continue to wait on me with their money. They can do so and leave me where I am. I have made the effort; It's now up to the ones that expect to permanently figure in baseball to get together.

7th Inning. The Navigator: We Are the Ship, All Else the Sea, 1920–1921

Foster's American Giants started off the 1920 season by defeating the Pittsburgh Pirates, 8–1, at Forbes Field. The paper reported, "The defeat of a big league club on its own grounds demonstrates the class of the Rube Foster aggregation."[1]

Kansas City Call, 20 February, 1920

Baseball Magnates Hold Conference
Sporting Editor of Defender Elected Secretary

Kansas City, Mo., Feb. 13.—Representatives of the baseball teams of the west arrived here today and went into session at the Y. M. C. A., with the following baseball magnates present:

J. T. Blount, Detroit, Mich., Detroit Stars;
W. A. Kelly, Washington, D. C., organized baseball of the national capital;
L. S. Cobb, secretary of the St. Louis Giants baseball team;
John Matthews, Dayton Marcos, Dayton, Ohio;
Joe Green, Chicago Giants, Chicago, Ill.;
C. I. Taylor, Indianapolis A.B.C.'s, Indianapolis, Ind.;
Elwood C. Knox of the *Indianapolis Freeman*, Indianapolis, Ind.;
Andrew ("Rube") Foster, American Giants, Chicago, Ill.;
Charles Marshall, *Indianapolis Ledger*, Indianapolis, Ind.;
J. L. Wilkinson, this city,
and Cary B. Lewis, sporting editor of the *Chicago Defender*.

Temporary Officers Elected

On motion of "Tenny" Blount, Detroit, Mich., Mr. Foster was nominated and elected temporary president. Cary B. Lewis of the *Defender* was elected secretary. The aim and object of the meeting was discussed and the plan for a circuit for the season of 1921 came up for consideration. Every manager was very enthusiastic and said he would carry the same enthusiasm back to his hometown. The outlook for 1921, they claim would be the greatest history of baseball.

Foster Springs Big Surprise

One of the big surprises of the first day's meeting was when "Rube" Foster uncovered the fact that he had a charter, incorporated, for a National Negro Baseball League. When "Rube" displayed the charter the "magnates" were dumbfounded. The league is incorporated in the states of Illinois, Michigan, Ohio, Pennsylvania, New York and Maryland. Then Mr. Foster and Mr. Blount discussed tentative plans for the circuit of 1921. Dr. Howard Smith met the delegations at the depot. A smoker and dinner has been arranged. The second day's meeting will be held tomorrow. The visitors are stopping at the "Y."

Kansas City Call, 27 February, 1920

Western Circuit organized; to Become Effective April 1, 1921

Kansas City, MO, Feb., 20.—A Western circuit, National Baseball League of the United States, was organized her last week in the rooms of the Community Center. Newspapermen and sport writers became the arbitrators for the baseball magnates. It was the first time in the history of a baseball meeting that there was exhibited so much harmony and good spirit. Andrew "Rube" Foster was chosen as the temporary chairman and secretary. He stated the aim and purpose of the gathering and then said he would leave it to the newspaper men at the meeting to decide all questions, select players for the various teams and write the by-laws and constitution for the league. No sooner had he said this than C. I. Taylor of the Indianapolis A.B.C.'s assented, also "Tenny" Blount of the Detroit Stars.

The Player Question

The player question was the first to come up for consideration. It is a well-known fact that some of the managers have been dickering with each other's players, which has caused a great deal of consideration during the past years. This was thrashed out and all agreed that the newspapermen should embody this question in the laws and constitution of the league. In the best judgment of the newspapermen all the players for the league were selected.

Writers of the Constitution

The writers of the constitution and by-laws of the new league were Dave Wyatt, *Indianapolis Ledger*; Elwood C. Knox, *Indianapolis Freeman*; Carry B. Lewis, *Chicago Defender*, and attorney Elisha Scott of Topeka, Kan. These men were up all Friday night and part of Saturday morning, framing the "baseball bill of rights" to guide the destiny of the future league.

At noon Friday it was brought before the conference. The preamble was read and adopted. The constitution was read by articles and sections, correction after correction was made and finally it was approved by Attorney Elisha Scott. The constitution was signed by Andrew Foster, American Giants, Chicago; C. I. Taylor, A.B.C.'s, Indianapolis, Ind.; "Tenny" Blount, Detroit Stars, Detroit, Mich.; Chicago Giants, Joe Green, Chicago; J. L. Wilkinson, Kansas City Monarchs, Kansas City, MO.; Lorenzo Cobb, St. Louis Giants, St. Louis, MO. Each manager paid his $500 fee to bind them to the league and constitution.

Will Operate Next Season

The Western Circuit, National Baseball league, will not operate until next season. This meeting is the foundation for next year. The circuit will not officially operate until each city has a park, either leased or owned and this will undoubtedly be by April 1, 1921. Those who had no lease this year claimed they would have one next season. Mr. Matthews of the Dayton Marcos, who was ill with the "flu" sent a special delivery letter stating that he would be in perfect harmony with whatever was done at the meeting. He sent his per ratio to pay for the expense of the newspapermen who acted as arbitrators. Several road teams had representatives and paid their part of the fee to play in the circuit as per schedule. Nat C. Strong of the Nat C. Strong Amusement Company, New York City, sent a letter stating that he was ready to do anything that would promote the best interests of baseball all over the country. After the Western Circuit is put into operation successfully Mr. Foster will then call a meeting of the organization of a National Baseball League, taking in every large baseball city in the east.

Newspaper Men Select Players

The newspapermen had the day at the meeting. No manager ought to say about players. They were selected on account of their RELATIVE STRENGTH to each team. The newspapermen will form an arbitration board to settle all disputes and act as publicity agents for games.

The following players were selected for the teams in 1921:

Detroit Stars—Pete Hill, Bruce Petway, Frank Warfield, Edgar Wesley, Joe Hewitt, Mac Eggerson [Eggleston], LeRoy Roberts, Henderson E. Boyd, [Bill] Holland, Richard Whitworth, Jimmy Lyons, [Charles] Lefty Hill.

Kansas City—John Donaldson, Joe Mendez, Frank Blukoi, ? Jackson, Walter [Dobie] Moore, Rube Currie, [Jose] Rodriguez, [Bartolo] Portuando, Sam Crawford, Wilbur [Wilber, "Bullet"] Rogan, W. Harris, [Bernardo] Baro.

St. Louis Giants—Tully McAdoo, Dan Kennard, Charles Brooks, Charles Scott, William [Plunk] Drake, [Ping] Dandridge, Felix Wallace, Charles Blackwell, Eddie Holt, John Tinner, [Johnson] Hill.

American Giants—George Dixon, Jas. Brown, Leroy Grant, Elwood [Bingo] DeMoss, Robert Williams, David Malarcher, J. E. [John] Reese, Thomas Johnson, Thomas Williams, Richard Lundy, Christopher Torentti [Cristobal Torriente], Edw. [Robert "Jude"] Gans.

Chicago Giants—Lawrence Simpson, Walter Ball, Lemuel McDougal, Edward Jones, John Beckwith, William Green, Thurman Jennings, Frank Jefferies, Horace Jenkins, Joe Green, Clarence [Bobby] Winston, Tom Clark.

Taylor A.B.C.'s—James Jefferies, Jim Taylor, Morten Clark, Russell Powell, [Hurland] Ragland, William Webster, Oscar Charleston, Ed Rile, Murray, William [Dizzy] Dismukes, Decatur Johnson.

[Author's Note: Tentative rosters for the Dayton Marcos and the Indianapolis ABC's were not listed. Newspapers gave no reason for their omission.]

The (Pittsburgh) Competitor, February 1920

The Future of Colored Baseball
By C.I. Taylor

Now that the "Hot Stove League" is in full blast there is, of course, much discussion pro and con from coast to coast about baseball which executed a remarkable "come back" last season after several years of rather indifferent attendance to the game due to the all-absorbing question of the war. With the great conflict definitely settled the national game immediately came into its own, and in every hamlet and every steaming metropolis more interest was displayed in it than had been manifest at any time before. Colored ball teams shared in the general prosperity along with the whites, and indications are that next season will be the greatest in the history of the sport.

With this prospect in view I have been asked to give my ideas regarding the status of baseball as related to the colored people. I am more of a "doer" than I am a "teller," but I shall endeavor to state as concisely as possible just what I think is wrong with the game insofar as colored ball teams are concerned.

First let me say this: I am an optimist. I have faith in my people, and their ability to accomplish all things. Baseball is their national game as much as it is the national game of the whites, because it is above all things an AMERICAN game. It abides deep in the sport loving natures of all Americans regardless of their creed or color.

In light of this truth why is baseball — I mean now the business operation of it — in such a chaotic condition with the colored people? We produce excellent teams, too, considering the very poor facilities we have in developing them as compared with the elaborate and carefully planned training camps that are maintained by the whites. But eliminating this and getting down to the concrete fact that we have good players and good ball teams, why do we grow so slowly? Why does the end of each season find us but little, if any, farther advanced than we were the year before?

The answer can be summed up in three words: Lack of organization!

We have the goods, but we haven't got the organization to deliver them. We are a good deal like the country was during the great coal strike. There was plenty of coal, but no way to get it to the consumer. The public is the consumer in baseball just as in everything else. So, granting that we have the players, and that we can perfect the teams, it's up to us to find a way to profitably present baseball on the diamond. And after something like a quarter of a century as a player, promoter and baseball manager, it is my frank opinion that the one and only thing necessary for the perpetuity of the game is organization.

My convictions in this respect are not of recent acquisition. For a great many years I have put in sleepless nights studying the problem and searching out ways by which some methods could be successfully employed to get the colored ball clubs organized into sound, self-supporting, well conducted leagues. By the same token I have written many times to men in all parts of the country who were active in the game, experienced in the affairs of baseball, and in the handling of clubs, ever urging that we get together — that we organize! I doubt if any other living colored man has carried on such an extensive correspondence in the interest of the sport.

For the most part a deaf ear was turned to my pleadings. In some instances I was referred to as a "dreamer." Many in reply would assert that we had no grounds in various cities on which to play; others opined that we hadn't the men to handle the clubs. My answer was and still is this: "We will always be in the same boat unless we launch out into an organization." Men don't seek out a battle ground before they form their armies. We will never have playing grounds until we can get an organization of such strength as to enable us to procure them, and to guarantee the public a standard schedule of games on those grounds after we get them.

It is somewhat gratifying to me today to know that the very men who in the past stood in the way of such an organization, have now reached the conclusion that it is the only hope, if we are to make anything out of baseball for the black Americans. No man ever traveled far unless he made a start. Organization is the intelligent beginning of all things, and the sooner we as a race recognize this fact, the quicker will we be acknowledged by other peoples; and the greater will be our stride in the game of life.

Organization means a combination of parts. Every ball club on the corner lot; in every school yard;

in the great pleasure parks and playgrounds for children is simply the bringing together of the boys of that community, thus forming an organization. Without this system neither pleasure nor benefit could be derived. There could be no progress.

The same thing obtains with the big colored ball clubs throughout the country. Each club is a composition of players who have to learn the game in the public schools; on the sand lots and at college. Each player is a component part of his club. And the club, with its rules and regulation intended to govern the actions and dealings of the men in the organization. This we can all readily see. No argument is required to convince the least thoughtful that all the foregoing is true; yet it seems hard to convert many to the realization that if the colored ball clubs are to grow into the really gigantic institutions that they should be, it is absolutely necessary that they in turn, should organize. Unless they do, nothing can be accomplished.

Let me illustrate just a few of the things that result without an organization of the clubs. Back in the years of 1915–16–17 and 1918, my baseball club, the Indianapolis ABC's represented what was hailed by many critics as a "perfect machine." I don't think I am exaggerating it when I say that that same club, if in the organized baseball conducted by the whites, could have been sold at a price ranging anywhere from 50 to 100 thousand dollars—or that the sale of these clubs as represented by the various years, would have netted me around two hundred thousand dollars. For lack of organization they didn't net me a single penny.

Under the conditions that now exist, each player is his own free agent, and can play wherever he pleases and for whatever sum that he and the club owner agree upon. At the close of each session the clubs disband and we have only the word of the several players as to their services the following year—without any way of forcing them to live up to their word. Without the club owner being aware of it three or four of the best men in his team may sign to play elsewhere, possibly after having been advanced quite a sum of money on the strength of the player's promise to be with the team again the next season. And, furthermore, it has been the ungentlemanly and dishonest practice of many of the self-styled "leading lights" in the game to promote just this sort of dealing among the players.

Whenever this happens it means that the old machine has been broken. It must be relegated to the scrap heap, and new men must be sought, with only two ways to get them. The first is to develop young players—an operation that requires a great deal of tact and patience—or to offer inducements to men who morally, if not legally, belong to another club, to "jump" the other club in order to fill the places made vacant by the men who have "jumped" your club.

And here's another phase! Most players are instilled with an ambition to play only in the big cities. They apparently prefer New York or Chicago at far less money than they might receive in the smaller cities. This may be natural to a degree, but it isn't good business policy, nor is it a thing that tends to help the game for the reason that this is a pretty big country outside of New York and Chicago, and baseball cannot thrive and flourish in these cities, which I use merely as a means of illustration, unless it is also prosperous elsewhere, for the people in New York or Chicago will not pay good money for any length of time to see their teams cross bats with inferior visiting teams. Here is where organization would come in, for it would serve to equalize the playing strength of the respective teams. Pitcher Jones or Catcher Smith couldn't migrate to New York or Chicago without the knowledge and consent of all the club owners in the league, and without the approval of the league directors.

I am glad to say that there is a rift in the clouds so far as this condition is concerned, and the players themselves are taking no minor part in forcing the issue. They are learning that they are their worst enemies in committing an act that in any way tends to prevent organization. They are fast coming to realize that if one or two big clubs can sign up all the stars, thus permitting a few players to romp around the country heralded as "world champions," half the time one afraid to play the other so that the people will know the truth as to who are the real champions, they are very likely to be left out in the cold themselves at a considerable distance from the spot light. They are waking up. They are failing to return to a "kind" of contract sent out with their signature attached. The "leading lights" are becoming alarmed and the slogan, "ORGANIZATION," is fast gaining ground.

For the enlightenment of the public I am doing this article with a copy of a letter which I wrote to Rube Foster in the spring of 1916 relative to organization, and which is a fair sample of many sent out, both public and private, from 1912 to 1918.

Dear Mr. Foster:

I am writing you again in regard to a matter that weighs so heavily on my mind that it is bordering on the impossible for me to hold my peace. You said in a letter to me last winter that Negro ball players as a whole, are a lot of ingrates—that they are enemies to their best friends, and would do almost anything to defeat the honest efforts of those who are rightly the leaders and promoters of their best interests. All these charges, and even many more, I am compelled to admit, are to a surprisingly large degree, the truth. Notwithstanding this I have a few suggestions to offer you, in my humble way, and I hope that you will think them over and see if they are practical and advisable.

I have thought considerably along this line and the more contemplation I give it, the stronger are my convictions that you are the man of the hour to strike the blow which will weld into one harmonious organization, the colored baseball clubs of this country. After spending many sleepless nights pondering over the conditions relating to baseball among us, it is my firm belief that we are at a crisis, the end of the old order is at hand, and the beginning of a new era is upon us. And the future of the national sport among us depends largely upon how we enter this new ear. The time is fully ripe for organization this year, if not permanently, tentatively.

I am not pleading to you thus for any individual or personal interests, but rather for the redemption and perpetuation of the great national game. I have long since laid aside petty jealousies, personal interests and selfish ambitions as I have told you in the past, and am using every legitimate argument in effort to create sentiment in favor of a Negro league. It must come if we are to keep alive the great sport among us, for it has been fully shown that we are barred from organized baseball as it exists today in this country.

Sentiment alone is sufficient to keep us out of the present day organized baseball, even though our ability and our many friends throughout the states speak volumes in our favor. To any well thinking man an organization of our own is the speediest and most effective remedy.

[Author's note: Below Taylor is holding Foster accountable.]

I say in view of your superior leadership, executive ability and thorough knowledge of baseball, your national reputation as the greatest organizer the game has produced coupled with the confidence of the baseball public throughout the country would have in an organization headed by yourself, you are particularly fitted to set this wheel in motion. A tentative league ought to be organized this year. We do not court failure, but 'tis better to have tried and failed than never to have tried!

There are good clubs in the following cities: St. Louis, Louisville, Indianapolis, Chicago (two clubs) and one road club — say the Cuban Stars, making six good clubs in all. I believe if you would issue a "call" for the representatives of these clubs to meet in Chicago about the middle of May for the purpose of perfecting a tentative organization to be tried out for three months you will find that you can preplan the entire thing, such as officials, schedules, salaries, players and the like are concerned, and it would be carried out to the letter; if it is never tried it will never be a success.

The Eastern clubs could easily be spliced in by giving you the power to switch the league schedule so as to keep all the clubs playing good attractions on Sundays. June 6 would be a fine day for the "Tentative" league opening. Let me hear from you.

C.I. Taylor

Since writing the above the geographical conditions have been changing somewhat, and other cities have come into the limelight which would eliminate several of those mentioned.

The above letter expressed my views as they were then, and I have since had no reason to reverse them. With an organized league in back of it, baseball would fill the place with the colored public that it should occupy, and I repeat, it's bound to come!

I said in the beginning that I am an optimist. I mean it! Let's organize!

The (Pittsburgh) Competitor, March 1920

National Baseball League Formed
By Ira F. Lewis

What was perhaps the most singular and noteworthy meeting ever held in the interest of our sport life as the meeting of the baseball men in Kansas City on February 13 and 14, when tentative agreements were signed for the formation of a national league of colored baseball clubs.

It is indeed a source of much satisfaction to know that after years of work on the right track but in the wrong direction, the big men in colored baseball are at last brought face to face with the same alternative which in time will eventually face every big Negro enterprise of the country — Organization.

Andrew "Rube" Foster, the Chicago mogul; and C.I. Taylor, the Indianapolis owner, came to the conclusion that further dissipation of their co-ordinate strength was useless, and they had better make steps and sacrifices not only for the perpetuity of the game, but for the conservation of their own business enterprise. The effort all along has only needed Mr. Foster's aid to make the try a success. And to his undying credit let it be said that he has made the biggest sacrifice of anyone. For be it known that his position in the world of colored baseball was reasonably secure, inasmuch as he controlled the situation pretty much not only in Chicago, where baseball is the fourth meal of the day, but in the Middle West. With ideal park location, and supported by unlimited backing both in money and patronage, Mr. Foster could have defied organization for many years. But, happily, he has seen the light — the light of wisdom and the spirit of service to the public. From now on he will begin to be the really big man in baseball, he should be, by virtue of his knowledge of the game from both the playing and business ends.

It is just possible that some of the events of the past season had something to do with Mr. Foster's move of flashing the signal that it was time to organize. Whether this is true or not, he deserves a world of credit for making the circuit a certainty by lending what he has in his storehouse of knowledge, experience, position and money.

Mr. Taylor sets forth a very lucid argument in the February number of *The Competitor* to the effect that the old order was passing and something should be done towards organization.

Both men have lent a life's study to baseball and it is decidedly refreshing to know that they both evidently feel that they owe the game something, other than the smile they give the turnstile.

There will, of course, be some disappointment when it is seen that the circuit includes only Western cities, but there really should not be any occasion for anything but rejoicing. Rejoicing for reason of the fact that we are getting to the place, at last, when we can see that it is decidedly advantageous to pool our interests, the other fellow on the other side of the fence to the contrary notwithstanding to work out our mutual interests. The workings of this league will be watched with more than passing interest by everyone, if it is successful as we all hope, look for further merging of colored business interests on a national scale.

It is fitting and proper that only Western cities should form the young league for the simple reason that everyone of the cities represented, has been tried and put through the acid test as good baseball town, and of course in those cities it is not so hard to pry a dollar away from a business man as an investment in baseball, because the business feature of the game in those cities is established. Then, too, the cities represented allow Sunday baseball, a feature which almost insures success.

The American League, generally considered the real major league of baseball, before the Frazee-Ruppert-Johnson snarl broke up the fine team work of the junior league, had all Western cities in its makeup prior to 1901, when the growth of the league and a popular demand for expansion caused Ban Johnson and his league to invade the East.

So with the new league, its hoped for success will, in time, attract, first Cleveland and Pittsburgh to the possibility of baseball as an amusement and business venture, and finally the East. But just now, the cities represented are so closely situated as to permit a shifting of teams without pouring all the receipts into the coffers of the railroads. Or, better still, with the generally loosening up with the restrictions on pleasures, as an offset to the prohibition amendment, Sunday baseball, we believe, will come in all the big Eastern cities. Then, it will be possible to form an Eastern wing of the league, and a real world's series, at the close of the playing season. This feature, however, is mere conjecture, and perhaps hinges on many possibilities, but it is at least possible, and not altogether improbable.

The feature of the new league which will appeal most keenly to the baseball loving population of the race, however, will be the fact that with a general distribution of the playing strength, more new men will be developed, by virtue of the multiplicity of opportunities. Under the old order of things with two stonewall teams in Chicago and Indianapolis and mediocre outfits in Dayton, St. Louis and other cities, colored baseball certainly presented a top-heavy aspect.

Teams outside of Chicago and Indianapolis were generally filled with men too slow for the American Giants or ABC's or youngsters with poor coaching and training, and with the resultant slim chance of advancement. With a distribution of playing strength and wholesale effort of co-operation, things should take a pronounced trend upward.

Under the watchful eye of a manager who is trying to make good; the ever present advice of a veteran who wants to be with a winning team in the league; and spurred on by the publication of his playing averages, which it is to be hoped our weekly papers will correctly carry, youngsters should develop rapidly into Petways, Grants, Hills, Reddings, Williamses, Charlestons, Taylors, etc.

Another side of the league should not be remiss in mentioning here and that is the players' contribution to the league itself. While the chance to play in organized baseball should afford them ample protection from the alleged practices of the past against their interest, it is to be hoped that the boys themselves will look upon the serious side of what is expected of them. Of course they are not asked to pay their own railroad fare or hotel bill, or pay anything for upkeep of the parks, but from the public and from their employers, unstinted loyalty and a 100 per cent effort will be required of them on and off the field. A strict observance of training rules, and gentlemanly conduct on the part of the players will do as much towards making the league a success as any amount of money put into the project. The ballplayer has the chance he has longed for and it is up to him to deliver the goods.

The player who can look over the benders and soak to safe territory the fast ones, after a night of carousing, is yet to be born. The *Competitor* wishes the new league success.

Corporate File, box 1779, no. 12478,
Dissolved Domestic Corporation Charters
Illinois State Archives

Articles of Incorporation for the Negro National League

Although the league started play in 1920, it was not until 1924 that the formal document was signed and registered with the state.

The Negro National League was chartered with $2500 in common stock at $25 a share. The shares belonged to the five directors: Willie Foster, Russell Thompson, Rube Foster, Walter M. Farmer, and J.L. Wilkinson. Wilkinson, owner of the Kansas City Monarchs, was the only white club owner and stockholder in the league. Currently, it is not known what role or relationship Thompson and Farmer had in the formation of the league and its charter membership. Willie Foster, Rube's younger half-brother, was majority stockholder.

Louis L. Emmerson, Secretary of State:

We, the undersigned, adult citizens of the United States, at least one of whom is a citizen of Illinois,

Willie Foster 3342–44 Indiana Ave., Chicago, Illinois.
Russell Thompson 3342–44 Indiana Ave., Chicago, Illinois.
Walter M. Farmer 184 W. Washington St., Chicago, Illinois.

Propose to form a corporation under an Act of the General Assembly of the State of Illinois, entitled, "An Act in relation to corporations for pecuniary [financial] profit." Approved June 28, 1919, in force July 1, 1919; and all Acts amendatory thereof; and, for the purpose of such organization, we hereby state as follows, to-wit"

1. The name of such corporation is The Negro National League of Professional Baseball Clubs.
2. The object is which it is formed is:

   Section 1. This organization has for its objects, the organizing, equipped and maintaining Baseball Clubs, composed of Colored Professional baseball players, sufficient to constitute and form a Circuit for the playing of championship games among the clubs belonging to The Negro National League of Professional Baseball Clubs.

   Its further object shall be to protect and promote the mutual interests of Colored professional baseball clubs belonging to The Negro National League of Professional Baseball Clubs as well as Colored Professional Baseball Players.

   Section 2. To establish and regulate professional baseball championship games under the supervision of the Board of Control of The Negro National League of Professional Baseball Clubs.

   Section 3. To maintain and own by purchase, gift or otherwise, amusement parks or buildings for the carrying out of the objects and purpose of The Negro National League of Professional Baseball Clubs.
3. The Duration of the corporation is Fifty (50) years.
4. The location of the principal office is 3342–44 Indiana Avenue, City of Chicago, County of Cook, and State of Illinois.
5. The total authorized capital stock is Common $2500.00.
6. The number of shares having a part value is One Hundred (100)
7. The name and address of the subscribers to the capital stock, and the amount subscribed and paid in by each, are as follows:

Stockholder	Address	No. of shares	Amt. Subscribed	Amt. Paid In
Willie Foster	3342 Indiana Ave., Chicago, IL	40	$1,000	$1,000
Andrew R. Foster	3342 Indiana Place	20	$500	$500

Stockholder	Address	No. of shares	Amt. Subscribed	Amt. Paid In
J. L. Wilkinson	4118 Agnes St., Kansas City, MO	20	$500	$500
Russell Thompson	3342 Indiana Ave., Chicago, IL	15	$375	$375
Walter M. Farmer	184 W. Washington St., Chicago, IL	5	$125	$125
		100	$2500	$2500

Document signed and dated by: Willie Foster, Russell Thompson and Walter M. Farmer and notarized by Aug. L. Williams, November 8, 1924.

[Author's Note: The following year, 1925, the number of directors was increased to eight, from its original five, to respectively represent the eight teams in the league.]

On June 4, 1929, the Negro National League was officially dissolved, by the "People of the State of Illinois at the Relation of Oscar E. Carlstrom, Attorney General."[2]

The (Pittsburgh) Competitor, Jan/Feb 1921

Baseball Men Hold Successful Meeting
Bacharach and Hilldale Join National Negro League.
Circuit Extended and Many Trades Made.
Columbus Displaces Dayton
By Ira F. Lewis

With all the pomp and splendor characteristic of the big noise in organized baseball, the owners and managers of teams representing the National Association of Professional Clubs, operating the National Negro League met in Indianapolis, Indiana, on Friday, December 3, to check up on the 1920 season and formulate plans for 1921.

The opening session was called to order by Chairman Andrew Foster, in the assembly room of the Indianapolis YMCA on Senate Street, at 10:30 AM. This open meeting was attended by Charles A. Mills, representing Homer G. Phillips, representing the St. Louis Giants; John Matthews, of Dayton, representing the Dayton Marcos; J. Tenny Blount, representing the Detroit Stars; Harry St. Clair, Dr. H.M. Smith and J.L. Wilkinson, representing the Kansas City Monarchs; Edward Bolden, of Philadelphia, representing the Hilldales; J.W. Connor, of New York City, representing the Bacharach Giants; C.I. Taylor, of Indianapolis, representing the ABC's; Jim Taylor, representing the Dayton Marcos; the American Giants, Chicago Giants and Cuban Stars being represented by Rube Foster.

A.M. Williams of Pittsburgh, and G.J. Tate and L.R. Williams, of Cleveland, were on hand sounding out the possibilities of securing franchises for their respective cities. Sol White and Nathan Harris, the baseball players of other days, were also on hand. Elwood Knox, of the *Indianapolis Freeman*, J.J. Gilmore, of the *Kansas City Sun*; A.D. Williams, of the *Sportsman's Weekly*; Dave Wyatt, of the *Chicago Whip*; W.H. Jackson, of the *Indianapolis Ledger*; Frank Young, of the *Chicago Defender*; and Ira F. Lewis, of the *Pittsburgh Courier* and *Competitor* magazine, were the newspaper men covering the big pow wow.

Chairman Foster in his opening address pointed out the wonderful success attending the first season of organized effort. He produced figures to show that not only had a greater amount of interest been shown in the game, but that all clubs had made money. Good money. His report showed that the eight clubs had played before more than 616,000 people during the season just past with every indication for a greater year in 1921.

The executive session of the association was of course held behind closed doors, but the information given out to the reporters was to the effect that there would be changes in the circuit next season.

The Dayton [Marcos] franchise will be transferred to Columbus with the widely known and popular Sol White as manager. An option was also held on Redland Field, the home of the Cincinnati "Reds" and the Cuban Stars will use that diamond while the Reds are on the road.

Perhaps the most singular stroke of the meeting was the taking in of the two strong Eastern teams, Hilldales of Philadelphia, and the Bacharachs of Atlantic City, as associate members of the Western circuit. This new arrangement will afford the Eastern fans the chance of seeing the Westerners in action as well as to give the fans from the sunset section a chance to see the seaboard teams perform. It is from the standpoint of protecting their interest against the unholy practice of contract jumping that makes this new alignment look so rosy with the owners. With eight clubs in the West and two in the East operating under a common law of understanding, it will make the players who think little of obligations to their club a chance to think things over before accepting advance monies and signing contracts promiscuously.

The David Harums were on hand as usual putting 'em over on one and another. The most important of which was the transfer of [George "Rabbit"] Shively from the ABC's to the Bacharachs, and the selling of Jimmy Lyons, the sensational outfielder of Detroit, to the American Giants for the veteran Jude Gans and the promising shortstop, young [Arvell] Riggins.

There was much talk over a proposed three-cornered deal between St. Louis, Detroit and Indianapolis, but "Chubby" Charley Mills was not inclined to bargain.

The reserve clause in all contracts between club and players was adopted and made a part of the contract. While this clause appears at times to work a hardship, it is in spirit the very heart of organized baseball. Were it not possible to exercise this right over a signed player the stronger clubs would gobble up all players after a short period with other clubs and thereby hurt the competitive spirit of the game.

Rube Foster's American Giants, of Chicago, were formally awarded the championship of the 1920 season and will float to the breezes, the championship pennant at Schorling Park next summer.

By the twenties, Chicago had become the Midwest's counterpart to Harlem in the East. With *The Defender* becoming the premier black newspaper of the Midwest, they promoted all segments of sports. Chicago's Harlem Globetrotters competed for national media attention against Harlem's Renaissance Five. Chicago boasted of being the home of champion boxer Jack Johnson. And the "Old Man" of football, Amos Alonzo Stagg, was coaching at the University of Chicago.

Foster had preached the wisdom of creating an organized black league. In 1887, the League of Colored Base Ball Clubs were formed with the Boston Resolutes, New York Gorhams, Philadelphia Pythians, Washington Capital Citys, Pittsburgh Keystones, and Louisville Fall Citys, but lasted less than a month. Later, in 1906, another league, the National Association of Colored Base Ball Clubs of the United States and Cuba, was formalized by several white owners. It failed to play one game.[3]

Following the 1907 season, The *Indianapolis Freeman* broadcast the challenge for a new league called the National Colored League of Professional Ball Clubs. The circuit was to be composed of eight teams with Cincinnati, Cleveland, Louisville, Pittsburgh, Chicago, Indianapolis, Kansas City, Toledo, Detroit, Milwaukee, Memphis, Nashville and Columbus, Ohio as prospective anchor cities. The League was to be led by Frank Leland, Elwood C. Knox, editor of the *Freeman*, and Ran Butler, owner of the Indianapolis ABC's. The league never materialized.

Although an outstanding pitcher, a dependable team owner and a brilliant manager, perhaps Rube Foster's most impressive fulfillment came in 1920. With the gate keepers controlling the purse strings, black teams were often exempt from making the really big paydays. Foster sought alternative solutions. Owners of the most stable black teams gathered in Kansas City, Missouri, at the Paseo YMCA, to discuss a structured league, game schedule and player contracts.

On the eighth day, they drank the Kool-Aid and created the Negro National League of Professional Baseball Clubs, better known as the Negro National League (NNL). It consisted of eight ships of hope to battle the sea of segregation. The league's motto was "We Are the Ship, All Else the Sea," borrowed from former slave and later abolitionist Frederick Douglass' quote, "The Republican Party is the ship and all else is the sea." Douglass added, "I am a Republican, a black, dyed in the wool Republican, and I never intend to belong to any other party than the party of freedom and progress."

Going against the tide of freedom and progress in developing a new league, Rube's voyage would become an obsession. Foster, the genetic Eve of black baseball, birthed a confederacy of clubs that embraced a permanent existence of quality baseball. It became the first league of color to survive a full season. Initially, the new league barely caused a ripple in the ocean of recognition.

For years, Captain Rube struggled without a life preserver in his attempts to keep his boat afloat. The human anchor gave IOUs, advances, and sometimes loaned players to struggling franchises, attempting to balance the talent pool around the circuit. Foster argued that their exclusion from the National Pastime was a symbolic rip in the red-white-and-blue flag. His struggles became successes, as black ball exploded in popularity and power, to boldly go where no black organization had gone before, ultimately becoming an integral part of baseball Americana.

As founder, secretary and president, Foster controlled the purse strings in the league as he set sail into his "home-of-the-brave" league with the patriotically named Chicago American Giants. As league president, Foster showed his true desire for success by sending his premier player, Oscar Charleston, and submarine hurler Dizzy Dismukes to the revamped Indianapolis ABC's. The Chicago Giants received over-the-hill pitcher Walter Ball and power hitter John Beckwith. The Detroit Stars got gate attraction veteran Pete Hill, Bruce Petway, Ed Wesley, Dick Whitworth and Jimmy Lyons, while the Monarchs got former All-Nation pitchers Jose Mendez and John Donaldson.

Pugilist Jack Johnson was still a gate attraction in 1921. Jack Johnson plays himself in this all-black sports melodrama about a physically weak young man, Joe Walker (Reed Thomas), whose girlfriend, Molly Moran (Blanche Thompson), is falsely charged with conspiracy to defraud a doctor. Learning self-defense and sportsmanship from the former heavyweight champion, Walker leads the Kansas City Monarchs to victory over the Detroit Stars (showcasing real players), and is also able to nab the villain who framed Molly, gang-leader Tom Atkins (Walter Simpson). Also note the promotion of Cristobal Torriente as the "Black Babe Ruth" (courtesy *Chicago Defender* 12 November 1921).

There was a time that Donaldson was the most feared pitcher on the planet. A *Mansfields News* (June 12, 1915) article reported that Donaldson had recently pitched 30 innings without allowing a hit or run. The article quoted John McGraw saying, "If Donaldson were a white man, or if the unwritten law of baseball didn't bar Negroes from the major leagues, I would give $30,000 for him — and think I was getting a bargain."

The *Mansfields* press continued, "Donaldson, just before establishing his record of pitching 30 innings without a hit, struck out 25 men in a twelve-inning game — an average of better than two strikeouts per inning."

For enduring personal sacrifices and hardships in formulating the league, Foster was hailed by writer Dave Wyatt as the "King of Baseball," in an April 1920 for *The Defender*:

> Foster broke up one of the greatest playing machines of all time. And citing the necessity of organization, he decided to advance a few strides farther in the game of sacrifice. When the idea of a foundation for a Colored Baseball League was conceived its sponsors at once hearkened to the popular demand for a circuit as evenly balanced in playing strength as was possible. It was seen that success could only be attained by the distribution of players so that each club in the circuit could at least acquire one, two or three players of such established prestige that it would be at once arouse the interest of the public to a point where there could be no possible doubt of a complete evolution of antiquated ideas into a full realization of modern methods of baseball government.

Kansas City Sun, 20 January 1921

Will Colored Baseball Survive the Acid Test?
By Andrew "Rube" Foster

The coming season will either permanently secure baseball among us or will destroy the good that has been accomplished. Unfortunately, the hardest job that could be imposed on any human was my acceptance to again head the league. This job is a gigantic position, and will test the best that is in me. Since I have accepted it, I am going to be successful regardless of any condition that may confront me. I am not easily discouraged and will work; failure is something I do not know the meaning of.

To be successful, all owners will have to do team work; they will have to pull together. Just the same as all leading clubs of players work together, their inside stuff is what will get them and baseball somewhere. Team work with me is the first letter of the alphabet and just as proficient as all my clubs have been in team work, discipline and deportment is just what I expect to develop the other owners to that same proficiency.

The most regrettable thing of a wonderful finish, breaking all records for Colored baseball, was the short-sightedness of some of the owners of our clubs. The Bacharachs have lost prestige which will take great effort to rebuild; the sending of the name Bacharachs to Cuba, with a combination of players from six different clubs ... was poor judgment. The wholesale fraud to the public that the Lincoln Giants are playing ball on the Coast, when in fact, only three players are out there, is bunk that the public could afford to not have, as they want the real results and truth. When they find this out, any legitimate story in the press, they will not believe and say, it's that such and such the paper said. The name Lincoln Giants has been benefited, inasmuch as the players on the coast that they have and the players they have from other clubs have played so far superior to what the Lincoln Giants can play, that they are the benefactor.

The public, who pays the toll at the gate, want the real article of baseball both from the playing standpoint and the right way it should be played. Several instances they past season have clouded their memories and they have asked me: "Why do you allow such, if it is wrong?" There are many ways to cure things, and it is not policy at all times to do the thing you know to be right; circumstances should always alter cases. The main trouble is that many of the owners are parading under false colors; their patrons think that because they own the club, they know baseball and they do many things that are wrong to substantiate that belief. It makes them sick when some fan who thinks he knows the game says, "Why is he letting Foster rough that over him? Don't stand for it." The others sitting around think that because he has seen much baseball or attended league games, or was a rubber for some league club, he knows more than Foster and demand of the owner to stop Foster, when, in fact a man can see league baseball all his life and still be dumb or a man can look at a physician operate for years and then not operate; you must study and experiment with everything you want to know.

We were playing the Bacharachs for the championship at Chicago. Up came a decision that manager Redding of the Bacharachs objected to. The umpire told him why he made the decision. Knowing Redding, I told him that the decision was right, but some of the ignorant players with him said, "You are just letting Foster rub it in, don't stand for it." Redding said, "Well I'm not going to stand for it; I will take my club off." I said to the umpire, "It's alright with me, reverse the decision." He said, "Are you

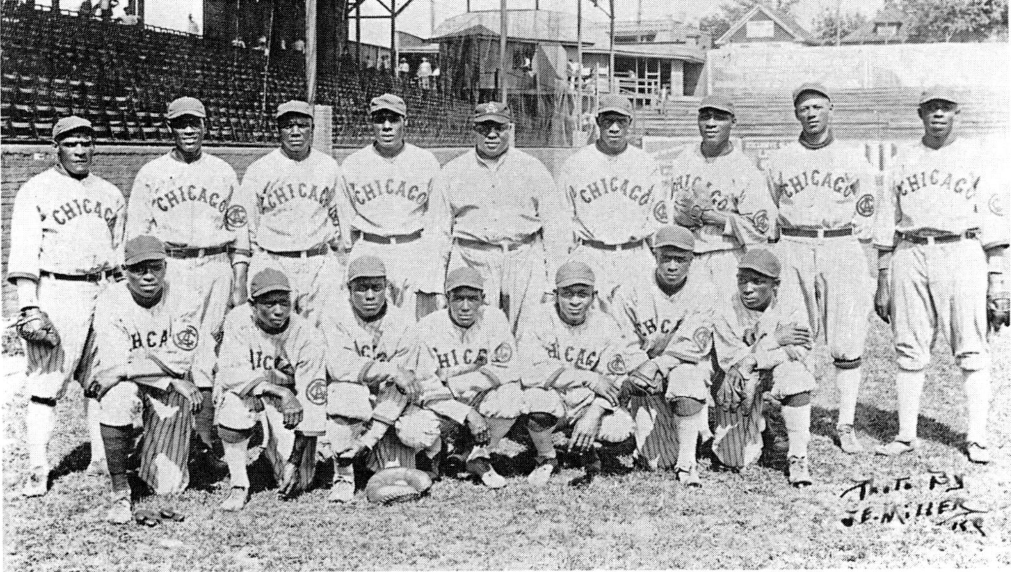

Top: **The Paseo YMCA on 18th and Paseo in Kansas City, Missouri, hosted the meeting of the Negro National League on February 19, 1920. Ten years earlier, Julius Rosenwald, a Jewish philanthropist, challenged the city to raise $75,000 to build a Negro YMCA, to which he would add $25,000. The funds were raised in less than ten days by the black community. The photo was taken in 1992.** ***Bottom:*** **1920 Chicago American Giants. Top row (left to right), Cristobal Torriente, Tom Johnson, Unknown, unknown, Rube Foster, Bingo DeMoss, Leroy Grant, Tom Williams, Jack Marshall; bottom row (left to right), Jim Brown, Otis Starks, George Dixon, Dave Malarcher, Dave Brown, unknown, John Reese (both photographs NoirTech Research).**

saying that because you think it wrong?" I said, "No, I just don't want them to quit." After the game he brought the rule book to them to show them that they were wrong and the next time such a decision comes up and the umpire rules it correctly, all of those that saw this one will call him a robber. Such men are not efficient to lead clubs of today.

A decision came up at Kansas City that lost one game and series for us. A man was on first, one on second and one man out. The batter hit a fair ball that struck the umpire before touching a fielder. He allowed the run to score from second. I objected, explained the rule to the umpire, but he said, "I have been umpiring for various leagues and know the rules." I asked him to ask one of the sporting writers of the daily papers who had come down and both agreed that I was wrong. I finished the game under protest. After the game, I showed them the rule, saying that unless all bases were occupied, no run could score. The fans booed me at Kansas City; said that I could do that in Chicago, but could not rough that stuff over them.

I am a believer that honesty is the best policy and will not allow anyone to lead me from this belief. My success has been that everything I do I do it knowing that I am right. Where there is a benefit of doubt, I never argue the point. The public at Chicago once thought I was taking advantage of clubs, but as they were educated up to the fine points of the game, they readily saw that I was doing the right thing and where they booed me, they applauded.

The jealously that exists between players, manager and owners must be a thing of the past. All of our future depends on just how much cooperation each will give to the other. I have never accepted any position that in any way I could be used as a figurehead. This goes with the job I have not accepted; all must pull together, agree on a policy, right or wrong, and play the team work behind whatever is accepted as the best policy. No player is greater than the game that created him, no owner more supreme than the confidence his patrons have in him. The public and fans have had 24 consecutive years to consider me; their great confidence in me has stirred me to greater things; instead of my hold diminishing with them, with understanding, they rallied tenfold for me. I would not betray this confidence to be President of the United States.

Now least all owners, players and the public pull together, with your combined cooperation, I will, with your assistance make the National Association of Colored Professional Base Ball Players the ship, all other opposition the sea. Something that when your children seek employment or want to become associated with, regardless as to their education, you can hope eternal, express your co-operated desire and feel that something great is to become of your son's future, where your mother, sister, wife and sweet say; I am sorry, I have an engagement, but my son is playing ball today, and we must all go to see him.

[Author's note: Foster's American Giants did pass the acid test. In an article by Howard V. Millard in the July 15, 1921, edition of *The Decatur Review*, he wrote the team "...would rank well with any major league club. The American Giants more than proved their ability Thursday in the first of a three game series with the Staleys, when they defeated the starch-workers 4 to 1."]

Millard added, "The colored boys didn't show the tremendous hitting power that you would see in the big show but they certainly field like a major league club and laid done some neat bunts. There wasn't a slow man on the club, while all of the infielders and outfielders had gun shot arms, Williams at short and Malarcher on third retired men at first after knocking down sure hits." Also, "Grant on first for the visitors put up a wonderful game, taking several bad pegs that were hurried to get runners, while he smothered Demmett's terrific drive in the fourth in easy style."

The Staleys were a semi-pro team owned by the Augustus E. Staley Company, a starch manufacturer. In 1920, their football team, led by George "Papa Bear" Halas, finished with a 10–1–2 record and joined the American Professional Football Association, which became the National Football League in 1922 in Canton, Ohio.

Halas took full control of the team in 1921 and moved the team to Chicago. As the "Chicago Staleys" they won the NFL championship that season. The following year they adopted the name Bears as a tribute to the baseball Chicago Cubs who permitted the Bears to play their games at Wrigley Field.

Also note, in the 4–1 loss to Foster's American Giants, the Staleys' sole run came on a homer by George Halas, his fourth in the last five games. In 1919 Halas played 12 games with the New York Yankees before a hip injury ended his baseball career. The next season, Babe Ruth took his position in right field.

The Staleys took the second game of the series by a 5–4 score with Halas getting two singles in four at-bats. In the rubber game, the Staleys put 50-year-old Joe "Iron Man" McGinnity on the mound. The future Hall of Famer had retired in 1908 at age 37. Called the Iron Man for his durability, in 1903, McGinnity started both games of double-headers, thrice in the same month, and won all six games, en route to a league-leading 31 wins.

However, Foster's men were not kind to the old man, as they scored eight runs in four innings pitched, on their way to a 14 to 5 victory. Cristobal Torriente touched the Staleys for a three-run homer and a triple, while Bingo DeMoss went 4-for-6, with Jelly Gardner adding a home run.

Overall, attendance was reported as 1,000 for the first game, 1,300 for the second game and 1,500 for the final contest, an excellent turnout for a city of roughly 70,000 inhabitants.

Chicago Whip, 12 November 1921

Foster Jailed for Fraud
Claim Rube Bilked His Ball Players
Atlanta Man Has Chicago Magnate Taken from Special Train and Arrested.

Atlanta, GA, November 12—Andrew "Rube" Foster, owner and manager of the American Giants of Chicago and president and moving spirit of the National Negro Baseball League was taken from this private train here last Thursday afternoon and arrested on charges of cheating and swindling.

Atlanta policeman boarded Foster's special train as it entered the station at 4:40 o'clock Thursday afternoon. The train consisted of a locomotive, baggage car, diner and three Pullmans. Rube was on his way to New Orleans to play for the championship of the South.

Taken to Police Station

The popular Chicago baseball magnate was hauled from his palatial special Pullman train and taken to the police station, where he was held.

Bond was quickly furnished by Ben J. Davis, well-known Odd Fellow, and editor of the *Atlanta Independent.*

Left Ball Players Stranded

The arrest was made at the instance of Atty. Roy C. Drennan, white, who was acting for Ben Harris, a former member of Rube's ball team.

Harris alleges that in the formation of the National Negro Baseball League last summer Foster recruited a number of players in Atlanta. The players were promised $125 monthly expenses, and a percentage of receipts, it is said.

When the league ended in Chicago several weeks ago, it is said, Foster abandoned the league and left the players stranded according to Harris' allegations. He also says the players were not paid their salaries for share of receipts.

After arranging the bond, Rube boarded his train again and left the city just as President Harding's special was pulling into the station.

Foster's destination is Cuba. He is taking two complete teams. After the New Orleans series, a complete schedule will be played in and around Havana. Foster emphatically denied all of the charges.

Chicago Defender, 10 December 1921

Rube Foster Tells What Baseball Needs to Succeed

First of Four Articles by President of the National Negro League Deals With Many Shortcomings and Suggests Way to Permanent Success

By Rube Foster

This article to one not familiar with baseball would be a difficult proposition to understand, but to one who has followed baseball for 24 years it is an easy matter; in going over the ups and downs of a career necessary for permanent success.

I am going to contribute four articles, the second one, "Why Colored Baseball Owners and Managers Have Been a failure"; third, "Colored Baseball Players As I Know Them," and the last, "Colored Umpires."

In the reading of these articles there may be many that may disagree with some of the things I may say, yet much weight must be given to what I say, as I have dealt practically with the subject longer, made a greater success and have been the only man of Color to remain continuously in the game for such a length of time.

It would really be unfair to tell you offhand what baseball really needs unless I give you a synopsis of what baseball has had.

What Baseball Has Had

Baseball, as far as our Race is concerned, has had many up and downs. There has been two great causes for this. First, the national game was put in disfavor by the narrow ignorance of leading people all over the country, who believed baseball was a game to be patronized only by the sporting element and not fit for their girls and boys to see. The caliber of players, the training they received, had much to do with encouraging this idea. I have seen the time when no respectable people would think of inviting a ball player to their home. I came up under these conditions. I made baseball a profession, later a business, yet my association has been such that I have wiped away much of that prejudice, so much so that I know of no men who have not felt it as much an honor to meet me as I felt it as much an honor to meet them from the most prominent men in the churches to our greatest educators and college professors. They have been my staunchest professors. Their homes are open to me and my home is to them.

Baseball needs more men of this type. They need men who in their home town can gain the confidence of all the people, men who can see some good in the worst element and have the power to draw that good out of them, thus making them useful to the rest of our Race.

There was a time in my memory when a denomination as large as the Baptist did not allow a Methodist minister in its pulpit, nor allow a Christian Baptist to take a sacrament in a Methodist church. Such were the teachings of our leading Colored divines at that time. Time has brought about many changes, education has done the rest until now we see the Baptists and Methodists communing together, Baptist and Methodist ministers visiting and exchanging pulpits and telling us this is the right way. The more enlightened we become the more we fall into the trend of the other highly intellectual nations. We now see things from an intelligent standpoint and not as we formerly have seen them.

There is not a denominational school that does not teach the students the value of athletics. We came into this after all of the white colleges, white churches and white social settlements placed baseball and other athletics upon their curriculum.

Baseball, among our people, has been poorly encouraged. Ball players who have come up under bad conditions have not had much over which to be elated. That is as far as encouragement from our leading citizens is concerned. They believed the better class of people though them inferior, which actuated their conduct in this capacity more to live up to the standard set up by public sentiment than for any other reason. Our men of thought and capitalists have as much to do with this condition as the ball players themselves.

Business Men Needed

What we need is a set of men in each city to form a stock company along the following lines: Ten men at $1,000 each or twenty men at $500 each, which would amount to $10,000; they could get a franchise in the league and operate a club. In this way any such set of influential men in any city would be able to realize at the lowest possible estimate more than 10 percent on the investment.

This amount of money at Detroit, St. Louis, Cleveland, Cincinnati, Indianapolis or Kansas City, would help conditions at these places.

The organization is here. The players are here. What we now need most is the moral support of men worthwhile in their cities. We have several men who control their clubs now who are financially able to carry these clubs, but with a season like the past season there is great doubt in my mind as to whether they could go along in harmony and work as they previously did.

I know of two men whose outlay of capital has not exceeded $3,000 [$36,500 in 2010], yet they have made over $30,000 with this $3,000 inside of two years. An individual making such profits with a limited baseball experience becomes a detriment when it becomes hard for him to see things rightly unless every season pays him the same pro rata as his first two years. Such individuals always find it necessary to make changes attempt to inaugurate a new system or block what has been done simply because men with better experience, who made all that they ever accomplished possible, have not accepted their judgment. These cities have drawn well and these owners believed it was due to their individual popularity.

In 1921, from his rocking chair Foster would write his four-part dissertation on the ills and challenges of the black baseball enterprise in the *Chicago Defender* (NoirTech Research).

I will give you an insight of the business ability of the men with whom I have been associated. After we drew up an agreement for organizing the league and worked under it for two years, we had reached a financial success that no one expected for at least ten years; while making money this system was a great thing. When the readjustment period came it became necessary for brains and experience to tide a business over that was fast sinking. The industrial situation which affected the entire world likewise hit baseball. These men found no other excuse for poor business than the system was wrong. They went so far as to say that Foster is president and he is the cause of it all and we have to be governed by him. He stays at Chicago all the time and makes us come there to play him. That is why he always wins the pennant. No logical man would make such a statement knowing the conditions under which we agreed to work.

We have eight clubs and only three parks—Detroit [Mack Park], St. Louis [Kuebler's Park], and Chicago [South Side Park]—where it is possible to play at all times. We operated and used three parks of the American Association. These parks were only available when the home clubs were not using them. We have two road clubs, the Cuban Stars and Chicago Giants, and it is necessary for them to be playing every Sunday. It was impossible to arrange any schedule where it was possible to put five clubs in three parks and play an equal amount of games. In the Association parks we were under agreement to use them on all open dates the home club was not in the city. This made it necessary to make these clubs, in order to live up to a contractual obligation, make unnecessary jumps and some clubs play more games than others. It was then agreed that only 15 games between each club in the league would be counted in the percentage column as league games, the other games beyond that number would be counted as exhibition games. We were compelled to play exhibition games in order to keep the clubs going. This was a wonderful thing for two years; everybody made money. Then came the industrial depression, and Foster was to blame for that; he was responsible for the financial depression all over the country. A child knows better than this. The same conditions, the same agreement that we worked under previously were the same conditions under which we worked this past season—no changes during the entire season.

A Sacrifice

Without the league the American Giants were a huge financial success; they would even be a greater success without the league now than heretofore. I felt it was a duty I owed my own Race to advance along the same lines as other baseball clubs, although I realized it would be at a financial loss. I had to change the percentage for the league clubs, and where I once had to pay $500 for clubs that played equally as well as these clubs, I had to pay the league clubs from $1000 to $1800. On top of this I reduced the percentage of the American Giants away from home 10 per cent. I reduced all the clubs' percentage what they were originally getting from the parks they played in from 5 per cent to 121/2 per cent. The park clubs under this system were paying less percentage than they did when they operated alone and were drawing three times the people that they formerly drew. In two instances I reduced a contact price 5 per cent where they had already contracted for the park for us. The park people after I explained to them what we wanted to do, reduced the percentage, as they knew that any plans we fostered that they would receive much more money on a cheaper percentage.

At the beginning of no season can we start to do business unless we start the season $10000 in debt; this amount of expense we carry in excess of any club in the league. Besides owning the stands, license, insurance and operating expenses of a plant as large as the American Giants' park, should it burn down we would have to pay $50,000 for the unexpired term of the lease we own. This is the amount of overhead expenses. We haven't a single other club in the league that cannot go out of business today and lose more than they had advanced the ball players and uniforms they used this year.

The men with whom I have associated have asked that I take such an expense and pool it the same as they do their clubs, that is to go away from home and play as often as other clubs. When they leave home they carry only traveling expenses and salaries. When I leave with a 10 per cent reduction of the former percentage, I must carry one of the highest paid baseball clubs and expense of the park. All this expense is on my shoulders together with traveling expenses and I have to accept 25 percent less than when at home. When men become this narrow their business ability can be easily determined. For any man to co-operate on an equal basis with anyone, he must carry equal liabilities. Had this stage been reached it would have been a fair proposition.

For 5 per cent I must schedule all games and worry with details. These inexperienced men know nothing of business nor baseball. I have been so engaged day and night in trying to keep other clubs going that I have not been able to see the American Giants practice all season. All of my time has taken up trying to do things for the other clubs. In addition to this I must schedule all games of the American Giants, hire a force of 22 men for each game, handle the most orderly baseball park in the country, schedule games for all other clubs, get them players and arrange their playing strength. Yet, handicapped as I am, I give the star player of the country to the other clubs and then have been able to run through their clubs like salt. This does speak well for their ability as baseball men.

People don't criticize me for any other reason than that they don't understand, and from ignorance all over the circuit, many of them have agreed with their spectators that Foster has too much power and that it is dangerous to give any one man so much power. In many instances this is true, yet in many cases power sometimes brings out the best there is in a man and makes him one hundred times more reasonable than he would be under opposite conditions. The men you hear criticize me must have some alibi, yet they admit that contact is a great asset. They did not find me too powerful or dangerous to give me so much power until by contact they knew that I had learned to my regret that they were useless.

Baseball's Necessity

All men who are possessed with positions of trust must always have a cabinet or some advisory board to whom they may go for advice. I cannot say this for the men with whom I have been associated. When consulted their advice is always, "Do as you see fit because you know best." I want to be relieved of this responsibility. If any set of men in any city can raise $10,000 I will be willing to come to their city, arrange a meeting and give them the plans to formulate and effect an organization and let them be responsible for the running of their own clubs and not let same rest upon my shoulders.

These clubs can be had, and surely with boasted talent and finance and the ability to listen to a straight forward business proposition with no such thing as losing money and at the same time help to raise the Race from the thought of being a thing of sympathy crying that the world is against him when he has made no effort to improve conditions many cities will be able to boast of a real baseball club.

I only wish first-class men to communicate with me. I am willing to take the time to come to the place to effect an organization. I have reached the conclusion that our men cannot peacefully get along as individual club owners. They can be made, however, to fit into our new plans. If not, we can afford to go along without them.

Chicago Defender, 17 December 1921

Rube Foster Tells What Baseball Needs to Succeed

The second Article by the President of the National Negro League Tells Why

Managers and Owners Have Been A Rank Failure

By Rube Foster

It would not be hard to point out many of the mistakes that have caused many owners of baseball clubs to fail. They have failed to learn the fundamental principles that would insure success in any undertaking. Owners would have made a success had they inaugurated a business system in the handling of the affairs of their club and let the success or failure rest upon the shoulders of the manager. Their failure to do this has handicapped their success and their business experience has proven the equal of their baseball knowledge.

If you will take all of the baseball clubs and their owners, from California to Maine, it will be surprising to know that only three men who own or control our ball clubs in the United States know anything about baseball as it should be played, the rules governing it or the ability of the players, yet we have hundreds of baseball clubs owned and controlled by men of our Race. Any player that they can secure to handle their club knows far more than the owners.

The fans in the different cities naturally think that any man who owns a ball club knows more about it than anyone on the club, and when any error is noted they go the owner and register their criticisms. The owner will go to the manager and tell him what he wants done. The manager in order to keep the club, tries to do the things the owner wishes, knowing at the same time it is wrong. This is why we have had such little success in handling the clubs. We have several smart players that would be a success as manager were they allowed to use their own ideas. With the exception of C.I. Taylor and myself I know of no other man connected with baseball as manager or owner that has the full say of everything pertaining to the club in its playing. Our success has been due to our ability to run our clubs as we see fit.

How to Select a Club

There are many men in all lines of business who are good salesmen, but not good buyers. There are also men in baseball who are not good judges of baseball players, but haven't the ability to direct them.

The majority of the present owners today have such little knowledge of baseball players that in organizing a baseball team the first thing they set out to do is to obtain the player of whom the papers speak most and herald as stars. They never consider habits, disposition, force of character nor ability. All they wish is the man the people believe to be a star. When a star goes to his town he realizes that the owner knows less baseball than he and he will not accept an instruction from him. The owner, in order to keep the good will of a ball player, permits him to break club rules and places the restrictions, fines and the like upon the young player of the club. No one can hope for success following such examples.

Owners' Poor Judgment Deplorable

With the weaknesses above mentioned one marvels at the success we have accomplished. When the star players wish to be transferred to another club and the owners want them they can go to the owners and make their own terms. When the owner finishes contracting for his own players he finds it impossible to make the money for which he has so contracted.

It is compulsory in our circuit for each owner to deposit $1,000. This amount of money covers the obligation for the club in the league and guarantees to the players any salary due them. Several clubs in the circuit have run their indebtedness up to such an extent that in order to pay off same would remove them from the association. This is particularly true in the case of St. Louis. Several owners of clubs now want to continue in the league, but do not think it advisable to keep up the deposit. Such steps, if allowed, would disband the organization. There are but few ball players who would accept position with owners unless we guaranteed them their money. The owners want to make big contracts with players, but if the business doesn't warrant same they are ready to jump down and make them accept any consideration they are able to offer. I would never be a party to such as this because it would be detrimental to all concerned.

An owner of a ball club should first itemize his contractual obligations for the season, lay aside a surplus to meet anything that may arise, like poor attendance, bad weather, etc., put this money aside not to touch for any other than the prescribed things it was intended for. If they do this they will not offer contracts in excess of what they can afford to pay. Follow these principles each year and they will be able to look the players in the face, meet their obligations when they are due and establish a stable enterprise.

I know of one club, which had contracts with the players for a salary exceeding $3,000 per month aside from the incidental expenses in operating a club whose checks came back for $25 marked insufficient funds. We now have checks from a corporation that has bought a ball park costing $50,000. Ball clubs have gone to this place and played the man did not have enough money at the park to pay the guarantee and gave a check for the amount due said checks was deposited and returned marked. "Not sufficient funds." These actions are embarrassing beyond measure and puts the entire profession in a bad light with the people. It is just such things as this that has made it compulsory for me to appeal to a business set of men to take and care for baseball clubs in many cities.

Managers Have Been a Failure

The failure of our managers has been due to make because of their intentions to try to make good with the owner instead of forcing the owner to accept them on their ability to either make good or fail. Having to accept positions as managers under these conditions as stated in this article, the managers have failed: this is way they are branded as being unsuccessful. No man has any business being appointed manager of a baseball club where the players know so much more than the manager that their ideas cannot coincide with his.

We have some of our leading baseball clubs of the country managed by men who cannot either read or write. Some men have reached the fourth grade in school, while others on this same club have played for years, graduated from colleges, and yet these players playing ability, educational advantages must be humbled to meet the demands of such management. This is deplorable and any owner who tolerates such, it is easy to fathom his knowledge of baseball and business. Ignorance can never predominate over intelligence, and it is useless to try.

How to Manage a Club

Managing a baseball club requires brains, patience, endurance and an open mind to deal with all the players on a baseball club squarely. I have had all of the temperamental stars, the majority of all the great ball players that have played baseball for the past 16 years, and have yet to find a player that is hard to manage. I have not had one disobey any instruction given to him. To be frank and honest all of my players play baseball as if they had no mind of their own or did not know what to do. I have sent them to do things, take chances when conditions were such that it appeared like suicide to take the chance. Yet they have gone willing, without fear and nine times out of ten it brought them success. These things were reached by the player playing under me being taught to believe. I knew what was the best thing to do. They are more particular in trying to do the thing I request or what they think would be the most pleasing to me, this underlines their success.

Our players are trained before the season begins. We have meetings and many of the things we do are the thoughts and advice of players on our clubs. In establishing any system of playing all of the men go over any angle just what should be done in each play. We sometimes spend two weeks discussing a play without making a decision. I give my ideas along with theirs but whether it is theirs or my idea as to how a play is to be done we agree upon the same and it is binding. I oftentimes accept the ideas of our players when they are against my better judgment. I would wait until the time this play came up and when the mistake was made we would call a meeting and I would show them why I allowed them to use their judgment and why I did not think the play should not have been as they agreed. Then I changed same to my way of thinking and they agreed with me that it was best. I did not do it in a way to make them feel bad, but merely stated I had tried their way and would like to have them try my way. Their reply would be, "Alright, chief, we will try to make the play as you see best." They try it, and when I see they have reached a degree of success following my advice as to the play I call another meeting. At this meeting I state that we have tried both ways and ask them if they wish to use their method or mine. Their answer is always, "The way you suggested."

This course is followed in all the rules of baseball. We discuss each rule and so far as to ask the different umpires who officiate wherever we play their interpretation of the different rules and plays. We get their interpretation, and if it does not agree with our system of playing we play the play as interpreted by the umpire.

"I never send a man to that to do anything that we have not rehearsed at least a season with that man. When a new man comes on the club he never gets signals or any instructions what to do. I tell the player and it is understood between all of the players on our club that anything he can do or think should be done to go ahead and do it. After the season is over I pick out all the things he has done that can fit into our system of plays, school him on these points and he becomes a valuable man to us.

I study my players to such an extent that I never send them up to do anything other than the thing I know they can do best under the conditions that confront us.

I make my pitchers pitch under instructions in all crises, direct the ball where it is to be thrown, with what motion how high or how low and how far from the plate. The minute this sign is flashed to the pitcher he throws the ball with so much ease and confidence that the batter is helpless before him. We have pitchers come to us who have their own ideas about pitching, about playing another position I allow them to be hit all over the field. I have allowed players to make numerous mistakes without a comment, then have them come to me and ask what is wrong, that whatever they throw they hit it. My answer to them is that they don't know how to pitch. This takes some of our stars off their feet. They say that they would not say that to me, but instead, why don't I show them how to pitch. My advice is that from their reputation, I thought they knew how to pitch and that anything that I may say would hamper them no doubt. However, I agree to tell them what I may know about pitching and that they may try it out. I practice with him and show him I even take him out and let him watch all the hitters hit, show him their weakness and tell him when he pitches again to try these out, and when in doubt to look over to me and that I will tell him how to pitch. This is why you see all the players on my club look over to me to get a signal as to the best thing to do. No man will ever be able to successfully manage a baseball club that doesn't manage a club along these lines.

I associate with my players. I go into their homes and study their dispositions and habits; find out the things that appeal to them most. If the places they frequent are bad, I go there with them and make a habit of frequenting places of this sort regularly. When they go to a place and find out I have been there if it is not the proper place they discontinue going. In this way I have broken up many of their bad habits. If they like whisky I buy it for them, and after they have taken one or two drinks I say, "Don't let this ruin you." I further inform them that but few men can drink and think accurately; that I hope they won't let the whisky interfere with their work; that I drink it but don't let it interfere with my work. One would think one doing such things would lose the respect of their men, but I know of no man who has the respect I receive from the ball players. If they have any bad association and they come in contact with me, whether it is in a saloon, cabaret or on the street they go to their company and say; "Look out, here comes Rube; be careful how you act and what you say." They either call me "Rube," "Chief" or "Jock." It would help our managers a great deal to study this system which I have used for years.

Chicago Defender, 24 December 1921

Colored Players Prove Serious Drawback to Baseball

Third Article of Series by President of the National Negro League on "Baseball and Way to Make It a Success"

To write about Colored baseball players as I know them is like living in a city for a long time, riding on a street car and knowing each street as you pass it. My association with them has been of such long duration that even t at my present age I have never lived at any place continuously as long as I have been associated with ball players.

We have many and various types of players. There are two sets of players with whom I wish to deal in this article: The players of 15 years ago and the younger generation of players of today. The older generation of players passed out of baseball without leaving anything for the younger generation to take up except their ability to think and hit. In Grant Johnson, Sol White and William T. Smith, 20 years ago three of the leading ball players of the world, we know they could hit, throw and field. They had the advantage of college education — all were graduates. They managed and handled the destiny of players of that day and had the future of the players of today in their hands.

As exceptional players, with their educational advantages, players of today may hope to profit; their superior baseball knowledge with years of training and experience and educational attainments superior to any of the players of the present time should make them towers of strength as managers of the younger set of players. Had they developed their ability, applied some practicality, their services now would be indispensable. As it is the players will not tolerate these men simply because they believe with the opportunities they have had, had there been anything great in them they would have been in control of baseball long ago.

Coming down to the present players of baseball. We have some few men with wonderful ability — that is, natural ability; they accidentally fit in some great plays at times, but none of them has the ability, with a few exceptions, to take the initiative in any play, drill it into the men and execute it.

Ball Player Ruining Game

The players of today with whom I come in contact are doing much to ruin the profession they have chosen as a livelihood; their conduct is far beneath their profession; they have not even the confidence of their conscience. They have run off with so many people's money, signed a contract with any manager who will advance them money, sign contracts and draw money in advance on these contracts, having the managers to keep them from starving until time to play baseball in the spring, then come to these managers with the proposition that "they have been offered more money that they would rather stay with them."

In these cases you either have to raise the salary to the offer they have made or dispense with their services altogether. The managers who make such offers are more at fault than the players. When other managers do this sort of thing they run to the people and their fans and tell them that other managers are trying to get all of their players and thus break up their club. It is impossible to teach a man how to run off with another man's money and expect him to be honest with you.

$166,000 Paid This Year

The Bacharach Giants, Hilldales, Royal Giants, Lincoln Giants, American Giants, Columbus Buckeyes, Indianapolis A.B.C.'s, Cuban Stars, Chicago Giants, Detroit Stars, St. Louis Giants and Kansas City Monarchs have paid the players $166,000 in salaries. Out of this $166,000 paid them the entire bunch of players who have received this amount have not saved collectively $2,000. In addition to this, $67,000 has been spent in transportation, room, board and street car service for these players. Aside from this two-thirds of the men have asked for advances and have received the same on their next season's work.

The players don't believe the owners can afford to pay them the amount of money they ask so they try to get as much money in advance as possible in order to hold the owners to their contract. They are rapidly killing the goose that laid the golden egg.

The industrial depression that has hit the entire country must receive readjustment in the players' salaries as in other lines of business. The government will not pay these men such a salary, the packing industry is hiring thousands of men at less than $20 per week who work eight hours and can save some money of this but the majority of our ball players don't save enough to pay one week's lodging after the close of the season.

Out of these twelve clubs four were able to make money, two broke even and the other six lost money. In the event the losing clubs tire of going into their pockets to give the players, knowing in advance it is impossible to make such. They are liable to go out of business. In such a case the market will again be flooded with players. The clubs that made money would then not be able to make one-half as much or probably not break even. If they did not have these clubs to play this would of necessity reduce the salaries of the players and would cause baseball to revert to that of three years ago.

It is amusing to hear the players discuss their owners. They claim owners know nothing about baseball. This they speak of publicly and freely discuss the subject among themselves and soon it becomes published gossip. On various occasions I have advised them as the inconsistency of such talk. Told the players that even if the owners did not know as much baseball s they claimed, that they were men who were able to hire them and pay them a salary, consequently, they must have more sense than they. If not they would not have been able to go into business and hire men.

I further stated to them that if we did not have men who were willing to go in to the baseball business risking the loss of much capital that at least 150 players would be out of jobs and that players must learn to earn what they get and cut out their criticisms.

Players' Conduct Must Change

Baseball among the whites was on a downward grade until the big league owners and scouts went into the colleges and brought out the college athlete, who purified the situation and brought baseball up to its present high standard. Our managers soon adopted the same method, went into the colleges and brought out a number of baseball players, believing their superior knowledge and educational advantages would raise the standard of other players, and do for us what the white college ball players had done for the white baseball profession.

With only a few possible exceptions our college ball players have degraded the profession. They have proven to be the greatest whisky drinkers. The greatest professional falsifiers, the biggest contract jumpers with whom I have come in contract are numbered among the boys that hailed from our colleges. They naturally have the confidence of the owners and the public as well. The owners have favored a number of them in giving them more money that other players who have three times their ability as ball players, but their conduct and association have been such as to lose the respect and confidence of the people that they once had.

A lot of owners have thought because a player was college bred he knew more baseball than the fellow who had not attended college. I know, however, that they do not know as much baseball and are harder to teach than the players without the advantage of a college education. It is absolutely impossible for a man to make a good ball player until he has had three years of training under some man or club who really knows baseball. Of all the players that I have ever had it took from two to five years to make them even valuable to the team.

Intuition makes ball players valuable. The hog, the rabbit and the monkey have intuition, yet none of them are educated.

Should Know Playing Rules

College players should know more about the rules of baseball than the average player. It should be easier for them to reason, study the technicalities of the rules than the other boys. It is in this that they have the advantages and should put it to use. If they did these they would serve as a tower of strength to the other players. If they are asked by a player who has not attended college, but who has had much experience and gained much through contact, what is their idea of such and such a rule and upon receiving the answer the players does not agree with him and asks for a further explanation in order that he may understand him better, the college chap states that "If he explained the matter differently, he would not understand him still." I have had some of the players tell me of these incidents. I make it my business to come in contact with these individuals who are so full of knowledge and ask them a few questions concerning the rules of different plays. Their brains become so paralyzed that they are unable to give any kind of sensible answer. I show them how little they know, but take the time to explain the things to them until they plainly understand.

Our college players have found that there is much to learn; that to read a rule and commit it to memory is just the beginning of their baseball knowledge; that the interpretation of any rule is based upon the interpretation sanctioned by the rules committees and in the absence of knowing the interpretation that it is useless to commit a rule to memory.

8th Inning. Black and White Arbitration in the New Colored Leagues, 1922–1925

Chicago Defender, 31 December 1921

Future of Race Umpires Depends on Men of Today

Fourth and Last Article by President of Negro National League Deals with Dark Skinned Arbitrators of Today and Their Future Possibilities

I know that the fans all over the country are waiting to get my opinion on "Colored umpires." They have patiently waited for a number of years. I have received hundreds of letters from the people, even sporting editors of some of the great papers have written to me advocating and in some cases condemning me because I have not inaugurated Colored umpires at Chicago and in the League.

Some have been unreasonable in their demands saying that I was the man that could do it and that it was a shame that I did not give our people the privilege of umpiring. It is doubtful if they understand the many obstacles that would have to be overcome in order to place Colored umpires in our league.

The leading thinkers of the country today admit that it was cruel and unjust for four million slaves, uneducated and ignorant, to be turned loose as a free people without safeguarding the necessary things in life for them, preparing and fitting them for the duties necessary as citizens and a free people; these same conditions confront baseball as far as umpires of the Race are concerned.

To be an official umpire the first great step for the umpire is to study the disposition and temperament of the players with whom he comes in contact; to be a good judge of human nature, to know the baseball rules, their interpretation and to be HONEST and SQUARE. These qualifications are sadly missing in the umpires that I have seen perform.

I don't expect our umpires to be able to interpret the technicalities of the rules as the leading baseball men of the country, but ball players who have played under umpires who understand such rules and make plays according to the interpretation of such rules and are called out or put out of the game on a decision they know is wrong invariably cause a bad game, displease the fans and the people gradually stop coming to the ball games.

Our fans have been led to believe that any decision an umpire makes is binding on a club and whatever he says must be taken for granted that it is right. An umpire's powers are limited; he is only supreme in decisions of judgment; when he makes any decision against the rules he is no more than an ordinary spectator at the ball game, but in order to not disappoint the people who come to the park the club accepts the decision given against them and plays the game out.

Heretofore no games could be protested, and time and time again games have been thrown away by the unjust decision of the umpire. We have tried to prevent this and instructed all of our clubs to play a game out regardless of the umpire's decision, if he made a decision against the rules inform him that they are playing the game under protest; notify the president of the league of the facts in the case and if the decision made by the umpire was against the rules the game would be thrown out and ordered played over. This was done on several occasions and when the decision was against the home club the manager and his players would say that the decision was made against their club because they feared their club would be beaten, therefore it was expected.

An umpire has more than the responsibility of the ball game on his hands; his actions are closely watched; he should not be swayed in his judgment by the applause of the home club's fans. This is noticeably true from the games in which I have seen them work.

It is the duty of a captain or manager to protest any decision that in his judgment conflicts with the playing rules; an umpire should tolerate such and be able to tell the captain or manager why he is wrong and explain the rule to him. When the umpire cannot do this then it is the duty of the captain or manager to protest vigorously and explain the rule to the umpire and if the umpire means to be fair he will abide by the rule.

Our umpires will not do this but instead will put the man out of the game, in many cases cause the manager or captain to withdraw his club from the field or start an argument. The result is a rotten game.

I have had much experience with Race umpires. The players and managers of the different clubs always instruct the umpire when I am coming to town to watch out for Foster, he is liable to trick him, that all of the umpires are afraid of him and that he always tries to show them up, also to show up the players. This is simply done because the players know I am familiar with the tricks and technicalities of the rules and my system of playing is such as to inveigle a club for a violation of the rules and take advantage of their inexperience and gain a point. They cannot protect themselves against such a system and they go to the manager or umpire. Some of the managers know less than the players and they go to the umpire who they will pay and tell him point blankly, "I don't want you to let Foster come here and run any game for us."

On my first occasion where I have to speak of a violation of the rules the umpire waves me away and attempts to embarrass me. I will illustrate to you what happened with three umpires in three different clubs. We were playing at St. Louis. I had received many complaints from the different clubs regarding umpires in St. Louis, but took no action, until we played St. Louis. I found the umpiring so rotten and deliberate I could hardly stand it. We beat the St. Louis Giants in Chicago and it was circulated all over town that we had robbed St. Louis in Chicago. Bobby Williams who is a very modest player and who no one has ever known to use profane language, got a base on balls and on leaving the plate he said to the umpire, "Gee I am lucky," the umpire went down to the first base and ordered him out of the game. This broke up the defense of our club. Later on in the game he missed what the St. Louis catcher believed was a strike on one of the American Giants, the catcher turned around, hit the umpire and shook him, but the umpire would not put him out of the grounds.

At Chicago before five times as many people than in St. Louis, Charleston came from center field and struck an umpire because he called a man safe at second base, the base-umpire had ordered Charleston out of the game, but the umpire-in-chief came down to the base umpire and said to him, "Don't put him out of the game, let him remain in the game so he can see just what the Chicago people think of him," and he called Charleston back. Charleston was sorry and from that day on has tried to get into the good graces of the umpires and the public at large.

We were playing Hilldale at Philadelphia; we won from them the first day, on the second day the score was 3–3, we had two men on base and two men out. Torriente hit a ball down to the left field line that everyone thought was fair, Williams who was on second base and Malarcher on 1st had scored before the ball was returned; the umpire called the ball foul; we didn't enter any protest against the decision, but Williams and Malarcher went across the diamond to first and second base, the Hilldale player threw the ball to second base and the umpire called the men out for not retouching base in reverse order. We argued with him and explained to him that the rules stipulate that on all foul balls base runners do not have to touch bases in opposite direction. We finally succeeded in getting him to go to the umpire-in-chief who was white and ask him to explain the rule; the umpire-in-chief told him the decision was wrong, the Colored umpire became angry and said they called a play like that against them at Hilldale and he would not change his decision; this cost us the ball game and eventually the series.

The Hilldale ball grounds has a ditch in the center and left field, a ball rolling down this is impossible to be seen by the umpire. The rules stipulate that on any field or on any part of the territory where the ball is out of sight of an umpire he must make ground rules. I once had an umpire in Philadelphia who decided to play the game by the rules; we beat Hilldale; the ballplayers and fans got on Bolden, who wanted to do the right thing, and told him he allowed us to come there and change his rules and allow us to beat them. Rules or no rules it is impossible to get Hilldale to play according to the playing rules.

We Need Race Umpires.

We need umpires of the Race very badly and can use them to a great advantage; they don't know all the technicalities of baseball rules to make an efficient umpire, yet the more they umpire the better they will be. There must be a beginning. It would however be unfair to give them positions unless we were in position to give them the protection they will need in doing their work.

Our baseball players are harder to handle than the white players. It seems characteristic of our race to act according to the size of the attendance, the larger the attendance the worst our actions. We don't feel that we have had a good afternoon until we can show off to the multitude how bad we can be. All the clubs hire their umpires; they don't need to be told that they are paid by the home club, but if he does anything that the players tell the manager is wrong, or the fans tell the manager they don't agree on his decision and that he is robbing him, the manager doesn't weigh the merits of the umpire, but gets a new man in his place; the new umpire knowing the fate of the other governs himself accordingly.

Under such a system our umpires are not near as much at fault as the club owners and managers; they have not had a fair chance to show their worth, they can be as easily developed as the ball players. Until we can get our club owners to consolidate and agree that an umpire should be hired and instructed by the President of their League, his pay to come from him and that he does not have to be unfair to any club in order to get his pay, but that the only way to draw his pay is to be fair and just at every place; we cannot hope for success with Colored umpires.

It is an easy matter for umpires and managers to get together and discuss the interpretation of any rule they disagree upon as it is for the manager and players to get together and agree upon a system; argue the point, thrash it out and whatever agreement is reached make it binding.

We draw wonderful crowds and have sometimes as high as 500 ladies; if you know the temperament of our men as I know them, you can surmise about what would happen if before fifteen thousand people a player would walk up on the diamond and slap one of the Race umpires in the face. Do you think that he would stop to consider the welfare of the people, the interest of the people who have their money invested, calmly walk away and motion the man to the bench? You may know of some who would, but I have yet to meet them. Those I have met would say, "Church is dismissed, pray for the lights to go out, for there is going to be a hot time on this ground today."

In studying the rules of baseball the umpires must learn to govern his temper and remember that fair play is an unwritten law of baseball, that that has more to do and is upheld farther than any written rule in baseball. It takes the precedent over all the rules written in organized baseball.

I do not want our umpires to think I don't want them, but they know the conditions as stated by me have hindered their success. With the elimination of these things I am sure they would be a success. I would have them in preference to white umpires, but I cannot allow my preference to run away with my business judgment of what I know to be to our best advantage at this present day and time.

Kansas City Call, 13 May 1922

Foster Should Have Declared Forfeit
Monarchs Lose Opening Series to American Giants

The Monarchs have met the enemy in his own dooryard and came off second best. The story of the series is full of bad breaks in favor of the Fosterites, questionable umpiring and is climaxed by the spiking of [shortstop Dobie] Moore, whose stick work was a dangerous factor, no matter who pitched.

Rube Currie opened for the Monarchs Saturday, and only allowed two hits. Moore dedicated the ball lot with the first home run of the season and incidentally, the longest hit ever made in that park. Score: Monarchs 5, Giants 1.

The outcome of Sunday's game was a disgrace to Rube Foster, as League president, and the Chicago fans. In the 9th inning, with the score tied and two on, Moore stepped to the plate, swinging his big stick. The fans remembered his circuit clout of the day before, and to prevent a repetition of the same, swarmed out on the playing field, thus preventing the game from continuing and keeping the Giants from losing.

Rube Foster, as president of the league and as owner of the park, was the only person directly responsible. It was his business to see that the ground rules for spectators were enforced, and after they could not enforce them, then, as a fair sportsman, and according to the custom prevailing in organized base ball the country over, the game should have been declared forfeited to the visiting team. That is the decision rendered by major league umpires and upheld by the league president in the few instances where the decision was necessary.

Foster, as president, should have instructed the umps to render such a decision and proved himself a sportsman, but he didn't and the game stands on the books a tie, 2 to 2. Whether or not it will ever be righted, we do not at present feel competent to say, but Kansas City fans will have this to add to the other incidents which go to make the Fosterites so unpopular in this town.

Chicago Defender, 19 August 1922

Change the Umpires
Decisions Become Rank — Union Arbitrators Rule —
Chicago Defender Leads the Public in Clamor For Change of Complexions
by Frank A. Young

Umpires bad, umpires rotten, fine games but bad umpiring. Our head swims, we hear it on all sides. Of course there are a number of fans who never will agree with any decision given by any arbiter but there are countless thousands who are impartial who go to ball games for the sake of the game, don't care which club wins, but who do wish to see and who do demand better decisions than have been given out at the American Giants park on 39th Street in Chicago and at other parks operated and controlled or owned by the Negro National league.

A good example of the above was pulled Sunday. In the first place let me acquaint the reader with the real facts. There is a union of umpires in Chicago known as the Baseball Umpires Association. The park management informs them when games are to be played and this association furnishes two umpires or rather two men who claim they are umpires. Usually the same two men are at the same park every Sunday. To the short-sighted fan I might say it is not necessary for a manager to come upon the field, in front of 3,000 to 5,000 people, to argue with an umpire, thinking he will cheat in favor of him, nor is it necessary to believe that every time he objects to a decision that the manager is in the wrong. If a manager wanted to be unscrupulous it would be easy enough to pull such a trick behind closed doors away from the view of the public.

Back to Sunday's game. The umpire behind the plate called Rube Foster in from the third base coaching box and told him he would have to remove the glove from his hand. There is nothing in the rulebook that prohibits a man in the coacher's box from wearing a glove and this matter has come up any number of times.

[Author's note: Foster employed this tactic in the 1916 series against the Indianapolis ABC's, resulting in a forfeit victory for the ABC's.]

Foster refused to remove the glove and the game went on. At first base when [Bingo] DeMoss slid back the base-umpire was not in position to see the runner's one foot on the bag, but made his decision from where he was standing on the strength that the other foot was off. In the ninth [John] Beckwith tried to make third on a double but a nice relay got the ball to [Oliver] Marcell in time to get the runner. Instead of Marcell tagging Beckwith with the ball he tagged him with his elbow. In Monday's game a short fly to center field saw the fielder come in and take the ball on a bound. That is, he got it as it started to bound, what players call a "trapped ball." The base umpire called the batter out. There is no player in the world that I have seen so far in my life that can make a shoestring catch without bending his knees. These things cause fans to become dissatisfied and attendance to drop off. The real truth of the matter is that the park management at the present time has to stand for this sort of umpiring or face a strike by the association and get no umpiring at all. Another plain truth is these umpires on hundreds of occasions have the decisions made and ready to call before the play is completed. Again on Monday the man behind the plate called a strike a ball and his attention was then called to the fact that the batter had swung at the offering. He changed his decision, but how did he look to those that pay to come through the gate?

"What is the remedy?" some ask. "How long must we stand for this?" others ask. Not long, dear brother, not long. You remember two winters ago, when the *Chicago Defender* came out with an article demanding umpires of color? Many said the time wasn't ripe yet. We have abided our time. The pot has been boiling and in the language of the street, "The darn pot is about to boil over."

We have men who are capable of handling games. Take [Caesar] Jamison in Baltimore. There are two in New Orleans. However, suppose there weren't any. Then what? Train them, I say. Train them. If you can train a chimpanzee to do things then you can train men. Give us some brownskin umpires. It isn't necessary for us to sit by the thousands watching 18 men perform in the national pastime, using every bit of strategy and brain work, to have it all spoiled by thinking it is impossible to have any other men officiating but pale faces. Give us a change. The sooner it comes, the better we will like it. The columns of this paper are open to the readers for discussion, pro and con. Confine your letters to 75 words.

Address Fay, in care of *Chicago Defender*, Chicago, Ill. Now let the mail man get busy.

Chicago Defender, 26 August 1922

I am glad of the opportunity to write concerning the umpires at the American Giants' ball park.

I am a regular attendant at all games played there and there is not a game but what I hear the question: Why don't they have Race umpires here?

I agree with the World's Greatest Weekly that the time is right and the present day is the time.

We have enough old retired ball players that have helped make the game the success that it is, who have outlived their usefulness as far as players are concerned, who are just as competent as the umpires that we have at this time at that park.

We have men of the Race who know baseball from all angles, and who would be able to maintain as much discipline on the field as any umpire I have ever seen in this park.

The writer could name any number of men of the Race who are well qualified to handle the indicator, and I think that the game owes as much to the old players of the Race as it does to Deneen and Walsh of the American league.

Yours truly, T. H. Eron, Chicago, Ill.

Chicago Defender, 26 August 1922

I am writing these few lines of congratulation and approval on your article on "Change the Umpires." Sure, change them; give us brown skins. They can be better and can't be worse. As a fan who witnesses all Sunday and week-day games and the decisions you have mentioned and others besides, I say change them. I am a loyal American Giant fan with more faith in Rube's team than Henry Ford has in a "lizzie." Perhaps a change will quiet the Giants knockers and friendly enemies.

Richard Johnson, 450 East 48th St., Chicago.

Chicago Defender, 2 September 1922

Dear Fay: Just finished reading your article in the *Chicago Defender* under the caption of "Change the Umpires."

This page in your paper is always very interesting to the Race fans of Washington, many of whom, as myself, buy it just for this page alone.

Indeed, it is quite disgusting to learn that our professional ball players are playing daily under the eye of pale skins.

Here in Washington as you may know, we have no professional Race teams, but they do visit here occasionally. Please let me inform you of the fact that when they do come no pale face dons a mask behind them.

Do you mean to say that in a city like Chicago there are no Race men capable of performing such a task?

Put them on the sand lots, teach them the theoretical, as well as the practical side of the game, let them work their way up as though they were ball players in a minor league trying hard to win a berth in the big leagues and watch the results.

Wishing you best results in your task and hoping to see next season bloom forth with Race men as officials.

A Fan, Washington, D.C.

Chicago Defender, 2 September 1922

If I use over 75 words I can't help it, the issue is too great to be cramped into such a small package.

I feel it my duty to join in with Mr. Fay of the *Chicago Defender* on this subject of Negro umpires.

I am not alone on the question, either. It takes someone other than the player who must start the real ball to rolling in order to accomplish a satisfactory result in the ranks of the players and among the fans.

A good baseball fan, in my opinion, is one who is really interested in every part which goes to make up the real game, beginning at the president and ending at the caddie of the bats. I therefore with pleasure take the liberty as an interested fan in every part of this great sport to suggest that when the president of the Negro baseball association begins to employ some of the Negro brains, who in the past years were some of the best ball players on the diamond and who were really a credit to the team they played with, then why in Heaven's name such men should not be employed, who still retain that same brain, to fill the station as an umpire for Negro baseball, just as the whites do. Now these suggestions, as others or I may make them, do not originate by any means from a source of prejudice, but from a standpoint of right and just. And it is a proper picture painted to behold as perfect by both white and black, the player and the fan. Thus the answer echoed creditable. A Negro institution and it manned out and out by Negro brain. There is not anything narrow or even selfish in it.

We have here in St. Louis men who are worthy of just such honors and attention, viz.: H. Holland and Owen Bradley and yet even others. I know there are some in the baseball city of Chicago and other cities counted in the circuit.

I don't think these umpires should be stationed permanent in any city. They should be shifted about at all times for the good of all concerned. Now, the last, but not least, one of the greatest and the most essential duty of the player and also the fan is to respect the station of the umpire, if not the person in it at the time. Decisions rendered some time or another may seem bad to you, but remember this, both player and fan don't disgrace the game or the grandstand. A hint to the wise sometimes awakens the foolish.

Benjamin F. Barrow, 3419 Pine street, St. Louis, MO.

Chicago Defender, 9 September 1922

Reading your piece in the *Chicago Defender*, must say that it is about the best piece of information you could give out to the public. There is only one thing a white man can be that a Colored man can't and that is president of the United States, and if we had justice, that wouldn't be either. There is never a week passes that I don't read the *Defender*. What we need is Colored umpires. I have been umpiring ever since I quit playing baseball. I would like to umpire for Mr. Foster one week without any pay to demonstrate to him I have the ability. I know the rules and study then. Ask Foster's pitcher, Owens.

James Small, Jackson, Miss.

Chicago Defender, 16 September 1922

Dear Fay:

I am not altogether in favor of your plan at the present. I realize bad decisions are given both clubs and that fans, especially those who do not know the game, think that decisions going against the home club are bought and paid for. My idea would be to let one Colored and one white umpire work, alternating in games behind the plate. I have seen some good arbitrators at the 39th street park and have seen some pretty darn bad ones. The whole trouble is the class of men from which the park owners in the city leagues and the Midwest league have to draw are not used to the class of play and the strategy used, nor the quickness of action that is pulled off at our park, or rather, the park which our men play in. Now, inasmuch as you have started the ball rolling and the *Chicago Defender* is first in really doing things, I hope you won't stop like you did two years ago but keep at it. I hope the fans here and throughout the country will heap letters into your office and into the office of the president of the league, until he makes the step that will please thousands of those who weekly pay to see the American Giants perform. Hurray for Brother Abbott and his newspaper! Hurray for the sporting editor, and hurray, hurray for the whole gang!

Chicago, W.G. Proctor.

Chicago Defender, 23 September 1922

To the Sporting Editor:

Dear Sir: I write this to inform you that we have a very nifty umpire in Los Angeles who ought to make good anywhere. He is a Colored lad named W.W. (Billy) Donaldson. Billy has been in the traces about four years, during which time I have frequently seen him in action.

During the winter season here many of the big leaguers come to Los Angeles. A number of them have been accustomed to form a team and play a series of games with the best Colored nine that can be mustered. In most of these contests the Colored team has been successful. The double umpire system is used, Donaldson usually officiating with a white umpire. These games draw pretty big crowds and the games are corkers.

I have watched Donaldson closely in many of these tilts and found him to be alert, impartial, and fearless. I have seldom seen him razzed for questionable decisions and this is one of the crucial tests of a good umpire.

We expect to have another winter league session here this coming December between the best white and colored clubs that can be gotten together. Among the whites will be Bob and Irish Meusel, Johnny Rawlings, Boeckel, Carey, Lou Blue and such high class players from the big leagues. Donaldson has already been engaged as one of the arbiters. It looks like a banner season at the present time.

Respectfully yours,
Ed O'Malley
Los Angeles Times Sporting Staff.

Chicago Defender, 7 October 1922

Dear Fay: Your article in the *Defender* on the subject of Race umpires was very good and it was also put forth at the right time.

The teams are now on their last lap and mistakes by the present officials might lead to trouble that might be avoided by the use of Race men and umpires in the National Negro league.

There is in Washington a Mr. Despert, a former star player and a good umpire. I am sure that the different cities have other such men, so why employ white men?

Let the president of our League call the best of these men together and I know that he can get from this group a number of men who will satisfy both public and players.

Yours for Race sports,
Preston A. Mason,
Sec'y Buffalo A.C., Washington, D.C.

Chicago Defender, 7 October 1922

Dear Fay: I would like to inform you that we have two Colored umpires, Mr. Danny Despert and Mr. Henry (Spike) Spencer, who can be compared with any in the country. These two men officiate in all of the games played here by visiting clubs. Mr. Despert has played professional ball a number of years with the Brooklyn Royals until he was hurt in a train accident. Mr. Spencer was never a professional but he is a very close student of the game.

Andrew Allen, Jr., Washington D.C.

Baltimore Afro American, 27 April 1923

Rube Foster Signs 7 Colored Umps
National League Opens Saturday with Colored Arbiters for First Time

Chicago, Ill. April 26 — The Negro National League through the offices of the president, Andrew Rube Foster, announces the signing of seven colored umpires to be used in the league games this season.

This is the outcome of a long fight on the part of the public, aided by some nationally known sports writers who have gone to the front in the past few years.

With Billy Donaldson at Kansas City for the opening series will be B.E. Gholston of Oakland, California, who has been officiating in a white league in Arizona. Leon Augustine of New Orleans and Lucian Snaer of the same city will start at Milwaukee on April 28, when the Cuban Stars who have just arrived in the States open a five-game series in the league race.

Caesar Jamison of New York City and William Embry of Vincennes, Indiana, will start work at Indianapolis when the Detroit Stars open the league season there on April 22nd for the American Giants and an officer in the 365th Infantry in France will be held in reserve.

In November of 1923, additional problems arose about whether to hire the white umpires or the more expensive black umpires. The extra expense was incurred from moving the black umpires from city to city and paying the colored crew a guaranteed salary, while the white arbitrators were only paid for the games they worked. This issue caused much concern among the budgeted-strain owners. The black umpires had cost the league an additional $4,000 than the hometown white umpires. Eventually the controversy was settled when the owners agreed that the previous season the officiating by the black umpiring crew was the best in league history. The black umpires were retained for the upcoming season. Later the umpires lobbied for a pay increase in 1925 and received a 20 percent salary raise.[1]

Chicago Defender, 17 November 1923

Big League Stories
By Billy Donaldson
Negro National League Umpire

Rube Foster

I believe that Rube Foster is one of the world's greatest baseball strategists and I believe my views are shared by the majority of those who have seen him at work upon the ball field.

He is not only a strategist but a baseball pioneer and organizer. He is the father and organizer of the Negro National League, the first organization of its kind where boys of our Race could get employment as players and make a place for themselves in the baseball world.

The forming of the Negro National League started the ball rolling and now we have several leagues in the country where it is possible for our boys to make a decent living at playing ball.

Race fans should be very thankful for a league and for their very best in turning out to the games in full force, showing their appreciation toward Mr. Foster and his league. They will find the same caliber of high class play that is dished up by the white major leagues.

The big-hearted Mr. Foster's next move after the league was two years old was to search the country over for Race umpires and after a very thorough search he secured eight efficient umpires who gave a very favorable account of themselves. These men knew the game, worked faithfully and their work was satisfactory throughout the league.

They handled their games the same as any major league umpire and it was not a very hard task for them to break in and show their wares as arbitrators, something the Race should be proud of.

The people of the coast could not understand how any team could beat Rube for the pennant and the first question they confronted me with was: "Why did Rube fail to win the pennant again?"

The general impression was that the umpires were favoring Rube in the past years.

Fair and Impartial

I found after my close association with the league this past season that there is not a more impartial person in baseball than Rube Foster and that all games were played on the square. The players always gave their best efforts and were gentlemen on and off the field, doing as they were instructed.

Rube is generally successful in winning small score and close score games because he has a smart ball club led by himself, a master strategist and he generally outguessed the other manager or players. In [Bingo] DeMoss, [Jimmy] Lyons and [Jelly] Gardner he has men who lay the ball down on either side of the diamond and beat it out. For brute strength or heavy hitting he has [Cristobal] Torriente, [John] Beckwith and [Jim] Brown, who certainly could murder the horsehide at critical moments, at the same time not leaving out [Dave] Malarcher, B. [Bobby] Williams and [Harry] Kenyon, who were timely hitters.

After trying out a dozen or more pitchers Rube was not so fortunate in getting what he wanted in pitching.

He had to depend on [Ed] Rile and [Percy] Owens to do the heavy work end of the hurling. T. [Tom] Williams, [Jack] Marshall and [Fulton] Strong took their turns in the box, but did not have such a successful season as Owens and Rile. Rube's brother, Willie Foster, a southpaw, tried out at the close of the season and showed much promise as a pitcher. He returned to school, however.

[Leroy] Grant, the old war horse [34 years old] and pepper sauce, is still with them.

Pittsburgh Courier, 11 January 1923

Foster Threatens Baseball War
Says Bolden "Sold" Colored Baseball to the East in Recently Formed Organization in Phila.

The Eastern Baseball Association from the papers will have six clubs, Hilldale representing Philadelphia and Camden, Baltimore, Bacharachs of Atlantic City, Royals of Brooklyn, and Cubans of Havana.

It's useless to try and camouflage the public; such an organization as founded means only to perpetuate the commission of [Nat] Strong who has taken 10 percent from the gross earnings of colored ball clubs for over twenty years, has never built a blank fence for them to use and never will. His [Brooklyn] Royals [Giants] must go from day to day as a club without a home.

Why Hilldale Club withdrew from National Association

Edward Bolden, president of Hilldale Club, came to our annual meeting and told me that he wished me to arrange it so he could withdraw; explained that they were going to organize a league in the East. In explaining my position I told him we have no objections. Only we would not associate with clubs out of the association, but if he could get an agreement from the league to respect our rights, and when such an agreement was signed I would recommend the return of the deposit of Hilldale Club, but if he resigned that would be impossible. He said, "I must tender the resignation," which was accepted.

National Association Agreement with Hilldale and Bacharachs

Our agreement with Eastern clubs did not call for any exchange of players nor was it compulsory for the Eastern clubs to come West. It was an agreement to respect each other's contractual rights as to players and the territory they played in and not to tamper with their players. Bolden, last year, tried the same thing but got cold feet. He had asked me to return his deposit of $1,000 and with Strong and Keenan tried and made efforts to take players from the league for retaliation.

I used the same medicine on him, and would have wrecked the Hilldale club, but Bolden rushed to Chicago and asked me to allow him to again place his deposit and to undo the things done to his club. We accepted him for the good of baseball, yet he had to relinquish claims to [Dick] Whitworth and turn him over to me.

Two 15 Cents Meals for Playing Ball

It's hard to believe that people can be so easily duped as our local fans in the East. I have played in the East under Strong when we received one hundred dollars for Sunday games yet drew as well as at present in New York. The whites took the players and paid them such small salaries as two fifteen-cent meals a day. I carried twelve men West with me and told them we could only exist with what we were getting, and I think one should not accept such conditions until he is convinced he could do no better. At twenty-one, the best players in the East left and came here with me. That one stand made me, nor have I changed from such.

Can you imagine a colored club playing to 10,000 people and receiving only the limit of five hundred dollars and then giving 10 percent of that to Strong to play in New York, and Bolden to play him must give him a percentage. I do not think much of a leader like that and such methods would not be tolerated with anyone who really thinks.

The *Philadelphia Ledger* is headlined, "Lloyd Signs with Hilldale." Can one fail to see why Bolden wanted to withdraw. He wanted to get with Strong. He could not tamper with his players from fear, but turns and signs one of Connor's men who belonged to the association and expects to bolster a club with players belonging to other clubs. He will start the war again. We have tried to avoid making player jump contracts.

They are now after more than men from our league and for one, I will not try to stop a raid on our players. But at the proper time will drive a blow that will not be easy to get rid of. I do not fear Strong or any man in the baseball business. They know if I play where the money is, I must share equally in it, so it's good reason they don't care to have me.

New York Amsterdam News, 16 January 1923

Edward Bolden Replies

The recent article published in various periodicals under the cognomen of Mr. Andrew (Rube) Foster, relative to the baseball situation in the East, reveals the fact that the self appointed " Czar " of Negro baseball is not satisfied with the unwieldy regime that he has set up in the West. But would, if possible, extend his autocratic reign to the Eastern situation. Using libelous propaganda in an effort to inoculate the public at large.

It is indeed surprising to find one in the exalted position of Mr. Foster to resort to the pernicious method of the poison pen, and the average fan cannot but wonder why one who has possibly attained the pinnacle in the Negro baseball world would stoop to such unscrupulous measures. I find the pressure of business such that it requires all of my time. Nothing is gained by ceaseless verbal battles, which is one of Mr. Foster's chief ways of playing in the galleries. Yet the attack upon a situation that is entirely foreign to him necessitates the exposure of facts that the average fan is entirely ignorant of and I am in a position to give and will gladly enlighten the followers of Negro baseball.

Mr. Foster begins with an unwarranted nefarious attack upon our new formed organization, The Mutual Association of Eastern Colored Baseball Clubs, which reveals the fact that he is suffering with a severe attack of the "green eyed monster" even injecting the race issue by calling attention to the fact that Mr. Keenan, secretary-treasurer of the Eastern Association is white. There are a few skeletons lurking in the closet of the Western Czar that have never been brought to light, and with the exception of a very few, the actual conditions are not known. It is indeed strange that Mr. Foster should take such a repulsive attitude to the fact that the Eastern Association is comprised of both colored and white officers. Why does Mr. Foster not publish the fact that Schorling Park and the American Giants are property of John Schorling, for whom the park is named, and Foster, a chattel of his white boss? Why does he not publish the fact that the secretaryship of the Western Association is held by Mr. Wilkerson [sic, Wilkinson], who is one of the opposite race? Why does he not publish the fact that the same Mr. Strong, whom he now seeks to hold up as a target, has letters from Foster entreating him to connect with the Western Association because of his known financial resources? Even stating in his letter of 11–24–21, that he and Mr. Strong were the only recognized leaders in Negro baseball. Very strange, some peoples opinion of racial devotion.

Again Mr. Foster assails the fact that Mr. Strong operates a booking agency, which many are cognizant of, and know as a legitimate business, but we have never paid Mr. Strong one cent for booking the Hilldale club. Why does Mr. Foster not publish the fact that he charges every club in the Western Association 5 percent of their gross earnings? Why does he not publish the fact that the Hilldale club paid him percentage for all clubs that came East, at the same time he charged the Western club a percentage, despite their heavy road expenses, a practice that is unheard of in the annals of bookings.

The situation in the West is such that a number of clubs are dependent upon Chicago, because of the Sunday games that they play at that city, and hence must submit to the gouging tactics of the Foster regime that are just as repulsive to them, but the situation is such that they must accept his terms.

Our club is too big to pay percentage for bookings, this being one of our chief reasons for resigning from the Western Association. His Sunday games in the West do not mean anything to us, as we have received more money for a twilight engagement in Philadelphia, where the players could walk to the park, than a Sunday game in the West, with over a thousand miles railroad fare to cover. Why does Mr. Foster not speak of the mid-week games in Chicago and Detroit, when the clubs play to empty benches? Why does Mr. Foster seek to cover the fact that the By–laws of the Western Association make provision for the visiting club to receive 35 percent of the gross receipts, yet the Eastern clubs (Bacharach Giants and Hilldale), were forced to pay 40 percent to all Western clubs, with the exception of the American Giants, that exacted 50 percent, while the Bacharach Giants and Hilldale received only 35 percent in the West and 5 percent of this was taken by the self-appointed Czar.

Why does Mr. Foster not publish how many clubs in the Western Association operated without placing their $1,000.00? Why does he not make known how many clubs beside Hilldale, including the American Giants, have put up their $1,000.00? These are facts that Mr. Foster will not give out. What kind of Association can run on the level with one meeting a year, one man to make up a schedule for ten clubs and juggle it to suit his own interests, one man heading an organization and holding the strings to its purse?

The owners of Eastern clubs are more than able to take care of the situation in their territory. The Mutual Association of Eastern Colored Baseball Clubs has been organized with the intention of giving the fans better baseball, which the public will decide the coming season. The Western Association could offer us no benefits, no protection, and we followed the only course that a sagacious one would pursue and resigned.

The East is responsible for the success of our club and all others in our organization, the West is beyond our jurisdiction. The Kaiser attempted to swallow the world with results, that are now history. If the self-appointed Czar of the West can digest the baseball situation in his territory, so good. But he surely will have to contend with the after effects of an epicurean who indulges in rarebit suppers if he attempts to include the East in his diet.

Second Conference Of The Mutual Association of Colored Baseball Clubs Held On January 20, 1923

The second important conference of the Mutual Association of Colored Baseball Clubs was held in the Christian Street Y.M.C.A., Philadelphia on Saturday, January 20. The movement to establish a league of the Eastern Colored Baseball Clubs has already met with favor throughout the East, and the full quota of commissioners of the organization were present. These commissioners are: Thomas Jackson of the Bacharach Giants, James J. Keenan of the Lincoln Giants, Charles P. Spedden of the Baltimore Black Sox, Alexander Pompez of the Cuban Stars, Nat C. Strong of the Brooklyn Royal Giants and Edward Bolden of the Hilldale club. Chairman Bolden appointed a committee to draft a well balanced schedule that will be advantageous to all member clubs. The selection of competent, unbiased umpires and officials was also taken up and discussed. These arbitrators of the game will come under the direct jurisdiction of the commissioners and will be vested with authority to run the games without molestation from players and managers of the clubs.

Colored Umpires Desired

An outstanding feature of the conduct of the New league is the fact that it will select its own umpires who will be registered and given full authority to settle all disputes and disagreements. Hence, there will be no walking off the field with the admission fee of hundreds of fans burnt up as has been the case before among some colored clubs seen here.

The league wants to get colored men to officiate in league games if competent men can be found, and Mr. Spedden and Mr. Rossiter intend to send in the name of Charles Cromwell, the local square deal arbiter, who has become famous among local fans for calling them as they is. If colored men cannot be found to fill the roster, then white men will be selected.

Baltimore Afro-American, 16 February 1923

Bolden Challenges Foster To Debate
Suggests Philadelphia Academy of Music So That Fans May Attend
Foster Admits Profits
Foster Declares He [Bolden] Got $22,000 in 1922 Out of Baseball

Rube Foster, head of the Negro National Baseball League in the West is on his way East to answer the challenge of Edward Bolden. He plans to stop in Pittsburgh, Cleveland and New York.

Flaying Rube Foster for keeping Hilldale's $1000.00 membership fee, now that Hilldale has departed the Western National League and joined the Eastern Colored League, Edward Bolden, manager of Hilldale, challenged Foster to a debate here.

Mr. Bolden said: Mr. Foster states he will come East and gladly meet Mr. Strong or myself on the merits and demerits of the two leagues. I accept his challenge. I suggest he take part of the one thousand dollars deposited by Hilldale, rent the Academy of Music in Philadelphia, so that thousands of fans may attend, and give the balance to a fund to help disabled ball players such as Richard Whitworth who was injured in his employee, and is now languishing in Wash. 42, County Hospital, Chicago. Illinois. A fine way to take care of deserving ball players.

Why does Mr. Foster charge fifty percent of his team and only allow the member clubs thirty five percent? Why has Mr. Foster thousands of chairs at Schorling Park, from which he claims visiting clubs cannot share profits? No wonder he has money in several banks. No wonder he wrote a letter to Mr. Strong under date of January 18, 1922, saying I am no four thousand dollar man. I made twenty two thousand dollars out of baseball last year.

How many board fences has he built for his teams to play behind? Why do most of the member clubs of his league have to play in parks where they give from twenty to twenty five percent of gross receipts to white men, and ten percent to Mr. Foster? No wonder four of his clubs have already failed. Mr. Foster may not fail, but he is digging his own grave through his greed for personal gain, unless he becomes fair and gives the teams an even break.

Despite his benevolent reputation, Foster was a constant subject of controversy and criticism. In 1923, the *Chicago Defender* published an anonymous letter from a disgruntled ball player stating that Foster was taking more than his fair share of the gate receipts and at times paying his players less than the contractual rate. The anonymous writer also suggested the powerhouse American Giants did not play up to their full potential, because of clubhouse dissension over low wages. The player further claimed this disharmony caused the team to lose its first league championship since its inception.

Unknown to the accuser, Foster had earlier in the season made arrangements with the black-owned Binga State Bank, founded by Jesse Binga, formerly a barber and Pullman porter, to bankroll his team. On May 4, he sent his captain Bingo DeMoss a letter announcing bonuses for the staff, citing:

> Dear Mr. DeMoss:
>
> I wish that you would have the following men to call by the Binga State Bank, where they will find bank books made out to their credit: Elwood DeMoss, John Beckwith, James Brown, Leroy Grant, James Lyons, Robert L. Williams, Cristobal Torriente, Floyd Gardner, Edward Rile, Louis Woodfolk and Richard Whitworth.
>
> Several of the men on our club deserve something not from present or past actions, but as long as they are good enough to be identified and retain the reputation as members of the American Giants baseball club, I feel that they are due some consideration.
>
> This money that they will find to their credit at the bank is given gratis and will not be charged.
>
> Yours Respectfully,
>
> A.R. Foster[2]

Additionally, other players were given unidentified sums of cash. Included in this group were three regular players fewer than 20 league games, one a sore-arm pitcher and two other outfielders. In review of the salary schedule of the 1923 American Giants roster, the lowest paid player was at $175 a month from May1 to the first of October, five months. And in most cases, over the course of the season, each player had received bonuses of at least $1,100 and upwards to $3,000.[3]

The average salary of a black ball player in the early 1920s was roughly $175 a month — ranging from $75 a month for rookies upwards to $375 a month for team stars, with $1.00 to $1.50 a day for meal money. Meanwhile, major league white players typically received from $300 to $2000 monthly and about $15.00 a day for meals. Competitively, wages for meat packing employees were about $80 a month, and $115 a month for government mail carriers for the period. By comparison, the federal government reported that the average income in 1924 was $1,266 per household or $105.50 per month.[4]

Offering a substantial income for the period and with five years of somewhat consistent play, the league would be incorporated on November 18, 1924 and renamed the Negro National League of Professional Baseball Clubs with a total authorized common stock of $2,500. Each share of stock was worth $25.00. The original board of directors and stockholders included Walter M. Farmer with five shares, Russell Thompson with 15 shares, and Andrew Foster and J.L. Wilkinson with 20 shares apiece. The politically astute Foster named his 20-year old brother Willie Foster as the majority stock holder of the corporation with 40 shares. Moreover, shareholders Willie Foster and Thompson listed, as their address, 3342 Indiana Avenue, conveniently residing in the same apartment complex as Rube.

Although the league was balanced talent-wise, Foster's American Giants captured the NNL title in the initial three years. In 1923, along came the Eastern Colored League (ECL), creating competition for America's top black talent. Their raiding war of players instigated a fight for bragging rights in Black America that inspired both leagues to higher standards for quality play and professional acumen.

With the formation of an established league, Foster had dreams that the winners of his new league play the winners of the white major leagues. The potential financial bonanza of his marketing idea would be unprecedented.

But Foster was not without his critics, who claimed that Foster's main purpose in

Hall of Fame pitcher Willie Foster was Rube's half-brother, after his father remarried. In the 1910 census, six-year old Willie is living with his uncle and aunt, Claude B. and Sarah Stuart in Rodney, Mississippi. The 1910 census says Willie was born in Texas. In 1924, the politically astute Rube named his 20-year-old brother Willie Foster as the majority stock holder of the corporation with 40 shares (NoirTech Research).

forming the league was to restrict Nat Strong, a prominent white Eastern booking agent, from controlling the black teams through lucrative financial arrangements. Black teams rarely received equitable compensation. Nevertheless, Foster, or "Jock" as he was called by players and friends, had a stable supporting crew of baseball executives and league officials. On May 2, 1920, Foster saw his vision become a reality when the Indianapolis ABC's beat Joe Green's Chicago Giants 4–2 before approximately 8,000 fans in Indianapolis in the first NNL game.

The alphabet team, behind the pitching of Ed Rile's seven-hitter, defeated 20-year barnstorming veteran Walter Ball and his Chicago Giants, 4–2. Big time Black baseball had finally arrived upon the national scene.

A dynamic combination of old and new stars for the Giants emerged in the league's early years. Cristobal Torriente, and speedsters Jelly Gardner and Jimmy Lyons, both from Arkansas Baptist College, patrolled the outfield. In December 1920, Lyons was picked up in trade with the Detroit Stars for outfielder Jude Gans, shortstop Orville Riggins and rookie pitcher William Force. Their pitching ace was Dave Brown, a lefty, for whom Foster had posted a $20,000 bond to get him parole from a robbery conviction back in 1919. Sadly, Brown was the league's best left-hander until 1925, when he fled from the Lincoln Giants to avoid a homicide charge. He later appeared in the upper Midwest under the alias "Lefty Wilson."[5] They also signed highly touted George "Tubby" Dixon at catcher, with Army veteran Leroy Grant at first, and the team Captain, Bingo DeMoss, at second. They added quick and reliable 5-foot-5-inch Bobby Williams at short and the dangerous switch-hitter Dave Malarcher, from New Orleans University (now Dillard U), to anchor the hot corner.

The Foster mystique was never more evident than in 1921 against the Indianapolis ABC's. Losing 18–0 after seven innings, Foster gave the bunt sign 11 times in a row. This strategy caused chaos among the ABC's infielders. Cristobal Torriente and Jim Brown each connected for grand slams in the inning, eventually tying the score, 18-all. The tied game was called because of darkness.

In the early years of the league, the Chicago American Giants were a power team. They had formed a team with speed, men that could really hit, superb pitching and excellent catching. Each man was selected for his attitude toward a commitment to domination.

The master was humble in recalling his days as manager in an interview with George E. Mason in his *Chicago Defender* article entitled "Rube Foster Chats about his Career" asked Foster did he have any favorite players. "No!" Foster replied emphatically, "I try to pick my players by their ability to play baseball. Real team work is necessary to make a winner, so every player must be up to the standard or in spite of personal friendship or public opinion, I insist on judging my men by their ability to playing winning ball."

Foster added, "I have been asked on several occasions: 'Where did the colored men learn to play ball?' They went out of curiosity to see them, little dreaming that they were by any means going to see a contest worthy of the name of baseball. To see our men daily defeat the best of their city representation composed of some of the most widely known players of the age, seven regular members being regulars in the past world's series. These people stood for hours and hours, paying enormous prices. If unsuccessful in gaining admission they were satisfied to remain to get a glance at the players who had achieved so much fame in their different league as to be picked to play in a contest for the championship of the world, representing to two best clubs of their race. Is it little wonder they were dumfounded? They never knew or had never seen their pictures in the paper. They had never read their records. They had never heard of men paying princely salaries to other men to train and teach them how to play ball and to see the pride of their nation humbled by men of an inferior race — it is to be marveled at."[6]

With the Negro National League firmly established with a solid constitution, the owners' primary concern was competition from another league. A competing league could entice players to abandon Foster's ship for higher pay. Probably the most important feature of the new constitution was Article 3, describing the league's policy on team jumpers:

> No player which has played with a club in either league for a season or part of a season shall be employed or permitted to play with a club in the same or other league during the season immediately following without a proper release from the club last employing him.

This ruling came in handy for the Cuban Stars of the Western League and prevented their star outfielder Estaban Montalvo from being retained by the Lincoln Giants of the Eastern League. Montalvo had asked for a $25 raise at the beginning of the 1926 season. Manager Agustin Molina refused to accede to his demand and Montalvo elected to remain idle throughout the 1926 season. At the close of the season, the secretary of the team failed to list Montalvo's name among the list of players under contract and the Lincoln team immediately grabbed the unclaimed star. This caused a protest from the Western League and from Commissioner James Keenan of the Eastern League.

At this time, Keenan announced that he would keep Montalvo out of the lineup. He did this with the expectation that the Westerners would send for him. But as time went on and no offer came from the West, the Lincoln owner became restless and decided to put Montalvo back into his lineup since the other club made no effort to secure his services.

Keenan was one of the founders of the Eastern Colored League back in 1922 with his club as an original member. Although he was secretary and treasurer, his association with the other commissioners had been anything but cordial over the past three years. As his team struggled for survival, Nat Strong, the other New York Commissioner, blocked his attempts to get new players.

Keenan and Strong were rival managers in New York City and each fought for territorial bragging rights. Being a part owner of Dexter Park in Brooklyn and booking agent for Farmer's Oval and several other parks in the Metropolitan district, Strong had an advantage over his rival, and his influence was used with the other commissioners against the Lincoln Giants owner.

Strong was even successful in having President Isaac Nutter change a decision he made earlier in the season declaring that the Lincoln Giants had a legal right to Montalvo's services. President Nutter eventually decided to return Montalvo to his Western club, the Cuban Stars.

For unexplored reasons on September 21, 1925, revisions to the NNL charter were filed, increasing the number of directors to nine from five members. Added were Steve Pierce (of Detroit), Joe Rush (Birmingham), R.S. Lewis (Memphis), Richard Kent, Dr. G.B. Keys (St. Louis), Warner Jewell (Indianapolis), and Agustin Molina (Havana), removing Willie Foster, Thompson and Farmer, and retaining Rube Foster (Chicago) and J.L. Wilkinson (Kansas City) as directors. The proposal was accepted on December 5 with the league now being represented by each team owner.

Going from the office to the dugout, Foster was still upset with his ace, Richard Whitworth, a sinker ball pitcher, for signing with Hilldale. Whitworth, along with Bill Francis (3b) and Jess Barbour (of) had signed with Bolden's club in November, 1919, before the initial meeting in February, 1920 to form the NNL. Foster accused Bolden of retroactive player tampering. Bolden countered that the bylaws of the league constitution against transfer of players was not effective until the 1920 season. Foster had also sent Bolden an itemized statement for $188.47, for unpaid advance money to Whitworth. Bolden refused to pay the charges, responding:

> Was not the aforementioned player led to believe that the indebtedness that he had subjected himself to, by accepting advance salary would be taken care of by you, released our club of any obligation.

After the 1922 season, Ed Bolden's team, the Hilldale Club, withdrew its associate membership from the Negro National League. Bolden cited that two of the league teams had refused to make the long, expensive trip to Darby (outside of Philadelphia) and league officials had not included the Hilldale team and other associate members in the league standings.

When Bolden withdrew his team, he demanded the return of his $1,000 good-faith deposit. The by-laws of the league constitution specifically stated that the deposit would be forfeited if a team withdrew. Bolden was furious when he discovered he could not receive his deposit and claimed some team owners had never made deposits. Bolden felt Foster had taken advantage of him, but Foster countered with a claim that Bolden had induced players to join his eastern team and the $1,000 was an advance payment for their contract releases.

Just before the Christmas holidays, on December 14, 1922, Bolden submitted a letter of resignation to the league's board, citing that the amendment for forfeiture of deposits was made when no associated members were present. In part, Bolden wrote,

> The hitch came when President Foster accepted the resignation but chose to juggle the funds, by refusing to return the $1,000 deposit of good faith belonging to the Hilldale Club, basing his ruling on an amendment that had been made to the constitution at a meeting that was not attended by a representative of the Hilldale Club and no copy of said amendment had been exhibited to the officials of the Philadelphia Club prior to the tendering of their resignation.
>
> As an associate member, we did not figure in the league standings, received only two attractions from the West, yet complied with all the requirements of the organization and owe nothing.
>
> We are far from satisfied with the manner in which our money has been withheld and unless the association speedily rescind their ruling, the officials are due for a legal shake down that will "rattle" the bones in the closet and someone will get much more publicity than they desire.

Two days later, on December 16, 1922, Ed Bolden and Nat Strong formed the Mutual Association of Eastern Colored Baseball Clubs, better known as the Eastern Colored League. Bolden was elected as chairman, and James Keenan as secretary-treasurer of the six-team league. The league consisted of the following teams:

> Bolden's Hilldale Club; Nat Strong's Brooklyn Royal Giants; Thomas Jackson's Atlantic City Bacharach Giants; Keenan's New York Lincoln Giants; Alex Pompez's Havana Cuban Stars; and Charles Spedden's Baltimore Black Sox.

Foster was not impressed with the fact that four of the six eastern club owners were white Americans (only Hilldale and the Cuban Stars were black-owned). Historically, many white owners had employed carnival methods to promote the game and enticed players to perform circus-baseball acts to entertain fans. The most prominent of these owners was Nat Strong. He was owner or part-owner of several Eastern powerhouse teams, the Brooklyn Royal Giants, the Philadelphia Giants, the Cuban Giants and the renowned white semi-pro team, the Bushwicks. Foster feared that Strong, a powerful New York booking agent, would economically exploit black baseball and eventually control all of black baseball in the eastern states. His fears were confirmed when black-owned franchises like the Richmond Giants and Harrisburg Giants split from the original body of the league because of their non-affiliation with power broker Strong. On January 13, the *Chicago Defender* questioned the alliance, writing "colored baseball in the East has gone back a decade when Nat Strong offered ball clubs $100 flat [fee] and two 15-cents meals for a Sunday game."

Some of Foster's fears were manifested on opening day of the 1924 season, when Strong refused to play the league's weak sister, the Harrisburg Giants. Later in May, Strong's Royal Giants refused to play Keenan's Lincoln Giants. It appeared that financier Strong only wanted to play teams that attracted large crowds. By unanimous vote from team owners, with Alex Pompez of the Cuban Stars voting by proxy, the Royal Giants were removed from the Eastern circuit. Eventually, because of Strong's influence in scheduling games with major league cities and their parks, the league's top power broker was reluctantly reinstated. Still, his team played only 41 "league" games, while the champion Hilldale Giants played 69 games that season.

The lack of a consistent schedule also plagued the Western League simply because most teams did not own parks. Teams from Chicago, St. Louis, Kansas City and Detroit usually booked games while the local white major or minor league teams were on the road. With the exception of the traveling Cuban Stars, the teams would rent minor and major league parks when available. In addition, intracity, intrastate and interracial rivalries often generated far greater revenue than regular league games. When given a choice between a league game and an exhibition game, teams usually chose the latter. The exhibition games, with the attraction of rivalries and local interest — especially interracial competition — produced larger, better paying crowds. Many team owners insisted that "race" games determined whether they would be able to survive into the next season.

However, Foster's greatest concern with Strong was his position on "contract jumping." For a player, contract jumping mentally freed one of his contractual obligations to the club, similar in effect to today's free agency. This practice of freely going to the highest bidder caused undesirable raiding wars by both leagues. Bolden eventually attracted marquee Western players like Biz Mackey from the Indianapolis ABC's, Clint Thomas and Frank Warfield from the Detroit Stars, and George Carr and Rube Currie from the Kansas City Monarchs to join his Hilldale team. The Eastern league teams were located in areas with significantly larger black populations than the Midwestern and Southern teams. This enabled the league to offer higher salaries to influence stars of the Western circuit, the Negro National League, to make the transition to the Eastern Colored League.

Mrs. Olivia Taylor, who inherited the Indianapolis ABC's team when her husband died in February of 1922, was victimized by the raiding. In 1924, her Indianapolis team was decimated by assault from the Eastern League teams. The lack of players made it impossible for her team to finish the season. They had already lost one of the league's stars, outfielder Oscar Charleston, a future Hall of Famer. Also leaving the ABC's were slugger "Crush" Holloway and submarine pitcher William "Dizzy" Dismukes, who had pitched no-hitters in 1912 and 1915. Although the ABC's were paid comparably well, they were attracted by the glamour and promise of big-time Eastern city baseball.

According to figures from Mrs. Taylor's payroll ledger in 1923, Oscar Charleston was the highest paid Hoosier at $325 a month, followed by:

> "Dizzy" Dismukes (p) at $200; George Shively (of) at $200; Henry Blackman (3b) at $180; Gerard Williams (ss) at $175; Wilson C. Day (2b) at $175; Fred "Tex" Burnett (c) at $160; Crush Holloway (of) at $150; Namon Washington (Utility) at $150; Darltie [Daltie] Cooper (p) at $150; Charles Corbett at $145; and Omer Newsome at $135 per month.

The players often took advantage of the soft-hearted Olivia, by requesting numerous cash advances, causing the Indy club to bathe in red ink. When the 1924 season started, many players sought the free agent market for financial security. Player dissension, team mis-management and an unwillingness of other owners to accept a female owner, forced Mrs. Taylor to dissolve her team. The team had an outstanding debt of $1,556.56 for operating expenses and Mrs. Taylor had a personal debt of $620.25 owed to Rube Foster. These debts, plus an unpaid room and board bill of $275.25 to a Chicago hotel, made it impossible for her to continue operating. The ABC's uniforms were held in lieu of payment by league officials.

In June, Taylor's Indianapolis club was succeeded by the Memphis Red Sox, (who reluctantly inherited the ABC's record of three wins and 19 losses) to complete the season. Because Mrs. Taylor's husband, Charles, had been instrumental in the formation of the league in 1920, the disbandment of the ABC's caused great concern among the Western League owners.

Withstanding the distraction of the once-solid ABC's leaving the league, neither Bolden nor Foster was willing to compromise his position on player jumping, making the likelihood of a World Series between the two leagues remote. Media pressure from such writers as Ollie Womack of the powerful syndicated Associated Negro Press, Frank "Fay" Young of the *Chicago Defender*, Wendell Smith of the *Pittsburgh Courier* and A.D. Williams of the

Indianapolis Ledger (former business manager for the Indy ABC's), bombarded the media with numerous editorials, calling for an end to the standoff.

World Series Arbitration
Chicago Defender, 5 January 1924

"Rube Foster has a Word to say to the Baseball Fans"

For fear that continued criticism appearing in various papers might lead you to form an opinion that would prejudice your patronage to see clubs in the Negro National league perform, would like to have you suspend your criticism against the clubs until you are convinced by proof that they have done better than expected.

League Has Done Well

With less than $12,000 to work with or on, all of this for individual clubs, not one cent was used for promotion. The league has been able to function and has paid out to players $428,000 and for the use of parks $165,000. For railroad fares, sleeping car fares and board, $130,000. This has nothing to do with the incidental expense of each club, advertising, balls, bats, equipment and help at the ball parks, umpires, etc.

There are only 27 Sundays and holidays in the playing season. It is a proven fact that on Sundays only have clubs been able to play at a profit.

Detroit and Chicago have 18 Sundays during the season that can be played at a profit. Kansas City, Indianapolis and St. Louis have 11 Sundays.

The weekdays have on many occasions been a complete loss and many times the clubs after playing have had to dig down in their pockets and pay an additional expense, the gate being too small to even pay expenses. Yet four years ago the combined salaries of the clubs we had West did not amount to $15,000. These are facts and are worthy of your consideration.

There is a demand for a schedule, the things the big leagues are doing and a continual knocking by giving comparison with what big leagues are doing, and why we should do the same things. Probably you have never taken into consideration that men who operate big league clubs are rich men. Their wealth can be counted in millions, that a man cannot own a big league club that has not millions of dollars, that we have only the faith in the weather man and cannot see our way clear to do so. We are willing and know what can be done, but have nothing to do it with. There are of plenty of places for sale on Sheridan Rd., also on the North side; plenty of places for sale in the Loop. You could own them easier than we could afford to operate as big league clubs or minor associations.

Constructive Criticism Is Just

Criticism often makes one stronger and many times prepares one to do better. We have been severely criticized by some, yet the same critics cannot even make a living themselves. When one so criticizes just ask him to show you what he has accomplished, or how many men's welfare he is responsible for. When he answers you, you will have a better chance to see why some people knock. If conditions are wrong I for one welcome a change, but don't break up something unless you have something equal to give in return.

Several articles have appeared in different newspapers that have been very detrimental. They have not been based on any truth, just deliberate lies, yet it was good news and went to the people. Our people mostly believe all they read, but are fast waking up to the belief that reading a thing does not make it correct, and are thinking some for themselves.

I take great pride when I refer to the American Giants. They have done wonders. When there were no other clubs in existence the Giants traveled thousands of miles to play ball. Each trip has brought renown to Chicago. Anyone familiar with such trips knows they are all taken with sure loss of money. Yet we believed a better day was coming and set out for California and the far Northwest to make the Colored players heard of. Our various successes are now history. The Giants have done more to keep friendly feelings between the Negroes and whites than any other institution of its kind in the world. They are the best in baseball from merit and accomplishment.

Color Line Not a Barrier

Mr. Schorling is one of the best and most honorable men I have ever come in contact with. He made it possible for us to enjoy baseball in the city. The park was built exclusively for us, has been used the same way, and is an investment that runs into thousands of dollars. He has allowed to be paid through my hands over $700,000 to Colored people alone. In our 12 years together there has never been a difference of opinion. He has never asked me why I did anything or censured me for any steps taken. He has paid me more than any man before; Has given me I knew did not come from the games, as it was just three years ago we were able to pay for the park.

You can see or better judge the type of man he is when you take into consideration that every game, all contacts and permission for the use of the park, what anyone receives, all help and employees, rental of grounds have been trusted to me and no one has been able to do any business with him until they came to me. This will give you better insight into how some men are made. When he wanted me he said, "I am fixing to invest lots of money in baseball. I want you with me. Name the terms." I told him. He said: "If that's what you want you must be worth it." That was our last business talk. This was 12 years ago.

Appreciating the many favors and patronage we have been accorded by the fans everywhere, especially at Chicago, I want you not to worry over rumors concerning the club. We will make efforts to continue. We have seen the stars leave here. Some criticized me for sending many of the best players in the world away, yet you had confidence enough to await developments, and have seen developed the greatest players in the country. None of these players made the American Giants. It is an institution and will live. Its resources can be depended on.

Men sometimes outlive their usefulness. They sometimes do things that are detrimental to the best interests of the club. Players leaving here have done this, hence the change. All players who have been asked to remain or tendered contract has signed. Leave the rest to us.

The September 6, 1924, issue of the *Chicago Defender* printed an undated letter from J.L. Wilkinson's business manager and secretary, Quincy J. Gilmore, pleading:

There has been considerable agitation on the part of the baseball fans throughout the country for a series of games to determine the Negro championship of the world between the winners of the pennant in the National Negro Baseball League and the Eastern League.

It seems that there has been a general hesitancy on the part of the management of the two prospective winners to issue a challenge for such a series. There seems to be a disagreement between the owners of both leagues which I hope for the benefit of the game and the fans in general, will not interfere with such an event.

On behalf of the Kansas City Monarchs, winners of the 1923 pennant, and the prospective winner of the 1924 pennant of the National Negro League, I herby issue a challenge to the winner of the Eastern League pennant for a series of games to determine the Negro world's championship.

This series to be arranged by a commission representing both leagues and to be carried out under the same plans as the world's series between the National and American leagues.

Respectfully, Q. J. Gilmore, Secretary.

Ironically, it was Judge Kenesaw Mountain Landis, major league baseball's embattled commissioner, who was asked to adjudicate this personal feud. Young Landis, born in Millville, Ohio, grew up in Logansport, Indiana. After failing an Algebra course he dropped out of high school. He later taught himself dictation to secure a job as a courtroom reporter. He eventually earned his diploma in night school and later received his law degree from the Union Law School of Chicago. A social illiterate, the tobacco-chewing, inarticulate, foul-mouthed Landis never went to college.

In 1905, he had been appointed a federal judge in Illinois by President Theodore Roosevelt. Later, he became nationally known for forcing millionaire John D. Rockefeller to testify in the much publicized case against his Standard Oil Company. Decidedly, Landis smacked the Rock with an unprecedented fine of over $29 million dollars. Rockefeller never paid the fine as he won the case on appeal.

The ultra-conservative Judge Landis also had exposure to baseball. In 1914, he had presided over the monopoly suit against the Major Leagues brought by the newly formed Federal League. After several years of appeals and months of deliberation, the case was settled out of court.

With damage to the image of America's national pastime brought on by the infamous

Black Sox Scandal in the 1919 World Series, Landis was pressured to accept a job as baseball commissioner. His no-nonsense approach to matters made him an ideal candidate. His salary rose from $7,500 as a judge to $50,000 as baseball commissioner.

As commissioner, Landis was often portrayed as an egotistical monarch with authoritative influence. He was often accused of a restricted outlook on America's game, particularly in matters of race relations. He had long been a proponent of segregated baseball, issuing a decree in 1921 to prevent white major league teams from competing against any black barnstorming teams in the postseason, especially the Babe Ruth All-Stars. Players rallied in support of the Bambino, threatening to form a union if not reinstated. Regardless, Ruth and Meusel continued to play against teams—predominantly black teams like Oscar Charleston's Colored All-Stars, in the Southern California League during the Spring of 1922—Landis eventually suspended the Yankees' bad boys, Babe Ruth and Bob Meusel (the second leading hitter on the team), and Wild Bill Piercy (a third-string pitcher), for 39 days, or until May 20 of the 1922 season, for not adhering to his dictum. Piercy would start the season with the Boston Red Sox.

His policies were often accepted, if not applauded by the baseball nation. While writers often viewed Landis as harsh and narrow minded, he was generally popular because of his steadfast efforts to maintain the integrity of the game that was seriously questioned during the World Series scandal. His rule became nearly absolute with the 1922 Supreme Court decision, *Federal Baseball Club of Baltimore, Inc. v. National League of Professional Baseball Clubs et. Al,* that exempted the major league cartel from anti-trust legislation.

Now the omnipotent Landis, in an unofficial capacity, was being asked by Bolden and Foster to arbitrate the remaining indecisions surrounding the first Colored World Series. Judge Landis agreed to draft an agreement similar to ones by the American and National Leagues. In substance, the agreement would decide all questions related to future drafts, contracts, players, salaries, post-season games and any protest filed by teams. In response to Landis' acceptance of the appointment, Rube Foster sent a telegram on September 2, 1924 to the *Pittsburgh Courier* newspaper, stating in part:

> Delighted at opportunity for peace ... Judge Landis will arbitrate each complexing situation, decide its merits, and draft an agreement between the leagues and pledge to accept whatever his decision will be, or will agree on lines agreeable through compromise between the leagues...
>
> Judge Landis sees no reason why peace should not be restored, for the good of the game, and sees no reason why the winners in Negro baseball World's Series should not meet winners in regular World's Series if the public demands same.
>
> Western fans want to see Hilldale and Kansas City meet this year. The Western League is willing to let the East keep contract jumpers now held providing some agreement of protection to both leagues can be signed for the future. Landis is willing to draw up agreements the same as protects the National and American Leagues.

The World Series participants appeared to be the Kansas City Monarchs, who would clinch the pennant on September 13, against Foster's Giants, and Bolden's Hilldale club, who had clinched the pennant on August 28.

The compromise agreement by outside arbitrator Landis was a major step in reconciling the differences between Foster and Bolden. The two leagues coming under the same umbrella of regulations meant the club owners had the right to develop men and to keep them under contract during the entire year. It also prevented the players from borrowing money on the strength of their contacts and then jumping to another league.

An amendment to Landis' constitution by the Negro National League stated additional rules:

While the public clamored for a World Series between the Negro National League and the Eastern Colored League, narcissistic league presidents Foster and Bolden fought over an entry deposit. Writers bombarded the newspapers with numerous editorials, calling for an end to the standoff (*Philadelphia Tribune* 6 September 1924).

1) To allow all players who have jumped contracts to remain in the Eastern League.
2) To respect and draw an agreement to respect contracts between players and clubs.
3) That each league who has contract jumpers to see that the money each player owes an owner is paid to that owner.[7]

On September 6, 1924, Edward Bolden responded to the Landis decisions in an open letter to the *Pittsburgh Courier* and the *Philadelphia Tribune*, stating in part:

> If the proposed World Series between colored clubs of the East and West does not materialize in 1924, you may put it down that it will not be due to any obstacle placed in the way by me...
>
> The player question, however, was not the seat of the trouble between the Hilldale Club and the Negro National League, but the fact that our deposit of good faith to the amount of One Thousand Dollars had been retained by the Western body, since we resigned from the Western League in 1922.
>
> This matter, of course did not set well with our organization and hitherto we were not in any mood to compromise. However, the matter, when compared to public opinion, is very trivial and I personally am far removed from standing in the way of popular sentiment. If any club in the Eastern Circuit has an axe to grind it is ours.
>
> You may put it down that I am waiting on the actions of our Commission and the advance from the West. The East will concede to the wishes of the fans.

With neither Bolden nor Foster willing to tarnish their image with the fans and the media, they were overcome with a spasm of pride and preceded to organize the first Colored World Series.

Louisianan Dave Malarcher succeeded Foster as boss in 1926 and quickly established himself as one of the best strategists in the game. Nicknamed "Gentleman Dave" because of his scholarly and soft-spoken manner, Malarcher won the Colored World Series in 1926, beating the Bacharach Giants.

Malarcher reflected on the early years with Foster in an interview with author John Holway:

> If you haven't got intelligence enough to fit into this play, you can't play here. That's all there was to it. It isn't generally known, but Rube was so superior in his knowledge of baseball that from 1920 to 1922, we were so far out in front of the league by July, they had to break the season up into two halves so there would be interest in the league the second half.

One of Foster's protégés, George Sweatt, while living in Chicago, recalled Foster's genius:

> Every time Rube Foster would come to Kansas City, he'd draw crowds down there. He liked to tell stories about what he was going to do to the Monarchs. He'd just brag and get crows. They'd have to have the police come so the traffic could move. He possessed shrewd sportsmanship. Shucks the Giants-Monarchs games were always sellouts.[8]

In a Dave Malarcher interview with author Charles Whitehead, Foster's managerial successor recalled the memory of this genius with an example. Jimmy Lyons might say, "Jock, bring me pair of $20.00 spikes, Spauldings. Size 10–D." Jelly [Gardner] would ask for, "jockey strap, size 30." The Cuban would say, "Me need new socks, Jock." Then Bingo [DeMoss] might say, "A new black glove," and so on. Rube Foster had neither pen nor pad, but when he returned, he had exactly what had been requested. "Not only was his mind imaginative and creative," Malarcher added, "it was photographic as well." Foster's "rain man" mentality was like a Rubik cube; complex, colorful and incredibly systematic. Foster had an incredible memory that recalled every instance of a game with facts that escaped the common man.

We are the ship, all else the sea was the league's mantra. With brains and influence, Rolodex Rube seemed invincible. In 1926, the czar-like dictator, with the booming baritone voice, succumbed to mental illness and was institutionalized in Kankakee, Illinois. Unable to float their boat, the entire league became soaked with more seepage than the Titanic. Like a ship without a sail, or a compass without a needle, the league was lost at sea. The league struggled without their Foster's life jacket — playing its last World Series in 1927 — along with several teams fading from existence.

Again, Malarcher spoke highly of his mentor in an interview with Charles Whitehead, author of *A Man and His Diamonds:*

> Rube was stern, but yet still fair. He was a religious man. He had a great memory. I had the two greatest teachers, Rube Foster and C.I. Taylor, the two greatest men ever to manage. I learned from C.I. how to put a ball club in condition. And I learned from Rube how to put them in condition and then how to direct them, which makes me know that Rube was the greater of the two. Rube was a master, he was a master. After I became manager I used to win so many ball games the fans would say to me, "You're a greater manager than Rube." You know what I said? "I'm just doing what the master taught me."[9]

Evidence was seen when the American Giants won pennants in the league's first three years of existence before the Kansas City Monarchs took control in 1923 and repeated as champions in 1924 and 1925.

The 1924 season was a landmark year, for the leagues played for the first official championship of black baseball. Foster's team lost out to the Kansas City Monarchs for the NNL title as the Monarchs went on to defeat the Hilldale Club of the ECL in a thrilling ten-game series, with the final game played on Foster's home turf in Chicago. The ten-games series was the longest on record in modern history. The first colored World Series was arguably the most dramatic, as well, as each team reeled off three wins in a row, four games were decided by a single run, and five games were won in the final inning.

Baltimore Afro-American, 22 November 1924

Rube Foster Reviews the World Series and Tells A Little Baseball History

It is impossible to enjoy a work of art without being mindful of the artist whose skill brought the treasure into existence. To be grateful for a gift without considering the philanthropist is vain. Likewise, people cannot look upon the development of Negro baseball without a genuine appreciation of the man whose ability and courage are mostly responsible for that advance.

This series was concrete evidence of the worth of a proposal which opens so many opportunities to Negro youths with brains and mechanical perfection.

The man, of course, is Andrew Rube Foster, of Chicago, the Daddy of Negro Organized Baseball. Feeling that our readers would like to know the reactions from the series, we wired Mr. Foster for his opinions in that and other matters. Regarding the series he says:

High Class Ball

Exclusive of the first two games at Philadelphia, I saw eight of the best played games of ball I have ever witnessed. One familiar with the struggle of the contesting players cannot be expected to agree with some who paid to witness the battles. I speak with an intimate knowledge of inside conditions.

I have seen a majority of all World Series games played and never did any of them have anything on our colored series. Lapse of memory, failure of stars to deliver when everyone thought they would their failure, and the player of whom nothing was expected saved the day by a great hit, a sensational stop, an unexpected steal, is what makes baseball the game it is, and this series electrified one by such incidents.

Hilldale Outfield Best

Hilldale had the most wonderful outfield I have ever seen. There may be men who can play as much outfield as these, but for 10 days I saw in them what I have never seen in any outfield playing ball. They worked in unison. If a catch had to be made with the bases full, whether standing on their ears, sliding for it, or going far back and never turning the second time, they did it time and time again. During the entire series of games the Hilldale outfield did not even fumble a ball and time after time they played hits to angles which should have been good for two bases.

[Outfielders were Clint Thomas, Otto Briggs and George "Dibo" Johnson].

Winters Shines

The pitching of [Nip] Winters, day after day was one of the greatest exhibitions I have ever witnessed.

Kansas City cannot be denied the honor of having a worthy champion. They won the series fairly and had a chance to make their victory more conclusive, but did not take full advantage of their opportunities. At times their errors of omission, which are the most damaging things to a club, might have beaten them.

[Author's note: The most valuable player in the series was perhaps Winters for his exceptionally fine pitching performance. He started and completed four games, winning three, with his only loss coming in Game seven, which went 12 innings. He struck out 21 batters in 38 2/3 innings, while compiling a diminutive ERA of 1.16.]

Painful to the west was the sign of this wonderful bunch of clouters feeding out of the hands of Hilldale's great hurlers. Some thought it was inferior pitching which had made the club's reputation as hitters during the regular session.

Mendez Hero

At last came the day of days, the series was tied up. The battle of the afternoon would decide the winner. K.C.'s pitching staff was a twisted mass of wreckage, ready for the scrap heap. Jose Mendez, considered too old and decrepit to hurl ten games a year, came to me and said, "I am going to pitch today."

I looked at the nervy Cuban and replied, "For the first time during the series you are doing the thing I think best. I would rather see you lose it, if lose it you must, than any other pitcher win it."

Mendez pitched with all the years of experience which were his. He had the Hilldale club believing each inning that they would get him in the next and their anxiety to do it instead of waiting him out beat them. Believe me. I am proud of that bird.

[Author's note: Mendez faced 30 batters in the title contest and yielded three singles and one walk, with no runner reaching second base in a 5–0 Monarch's win.]

[Author's note: Statistically, Hilldale scored more runs, had more hits, more RBIs, and received more walks. They hit for a higher average and made fewer errors in the field. Their pitching staff had a lower ERA, gave up fewer hits per inning, struck out more batters, and walked fewer hitters, but still lost the series. The deciding factor may have been that Hilldale abandoned 86 men on the bases while the Kansas City Monarchs had the home field advantage in the last six games.]

A Truthful Review of Baseball

So much has been said as to what should be done in baseball, so much from men who know nothing of baseball or business, but are hardly responsible for their shortcomings, yet they have a multitude that join them in destroying what little good anyone accomplishes.

I am partial to baseball, have followed it from a child, have never been identified with any other business but baseball, rode freight trains; have been barred away from homes on account of it, as baseball and those who played it were considered by Colored as low and ungentlemanly.

I left school at the eighth [sixth] grade to try and make a living at baseball. Although I have seen some bitter, heart breaking ventures in it, have never even during the war stopped. I have found one thing that gives me more pleasure than anything else. Baseball allowed me to make many change their minds. I have as friends from president to priests and some of the most influential men in all walks of life. They all know I am still fooling with baseball.

It is just as much an honor to meet the ball player, as for the ball player to meet any man. I have wanted all ball players to do the same. They are daily changing. I have paid men more to play ball, who could not read or write than many college professors, and have seen players draw more money for their skill, than men in any other line of endeavor paid them by white or black.

I am going to force the organization, and turn things over, so all will be the beneficiaries.

In 1920, before the forming of the Negro National league, there were fixed salaried Colored clubs in the United States: Hilldale, [New York] Lincoln Giants, [Brooklyn] Royal Giants, [Atlantic City] Bacharach Giants, American Giants. The entire profession at this time drew less than $50,000 for all of them. National league organized 1920 leaving four clubs East one West American Giants. I organized A B C's Detroit St. Louis, Cuban Stars, Dayton Marcos, Kansas City, Chicago Giants and wrecked playing strength of the then powerful American Giants to equalize clubs.

1920 eight clubs 80 per cent gross receipts received	$ 206,520.90
1921 eight clubs 80 per cent gross receipts received	$ 251,724.97
1922 eight clubs 80 per cent gross receipts received	$ 428,291.94
1923 eight clubs 80 per cent gross receipts received	*$ 193,669.17*
Total receipts first four years	$1,080,206.98

The players have been paid in the four years $192,000 by the eight clubs. This does not include the season of 1924.

The East from all reports has done as well. The most ridiculous part of this is we have not the men capable of handling such a situation. Even the past season of the 14 clubs, 10 of them lost money. All clubs in the West lost money. We need business men and some strong enough to place baseball on a basis where economics are known to mean something.

Railroad fares have doubled, salaries doubled everything yet not a raise in prices, less attendance and strong clubs suffering by the failure of the weaker ones. Rain this year has about brought the men to their senses. One man had not enough money as a league would have him to do as a league would have him to do. It's too big a loss when you catch bad weather. All of this has been accomplished in the West. It was done in 27 days of the year, the week day games have not paid the expense of operation. Here is a real money making proposition. Based on business principles it can be made a wonderful thing. The owners and players are not getting results from such methods. The men who have been in baseball a long time are still here. Those who have fallen which are many did so because they tried to improve on a system that was not practicable.

Men can own ball clubs and be successful if they would only hire some brains to run their clubs.

The Monarchs repeated as league champions in 1925, before yielding starboard control to Foster's American Giants in 1926 and 1927, now managed by Foster's protégé, Gentleman Dave Malarcher.

The Giants got their revenge in the 1926 playoffs, beating the Monarchs 5 games to 4. On the final day of the playoffs, Foster's half-brother, Willie, won both games of a double-header. He defeated the Monarchs' pitching master and manager, Bullet Rogan, twice, 1–0 and 5–0. Iron men Rogan and Foster pitched complete games in the twin bill, a first in playoff history.

Willie Foster spoke greatly of brother Rube in an interview with historian Charles Whitehead:

Rube should have been the first Negro into the Hall of Fame. He organized the Negro Leagues and some say he revolutionized the game. He should be credited with the catcher running down to back up the first base on a hit ball. Pitchers throwing sliders, drop balls, or drag bunting? Rube had a great personality and would treat you fair. He wouldn't cuss anybody and paid your salary on time. You had to respect the man, and love the man. A young man would be glad to come on the team for $175 a month. Rube Foster was a legend. He was a great man.[10]

After seeing José Mendez beat aces Christy Mathewson and Nap Rucker in a 1908 series, New York Giant's manager John McGraw boasted, "I have just seen the greatest pitcher of all time." Mendez often sported a red sweater, a gift from McGraw (*Washington Post* 21 January 1912).

Chicago Defender, 29 November 1924

"Rube" Foster's Timely Talks on Baseball

Answering another question by this paper as to the past and future of our national game, Rube Foster, Daddy of Negro Organized Baseball wired:

"We have played the series, met the demand of the public, and when the two leagues meet in Chicago next month much hard work must be done. It is a tough job and I believe we need more wisdom than that possessed by both leagues. Much has been said as to what should be done in baseball by those who have no experience in either baseball or business. They are hardly responsible for their shortcomings yet a multitude joins them in trying to destroy what little good we have tried to accomplish.

The skeptic will criticize as long as there is a chance to pick a flaw. The chronic knocker who likes to break images because he cannot build them, will forever have a pet peeve. But people who know the general run of fans and live, red-blooded folks who like to see a good job done, will appreciate more and more the mutual benefit accruing to the whole race from baseball. Our part in this program is to give it our healthy patronage. Remember that Negro baseball is helping so many hundreds of our boys in a material way that we ourselves must grow bigger and more worthwhile along with its continued success.

I am partial to baseball, have followed it since a child and have never been identified with any other business. I have ridden freight trains, have been barred from certain homes on account of baseball and those who played it, have been considered by colored folk as low and ungentlemanly. I left school in the six grade to try to make a living at the game I loved so well.

[Author's Note: Foster attended the lab school at Tillotson [now Huston-Tillotson] College in Austin, Texas. Historically black colleges, like Tillotson, usually offered educational opportunities for black children segregated from white-only schools. The "separate but equal" doctrine put forth by the 1896 Supreme Court decision of Plessy v. Ferguson was standard dogma for the period, leaving some black youths with few institutional options. The school's office of registrar reported in a letter dated July 11, 1989, to the author, that Foster attended the sixth grade in 1896/97 (listed as Andrew A. Foster) and 1897/98 (listed as Andrew O. Foster), about the time he joined the Austin Reds, the college's baseball team. Today, Huston-Tillotson is a member of the United Methodist-United Church of Christ Affiliated College, the same religious body that christened Rev. Andrew Foster.]

I have seen a bitter, heart-breaking time in it and I have never stopped, even during the war. I have found one thing that gives me more pleasure than anything else. Baseball allowed me to make many change their minds. I have as friends from presidents to priests and some of the most influential men in the all walks of life."

They all know I am still fooling with baseball. It's just as much an honor to meet the ball player as for the ball player to meet the civilian. I have paid men who could not read or write more money to play baseball than some college professors receive. I have seen men draw more for their skill in baseball than men in any other endeavor, black or white.

These major conflicts and Foster's perennial role as a manager, owner, and general manager of the Chicago American Giants, only compounded problems. Meanwhile, Foster's responsibilities also included league president and treasurer, resolving player contract disputes and futile attempts to save financially troubled clubs. The lack of team-owned ballparks and an inconsistent scheduling of playing dates proved to be too demanding for this baseball genius.

Chicago Defender, 27 December 1924

Foster Gives Reasons for Resigning

Foster's letter of resignation was addressed to the various club owners and read:

This letter will serve notice upon you that I no longer care to officiate as president of your league.

The American Giants will not affiliate with any organization that you care to function. I have decided it is best for me to go along lines that are more agreeable to me, and will give greater satisfaction.

I wish to have you complete all accounts, so that I can make a complete statement of my regime in office.

It has been difficult for me to get along with you, and you have done everything to handicap me. As long as I thought these things were done because you did not understand, I was content to go ahead and do the best I could. Your actions this season have so discouraged me I have many times asked myself the question, "Why should I continue to fool with a set of men who have neither reason or understanding?"

It is evident to me that with such co-operation I could not do any good, and would prefer taking my chances with your opposition, than with the co-operation I have received from you.

I have many times gone against the ideal of practical common sense in order to try and appease some of the men. You have not given me any support; you have been too weak in manhood to co-operate or help me, when you knew I was doing the best it was possible to do.

I am organizing along lines that I believe will give me more peace of mind and a better financial backing than can possibly be had in continuing with the majority of club owners of our organization. Get these reports paid up, and I am preparing a public statement as to why I am taking the steps I have decided to take, and will give a complete history of the work done and its failure, the cause of such, so there will be no misunderstanding as to my efforts on the decision I have made.

I have never taken an order or suggestion in my life. I was a success long before any of you men came into the business. I do not need you to decide my future. I do not want to decide yours.

Respectfully yours,
Andrew R. Foster
Pres. N.A.C.P.B.B Co. [National Association of Colored Professional Base Ball]

Chicago Defender, 27 December 1924

Rube Foster Resigns as League Head
N.N. League Disbanded — Blount Claims He was systematically Robbed by Booking System

Chicago, Ill., December 24 — What is perhaps the biggest baseball scandal of all times broke here last week with the announcement that Andrew "Rube" Foster had tendered his resignation as head of the Negro National League, and that the organization had automatically disbanded, with the withdrawal of the deposits of the different clubs, which is in reality the only binding cord.

Tenny Blount, former owner of the Detroit Stars, has exposed an alleged hotbed of graft and corruption. Blount writes, "I shall attempt to tell you how and why 13 ball clubs have failed or been forced to quit the Negro National League. I feel that I owe it to my many friends to explain my reasons for leaving the league. I shall tell them of the things I was compelled to put up with for six years and let them decide for themselves— it is a wonder how I put up with it for such a long time.

By J. Tenny Blount

First, let me say here I am not ungrateful and am duly mindful of the things Mr. Foster did for me, although I admit I would not have permitted him to do them had I known his real motive.

It was in 1919 when Foster found himself obligated to enough baseball players to form three clubs, due to the fact that the war had just released them and they came to Chicago seeking employment. I agreed to take some of the players and start a ball club in Detroit. You will remember there was only two clubs in the West that year, Detroit and Chicago. I had honor and character and believed most of the men possessed the same. Crookedness of heart had never crossed my mind as being the by-word of some individuals, but I know that same exists now. For this reason I trusted Foster and allowed him to draw up an agreement between himself and I that called for 10 percent of the gross receipts of all games played by my club as his share for booking.

Leases Mack Park

Foster's first crookedness came to my attention when we set out to lease Mack Park from John Roesink, the owner. In this agreement to which Foster was so careful to place his signature to, it was plainly stated that Rube Foster was co-partner in the lease, but also said that Foster would assume no responsibility for maintaining the lease and games at the park except through and by the sanction of the Foster Booking Agency. For this consideration the Foster Agency was to receive 10 percent as Mr. Foster's share. For rental of the park I was to pay 20 percent of the gross, leaving only 70 percent of the gross to pay all expenses from and divide with the other club.

For awhile I went along, losing money because the weather had been decidedly against me, almost every Sunday it rained. I then began figuring how I could earn some money to offset heavy expenses and the thought struck me that I might stage some small prize fights at the park when not playing baseball. After the first fight, Foster wrote me asking for his 10 percent of the gross receipts, to which I replied, they are small, but will go at least a short way toward helping me meet the expenses that you are helping to place upon my by demanding a big percentage for booking. Foster replied, "Unless you send me the 10 percent I shall cancel all games at your park for the season and further will prohibit you from booking any."

My next communication from Foster was in regards to a game to be played in Detroit by the Chicago club. He wanted the game played in Navin Field [later named Briggs Stadium from 1938–1960 after owner Walter Briggs and later Tiger Stadium, when John Fetzer took majority ownership in 1961], the home of the Detroit club [Tigers]. I pointed out to him that the rental on the park would be 25 percent of the gross and that besides I would have to pay Roesink the 25 percent for Mack Park to protect my lease. It meant I must give away a total of 50 percent of the gross receipts before figuring on my expenses, after which the American Giants must have 40 percent exclusive of the 5 percent for booking the game. It meant the game would have netted me absolutely nothing and the expenses of my ball players must be met. I made attempt after attempt to show him how utterly impossible this was, but Rube could see only the greater 10 percent of the gross, notwithstanding the fact that I must stand double expenses. His argument was based on the belief that more fans would see the game at the White Park. It was a blow to me, but I again consented after his usual threat to stop booking attractions to my park.

House of David Comes

A short time later the House of David, best attraction to come to Detroit, was scheduled to play a game at my park on Sunday and in submitting the contract they stated plainly that no fee for booking the game would be allowed. I sent this contract to Foster, whose reply was: "Unless I receive my fee for booking, the game must be cancelled." This was Friday of the week before the game, so what was I to do? With Foster demanding the fee and the House of David declaring they would not pay it. However, the game was played and I sent him my 5 percent, but the House of David did not, so he wrote me: "Unless I receive check for the House of David game I shall cancel all games at the park for the season." After much correspondence the House of David's secretary sent Foster the check, declaring, "Never again!"

Much has been said about Foster collecting a percentage of the receipts from clubs in this league, but few know the real facts. For every game played by clubs in the Negro National League Rube Foster receives 10 percent of the gross. That is if I play a series with Kansas City I must send him 5 percent making a total of 10 percent. It is hardly conceivable that the games played by Mrs. Taylor's A.B.C. club along with the close of her affiliations with the league netted Foster 10 percent of the net for the games were always a losing proposition and a matter of getting railroad fare and meals for her club.

Many times Birmingham and other good drawing attractions have been compelled to take long jumps to Detroit and other cities simply because it meant a larger gross and percentage for Foster. A six thousand gate with an expense of five thousand meant more to Foster than a three thousand gate with a one thousand expense. He never considers the expense, it is always that 10 percent of the gross that is coming to him.

Going to Chicago

Many wondered why I did not come to Chicago early in the past season. It was imbedded in my mind that what's fair for the goose is equally fair for the gander. You see when Rube comes to Detroit he takes besides his 5 percent for booking, 40 percent of the gross on all tickets sold. But when you go into Chicago he only allows you 35 percent of the gross. And besides he takes off 10 percent for war tax, figuring your percentage on a 65 cent admission, while other parks he takes of a percentage of 67 cents, allowing only 8 cents for war tax, which is the correct figure. It seem rather small, but when you figure that Foster gets 2 cents on every admission in his own ball yard without anything being taken from it for the government or the other clubs, it is a swell lift toward buying those expensive cars the old boy has.

It was in September that I informed Foster that I was through and had disbanded my ball club. But several days later I received a shipment of 12 dozen balls with a bill for $120. I ask Foster to take them back, as I had already informed him that I was through, but he would not do so. It was plain to me why he wouldn't, inasmuch as he gets a percentage on all balls bought from the company, so for a measly rake-off he forced to me to take 12 dozen balls after I had disbanded my club. Of course, my $1000 deposit was up with him and I was forced to pay the bill.

But the real break came in Chicago the past week when I approached him about the statement that he was going to break me. His reply was "Well, anything I say I'll do, I come pretty darned close to doing." But I said, "You won't break me for I have already quit your league on September 26."

As the Blount allegations of Foster's ultimatum to control the Detroit franchise made waves throughout the black press, fans wondered about the chances of ever having another productive season. With so much internal turmoil among the owners they met in Chicago, at 3435 South Indiana (one block south of Foster's home at 3342 S. Indiana), on December 4–6 (Thursday-Saturday) to assess damage control and make future plans. At the top of the meeting agenda was not Blount's claims about Foster's threats to cancel his games unless he paid the contracted booking fees at Mack Park, but Blount's treatment of his players the last two weeks of the season.

On September 16, two weeks before the seasons ended, Blount called his players into the office and told them he was resigning as an officer of the league. The players would be allowed to play some barnstorming games, if they paid Blount one dollar each to rent the uniforms.[11] He explained the players had agreed to the co-op plan, but league officials demanded that he give the Detroit Stars the two weeks of salary as originally contracted.

Before league officials would vote that Saturday, Blount returned to Detroit on Friday, leaving Dr. George B. Keys of St. Louis with his proxy. Other representatives included Birmingham, American Giants, Cleveland, and Kansas City, with the Cuban Stars voting by proxy. The Memphis club was absent because owner R.S. Lewis had an $800 debt and was not permitted to attend or vote. Blount was voted out as league vice-president and replaced by Dr. Keys. The directors also issued a decree that Blount must pay the players by January 1, or present signed affidavits by each player stating they agreed to the play the final two weeks of the season without pay, relieving Blount of any payment obligations.

Before Blount escaped to Detroit, Foster challenged the directors to accept his resignation. He demanded that all indebtedness due him be settled. Foster returned the $1,000 deposits to each franchise, minus any outstanding debt. He then made a motion to make Dr. Keys the chairman of the audit committee to examine his books. The motion died as no one seconded it, included Blount. Foster was re-elected president of the NNL by acclamation.[12]

Subsequently, Foster provided a typed statement entitled, "Donations from Foster for the welfare and operation of the National Negro League" which listed the following expenditures:

Toledo and Milwaukee	$ 906.56
Players	3,061.00
Commission	2,164.00
Columbus, Ohio	5,258.00
League Expenses	3,216.00
Indy ABC's	1,556.00
Players Stranded	450.00
Owners	*7,550.00*
Total	$24,612.06

"Reports, counter-reports and charges do not disturb me," Foster claimed. "I know the facts and have the figures." He also shared his 20-hour workdays and paid expenses for all telegrams, long distance phone calls, office rental and clerical help.[13]

Additionally, Foster claimed Blount refused to play the league-financed and last place Cleveland Browns because of the typical poor gate receipts. Foster issued his order of "no-show, no dough" and requested Blount's resignation. In Blount's absence, Foster demanded the league move forward so at the February 2 directors' meeting at the Pine Street YMCA in St. Louis, the Detroit franchise was taken over by Steve Pierce, who had owned the Pierce Giants in Oakland, California.[14]

Ten days later, league officers met again in St. Louis and issued the following decree in support of Foster:

> We, the undersigned, owners of clubs, members of the Negro National League, Incorporated, composed of the following clubs and cities: Birmingham, St. Louis, Kansas City, Memphis, Chicago, Indianapolis, Detroit and the Cuban Stars, have examined the books, accounts and records of the said Negro National League, Inc., which have been under the direct supervision of the president since the organization of the leagues, and find everything in good order and that every act has been for the best interest of the league — the owners, collectively and individually, and that we do

hereby go on record as endorsing and sustaining the records of the league and the handling of same.

Therefore, as said owners are here and pledge our whole-hearted support to the president, Mr. A.R. Foster in his efforts to build a bigger and better Negro National League. We further pledge our support to the any movement that has for its purpose the advancement of the game, the players and the interests in general for which we have banded ourselves together to obtain better baseball and baseball conditions among that portion of the American citizenry know as the Negro.

Signed: Joe Rush, Dr. G.B. Key, J.L. Wilkinson, R.W. Kent, G.I. Hutchinson, R.S. Lewis.[15]

In addition to the written endorsement of Foster, league officials added $4,000 to their $1,000 franchise fee to insure "the living up to league rules and regulations in order that there will be slight chance for a recurrence of the Detroit case by any member of the league."[16] They also voted to play a split schedule for the 1925 season, with each winner of the half seasons to have a playoff series to determine the league champion and meet the Eastern Colored League champion (ECL).

The Kansas City Monarchs won the first half of the season with 31–12 record, and the St. Louis Stars won the second game with a 38–12 record. They met in a seven-game series with the Monarchs prevailing in four games to face the Hilldale Club of the ECL. Note, divisional play in Major League baseball would not happen until 1969, some 44 years later.

On February 11, 1926, Foster met with Ban Johnson, president of the American League, and John McGraw, manager of the New York Giants, both of whom were long-time acquaintances. Over the years, there has been much speculation as to what occurred in this meeting. At the time, rumors circulated that the mental burden of trying to convince white baseball officials that the Negro Leagues were a quality product, worthy of integration into the big leagues, had overcome Foster. It's believed that the meeting was the last time Foster served in an official baseball capacity.

9th Inning. The Vision Fades, 1926–1930

Earlier, in May of 1925, Foster had narrowly escaped carbon monoxide poisoning while staying at the Eubanks Boarding House in Indianapolis. Foster was found unconscious in the bathtub by a team member delivering an important telegram. He had accidentally inhaled fumes from a leaking gas pipe from the hot water heater. Foster was immediately taken to Battles Sanitarium and listed in serious condition. After a week's stay, Foster was released.

Chicago Defender, 6 June 1925

Gas Nearly Kills Andrew Rube Foster

Andrew Rube Foster, 4131 Michigan Ave., narrowly escaped death by asphyxiation May 26 in Indianapolis, Ind., when a leaking gas hose in the bath room of Mrs. Frieda Eubanks, 706 N. West St., caused the baseball magnate to be overcome. The near tragedy occurred about 6 o'clock in the morning when Mr. Foster entered the room to take his bath.

When the ball players of the American Giants failed to see their leader up and around at 10 o'clock they became alarmed and went to his room, thinking that he was ill. Gaining no response they pushed the door open only to find the room vacant and clothes laid out as if to use that day. They went to the bath room where at once the odor of gas could be detected. Bingo DeMoss, who is captain of the team, and others broke open the door and Foster was found lying against the gas heater unconscious, his left arm badly burned and the heater still lighted.[1]

Rushed to Hospital

An ambulance was called and Drs. M.O. Batiste of 2116 Boulevard Ave, and Homer Wales of 511 1/2 Indiana Avenue rushed the injured man to Batiste Hospital, where he regained consciousness about 1 o'clock in the afternoon.

In the meantime, Mr. DeMoss got in touch with Mrs. Foster over long distance telephone and she left at once for the Hoosier capital upon the urgent plea that "If she wanted to see her husband alive to come at once."

Mr. and Mrs. Foster returned to the city the next day. In an interview with a Defender reporter Mr. Foster stated that he remembered drawing water and getting in the tub for a bath, but remembers nothing else. His arm is very sore and is covered with cotton. He insisted on joining his club in Kansas City and left late Wednesday night for that city.

Praise Doctors

Mrs. Foster had nothing but the highest praise for Drs. Batiste and Wales and said it was their heroic work that saved her husband. Mr. Foster's wonderful constitution helped greatly in the battle between life and death.

From reports that soon went the rounds, all Indianapolis had it that Mr. Foster was dead and it took some time to quiet such rumors.

This would not be Rube's last visit to a hospital. Former Monarch and Giant George Sweatt lived in the apartment just above Foster's place on Michigan Avenue. Sweatt's autobiography, provided by his hometown Humboldt Historical Museum, recalled:

> I was traded to the Chicago American Giants for Torriente, an excellent outfielder and hitter. I reported to Rube Foster, the spring of 1926. He had made arrangements for my lodging with Mr.

and Mrs. James Johnson, an elderly couple. They rented the second floor of Rube's building at 4131 S. Michigan Avenue. Rube's wife Sarah, his son Earl and his half brother Willie occupied the first floor. I don't recall who rented the third floor. When Russ, a young catcher from college came, he and I were roommates and we became fast friends. The Johnsons treated us as if we were their own children. When school at Pittsburg (Kansas) was out, my wife joined me. A week later, Russ's wife (Mary Richards) arrived.

All of us camped with the Johnsons. Mr. Johnson taught us how to play a card game, called 500. If we sometimes happened to beat him, he would alter the rules in his favor. They were the nicest people I have ever known. Mr. Johnson could entertain you for hours telling stories; like the time a fellow he knew sold a newcomer one of the bridges.

Two or three times when I was returning to our apartment, I would catch up with Rube and we would walk home together. I noticed that he would be walking alright, when all of a sudden he would start to run and I would have to catch him. I told Mr. Johnson of this and he said that he had rumors, that Rube was a sick man. About a week later, as we were sitting down to our card game, we heard Mrs. Foster scream, "Oh no, don't do that!" So I ran down and knocked on the door. I said, "Mrs. Foster, is there anything wrong?" She said, "There's something wrong with Rube. He's just going crazy down here. I'm going to have to call the law." They took Rube away in the police wagon.

This was a terrible thing to witness; here was a brilliant man, being removed from his own home. He was put in the hospital and finally removed to an insane asylum. That year we won the pennant and the World Series from the Bacharach Giants of Atlantic City. In retrospect, I often think of Rube Foster, a man who had organized a league to where it was a profit making business and had built his team up to where they were contenders and winners of the third World Series. And to think that he didn't realize his ambition to be champion had come too late.

I have often remembered him, standing in front of the Street's Hotel in Kansas City, telling his listeners how his team, the American Giants, was going to beat the Monarchs. I can vision him now, standing in front the hotel where we stayed in Atlantic City, kidding the spectators, how he was going to beat them. What a Man! A Genius, if there ever was one.

Chicago Defender 10 September 1926

Rube Foster Sent to Asylum at Kankakee
Negro National Baseball League President is Confined in Illinois State Institution
Vice-Pres, Keys in Chair Temporarily
Organization Will Continue to Function and Strive for Improvement. Regular Meeting in December

Associated Negro Press

Chicago, Ill, Sept. 8—After a confinement of eight days in a local Psychopathic Hospital for observation and examination, Andrew "Rube" Foster, president and founder of the Negro National League and manager of the American Giants was declared mentally irresponsible and transferred to Kankakee, Illinois, last Thursday afternoon.

Mr. Foster, according to those close to him in his work, has been showing the effects of his strenuous labors for some months and friends repeatedly advised a long rest for him, but he refused to stop, saying that the game needed him and more so at that time than at any other period. However, he finally went to Michigan for a couple of weeks only to be brought back to Chicago on account of urgent business of the league. He never returned. The crash came within thirty days after his return to Chicago. It will be remembered that last year Mr. Foster, while in Indianapolis with his club was severely gassed in a bathroom where he was stopping at that time due to a leak in the gas pipe of a hot water heater. He suffered very much from this adventure and it is thought that the effects of this experience coupled with the many worries of his ball club and the business of the league caused his breakdown.

Fought Way Upward from Ranks

The rise of Andrew "Rube" Foster in the baseball world reads like a work of fiction. Born in Calvert [Winchester, 18 miles NW of La Grange], Texas, 47 years ago, Rube adopted baseball as his life work and made steady progress until he reached the uppermost crest of the peak. He started out in baseball as pitcher and in a short time he had a reputation of being the best in the U.S. The late Frank C. Leland brought Andrew to Chicago in 1901 to pitch for the Leland Giants. He pitched for Leland for two months and never lost a game. He left Chicago after this and finished the season in Michigan with a white club without suffering a defeat. The next season found Foster in New York with the Cuban Giants under E.B. Lamar. Rube lost his first game in New York, 14–0. He knew something was wrong with him or the club. He thought it over a while and the next time he went to the mound they had a new catcher. With his new catcher he ran up a string of 44 wins in a row. He was never defeated in any championship games and retired from pitching having lost but six games in twenty-four years to Colored clubs.

[Author's Note: See Appendix C for a list of daily games Foster pitched for a more accurate assessment of his career.]

Organized Giants and Later a League

Rube started forging ahead in a big way in Chicago in 1911 when he organized the now famous American Giants baseball club and by bringing to bear his knowledge of the game from all angles he soon had the club going in great style and know from Coast to Coast. It was the first club to create a desire in the fans to have other clubs of this type formed into a league.

Mr. Foster added the final jewel to his crown when in February 1919 [sic, 1920], he founded the Negro National League at Kansas City, MO, along with the late C.I. Taylor and others. At the time of the organization of the League there were only three Colored ball clubs in American on a salary basis, which combined did not equal $30,000 annually.

Salaries Jump from $30,000 to $275,000

Since the advent of the Negro National League, the eight club owners pay in salaries to players on an average of $120,000 per each six months playing season. With the organization of the East and South following in the wake of the National League the salaries were boosted to an average of $275,000 per season for the entire organized force. These figures alone should endear Foster to baseball players and club owners all over the country. He was been a real friend to ball players and has befriended many players whom he came in contact with and whom he never expected to get anything in return for his consideration.

Promoted First World Series

The honor of promoting the first Colored World Series goes to Andrew "Rube" Foster who finally arbitrated with the East and made this series possible by bringing peace between the two leagues after several years of worry to both leagues, causing by players of both sections jumping clubs and going into another section to play. This has been definitely settled and now no player in the West or West can leave and go in either league without the consent of the league officials.

It was one of the fondest hopes of Mr. Foster that his club, the American Giants would win the pennant this year and play the Eastern pennant winners for the World Championship. Right now it looks as if his hopes are to be realized as the Giants are leading the league and should they beat Kansas City in the play-off series they will play in the World Series.

Great Loss to Baseball

The passing of Foster from the active service in the baseball world will be felt and regretted by thousands who know and love this genial big-hearted sportsman, business man, and above all, gentleman. His loss will perhaps be felt more keenly by his associates in the baseball world. He had for seven years been their guiding hand and leader and his place will not be filled very easily. His friends are numbered by thousands among white and colored in all walks of life.

Effects on League

Just what will be the effect upon the league is not known at this time and probably will not be known until the league meeting in the fall. However, it goes without question he will be missed very much during the period which is sure to follow in the wake of his withdrawal from active service in baseball and the league. From present indications the club owners are going to carry on the league as heretofore with whatever changes they deem necessary to adjust the league to the new order. Dr. G.B. Key, St. Louis, who is the vice-president of the league, will finish out the season in the place of Mr. Foster.

On September 1 (1926), after suffering memory lapses, Foster was admitted to Chicago's Psychopathic Hospital for observation. After eight days of examinations, he was diagnosed as having indications of memory lapses with unbalanced behavior, coupled with occasional outburst of violence. In Foster's absence, league Vice-President, Dr. G. B. Keys, was voted as interim president, until the annual December meeting of the Board of Directors.

The once astute Rube Foster was committed to a mental institution in Kankakee, Illinois. Foster spent four years at the Institution of Rehabilitation before dying at the age of 51, on Tuesday, December 9, 1930. Death came on the eve of the midwinter meetings of the league which he founded. Foster's body was transported to St. Mark's United Methodist Church in Chicago, for funeral services. Thousands upon thousands of worshippers viewed Foster's casket that Friday evening and all day Saturday, as he lay in state at the Washington funeral parlor on 47th and St. Lawrence Avenue. On Sunday, December 15, funeral rites were held at three o'clock, the same time that Foster's Chicago American Giants took to the diamond on Sunday afternoons.

Foster was survived by his widow, Sarah, his son Earl Mack, who was attending Wilberforce University in Ohio, two sisters, Geneva T. Foster of Sapulpa, OK, and Gertrude Edwards of Santa Monica, CA, and his step-brother Willie.

Relatives, fans and business acquaintances sent scores of floral arrangements. The directors and league officials contributed for a stunningly large baseball wreath, made up of small, white chrysanthemums with red roses delicately placed, denoting baseball seams. The arrangement reportedly weighed over 200 pounds. The American Giants Booster Association sent a green baseball diamond with white carnations for the base paths, with Foster's initials, A.R.F., placed in the center of the diamond. They added two crossed bats just above the diamond in white roses.

The Reverend John B. Redmond presided over the funeral services, quoting scripture from the tenth chapter of Mark and the 21st verse, "Then Jesus, beholding him, loved him, and said unto him, 'One thing thou lackest: go thy way, sell whatsoever thou hast, and give to the poor, and thou shalt have treasure in heaven: and come, take up the cross, and follow me.'"

Dr. Redmond intimately recalled Foster's humble beginnings in Calvert [Winchester, 18 miles NW of La Grange], Texas,[2] on September 17, 1879, as the fifth child of Rev. Andrew and gospel singer Evaline Foster. Also recalled was November 9, 1924, when Foster joined the church during a rendition of "What a Friend I Have in Jesus," with an affirmation of his faith saying, "I have reached first base and I want your help and God's help to reach home plate."

Frank (Fay) A. Young, sports editor of *The (Chicago) Defender*, who followed Rube's career for many years, spoke at the funeral calling Foster "One of the most brilliant figures that the great national sports has ever produced. Rube knew every technicality of the game, how to play it and how to make his men play it. A true master of the game."

The overflowing crowd of over 3,000 worshippers joined in singing the traditional Negro spirituals: "Rock of Ages" and "The Rosary." "The Rosary" was sung by Mrs. Mabel Malarcher, wife of Dave Malarcher, one of Foster's protégés and his successor as manager. Andrew Foster was laid to rest in Lincoln Cemetery. The local black newspaper, *The Defender* wrote, "he died a martyr to the game, the most commanding figure baseball has ever known."

As the nation mourned the death of one of baseball's greatest icons, Foster's wife, the former Sarah Watts, from Temple, Texas, had suffered immense grief during Foster's hospitalization. Two years earlier, co-owner Schorling sold the Giants team to a white florist, William E. Trimble. Trimble's unpretentious occupation was pari-mutuel gambler.[3] Mrs. Foster was told that no written legal agreement existed between Foster and Schorling and therefore she would not share in the profits derived from the sale.[4] Since October 29, 1908, when they were married, Sarah had had little knowledge of her husband's business dealings, and was left with nothing after his death.

Thousands of Chicago area residents viewed Foster's body and three thousand mourners were present for his funeral. The white chrysanthemum baseball sent by the Negro National League directors and officers weighed about 200 pounds, while the American Giants Booster Association sent the floral baseball diamond bearing Foster's initials. The floral arrangement bearing "Our Heart" was from his immediate family. Future owner and florist William E. Trimble sent a large floral piece of white and yellow roses that covered the coffin (courtesy Doris Foster).

The czar-like Foster was a 6' 4" baritone-voiced giant. He usually weighed from 210 to 290 pounds, dapperly dressed in a three-piece suit, with a dangling chained-watch in his vest pocket, sporting his trademark "big apple" cap. The gracious, ever-smiling Rube normally greeted men and women, in a Southern drawl, with the salutation of "darling." He made only one exception — his wife, Sarah. He called her "Smoochie." On leisure days, Rube and Smoochie toured the Windy City in their horseless carriage, a 1914 Runabout Apperson Jackrabbit Sedan.

The car was billed as the "Wizard of the Hills" featuring a four-cylinder engine and generally priced between $1,785 and $2,500. The five-passenger convertible was considered a luxury mobile as the average Ford Model T sold for about $500 that year.

The Fosters had two children, a girl, Sarah Watts (named after Mom), who died (1921) at age five of toxic poisoning, and a son, Earl Mack. In an interview with sportswriter A.S. "Doc" Young, Earl said:

> "Father respected his home and demanded respect for it. We never served a drink here." Earl added, his father was a "square shooter," who loved his home. "If he had $100," Earl recalls, "he might blow $5 — but $95 of it would go into the home."
>
> His mother, Sarah, said, "Rube spent the afternoons at the ball park. But he always knew where

Left: The fifth child of Rev. Andrew and Evaline Foster Bishop was later renamed Andrew. Rev. Foster served as presiding elder for the United Methodist Churches around central Texas and was called Andy by his close friends (courtesy Doris Foster). *Right:* The woman referred to by historians as the "Mother of the Negro Leagues," Sarah [Watts] Foster. While Rube was taking care of the operation of the league, Sarah could be found taking care of the players. There are numerous accounts of Mrs. Foster extending her hospitality to the American Giants and players from visiting teams (courtesy Doris Foster).

> home was. He never wanted to miss eating with the family. He was always home by eleven o'clock when he was in town."
>
> Sarah Foster recalled the bittersweet memories "We enjoyed many simple pleasures. When the weather was hot and humid like it is now, we'd go out on the Midway at night and eat ginger snaps and ice cream." She added that Rube was the "best husband a woman ever could hope to find."[5]

Without Foster's leadership, the Chicago American Giants never resembled the powerhouse team of the twenties. Judge W.C. Hueston emerged as league president, but he was unable to keep economically induced league problems from escalating. Player raids became more prominent and with scheduling conflicts and limited finances brought on by the Great Depression, the leagues were in serious jeopardy. Joe Green, former owner of the Chicago Giants, said, "When Rube died, the league died with him." The passing of the golden goose forced the league to scramble the once-stable financial omelet. By 1932, the once-prestigious black leagues were absent from many sports pages. A renewed menu for league stability occurred the following year, but the flavor of the game had become stale.

Perhaps Rube is the exception to philosophy's law of the excluded middle, which says that no one thing can be another thing at the same time. He was a walking contradiction; loud, rude, opinionated, witty, condescending, magnificently kind and generous, loving, with self-mocking humor. The paradoxical Andrew Foster was ordinary and extraordinary simultaneously.

Rube Foster was possibly black baseball's most influential figure. He raised the Negro Leagues from obscurity to respectability, from anonymity to notoriety. And despite the beliefs of some of his critics and doomsayers, an eloquent testimonial to his greatness can be found among a generation of fans and players. Although Rube's ultimate goal of achieving parity with the white major leagues was never realized during his lifetime, he took barnstorming teams and talented local clubs and molded them into a stable and prospering league.

Long before Jackie Robinson earned sports immortality for breaking the color barrier, Rube Foster was the driving force of the Negro Leagues and a proponent of integrated baseball. His dominating influences were the keys to better playing facilities, increased attendance and regular salaries for the once-cardboard black teams. From this crucible came the genesis of bronze stars that decorated future major league rosters. He whipped up a recipe, rich in razzle-dazzle to please fans.

Overall, Foster's life history was a real page-turner. His successes and failures were tabloid copy, with the true folklore somewhere in between. Foster was a phenomenal pitcher, a magnificent manager, a powerful organizer and even greater humanitarian. His DNA revealed the face of a Koala bear, the heart of laborer John Henry, the smile of Billy Dee Williams, the essence of Malcolm X, the vision of Dr. Martin Luther King, Jr., the oratorical skills of James Earl Jones and the creative genius of Ray Charles. Simply put, Rube Foster was the most robust blend of baseball expertise ever assembled.

In all sports, it was the game's hero we hoist on our jubilant shoulders in celebration of the ultimate victory. However, it was Rube Foster who shouldered the responsibility for carrying our future heroes to unprecedented heights, respectability, and reluctant recognition by major league gate-keepers. His mantra, "We are the ship, all else the sea" became his dream deferred until baseball's gate-keeping opened its doors to black players. And for his efforts, baseball has become a better sport, on and off the field, and a proven example of how dreams deferred really *can* become reality.

Extra Innings. Obituaries, Honors, Landmarks and Tributes, 1930

Chicago Defender, 13 December 1930

"Rube Foster: Master Mind of Baseball, Passes Away"

He leaves behind sister Gertrude Edwards of Santa Monica, California, and one brother Willie Foster, now pitching baseball in Los Angeles.

He was a member of St. Marks M.E. church, the North Star lodge No. 2 [or No. 1] of Masons in Chicago and the Stranger lodge No. 23 of Calvert, Texas.

Foster founded the American Giants in 1910 and played all comers, including all-star teams with such major league players on their roster as Jimmy Callahan, later manager of the Chicago White Sox; Jimmy Hutton, now head of the Post Office League; the late Jake Stahl, who afterward went to manage the Boston American League club; Mike Donlin of the New York Giants, Percy Skillin, Gus Munch, McNickols and others.

In 1920 he founded the Negro National League. It was a child of his brain, and Foster not only invested time but lost considerable money trying to assist promoters of teams in Milwaukee, Cincinnati, Columbus, Toledo and other cities. In fact, he was not only the brains of the league but was the league itself.

He gave away enough ball players to make four first-class clubs, asking nothing in return. He was president of the league at the time, two [sic, four] years ago, when his health forced him to give up the game and seek a rest.

Rube Foster's name is not only written in the baseball history of his Race, but he is known wherever baseball was played between 1900 and today. He knew more big league players and owners than any other individual and knew perhaps more newspaper men than any of the present-day players with the possible exception of Babe Ruth, who is the only man to have more space devoted to him in the daily newspapers than Mr. Foster.

His death comes on the eve of the midwinter meeting of the league which he founded. His loss is more than a loss to baseball—it is a loss to mankind.

Chicago Defender, 20 December 1930

Rube Foster Dead

Baseball's Most Colorful Figure is Called Out

Andrew "Rube" Foster, the master mind of baseball, perhaps the most colorful figure the game has ever known, was called out by Umpire Father Time, following a lengthy struggle to overcome illness.

In 1920 he founded the Negro National League. It was a child of his brain and Foster not only invested time but lost considerable money trying to assist promoters of teams in Milwaukee, Cincinnati, Columbus, Toledo and other cities. In fact, he was not only the brains of the league but was the league itself.

Rube Foster's name is not only written in the baseball history of his Race, but he is known wherever baseball was played between 1900 and today. He knew more big league players and owners than any other individual, and knew perhaps more newspaper men than any of the present-day players with the possible exception of Babe Ruth, who is the only man to have more space devoted to him in the daily newspaper than Mr. Foster.

His death comes on the eve of the midwinter meeting of the league which he founded. His loss is more than a loss to baseball—it is a loss to mankind.

Greatest: Rube Foster

He was the greatest pitcher our Race has ever known. He ranked with Cy Young, Christy Mathewson, Joe McGinnity, and other greats. He was a mastermind of baseball and was ranked by the daily newspapermen as one of the greatest managers of the country. The other two were John McGraw of the New

York Nationals and Connie Mack of the world champion Philadelphia American Leaguers. Foster was also the brains and the founder of the Negro National Baseball League, and it was due to his long hours and hard work plus the worry of running the league that caused him to lose his life.

Foster's headstone in Lincoln Cemetery at 12300 Kedzie Avenue, Blue Island, Illinois 60406; Section 6 (Latitude: N 41° 40' 15.7"; Longitude: W 87° 42' 04.9"). The *Chicago Defender* stated, "He died a martyr to the game, the most commanding figure baseball has ever known" (courtesy Jerry Malloy).

Rube Foster Passes

With the death of Rube Foster last week one of the most colorful figures in the history of baseball, the great American pastime, passed into history. Coming as he did of lowly parentage in an obscure Texas town, and rising to the heights attained by few men in his chosen profession, Rube Foster established for himself a reputation which will be difficult to overshadow, even in his death.

Foster was not a "Colored" baseball man — he was a person of consequence wherever baseball was discussed. He proved to a doubting public that white people have no monopoly on baseball, either from the playing or box office point of view. He proved that persistency, ability and knowledge of the game are all the attributes essential to a successful undertaking in any game. Even the color of his skin was no barrier to the success of Rube Foster — it may be said that he profited by it. Certainly he climbed the heights untried before by a baseball man of his color, and he made some steps that have already proved most difficult to follow.

We hesitate to predict the future of the infant baseball industry which Mr. Foster nurtured among our people. Already it seems a bit groggy and appears toppling. But that is another story. That any man could do for the game what Foster has done is worthy of mention and high praise. That he had to pass on while it was yet so young is the tragedy of the story.

Chicago Defender, 20 December 1930

Thousands Attend Last rites for Rube Foster

Andrew "Rube" Foster was buried at Lincoln Cemetery Monday just as the church bells were tolling the hour of day at noon.

Ball players and intimate friends of the family, the brave little widow, Mrs. Sarah Watts Foster; her mother, Mrs. Frank Mason; Earl Mack Foster, the son; two sisters Miss Geneva Foster of Sapulpa, Oklahoma, and Mrs. Gertrude Edwards of Santa Monica, California, and Masons from the North Star Lodge No. 1 [or No. 2 as reported by some newspapers] stood ankle deep in the snow as the body was committed to the grave by Rev. John B. Redmond, pastor of St. Mark's church, of which Mr. Foster was a member, and the Masons.

Two automobile loads of flowers preceded the hearse, which was followed by the funeral procession a half mile long, to the cemetery.

And they buried Andrew Foster like the hero of many a hard baseball game should have been buried. They buried him amid the flowers which were banked on each side of the bronze coffin and high on the altar at St. Mark's Methodist Episcopal Church at 50th and Wabash Avenue.

These flowers, which included a huge baseball made up of small white chrysanthemums with roses for the seams and weighing over 200 pounds, and which was sent by the directors and offices of the Negro National league, the brain child of the deceased which he helped to found in 1920, and another huge floral offering from the American Giants Boosters association, a green baseball diamond with white carnations for the paths between the bases, with Mr. Foster's initials, A.R.F., in the center of the diamond. Perched above the green diamond were two crossed bats of white with a baseball, all flowers in between. A huge white heart-shaped design with the words "Our Heart" was from the family.

From Princeton, Illinois came a huge piece of white and yellow chrysanthemums to cover the coffin. They were from W.E. Trimble. There were other floral pieces too numerous to mention. All these were tokens of esteem in which the public held the former king of baseball pitchers and friend of man.

The funeral services Sunday were held at 2 o'clock, the hour which the deceased had on thousands of occasions strolled to the pitcher's box to hurl a game of baseball, the same hour at which countless thousands had time and again sat comfortably in their seats in the ball park and had awaited the thrill of Foster's masterful pitching—and that thrill was never denied them.

And the services closed at the hour that the usual ball game ends. Even the Masonic rites which followed the simple, impressive and sad service might have been called an extra inning. It ended, as Foster's life had, between the twilight and eventide.

Mr. Foster had died on Tuesday, December 9, at 9 o'clock, after a vain effort to regain his lost health. His body lay in state all day Friday and Saturday at Washington's undertaking parlors at 47th and St. Lawrence Avenue. Thousands viewed the remains on those two days and on Sunday between the hours of 10 and 2 o'clock three thousand passed the bier. Long before the hour of service at the church crowds gathered, but the main floor of the edifice had been reserved for the family, close friends, the Masons, the honorary pallbearers, many of whom had been with the "Old Master," as Mr. Foster was known, since his coming back to Chicago in 1907.

There were representatives from the Negro National League, the St. Louis Stars, the American Giants Boosters Association, the Pittsburgh Homestead Grays, the Chicago Giants and other baseball clubs. The American Giants ball club, which Mr. Foster founded in 1910 and was manager of up to the time he lost his health, attended in a body. R.P. Gilkerson of the Union Giants of Spring Valley, Illinois; Nate Harris, who came West with Mr. Foster in 1907, and John Reese, manager of the St. Louis Stars attended. Mr. Harris came here from Ohio for the funeral. William J. O'Brien of the Umpires Protective Association represented that body, and James Hutton, president of the Post Office League, were among those in attendance.

When the serviced started a full three thousand people were packed in the main part of the church and the annex and outside in the snow and rain stood three thousand more, who were unable to gain admission, but who stood patiently awaiting their turn to view the remains after the service. And as the thousands inside wept as the white robed choir sand "Rock of Ages," the thousands outside caught the refrain from the open windows and they too wept as the heavens dropped nature's own tears in the form of falling rain.

Rev. A.D. Skelton, pastor of the Indiana Avenue A.M.E. church, opened the services with a scripture reading, which was followed by a prayer by Rev. A. Wayman Ward, pastor of Greater Bethel A.M.E. Church. Resolutions were offered by American Giants Boosters Association, Jefferson Davis, president, and by the Negro National League, Inc., by Harry Sinclair, secretary. Madison C. B. Mason, Jr., read the obituary.

Rev. John B. Redmond, in preaching the funeral services took for his text the 10th chapter of the book of St. Mark and the 21st verse, "Then Jesus beholding him, loved him." He then dwelt immediately, although briefly on the life of the deceased, who was born in Calvert [Winchester], Texas, in 1879, the son of Rev. and Mrs. Andrew Foster, the father a presiding elder in the [United] Methodist Church.

Back over Mr. Foster's life Dr. Redmond went from the time when the deceased was born in the parsonage in Texas until the day he died, sketching here and there the true character of the man who now lay beneath him on the soft white silken cushions within the bronze casket—a corpse—telling even his most intimate friends the goodness of the man that they, his friends, did not know.

Dr. Redmond was the pastor of St. Mark's church the Sunday morning of November 9, 1924, when after the service he had asked for converts and while the choir chanted "What a Friend We Have in Jesus," Mr. Foster voluntarily walked down the aisle of the church, placed his hand in that of the minister and said: "I have reached first base and I want your help and God's help to reach home plate."

"Mr. Foster's loyalty to the church and to this fellow man, and his squareness all ranked far above his ability as a baseball player and manager second to none in the country," said Dr. Redmond. Then he turned to the widow to give consolation and then to the two sisters. To the son he pointed out that his illustrious father had led the way for him to fellow.

A solo, "The Rosary," by Mrs. [Gentleman Dave] Mabel Malarcher, and the benediction followed.

The thousands within and without the church took his last look at the man who had succeeded in life that the game which made him famous, one who had given every ounce of strength in an effort to place baseball as played by his own people on an equal footing as that played by the major leagues.

The North Star lodge of Masons held their burial services which lasted about 40 minutes, and the body was returned to the Washington undertaking parlors, where the casket was opened again to allow a long line to view the remains.

[Author's note: Below is the complete text of scripture and songs from Rube Foster's funeral.]

"What a Friend We Have in Jesus"

1. What a friend we have in Jesus,
All our sins and griefs to bear!
What a privilege to carry
Everything to God in prayer!
Oh, what peace we often forfeit,
Oh, what needless pain we bear,
All because we do not carry
Everything to God in prayer!

2. Have we trials and temptations?
Is there trouble anywhere?
We should never be discouraged—
Take it to the Lord in prayer.
Can we find a friend so faithful,
Who will all our sorrows share?
Jesus knows our every weakness;
Take it to the Lord in prayer.

3. Are we weak and heavy-laden,
Cumbered with a load of care?
Precious Savior, still our refuge—
Take it to the Lord in prayer.
Do thy friends despise, forsake thee?
Take it to the Lord in prayer!
In His arms He'll take and shield thee,
Thou wilt find a solace there.

4. Blessed Savior, Thou hast promised
Thou wilt all our burdens bear;
May we ever, Lord, be bringing
All to Thee in earnest prayer.
Soon in glory bright, unclouded,
There will be no need for prayer—
Rapture, praise, and endless worship
Will be our sweet portion there.

"The Rosary," has sung by Mabel Malarcher.

The hours I spent with Thee, Dear Heart!
Are, as a string of pearls to me,
I count them over, every one apart,
My rosary, my rosary...

Each hour a pearl, each pearl a prayer,
To still a heart in absence wrung,
I tell each bead unto the end,
And there a cross is hung...

O' memories that bless and burn,
O' barren gain and bitter loss,
I kiss each bead and strive at last to learn,
To kiss the cross, Sweet Heart,
To kiss the cross...

I kiss each bead and strive at last to learn,
To kiss the cross, Sweet Heart,
To kiss the cross... (to kiss the cross)

Mark 10:21

Then Jesus beholding him loved him, and said unto him, One thing thou lackest: go thy way, sell whatsoever thou hast, and give to the poor, and thou shalt have treasure in heaven: and come, take up the cross, and follow me.

A final tribute came from Dave Wyatt. A life-long companion of Rube Foster, Wyatt discovered the pitching wonder in 1897 when he and his teammates on the Arlingtons of Hot Springs, Arkansas, met the Waco Yellow Jackets. Wyatt claimed the Yellow Jackets had two outstanding pitchers—Sol Chew and Andrew Foster.[1]

Chew and Foster had been fellow competitors. In 1899, Sol Chew was the ace of the San Antonio Rosebuds and often faced Rube Foster when he was with the Waco Yellow

Jackets. On August 11, 1899, Foster struck out 20 Rosebuds, on a one-hitter, to take an 8–0 victory. The *San Antonio Daily Light* regularly reported the intense rivalry between the two teams, and their play in San Pedro Park. Unfortunately, the visiting Yellow Jackets were the most victorious.

Wyatt thought Chew was the better of the two men. He claimed, "Foster looked the class, but he had a bad fault; he always insisted on piddling and talking to the crowd while pitching and it affected his work. I was about to decide that Chew would be the best experiment when Will Page, a well known business man of Hot Springs, told me that Foster would prove the best with a little work on his rough spots."[2]

Despite Dave Wyatt's claim that he wrote the league constitution, the credit should go to Elisha Scott, the Topeka, Kansas-based attorney. The 1916 graduate of Washburn Law School wrote the Constitution and the By-Laws for the Negro National League in 1920 at the Paseo YMCA in Kansas City, Missouri. His son, attorney Charles S. Scott, Sr., served with future Supreme Court justice Thurgood Marshall in the landmark 1954 case of Linda Brown vs. Topeka (KS) Board of Education (courtesy Charles S. Scott Collection, Kansas Collection, Spencer Research Library, University of Kansas Libraries).

In an article to the *Pittsburgh Courier*, Wyatt gave his account of writing the league constitution in 1920. Wyatt claimed, "In February 1920, the movement was finally launched. At the time Foster was at outs with [C.I.] Taylor, this writer and Charles Mills. The latter did not attend the meeting had in Kansas City. L.N.S. Cobb represented the St. Louis club for Mills. The meeting was called at 11 A.M. on a certain day and when under way for about 30 minutes and after Foster had been installed as chairman they decided on a committee to draw up bylaws, constitution, etc. Foster at once named Wyatt [currently with the *Chicago Whip*], C.I. Taylor, Cary B. Lewis of the [Chicago] *Defender*. At 11 o'clock that night nothing had been accomplished. At 12[midnight], Wyatt was left along on the job."

Wyatt added, "At 11 A.M. the following morning this writer handed in the constitution and it was adopted at 5 P.M. after Elisha Scott, a well-known lawyer of Topeka, Kansas, who had been sent to represent Bob Gilkerson of the Union Giants, Smith Valley, Illinois, smoothed out the tough spots."[3]

Several references also list Elwood C. Knox from the *Indianapolis Freeman* and Charles Marshall of the *Indianapolis Ledger* assisting in the framework design of the league constitution, with Elisha Scott as the major writer and framer of the constitution despite Wyatt's claims. Elisha Scott, a 1916 graduate of Washburn Law School, was known for his charismatic courtroom wit and dramatization. In 1954, his two sons, John J. and Charles Sheldon, Sr., assisted future Supreme Court Justice Thurgood Marshall in winning the landmark Supreme Court case of Brown v. Board of Education, involving integration of public schools.

Honors & Landmarks

The Rube Foster Memorial Baseball Field Dedication, 1943

Although Foster never served in the military, Fort Huachuca (Hwa-CHOO-ka, with

On July 18, 1943, at Fort Huachuca, Arizona, home to more than 15,000 African American servicemen, Rube Foster Memorial Field is dedicated. From left to right are Colonel Hardy, Mrs. Sarah Foster, Brigadier General Benjamin O. Davis, Sr., and Major General Edward M. Almond, commanding general of the 92nd Infantry Division. Mrs. Foster spoke at the dedication saying, "I learned that for a woman married to a public figure there are a lot of things to consider. The most important thing to consider is that your husband doesn't belong to just you" (courtesy Steve Gregory and the Fort Huachuca Historical Museum).

a soft h) of Arizona, dedicated a baseball diamond in his honor. The Field was named by the post commander, who sought to give the 15,000 African American troops training there a source of identification and inspiration.[4] On July 18, 1943, Post Commander Colonel E.N. Hardy and Brig. General Benjamin O. Davis, Sr., the first black general in the army, dedicated Foster Field in the presence of his widow Sarah.[5] Col. Hardy explained, "This field had to have a name and I talked to people searched the records and I believe that in naming it Rube Foster Baseball Field, we have given it the best name possible."[6]

The dedicatory address for the estimated $20,000 field was given by Col. Hardy, before an estimated 15,000 witnesses. The final speech was given by Brig. General Benjamin O. Davis, Jr., from the Inspector General's office. Highlights of the program included the Fort Huachuca theme song, "Huachuca," sung by baritone Sgt. Lawrence Whisonant, who also led the audience in the singing of "America, the Beautiful." Whisonant was formerly the understudy to Todd Duncan, star of "Porgy and Bess," the critically acclaimed opera first performed in 1935 with an entire cast of classically trained African-American singers.

The tribute was given by Lt. Baxter S. Scruggs, Fort Huachuca Library and Service

Top: Mrs. Sarah Foster throws out the first pitch at the Rube Foster Memorial Field. Post Commander Colonel Edwin N. Hardy (far right) felt that naming the field after Foster would provide inspiration to the African American soldiers stationed there (courtesy Steve Gregory and the Fort Huachuca Historical Museum).

Bottom: Mrs. Foster speaks at the dedication ceremony. Seated directly behind her is the first African-American general in the U.S. Army, Benjamin O. Davis, Sr. Over the years, Foster Field was downsized to a Little League field. In 2008, lights were removed. It was demolished in 2011 to make way for a new middle school (courtesy Steve Gregory and the Fort Huachuca Museum).

As part of the ongoing dedication of Foster Field, on August 21, 1943, singer and actress Lena Horne poses with Service Command Unit #1922 baseball team just before their game with the Douglas (Arizona) Air Base Nine. Horne watched the ground troops beat the air men, 7-4. A month earlier, 20th Century Fox produced the megahit musical film *Stormy Weather*, which featured Ms. Horne, Cab Calloway, Bojangles Robinson and the Nicholas Brothers, all of whom had connections to baseball teams (courtesy of Steve Gregory and the Fort Huachuca Museum).

Clubs Officer, who served in World War I with the 92nd Infantry Division (Buffalo Soldiers), soldiers who lived by the motto "Deeds, not Words." "As a baseball player and as a manager he won for himself a place in baseball's diamond-studded hall of fame. The dedication of this field at Fort Huachuca in his memory is also a testimonial of his courage, his faith and his character," declared Lt. Scruggs.[7]

Over the years, the field was scaled down to accommodate surrounding construction. Today, in typical military fashion, only a number—#48222—on a plastic and steel reinforced sign represents Foster Field. The green lettering on the white, 12-by-four inch sign is displayed on the first base dugout. Another sign shows "YA Field, Reservations Only, Tel 538–1026." While the "YA" stands for Youth Activities, it is doubtful if many youngsters-hit the long ball here. To the left field bleachers it is 346 feet, while right field measures 347 feet, and straightaway center is 466 feet. The power alleys were probably close to 400 feet. According to Arizona historian and educator, David Skinner, "These incredible distances apparently date from a time when the field was used by soldiers, and not their kids."[8]

Rube Foster Day, 1951

On July 29, 1951, another tribute to the "FATHER OF BLACK BASEBALL" was performed in Comiskey Park. The president of the Old Timers' Baseball Association, William C. Nielsen, presented Foster's widow Sarah with a plaque in memory of her husband. Nielsen was the former owner of the Chicago Gunthers for 25 years, and one of Foster's foremost opponents in the old Chicago city league. Also present for the ceremony were Bingo DeMoss, the Giants' field captain from 1919 to 1925, Dave Malarcher, manager from

1926 to 1928 and 1932 to 1935, and earlier Foster recruits, Floyd "Jelly" Gardner and Jimmy Lyons.

For years Tweed Webb, noted St. Louis historian, who has compiled data on the Negro Leagues for over half a century advocated a letter-writing campaign for the induction of Rube Foster into the National Baseball Hall of Fame. Webb, recorded in the July 8, 1975, *Congressional Record*, claimed:

> Andrew Foster was the greatest pitcher, manager and president we ever had in yesteryears, the era before Satchel Paige days. I have seen all the black greats of yesteryears since 1912 and have been a keen baseball observer for 55 years. Foster was the "Father of Negro Baseball" and manager from 1910 through 1922 of one of the greatest black team I ever saw, the Chicago American Giants.

Six years later, in 1981, Webb's efforts were rewarded when Foster became the first former Negro Leaguer to be selected to the National Cooperstown's Baseball Hall of Fame by the Veterans Committee, and not by the special Negro Baseball Leagues Committee, created in 1971. Foster lived 51 years. A second lifetime of 50 years had passed from his death in 1930 until 1981, before he would be honored for his eternal contributions to the national game.

Foster's son Earl Mack accepting the Hall of Fame plaque from Commissioner Bowie Kuhn in 1981. Rube Foster was the first Negro League veteran to be elected by the Hall of Fame's Committee on Baseball Veterans after the disbandment of the special Negro Leagues Committee. Foster was inducted as a baseball executive for the founding and operation of the first black league to survive a full season (courtesy the National Baseball Hall of Fame Library).

1981 Hall of Fame

Bowie Kuhn: Our first inductee began his baseball career in 1896 at the age of 17 as a pitcher for a traveling black professional team. His playing career which lasted until 1915 overlapped with a managerial career that began in 1910 when his Chicago Leland Giants lost only six times in 129 games. His most significant achievement was the founding of the Negro National League. Buck O'Neil, a member of the Hall of Fame Committee on Veterans, described him as a combination of Connie Mack and John McGraw, but here in Cooperstown he represents something more. He represents the people of the Negro League, players and leaders. Men who worked in near anonymity for many decades, they should be remembered and here in Cooperstown and in the heart of the American public they will always be remembered. The official language of his plaque says this:

> Andrew Rube Foster. Rated foremost manager and executive in the history of the Negro League. Acclaimed top pitcher in black history for nearly a decade in the early 1900s. Formed Chicago American Giants in 1911 and built them into Midwest's dominant black team. In 1920 he organized the Negro National League. Headed the league and managed the Chicago team until retirement following the 1926 season.

We are pleased to have with us today to receive the plaque for his father, Earl Foster.

Earl Mack, Rube Foster's son, complete induction speech:

"Good evening, to the Commissioner of Baseball and his staff. I would thank you and thank you and thank you. The staff has been very kind to me and my family. I can't exactly tell you how much it has meant to me and my family, but I have one other person that is very, very important in the scheme of things, my wife. She was magnificent — or whatever you want to call it. You believe that. So I'm not going to try to take up your time — they gave me a little speech I'm supposed to say — and I don't think I can make it anyway. I want to thank you, thank you."

Foster's Hall of Fame election was overdue and drew criticism by many worshippers, among them A.S. "Doc" Young, writer for the *Los Angeles Sentinel*. After Cool Papa Bell was justly inducted to the Hall in 1974, Young wrote, "After Cool Papa is inducted, this program should be ended, unless a comprehensive committee is formed, detailed research is done, and then in one final ceremony, the 20 to 25 deserving people who have so far been ignored are inducted in one mass ceremony." Young continued, "As I have pointed out many times, the first man the committee should have honored is the late Andrew (Rube) Foster. If Rube Foster isn't going to be honored, nobody should be honored. Foster was a great baseball promoter, team operator and league head as well as an outstanding pitcher. If he had been white, he would rank today with John McGraw, Judge Landis, the Comiskeys and Branch Rickey."[9]

Young later wrote in 1981, after the election, "Oh, Happy Day! Happy because I had campaigned for this, primarily in the Midwest and the East, over a period of years during which I often felt so exasperated I couldn't see straight and certain people in baseball got so disgusted with me they couldn't see straight."

Young added, "My campaign and my arguments were based on what seemed to be simple logic: Since Rube Foster was the greatest single force in the history of Negro League baseball, he should have been the first one elected to the Hall of Fame by the Negro League Committee. But, for various reasons, others disagreed and Leroy 'Satchel' Paige was the first honoree under the Negro League Committee's aegis."

"As the years passed and Rube Foster still was ignored, I became a man obsessed."

"I wrote a letter to baseball commissioner Bowie Kuhn. I publicly criticized the election of Monte Irvin — before Rube Foster got a shot. So, now, it was Wednesday morning, March 11, and Monte Irvin was calling from the Office of Baseball in New York City. He wanted to tell me the good news. But, I was out. By the time I received the message, Monte had gone home to New Jersey. But on Thursday, March 12, I returned Monte's call and he said, "I know you're happy."

And, I said, "Yes I am. Very happy!"

Truth to tell, I was as happy as a kid who had just inherited a chocolate chip ice cream factory."[10]

Rube Foster was inducted along with pitcher Bob Gibson and slugger Johnny Mize. Gibson collected 337 out of a possible 401 votes from the Baseball Writers Association of America, in his first year of eligibility. Mize and Foster were selected by the Veterans Committee, which reviews the careers of executives and players passed over by the baseball writers during the 20-year eligibility period.

Andrew Foster Tribute Marker & Sign, installed in 1996

W. Pershing Rd. & S. Wentworth Ave. [39th and Wentworth Avenue, Chicago, IL 60609–2839]

N41° 49.4192', W087° 37.881' Northwest corner

His team, the Chicago American Giants, played at Schorling's Park, formerly located at S. Wentworth Avenue & West Pershing Road in Bronzeville. Bronzeville is a neighborhood located in the Douglas and Grand Boulevard community areas on the South Side of city of Chicago around the Illinois Institute of Technology and Illinois College of Optometry. It is accessible via the Green, Red Lines of the Chicago Transit Authority or the Metra Electric District Main Line. Victory Monument and Ida B. Wells-Barnett House In the early 20th century, Bronzeville was known as the "Black Metropolis," one of the nation's most significant landmarks of African-American urban history. Between 1910 and 1920, during the peak of the "Great Migration," the population of the area increased dramatically when thousands of African-Americans fled the oppression of the south and immigrated to Chicago in search of industrial jobs. Many famous people were associated with the development of the area including: Andrew "Rube" Foster, founder of the Negro National Baseball League; Ida B. Wells, a civil rights activist, journalist and organizer of the NAACP; Bessie Coleman, the first African-American woman pilot; Gwendolyn Brooks, famous author and first African-American recipient of the Pulitzer Prize, actress Marla Gibbs, the legendary singers, Sam Cooke and Lou Rawls, and Louis Armstrong, the legendary trumpet player and bandleader who performed at many of the area's night clubs. The neighborhood contains the Chicago Landmark Black Metropolis-Bronzeville District. 47th Street was and remains the hub of the Bronzeville neighborhood and in recent years has started to regain some of the former glory of years gone by. Gone though for good is the Regal Theater (demolished in 1973) where many great performers took the stage. During the 1950s and 1960s, a decision was made to replace the "slums" with several straight miles of high-rise public housing projects, managed by the Chicago Housing Authority, essentially isolating and simultaneously concentrating the poor black population in this section of the city. The largest complex was the Robert Taylor Homes, where Foster's granddaughter Doris Foster once lived.

Andrew Foster Tribute Marker & Sign. Installed in 1996 and located on the Northwest corner of W. Pershing Road and South Wentworth Avenue in Bronzeville was the home of Schorling Park (NoirTech Research).

Dedicated on August 20, 1999, in Atlantic City, New Jersey, this unique work of art, which stands outside of Sandcastle Stadium, took noted sculptor Jennifer Frudakis 10 months to create in clay. "This was something I really had to research, but I enjoyed that part of it as well as the sculpting" (courtesy Larry Hogan and Michael Everett).

Source: *http://www.hotelplanner.com/Attractions/5705-Things-to-do-in-Elmwood-Park-IL*

1998 Texas Sports Hall of Fame

Foster was inducted with his brother Willie Foster, five-time Cy Young Award winner Roger Clemens, and Houston Astros manager Larry Dierker. Other non-baseball honorees included Clyde Drexler, Sandra Meadows, Hakeem Olajuwon of basketball fame, and golfer Judy Rankin.

The Texas Sports Hall of Fame was organized in 1951 by the Texas Sports Writers Association. Each year the honorees are inducted into the Hall of Fame at a gala dinner. The hall was originally in Grand Prairie in the Dallas-Fort Worth area. The Hall of Fame was closed in 1986 for financial reasons, and reopened in 1991 in Waco. In addition to memorabilia, the new location also houses archives. *www.tshof.org*

"Out from the Shadows: Negro League Baseball in America" Bronze Relief Dedication, August 30, 1999

Sandcastle Stadium, Black Horse Pike — Route 40, 545 Albany Avenue
Atlantic City, New Jersey 08401

6'×8' bronze relief is a montage of images from the history of Negro League baseball and the culture in which it was played. The sculpture not only represents great athletes of America's era of the color line, but it also symbolized the pride these Negro League players took in playing a game they loved, and their participation in our nation's struggle against racial discrimination. The composition of the relief draws the viewer in with a powerful central figure of Andrew "Rube" Foster, Father of Negro League Baseball. The detailed images surrounding Foster represent key players responsible for changing the social fabric of American society."

This unique work of art took noted sculptor Jennifer Frudakis 10 months to create in clay. "This was something I really had to research, but I enjoyed that part of it as well as the sculpting."

Frudakis, a native of Ventnor, NJ, is a graduate of the Pennsylvania Academy and Frudakis Academy of Fine Arts. Public works include sculptures at The Atlantic City Press, Holy Family College and Kean University.

The artwork legend:

1 **Marian Anderson** "A voice heard once in a 100 years"

2 **Barnstorming** Playing everywhere for the love of the game

3 **Martin Dihigo** A Latin Jewel — most versatile ever to play the game

4 **Larry Doby** First Black player in the American League

5 **Andrew "Rube" Foster** Father of Negro League Baseball

6 **Josh Gibson** Greatest baseball slugger of all time

7 **Monte Irvin** Newark Eagles, NY Giants, National Baseball Hall of Fame

8 **Reverend Dr. Martin Luther King** Inspired Modern Civil Rights Movement

9 **John Henry "Pop" Lloyd** Atlantic City's own — "greatest athlete ever produced by our national game"

10 **Maxwell Manning** Newark Eagles ace — mentored by "Pop" — mentor himself

11 **Willie Mays** Birmingham Black Barons, NY Giants, National Baseball Hall of Fame

12 **Page Fence Giants** Great 19th century Negro barnstorming team

13 **Leroy "Satchel" Paige** The Legend! First Negro Leaguer in National Baseball Hall of Fame

14 **Jackie Robinson** The Incomparable One — Breaker of the color barrier

15 **Segregation** The Era of Jim Crow

16 **Moses Fleetwood Walker** 19th Century Black Major Leaguer

17 **Smokey Joe Williams** "Greatest" Negro League Pitcher

18 **World War II Recruiting Poster** "Double V" — Victory Abroad! Victory At Home!

This artwork was commissioned by the John Henry "Pop" Lloyd Committee and sponsored by CRDA and Bally's Park Casino Hotel.

"Placing art in public places reinforces the idea that art should be made more accessible, that people should not have to only go to museums and galleries to view art," wrote Giles. Public art also enables viewers to experience the art up close. For many years, parks were the places that were best utilized for displays of public art. More recently, however, we are finding art in places where athletic events are held — stadiums and arenas, venues that draw numbers of people. And what better place to put a piece of sculpture than in front of this magnificent baseball stadium where it can be seen by countless baseball fans who represent a cross section of the American public?

But this isn't just any piece of sculpture. Rather, it is one that is also important because it exemplifies the tradition of commemorative art. It honors and pays tribute to the great history of Negro League baseball. In doing so, it is instructive, it teaches us about the past, helping in the process to ensure that the names, places and images associated with the extraordinary history of Negro League baseball will come to rest in the collective memory of future generations.

> Adding to the significance of this work is the fact that it is being located here in Atlantic City. How appropriate, for this community, too has a tradition. Few New Jersey cities have a more storied and rich past, especially as it pertains to African Americans. As an historian I was particularly struck by the non-baseball depictions found on this bas-relief— the symbol of segregation; Martian Anderson singing in 1939 at Lincoln Memorial; the Black community's Double V Campaign of World War II; and Martin Luther King, the pre-eminent civil rights leader of the 20th century. Through these depictions there resonates in this sculpture the linkage of black baseball to the larger black community and its historical quest for social justice, a quest that included the story of the Negro Leagues.
>
> The John Henry "Pop" Lloyd Committee began its work in the early '90s with the initial mission of restoring the Atlantic City baseball field dedicated in 1949 to honor the playing career and community service of National Baseball Hall of Fame great, John Henry "Pop" Lloyd. The Committee continues to extend this legacy so that the youth of America may benefit from the values engendered from "Pop" Lloyd, all those that played Negro League baseball, and the culture in which it was played.

http://www.popsballyard.org/index.html

Information provided by co-chairs Dr. Larry Hogan and Michael Everett of the John Henry "Pop" Lloyd Committee, Atlantic City, New Jersey.

2003, The Negro League Café— 301 East 43rd St.

On November 17, 2003, The Negro League Cafe, a new restaurant celebrating black baseball history, opened at the corner of 43rd and Prairie in Chicago, Illinois, in Bronzeville, 60653.

The Negro League Café as it stood in the summer of 2010. Owner Don Curry, a Negro League enthusiast, created a special martini called the "Original Rube Foster" which consisted of Minor League Gin, Mathilde Framboise and Pineapple Juice (courtesy Donald R. Curry).

The upscale restaurant serves Caribbean–influenced soul food and features artwork by father-and-son artists John D. Wolfe and John A. Wolfe. John D. produced an oil painting entitled *Chicago American Giants— Rube Foster* for display in the restaurant.

Owner Don Curry, a Negro League enthusiast, created a special martini called the "Original Rube Foster" which consisted of Minor League Gin, Mathilde Framboise and Pineapple Juice.

In 2005, attendees of the Jerry Malloy Negro League Conference made a field trip to the chic museum-café. Before closing in 2010, the Café's theme was "Enjoy the Food, Digest the History."

2004 Texas Baseball Hall of Fame

Texas Baseball Hall of Fame was established in 1978 by the late Texas baseball pioneer George Schepps. It was founded for the purpose of recognizing those who have contributed greatly to the rich history of our national pastime in the Lone Star State.

Their Rube Foster biography stated:

> No man better merits the title of "the father of black baseball." Foster was a visionary and one of baseball's genuine Renaissance men. He had an eye for raw talent and he was an ingenious innovator of strategy. Without the organization Foster imposed upon black baseball, the Negro Leagues could never have survived and prospered.
>
> In spite of the racist color line, Foster earned the respect of his white counterparts. John McGraw retained him as a pitching tutor for his Giants staff in 1901. Foster supposedly taught young Christy Mathewson how to throw his famous fade-away pitch, the pitch that Christy then rode to the Hall of Fame. Foster earned the nickname "Rube" by out-pitching Rube Waddell of the Philadelphia Athletics in a 1903 exhibition game.
>
> As a Negro League manager, Foster built his teams on speed and smarts. Arthur Hardy, a pitcher for Foster, once said, "Rube wasn't harsh, but he was strict." Managers from the white big leagues commonly came to learn strategy by watching Foster at work.
>
> In 1919, Rube joined a number of club owners to form the Negro National League (NNL). Not surprisingly, Foster was elected president and secretary. The slogan on the NNL letterhead read, "We are the ship, all else the sea." Rube Foster was inducted into the National Baseball Hall of Fame in 1981.

Source of biography above: *http://www.tbhof.org/bio/2004/biofoster.htm*

2000, Sports Illustrated's 50 Greatest Sports Figures by States: 21st in Texas

Native Texans who finished ahead of Foster were: Babe Didrikson Zaharias, Ben Hogan, Doak Walker, Rogers Hornsby, Sammy Baugh, Nolan Ryan, Bryon Nelson, Jack Johnson, Ernie Banks, Michael Johnson, Earl Campbell, Lamar Hunt, George Foreman, "Mean" Joe Greene, Tom Landry, Tris Speaker, Dick "Night Train" Lane, Forest Gregg, Roger Clemens, and A.J. Foyt.

Source: December 27, 1999 — January 3, 2000 issue, pages not numbered.

2008, Rube Foster Night

April 12, 2008. The Lorain Parks and Recreation Department of Lorain, Ohio, hosted the first annual "Andrew Rube Foster Night" at the Pipe Yard Stadium, on 2840 Meister Road, about 30 miles west of Cleveland. The event included a full day of youth league baseball games. The Admiral King High School (Admirals) and the Lorain Southview High School (Saints) wore commemorative uniforms of the Homestead Grays and the Chicago American Giants. Former players attending this inaugural event were Ernie Nimmons (1952 Indianapolis Clowns), Bobby Sanders (1957–59 Birmingham Black Barons and Memphis Red Sox), and Chuck Burton (1950 Cleveland Buckeyes.)

The organization annually awards four scholarships in honor of Rube Foster, based on the following criteria: 1) Grade Point Average, 2) Work Ethic, 3) Leadership and ability of being coached and 4) Impact felt on the overall program. The first recipients were: Matt Toth, Cody Buckholz, Mykel Rosario and Cameron Castro.

Black History Month, February 2009

Rube Foster is named by more than two dozen baseball historians as the top executive in the Negro Leagues by MLB.com. The four runner-ups in order were J.L. Wilkinson (Kansas City Monarchs), Cum Posey (Homestead Grays), Gus Greenlee (Pittsburgh Crawfords), and Foster's most competitive rival, Ed Bolden, owner of the Hilldale Club. The list was compiled by MLB.com writer Justice B. Hill.

LAST WORDS

Final written tributes to Rube Foster

When the names of baseball's great pitchers are mentioned, they include Andrew "Rube" Foster of Leland Giants and American Giants fame and Leroy "Satchel" Paige, made famous with the Pittsburgh Crawfords and later with the Kansas City Monarchs of the Negro American League.

Foster lived 20 years too soon. He died in 1930. Paige, whose mother says he is 44, almost "missed the boat." He was signed to pitch for the Cleveland Indians, the first Negro to pitch in the American League and the first of his race to be credited with a victory in that circuit.

Our answer was "No."

No sooner had we taken our eyes off the score book when a younger fan sat down. "Ain't Satchel Paige the greatest Negro pitcher who ever lived?" he asked. We couldn't agree with him. We knew Rube Foster, Walter Ball, Dick Whitworth, Dave Brown, Smokey Joe Williams, [Pat] Dougherty, Jude Gans, [Frank] Wickware, Bill Lindsey, Ed Rile, [Cannonball] Dick Redding, [Jose] Mendez, John Donaldson and many others.

Foster came along when ball players had to beat the other nine men and the umpire or umpires. Most of the time there was only one man and he stood behind the pitcher. Today there are at least two; most of the time three in Negro league games and sometimes four in intersectional or the so-called all star contests, one which is played in Chicago and counts in the series standing and one which is played in the East and doesn't rate in the series.

Likewise Foster played baseball when there were more than an abundant amount of 1 to 0 victories. One or two runs were good enough to win a ball game and sometimes a run could be made with only one hit in that inning. One-hit, two-hit and three-hit games were common. And nobody got excited when a no-hit, no-run game was turned in. To go from first to third on a bunt laid down third base line for a sacrifice out at first was not unusual.

Schooled His Men

Men like Jimmy Lyons, Jelly Gardner and others were schooled in the department, for two hours on some mornings at the old park at 39th and Shields. Foster worked out his men. When his signal called for a hit to right behind a runner going from first to second, it meant that and nothing else. If he said steal, he meant it whether it was second base or third, and he could figure a squeeze play to perfection, especially if only one was out. He would "take" an out to get a run across knowing most of the time that run would be enough for victory. And once in the lead, he didn't run up 16–5 and 12–1 scores. He always said the home team was the idol of the hometown fans and it was his opinion that it was not quite the wisest thing to do to humiliate the home team.

Therefore, whatever place Foster's club played, he could always go back. He was a pitcher. His hitting kept him in the contest when not selected for mound duty.

Chicago Defender, 7 August 1948
Through the Years by Fay Young

Rube Foster was the founder of organized professional ball along with the lamented C.I. Taylor. Besides being a pitcher and manager, he holds high rank as a strategist, and measures with Connie Mack and [John] McGraw as a manipulator of inside baseball. At one time Rube served under McGraw as coach of pitchers for the New York Giants. He at another time pitched for his club against Rube Waddell and the Philadelphia Giants. He was the first of colored managers to match colored teams against the big league clubs in post season tilts.

The Negro in Sports, 1949
Edwin Bancroft Henderson

There was Andrew "Rube" Foster, a round, friendly faced, bass-voiced giant who was first a great pitcher, next a superb manager, and finally an outstanding administrator. It was he who lost the most by the Jim Crow bar, for it was he who had the most to offer.

He was the man New York Giants manager John McGraw engaged briefly as a pitching coach, after failing in his efforts to sign him as a hurler. Among Foster's "pupils" was Christy Mathewson, one of the three or four best pitchers in major league history.

As a team manager, Foster was tough, shrewd, and cocky. He belonged to the McGraw school of wanna-win guys; and he was smart like [Casey] Stengel, [John] McCarthy, and [Leo] Durocher. As a league president (Negro National League), he was strong, perpetually in charge, stern, iron-fisted, in fact; imaginative and able.

Great Negro Baseball Stars, 1953
A.S. "Doc" Young

A stupendous pitcher at the turn of the century. Pitched exhibition ball, first drew attention by out-pitching the great Rube Waddell. A big man with a flare for showmanship. In 1905, won 51 of 55 exhibition games he pitched. Organized the Chicago American Giants, became a slick, stern-fisted character in dual role as owner and hurler.

Great Black Athletes, 1971
Jocko Maxwell

There have been many accolades attributed to the phenomenal success of Rube Foster. Robert Peterson in his required reading "Only the Ball was White" wrote it best: "If the talents of Christy Mathewson, John McGraw, Ban Johnson and Judge Kenesaw Mountain Landis were combined in a single body, and that body was enveloped in a black skin, the result would have to be named Andrew 'Rube' Foster. As an outstanding pitcher, a colorful and shrewd field manager, and the founder and stern administrator of the first viable Negro League, Foster was the most impressive figure in black baseball history. From about 1911 until 1926, he stood astride Negro baseball in the Midwest with unchallenged power, a friend of major league leaders, and the best known black man in Chicago. Rube Foster was an unlettered genius who combined generosity and sternness, the superb skills of a dedicated athlete and an unbounded belief in the future of the black baseball player. His life was baseball. Had he chosen otherwise, baseball would have been the poorer."

Only the Ball Was White, 1971
Robert Peterson

Very few people sing the praises of Andrew "Rube" Foster, the man who, for a long period of time, was Negro baseball. As a star pitcher, an outstanding and knowledgeable field manager, and as the founder and top executive of the Negro National League, Rube Foster, many will argue, was the outstanding individual in Negro baseball. For approximately two decades, Andrew "Rube" Foster was the power that propelled Negro baseball, and very little about it could move without his say. He was easily the most well known and most famous Black sportsman of this time.

Historically Speaking...
***Black Sports*, February 1972**

If Sol White can be called the chronicler whose literary efforts forged a needed link to the saga of early Negro baseball history, then Andrew Foster most certainly was the administrative genius who demonstrated that Negro baseball, properly organized, could be a money-making business. He was at one time or another, an exceptional right-handed pitcher, charismatic leader, canny baseball tactician, and a sound administrator.

***Pioneers of Black Sports*, 1975**
Ocania Chalk

As I have pointed out many times, the first man the committee should have honored is the late Andrew "Rube" Foster. If Rube Foster isn't going to be honored, nobody should be honored. Foster was a great baseball promoter, team operator and league head as well as an outstanding pitcher. If he had been white, he would rank today with John McGraw, Judge Landis, the Comiskeys and Branch Rickey.

***Los Angeles Times*, February 28, 1974**
John Hall

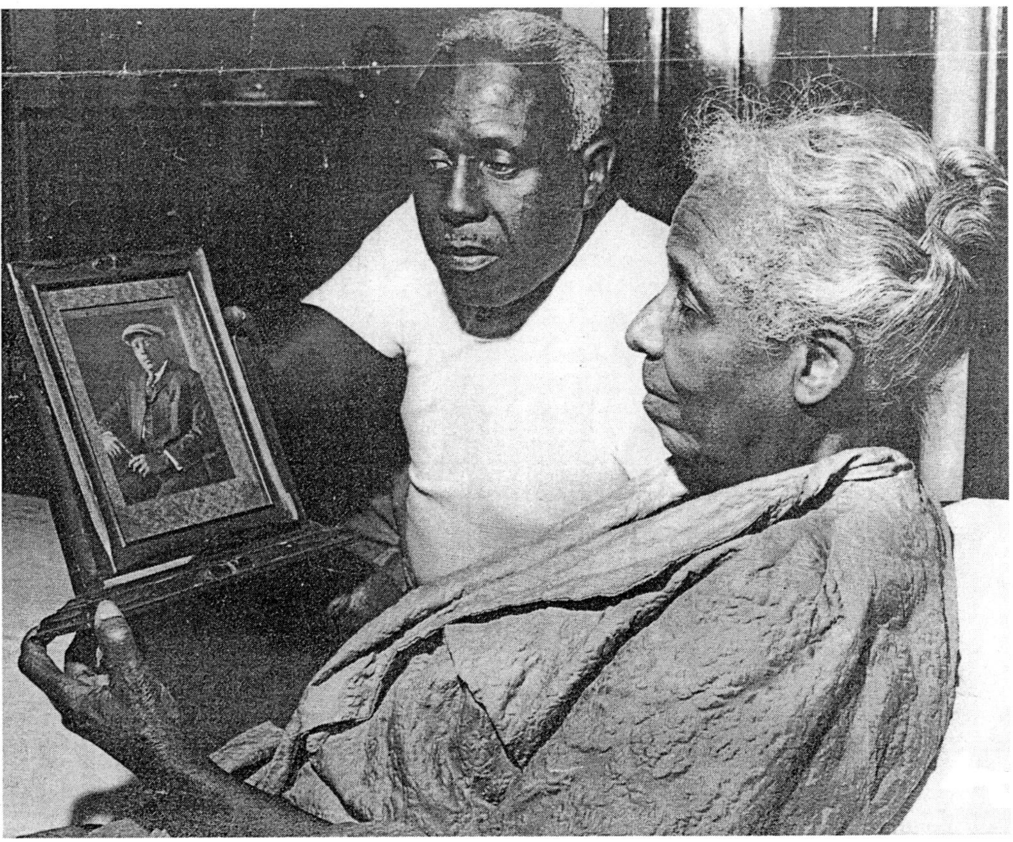

Earl Mack Foster and his mother, Sarah, view the classic pose of Rube Foster in the Robert Taylor Homes on Chicago's South Side (courtesy Doris Foster).

As an administrative impresario, Rube Foster was a much as force — in his time and in his arena — as Ban Johnson, the founding President of the American League. As a pitcher, he best approximated his contemporary, Christy Mathewson. And as a manager, he was on a level with his friend, John McGraw. That Rube Foster has not been elected to baseball's Hall of Fame by the special committee on Negro Leagues, that he has not even been mentioned publicly as a likely candidate, is— sadly — a measure of how the rich, bittersweet lore of Negro baseball has faded with the passing years."

Sports, May, 1975
Robert Peterson

Beyond the shadow of a doubt, one of the most colorful and multi-talented individuals who ever played and administered the game of baseball was big and fearless Andrew "Rube" Foster, son of a Texas Methodist preacher.

***Blacks in Baseball*, 1980**
Leon Herbert Hardwick

In the annals of baseball there are certain names such as Cy Young, Kenesaw Mountain Landis, Connie Mack, and John McGraw that are immediately recognized, even today. Yet, there was one baseball great, Andrew "Rube" Foster, who was reported to be greater than any of the aforementioned, but who because of his race, is today almost forgotten.

A Man and His Diamonds, 1980
Charles E. Whitehead

Appendices

A: No-Hitters by Rube Foster

#1 July 21, 1901, Fort Worth Colts defeated Corsicana (TX), 5–0. Box score was not printed.

#2 August 2, 1901, Fort Worth Colts defeated the Arlingtons (Hot Springs, AR), 6–1. Box score was not printed.

#3

July 7, 1904
Philadelphia, PA
Called after 7½ innings due to rain.

Mt. Carmel A.A.	R	H	P	A	E
Taylor, 2b	0	0	4	1	0
Smith, 3b	0	0	0	1	1
Devere, rf	0	0	3	0	0
Morgan, lf	0	0	1	0	0
O'Neil, cf	0	0	2	0	1
M'Dade, 1b	0	0	3	1	1
Long, ss	0	0	2	1	0
Josey, c	0	0	4	0	0
Vaughan, p	0	0	2	2	0
Total	0	0	21	6	3

Philadelphia Giants	R	H	P	A	E
Grant, 2b	0	1	2	2	0
Monroe, ss	0	2	0	0	0
White, rf	0	0	1	0	0
Payne, lf	1	1	2	0	0
P. Hill, cf	1	2	2	0	0
G. Johnson, 1b	1	0	4	0	0
Rube Foster, p	1	2	0	1	0
J. Hill, 3b	0	1	0	2	1
Footes, c	0	0	10	0	0
Total	4	9	24	5	1

Mt. Carmel 0 0 0 0 0 0 0 0 x—0
P. Giants 0 0 2 1 0 1 0 x x—4

Batting & pitching details were not reported.

#4

July 25, 1904
Philadelphia, PA

Trenton (NJ) YMCA.	R	H	P	A	E
Klein, p	0	0	2	3	2
Bennett, 3b	0	0	1	0	0
Horton, cf	0	0	0	0	1
Ross, lf	0	0	3	0	0
McCune, c	0	0	9	1	0
Travers, 1b	0	0	8	0	0
Young, 2b	0	0	1	1	0
Hanford, rf	0	0	2	0	1
Bratton, ss	0	0	1	2	0
Total	0	0	27	7	4

Philadelphia Giants	R	H	P	A	E
Grant, 2b	0	0	0	2	0
Monroe, ss	0	3	1	2	0
White, 1b	0	1	8	0	0
Payne, lf	0	1	0	0	0
P. Hill, cf	0	1	0	0	0
Johnson, c	0	0	17	0	0
Rube Foster, p	1	3	0	3	0
J. Hill, 3b	0	1	1	1	0
Footes, rf	0	0	0	0	0
Total	1	10	27	8	0

YMCA 0 0 0 0 0 0 0 0 0—0
P. Giants 0 0 0 0 0 0 0 0 1—1

Two base hit—Foster, Base on balls, off Foster 4. Struck out—by Egner 1; by Klein 6; by Foster 17; Stolen bases—Monroe, White, Hanford, Sacrifice Hits—Payne, Johnson, Bennett. Double play—Travers, unassisted.
Time—1:40
Umpire—Konover
Attendance—400
Note: The Giants scored their only run (unearned) on a wild throw by pitcher Klein to second base.

#5

August 22, 1905
Camden, New Jersey

Camden	R	H	P	A	E
Meehan, cf	0	0	2	0	0
Miller, c	0	0	2	0	0
Zollers, ss	0	0	4	5	2
Slack, 1b	0	0	14	1	1
Verga. 3b	0	0	0	2	1
Cross, 2b	0	0	3	0	0
McManus, lf	0	0	1	1	0
Brown, p	0	0	0	7	0
Robinson, rf	0	0	1	1	0
Total	0	0	27	18	4

Philadelphia Giants	R	H	P	A	E
Grant, 2b	0	1	1	2	0
Johnson, ss	0	0	0	0	0
Hill, lf	1	1	2	0	0
Monroe, cf	1	0	2	3	0
Moore, cf	1	1	2	0	0
Rube Foster, p	0	0	2	5	0
Bowman, rf	0	1	1	1	0
Washington, c	0	0	5	0	0
Thomas, 1b	0	0	12	1	0
Total	3	4	27	12	0

Camden 0 0 0 0 0 0 0 0 0—0
P. Giants 0 1 0 2 0 0 0 0 0—3

Two-base hits—Hill, Bowman. Sacrifice Hits—Brown, Foster. Left on Bases—Camden 3; Giants 3. Struck out—by Brown 2; by Foster 5. Bases on balls—by Brown 1; by Foster 2.

Time—1:30
Umpire—Osborn
Attendance: not reported

#6

September 22, 1907
Auburn Park, Chicago, Illinois

South Chicagos	R	H	P	A	E
McKee, cf	0	0	2	0	0
Staton, ss	0	0	2	6	0
Babcock, lf	0	0	3	0	0
Brading, rf	0	0	2	0	0
Laxea, 3b	0	0	0	0	1
Callahan, 1b	0	0	9	0	2
Hill, 2b	0	0	2	2	0
Tannon, c	0	0	4	1	0
Hillebrand, p	0	0	0	2	0
Total	**0**	**0**	**24**	**11**	**3**

Leland Giants	R	H	P	A	E
Winston, lf	1	1	0	0	0
Harris, 2b	0	1	3	3	0
Payne, cf	0	0	0	0	0
Wright, ss	0	0	3	5	0
Moore, 1b	0	1	14	0	0
Rube Foster, p	0	0	0	5	1
Booker, c	0	0	7	1	0
Talbert, 3b	0	0	0	1	0
Rose, rf, cf	0	0	0	0	0
Gatewood, rf	0	0	0	0	1
Total	1	3	27	15	2

Chicagos 0 0 0 0 0 0 0 0 0—0
Lelands 0 0 0 0 0 1 0 0 x—1

Stolen bases—Winston, Talbert. Double plays—Foster to Wright to Moore. Struck out—by Foster 7; by Hillebrand 3. Base on balls—off Foster, 3. HBP—Harris.
Time—1:50
Umpire—McCarthy
Attendance—4,500

#7

August 28, 1908
St. Paul, Minnesota

Hibbing Colts	R	H	P	E
Giselman, cf	0	0	1	0
Monahan, ss	0	0	2	0
Booth, 1b	0	0	7	0
Carroll, c	0	0	3	0
Brookings, 3b	0	0	3	0
Fagan, lf	0	0	0	0
Billings, rf	0	0	2	1
Calligan, 2b	0	0	6	0
Gilligan, p	0	0	0	1
Total	0	0	24	2

St. Paul Gophers	R	H	P	E
Wallace, 2b	1	1	1	0
Johnson, 1b	0	2	11	0
Davis, ss	0	1	5	0
Barton, cf	0	0	1	0

St. Paul Gophers	R	H	P	E
Rube Foster, p	0	1	0	0
Lydie, rf	0	1	2	0
Rose, c	1	3	6	0
Jones, lf	1	1	1	0
McMurray, 3b	2	2	1	1
Total	5	12	27	1

Hibbing	0	0	0	0	0	0	0	0	0	—0
Gophers	0	0	1	0	0	4	0	0	x	—5

Two base hits—Lydie, McMurray, Johnson, Rose; Stolen bases—Booth, Brookings, Lydie, McMurray (2), Johnson, Jones, Davis. Wild pitch—by Gilligan; Bases on balls—by Gilligan 1; by Foster 2. Hit by pitch—by Foster 1.
Time—1:45
Umpire—Thompson
Attendance—1,600

B: Team Depth Charts, 1902 to 1918

The depth charts provide insight on Foster's overall playing time and his place in the starting rotation. Based on box scores found, it appears Foster was the staff's pitching ace on the 1904–05 Philadelphia Giants, and 1907 Leland Giants. By 1913, it seems Foster's time on the mound with the Chicago American Giants was starting to diminish, as Dicta Johnson, Lee Wade, Frank Wickware, Tom Johnson and Cannonball Dick Redding took their respective turns in the lead role in subsequent years. The depth charts also reveal that Foster spent his non-pitching days mostly in right field, or at first base

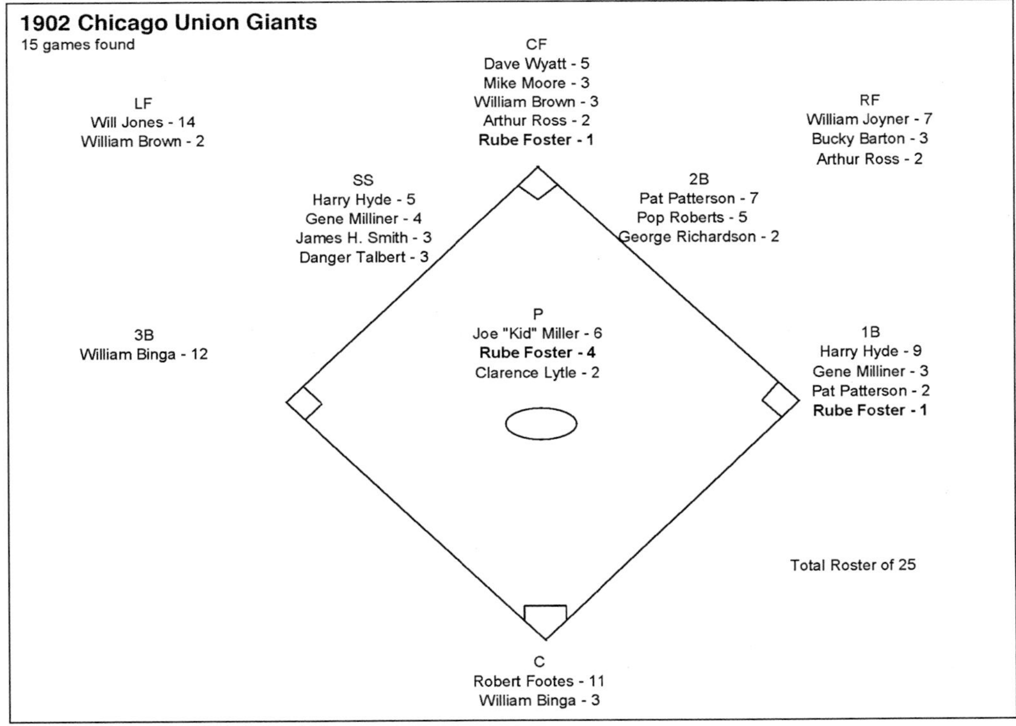

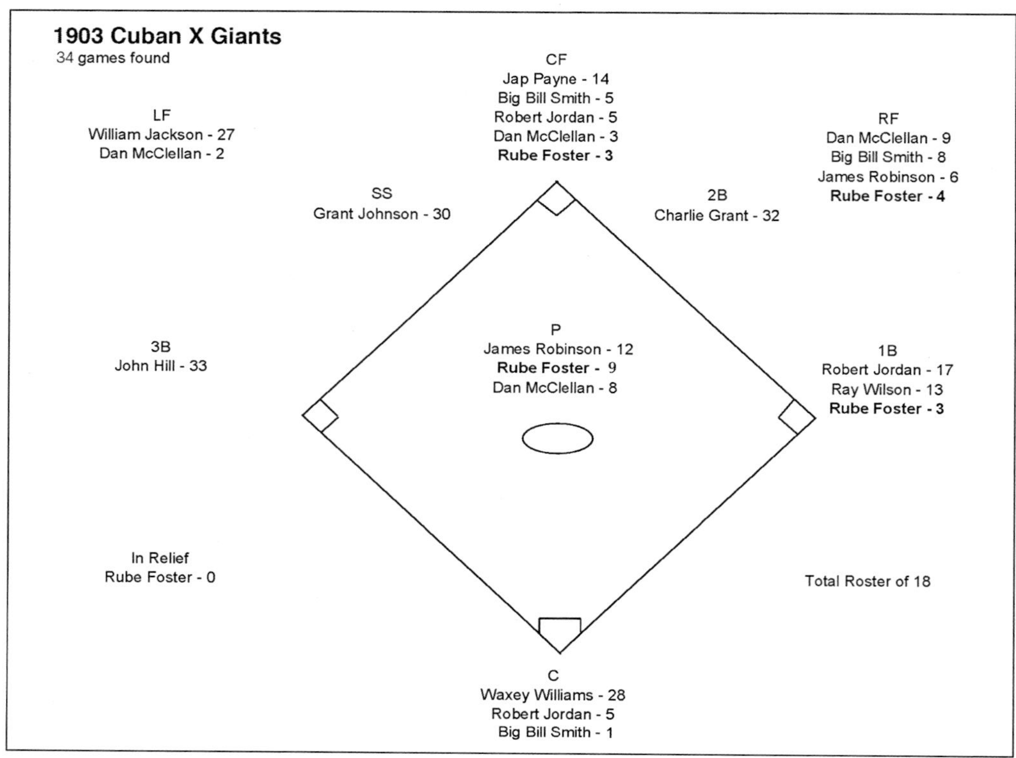
1903 Cuban X Giants
34 games found
CF
Jap Payne - 14
Big Bill Smith - 5
Robert Jordan - 5
Dan McClellan - 3
Rube Foster - 3
LF
William Jackson - 27
Dan McClellan - 2
RF
Dan McClellan - 9
Big Bill Smith - 8
James Robinson - 6
Rube Foster - 4
SS
Grant Johnson - 30
2B
Charlie Grant - 32
3B
John Hill - 33
P
James Robinson - 12
Rube Foster - 9
Dan McClellan - 8
1B
Robert Jordan - 17
Ray Wilson - 13
Rube Foster - 3
In Relief
Rube Foster - 0
Total Roster of 18
C
Waxey Williams - 28
Robert Jordan - 5
Big Bill Smith - 1

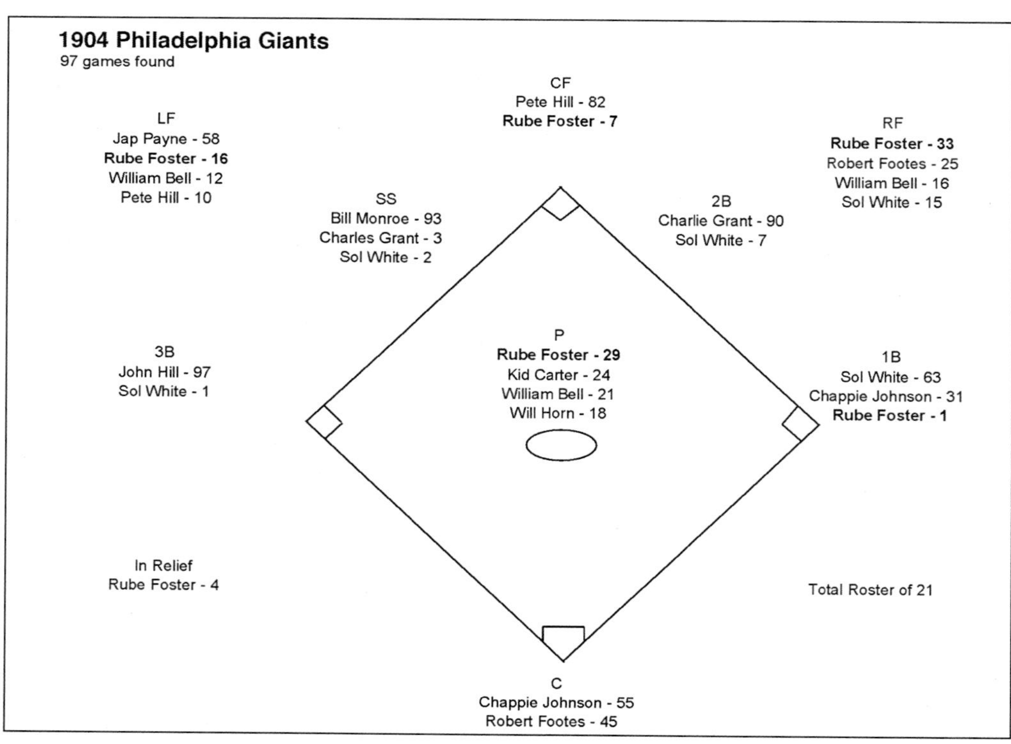
1904 Philadelphia Giants
97 games found
CF
Pete Hill - 82
Rube Foster - 7
LF
Jap Payne - 58
Rube Foster - 16
William Bell - 12
Pete Hill - 10
RF
Rube Foster - 33
Robert Footes - 25
William Bell - 16
Sol White - 15
SS
Bill Monroe - 93
Charles Grant - 3
Sol White - 2
2B
Charlie Grant - 90
Sol White - 7
3B
John Hill - 97
Sol White - 1
P
Rube Foster - 29
Kid Carter - 24
William Bell - 21
Will Horn - 18
1B
Sol White - 63
Chappie Johnson - 31
Rube Foster - 1
In Relief
Rube Foster - 4
Total Roster of 21
C
Chappie Johnson - 55
Robert Footes - 45

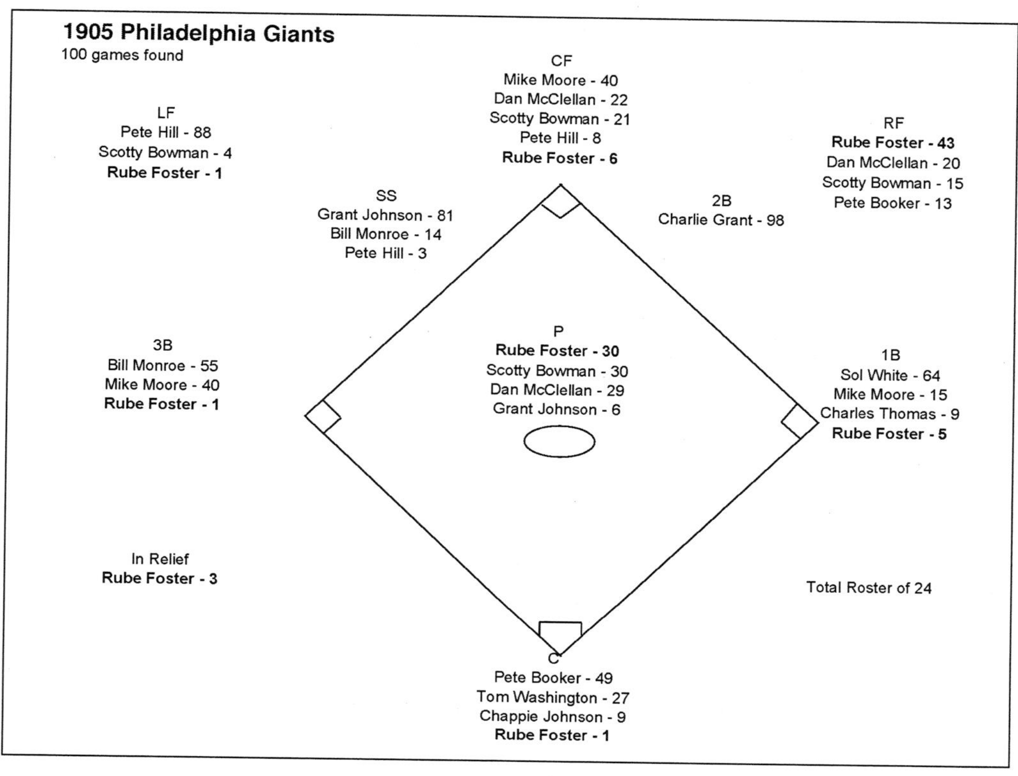
1905 Philadelphia Giants
100 games found
CF
Mike Moore - 40
Dan McClellan - 22
Scotty Bowman - 21
Pete Hill - 8
Rube Foster - 6
LF
Pete Hill - 88
Scotty Bowman - 4
Rube Foster - 1
RF
Rube Foster - 43
Dan McClellan - 20
Scotty Bowman - 15
Pete Booker - 13
SS
Grant Johnson - 81
Bill Monroe - 14
Pete Hill - 3
2B
Charlie Grant - 98
P
Rube Foster - 30
Scotty Bowman - 30
Dan McClellan - 29
Grant Johnson - 6
3B
Bill Monroe - 55
Mike Moore - 40
Rube Foster - 1
1B
Sol White - 64
Mike Moore - 15
Charles Thomas - 9
Rube Foster - 5
In Relief
Rube Foster - 3
Total Roster of 24
C
Pete Booker - 49
Tom Washington - 27
Chappie Johnson - 9
Rube Foster - 1

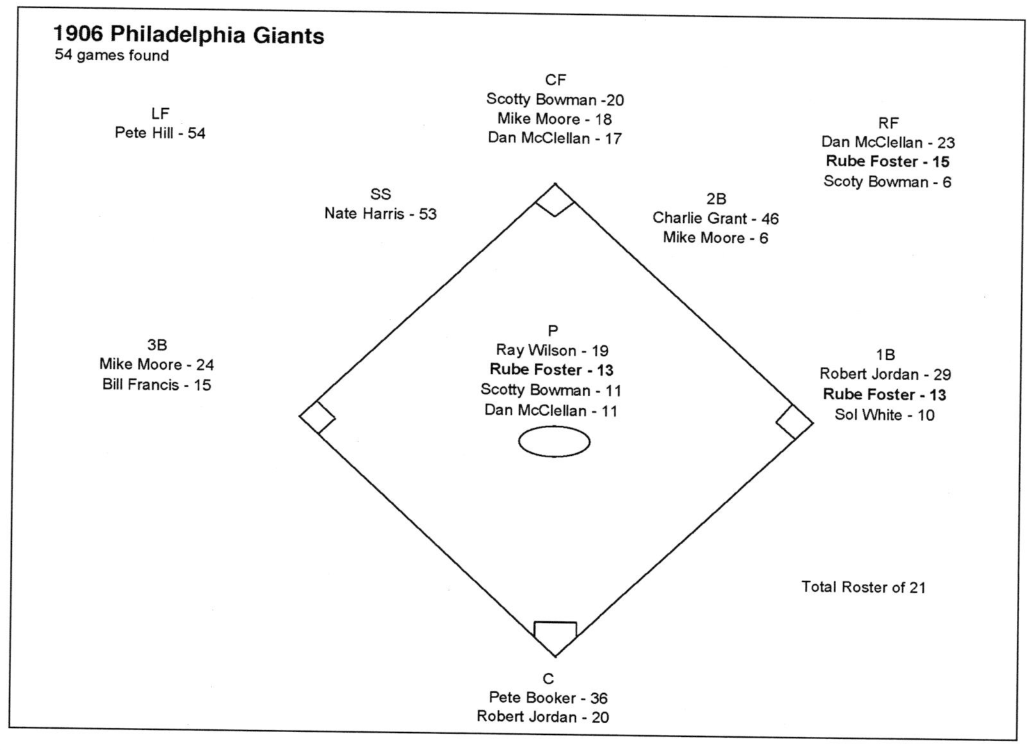
1906 Philadelphia Giants
54 games found
CF
Scotty Bowman -20
Mike Moore - 18
Dan McClellan - 17
LF
Pete Hill - 54
RF
Dan McClellan - 23
Rube Foster - 15
Scoty Bowman - 6
SS
Nate Harris - 53
2B
Charlie Grant - 46
Mike Moore - 6
P
Ray Wilson - 19
Rube Foster - 13
Scotty Bowman - 11
Dan McClellan - 11
3B
Mike Moore - 24
Bill Francis - 15
1B
Robert Jordan - 29
Rube Foster - 13
Sol White - 10
Total Roster of 21
C
Pete Booker - 36
Robert Jordan - 20

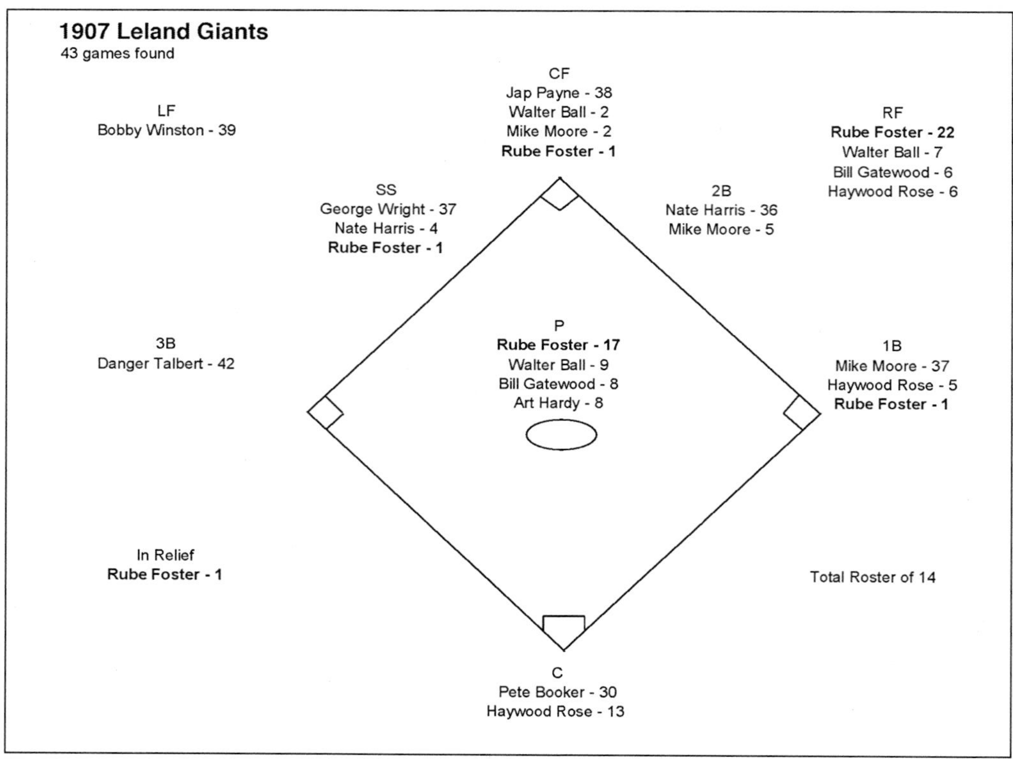

1907 Leland Giants
43 games found
CF
Jap Payne - 38
Walter Ball - 2
Mike Moore - 2
Rube Foster - 1
LF
Bobby Winston - 39
RF
Rube Foster - 22
Walter Ball - 7
Bill Gatewood - 6
Haywood Rose - 6
SS
George Wright - 37
Nate Harris - 4
Rube Foster - 1
2B
Nate Harris - 36
Mike Moore - 5
3B
Danger Talbert - 42
P
Rube Foster - 17
Walter Ball - 9
Bill Gatewood - 8
Art Hardy - 8
1B
Mike Moore - 37
Haywood Rose - 5
Rube Foster - 1
In Relief
Rube Foster - 1
Total Roster of 14
C
Pete Booker - 30
Haywood Rose - 13

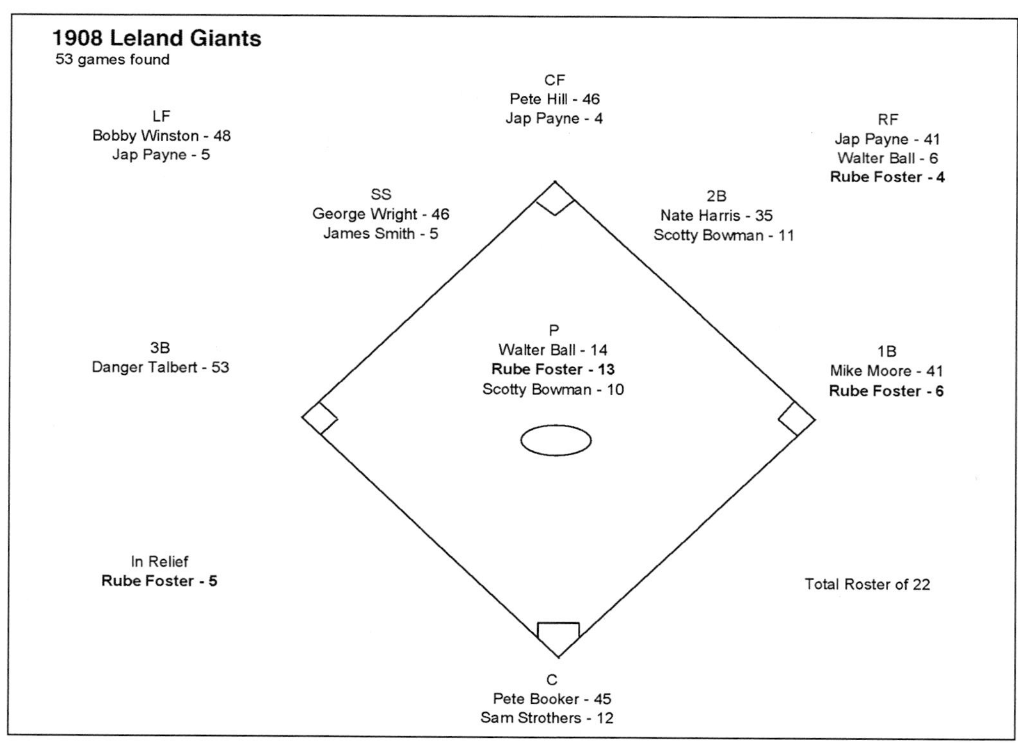

1908 Leland Giants
53 games found
CF
Pete Hill - 46
Jap Payne - 4
LF
Bobby Winston - 48
Jap Payne - 5
RF
Jap Payne - 41
Walter Ball - 6
Rube Foster - 4
SS
George Wright - 46
James Smith - 5
2B
Nate Harris - 35
Scotty Bowman - 11
3B
Danger Talbert - 53
P
Walter Ball - 14
Rube Foster - 13
Scotty Bowman - 10
1B
Mike Moore - 41
Rube Foster - 6
In Relief
Rube Foster - 5
Total Roster of 22
C
Pete Booker - 45
Sam Strothers - 12

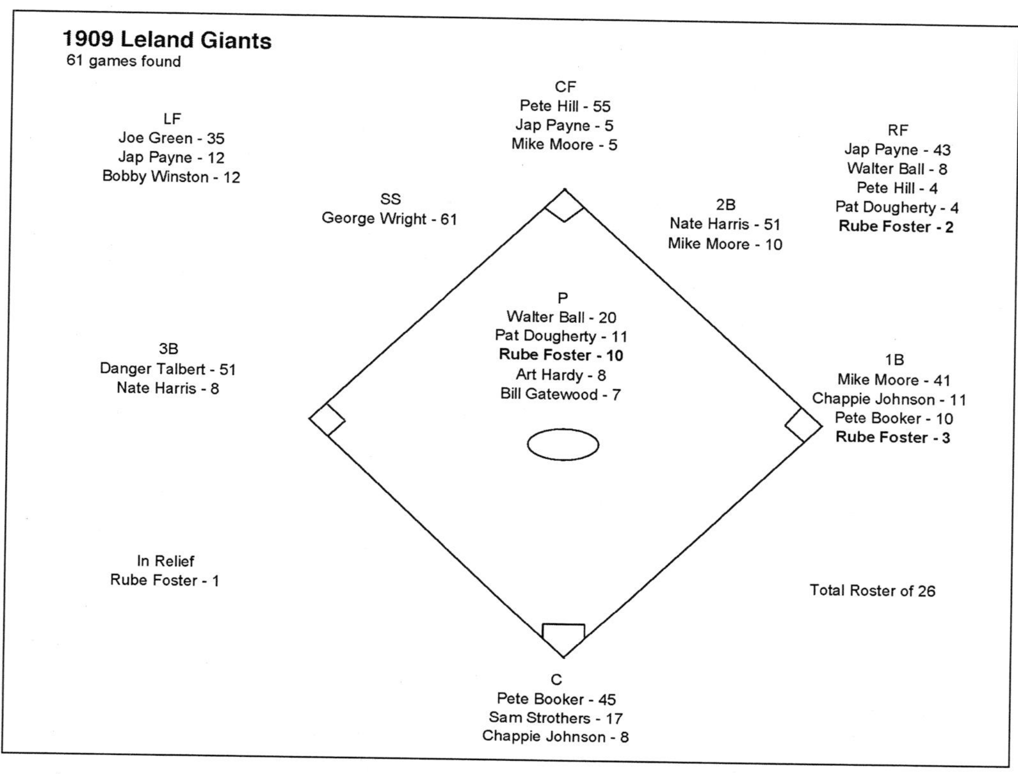
1909 Leland Giants
61 games found
CF
Pete Hill - 55
Jap Payne - 5
Mike Moore - 5
LF
Joe Green - 35
Jap Payne - 12
Bobby Winston - 12
RF
Jap Payne - 43
Walter Ball - 8
Pete Hill - 4
Pat Dougherty - 4
Rube Foster - 2
SS
George Wright - 61
2B
Nate Harris - 51
Mike Moore - 10
P
Walter Ball - 20
Pat Dougherty - 11
Rube Foster - 10
Art Hardy - 8
Bill Gatewood - 7
3B
Danger Talbert - 51
Nate Harris - 8
1B
Mike Moore - 41
Chappie Johnson - 11
Pete Booker - 10
Rube Foster - 3
In Relief
Rube Foster - 1
Total Roster of 26
C
Pete Booker - 45
Sam Strothers - 17
Chappie Johnson - 8

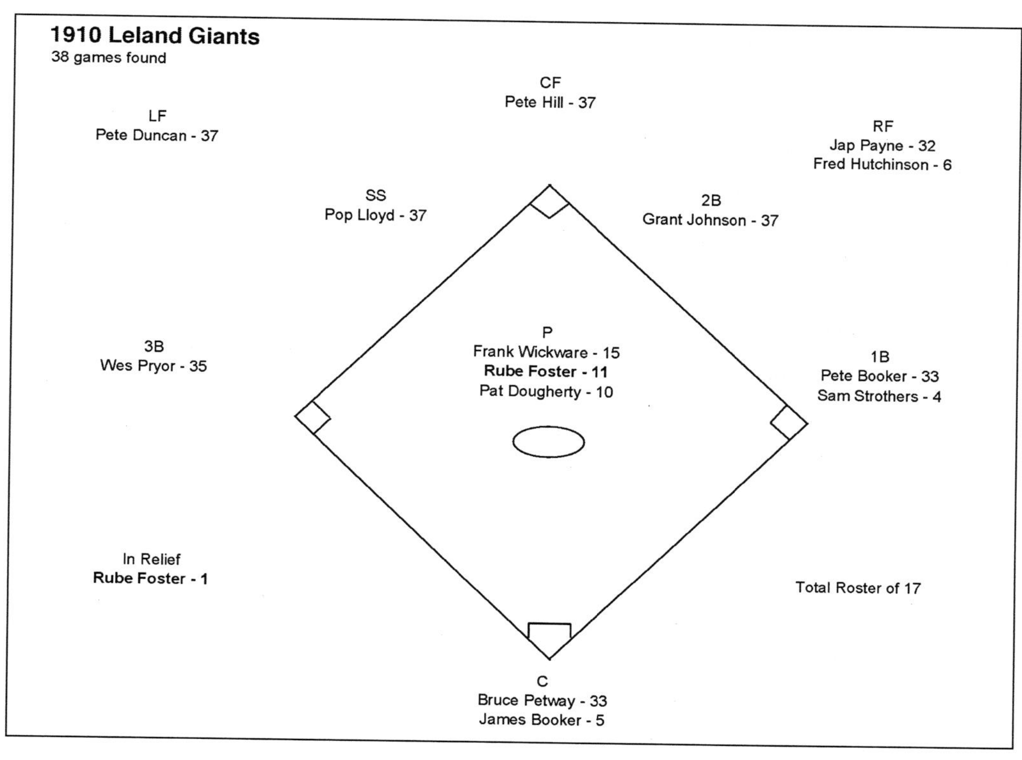
1910 Leland Giants
38 games found
CF
Pete Hill - 37
LF
Pete Duncan - 37
RF
Jap Payne - 32
Fred Hutchinson - 6
SS
Pop Lloyd - 37
2B
Grant Johnson - 37
P
Frank Wickware - 15
Rube Foster - 11
Pat Dougherty - 10
3B
Wes Pryor - 35
1B
Pete Booker - 33
Sam Strothers - 4
In Relief
Rube Foster - 1
Total Roster of 17
C
Bruce Petway - 33
James Booker - 5

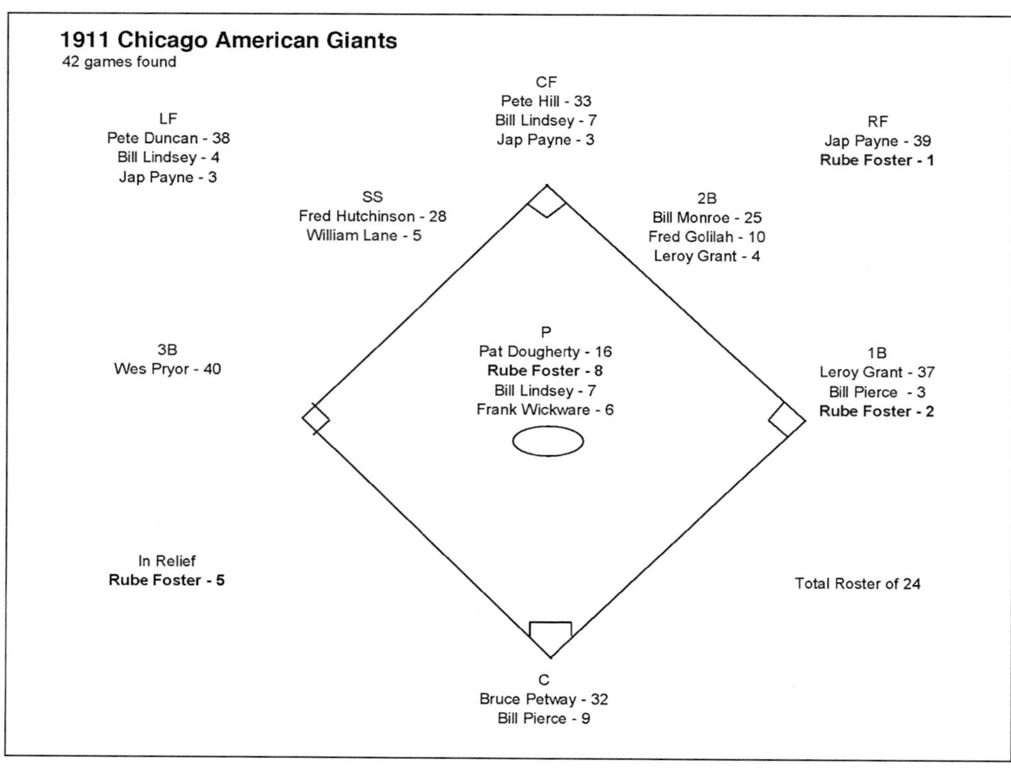
1911 Chicago American Giants
42 games found
CF
Pete Hill - 33
Bill Lindsey - 7
Jap Payne - 3
LF
Pete Duncan - 38
Bill Lindsey - 4
Jap Payne - 3
RF
Jap Payne - 39
Rube Foster - 1
SS
Fred Hutchinson - 28
William Lane - 5
2B
Bill Monroe - 25
Fred Golilah - 10
Leroy Grant - 4
3B
Wes Pryor - 40
P
Pat Dougherty - 16
Rube Foster - 8
Bill Lindsey - 7
Frank Wickware - 6
1B
Leroy Grant - 37
Bill Pierce - 3
Rube Foster - 2
In Relief
Rube Foster - 5
Total Roster of 24
C
Bruce Petway - 32
Bill Pierce - 9

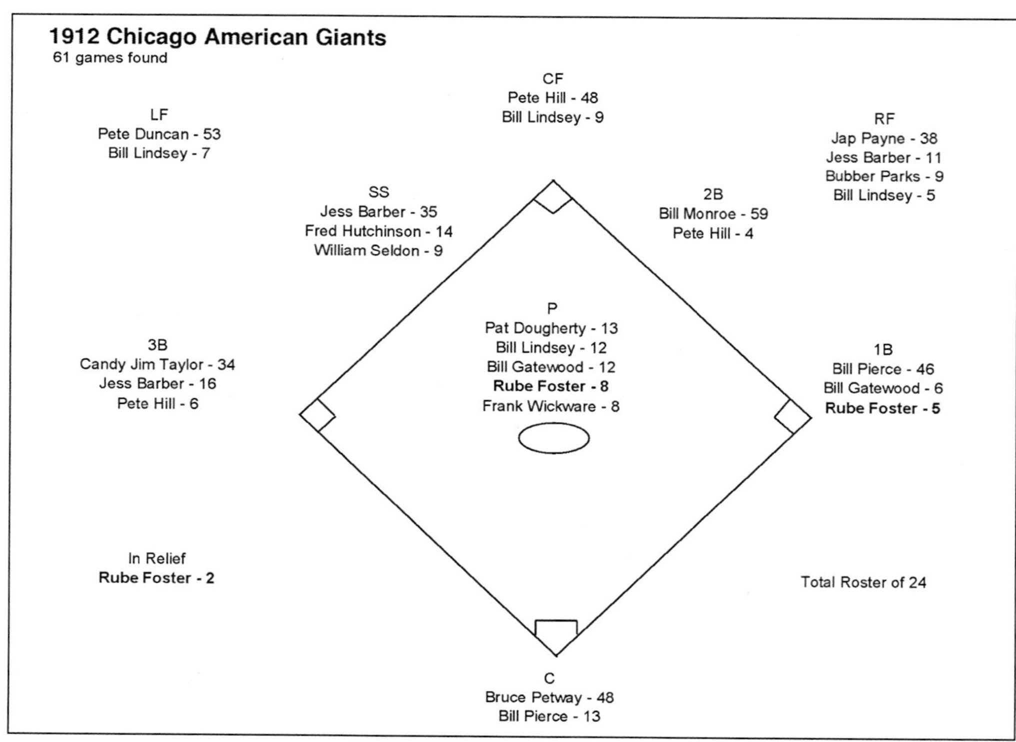
1912 Chicago American Giants
61 games found
CF
Pete Hill - 48
Bill Lindsey - 9
LF
Pete Duncan - 53
Bill Lindsey - 7
RF
Jap Payne - 38
Jess Barber - 11
Bubber Parks - 9
Bill Lindsey - 5
SS
Jess Barber - 35
Fred Hutchinson - 14
William Seldon - 9
2B
Bill Monroe - 59
Pete Hill - 4
3B
Candy Jim Taylor - 34
Jess Barber - 16
Pete Hill - 6
P
Pat Dougherty - 13
Bill Lindsey - 12
Bill Gatewood - 12
Rube Foster - 8
Frank Wickware - 8
1B
Bill Pierce - 46
Bill Gatewood - 6
Rube Foster - 5
In Relief
Rube Foster - 2
Total Roster of 24
C
Bruce Petway - 48
Bill Pierce - 13

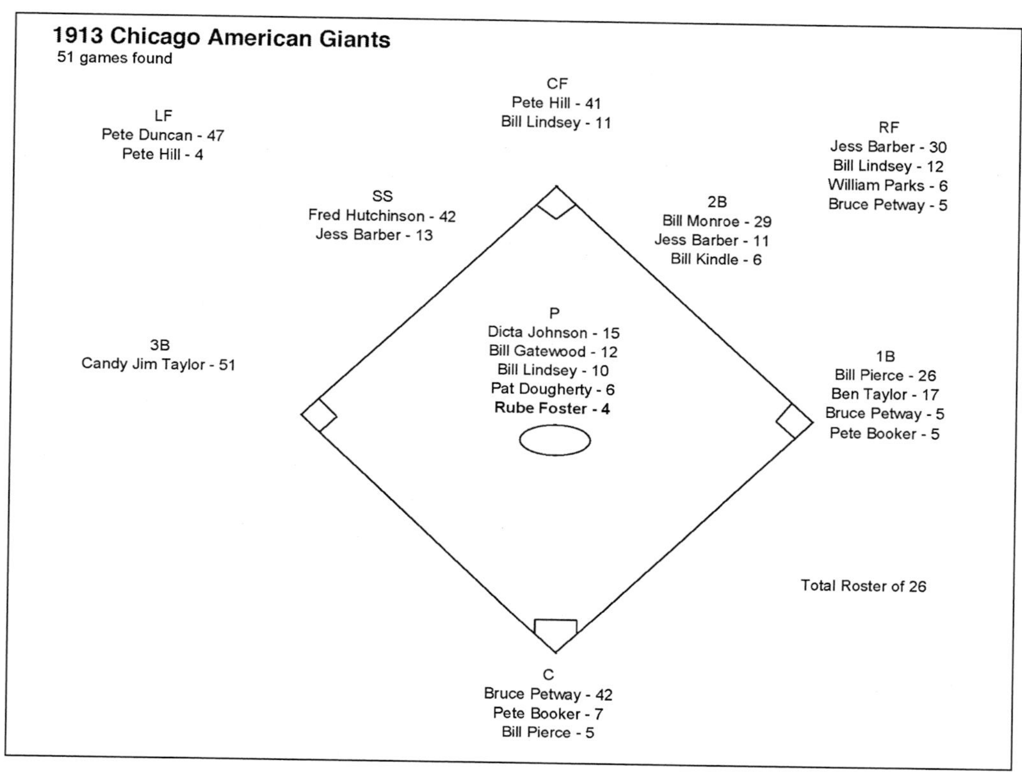
1913 Chicago American Giants
51 games found
CF
Pete Hill - 41
Bill Lindsey - 11
LF
Pete Duncan - 47
Pete Hill - 4
RF
Jess Barber - 30
Bill Lindsey - 12
William Parks - 6
Bruce Petway - 5
SS
Fred Hutchinson - 42
Jess Barber - 13
2B
Bill Monroe - 29
Jess Barber - 11
Bill Kindle - 6
P
Dicta Johnson - 15
Bill Gatewood - 12
Bill Lindsey - 10
Pat Dougherty - 6
Rube Foster - 4
3B
Candy Jim Taylor - 51
1B
Bill Pierce - 26
Ben Taylor - 17
Bruce Petway - 5
Pete Booker - 5
Total Roster of 26
C
Bruce Petway - 42
Pete Booker - 7
Bill Pierce - 5

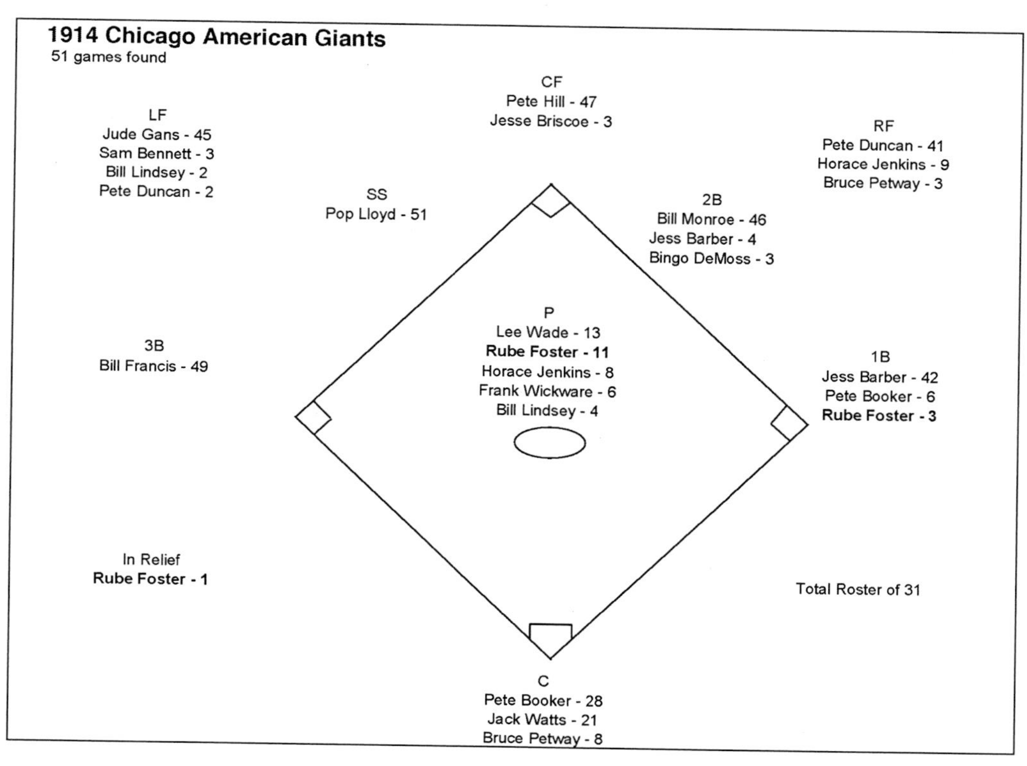
1914 Chicago American Giants
51 games found
CF
Pete Hill - 47
Jesse Briscoe - 3
LF
Jude Gans - 45
Sam Bennett - 3
Bill Lindsey - 2
Pete Duncan - 2
RF
Pete Duncan - 41
Horace Jenkins - 9
Bruce Petway - 3
SS
Pop Lloyd - 51
2B
Bill Monroe - 46
Jess Barber - 4
Bingo DeMoss - 3
P
Lee Wade - 13
Rube Foster - 11
Horace Jenkins - 8
Frank Wickware - 6
Bill Lindsey - 4
3B
Bill Francis - 49
1B
Jess Barber - 42
Pete Booker - 6
Rube Foster - 3
In Relief
Rube Foster - 1
Total Roster of 31
C
Pete Booker - 28
Jack Watts - 21
Bruce Petway - 8

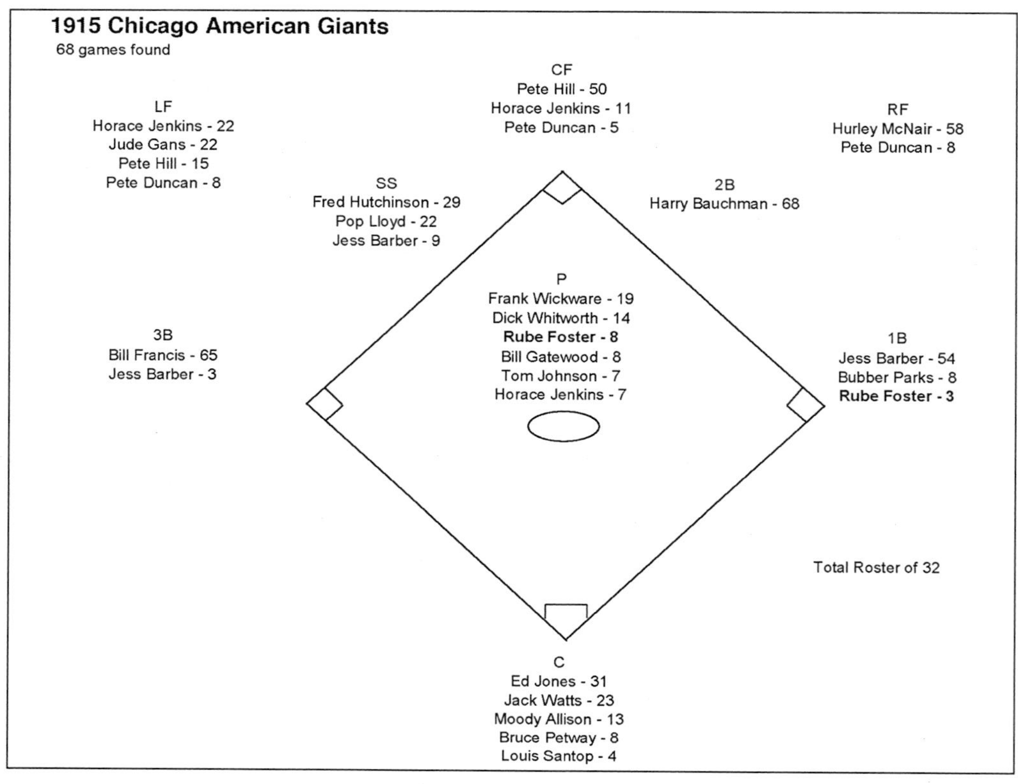
1915 Chicago American Giants
68 games found
CF
Pete Hill - 50
Horace Jenkins - 11
Pete Duncan - 5
LF
Horace Jenkins - 22
Jude Gans - 22
Pete Hill - 15
Pete Duncan - 8
RF
Hurley McNair - 58
Pete Duncan - 8
SS
Fred Hutchinson - 29
Pop Lloyd - 22
Jess Barber - 9
2B
Harry Bauchman - 68
P
Frank Wickware - 19
Dick Whitworth - 14
Rube Foster - 8
Bill Gatewood - 8
Tom Johnson - 7
Horace Jenkins - 7
3B
Bill Francis - 65
Jess Barber - 3
1B
Jess Barber - 54
Bubber Parks - 8
Rube Foster - 3
Total Roster of 32
C
Ed Jones - 31
Jack Watts - 23
Moody Allison - 13
Bruce Petway - 8
Louis Santop - 4

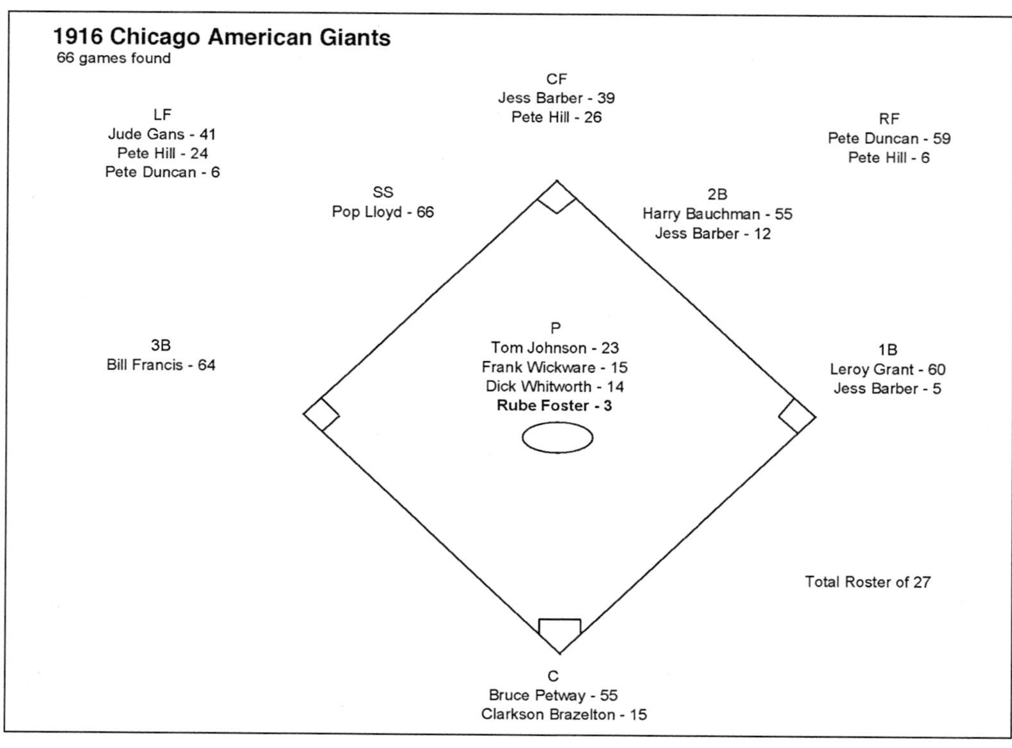
1916 Chicago American Giants
66 games found
CF
Jess Barber - 39
Pete Hill - 26
LF
Jude Gans - 41
Pete Hill - 24
Pete Duncan - 6
RF
Pete Duncan - 59
Pete Hill - 6
SS
Pop Lloyd - 66
2B
Harry Bauchman - 55
Jess Barber - 12
P
Tom Johnson - 23
Frank Wickware - 15
Dick Whitworth - 14
Rube Foster - 3
3B
Bill Francis - 64
1B
Leroy Grant - 60
Jess Barber - 5
Total Roster of 27
C
Bruce Petway - 55
Clarkson Brazelton - 15

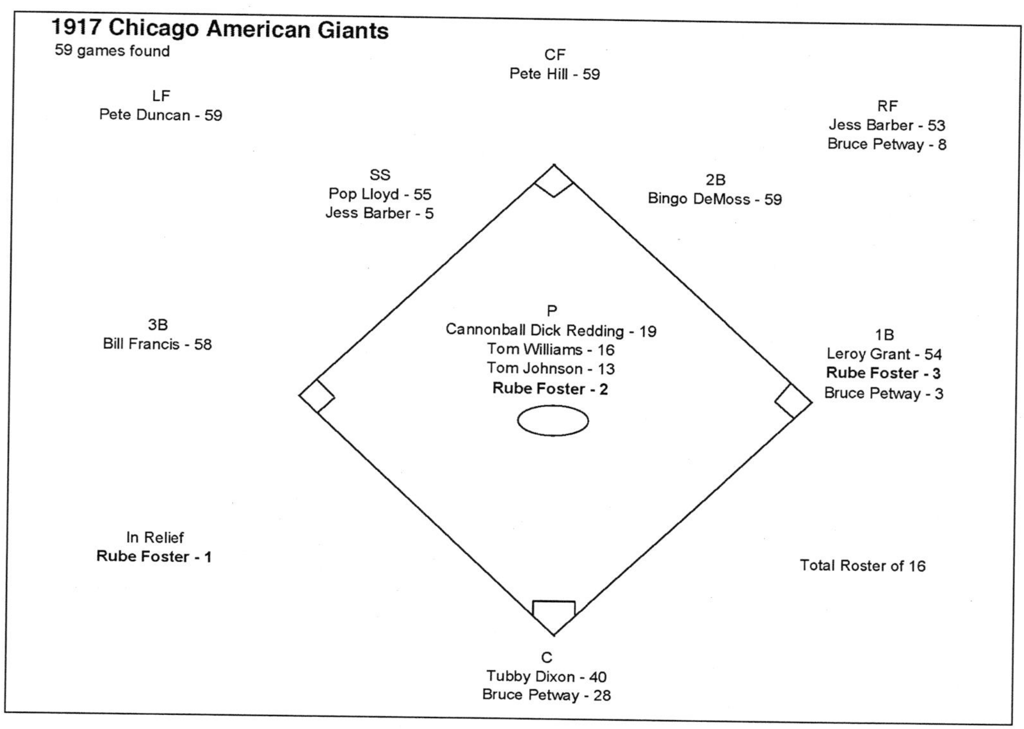

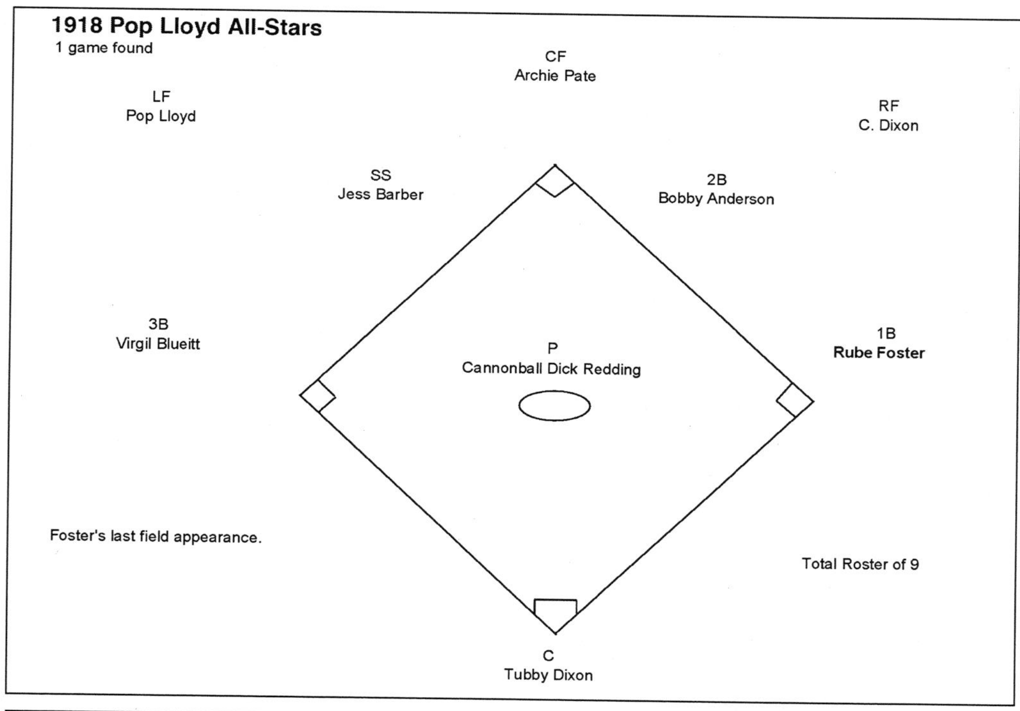

C: Foster's Daily Pitching and Batting Records

next page →

Daily Pitching Records

Team	Opp	Age	Date	DH	GS	CG	SO	W	L	PCT	IP	H	K	BB	WP	HB	RS	RN/9	ER	ERA
Waco (TX) Yellow Jackets	CIT	19	11-Aug-99		1	1	1	1	0		9.0	1	20	0	1	1	0	0.00	0	0.00
			1899		**1**	**1**	**1**	**1**	**0**	**1.000**	**9.0**	**1**	**20**	**0**	**1**	**1**	**0**	**0.00**	**0**	**0.00**
Palestine (TX) Yelw Jackets	CIT	20	06-Aug-00		1	1	0	0	1		9.0	14	0	0	0	0	7	7.00	7	7.00
Palestine (TX) Yelw Jackets	CIT	20	26-Aug-00		1	1	0	1	0		9.0	4	15	0	0	0	2	4.50	2	4.50
Palestine (TX) Yelw Jackets	CIT	20	01-Sep-00		1	1	0	1	0		6.0	10	0	0	0	0	5	5.25	2	4.13
			1900		**3**	**3**	**0**	**2**	**1**	**.667**	**24.0**	**28**	**15**	**0**	**0**	**0**	**14**	**5.25**	**11**	**4.13**
Waco (TX) Yellow Jackets	CIT	21	21-Jun-01		1	1	0	1	0		9.0	6	0	0	0	0	3	3.00	3	3.00
Waco (TX) Yellow Jackets	CIT	21	04-Jul-01		1	1	1	1	0		9.0	4	0	0	0	0	0	1.50	0	1.50
Fort Worth Colts	CIT	21	07-Jul-01		1	1	1	1	0		9.0	3	17	0	0	0	0	1.00	0	1.00
Fort Worth Colts	CIT	21	21-Jul-01		1	1	1	1	0		9.0	0	0	0	0	0	0	0.75	0	0.75
Fort Worth Colts	CIT	21	29-Jul-01		1	1	1	1	0		9.0	1	0	0	0	0	0	0.60	0	0.60
Fort Worth Colts	CIT	21	02-Aug-01		1	1	0	1	0		9.0	0	0	0	0	0	1	0.67	0	0.50
Waco (TX) Yellow Jackets	CIT	21	16-Aug-01		1	1	0	0	1		8.0	9	8	0	0	0	3	1.02	2	0.73
			1901		**7**	**7**	**4**	**6**	**1**	**.857**	**62.0**	**23**	**25**	**0**	**0**	**0**	**7**	**1.02**	**5**	**0.73**
Chicago Union Giants	CIT	22	11-May-02		1	1	0	0	1		8.0	12	1	10	0	2	11	12.38	6	6.75
Chicago Union Giants	CIT	22	22-Jun-02		1	1	0	1	0		9.0	10	7	4	0	0	5	8.47	2	4.24
Chicago Union Giants	CIT	22	13-Jul-02		1	1	0	1	0		9.0	4	8	1	0	1	2	6.23	1	3.12
Chicago Union Giants	CCG	22	27-Jul-02	1	1	1	0	1	0		9.0	5	10	5	0	0	3	5.40	1	2.57
Chicago Union Giants	CCG	22	03-Aug-02	3	1	1	0	0	1		9.0	10	5	2	0	0	4	5.11	2	2.45
Otsego Michigan	CIT	22	07-Aug-02		1	1	0	1	0		9.0	3	11	0	0	0	2	4.58	2	2.38
Otsego Michigan	CIT	22	15-Aug-02		1	1	0	0	1		9.0	5	13	0	0	1	2	4.21	1	2.18
Otsego Michigan	CIT	22	20-Aug-02		1	1	0	0	1		9.0	9	12	1	0	1	4	4.18	2	2.15
Otsego Michigan	CIT	22	22-Aug-02		1	1	0	0	1		10.0	4	11	1	0	0	4	4.11	2	2.11
Otsego Michigan	CIT	22	25-Aug-02		1	1	0	1	0		9.0	6	11	2	0	1	1	3.80	1	2.00
Otsego Michigan	CIT	22	28-Aug-02		1	1	0	1	0		9.0	4	0	0	0	0	2	3.64	2	2.00
Otsego Michigan	CIT	22	01-Sep-02		1	1	0	1	0		9.0	5	0	0	0	0	1	3.42	0	1.83
Otsego Michigan	CIT	22	13-Sep-02		1	1	0	1	0		9.0	7	0	0	0	0	1	3.23	1	1.77
Otsego Michigan	CIT	22	17-Sep-02		1	1	1	1	0		9.0	1	6	0	0	1	0	3.00	0	1.64
			1902		**14**	**14**	**1**	**9**	**5**	**.643**	**126.0**	**85**	**95**	**26**	**0**	**7**	**42**	**3.00**	**23**	**1.64**
Cuban X Giants	MIN	23	25-Jun-03		1	1	0	0	1		8.0	4	5	2	0	0	2	2.25	1	1.13
Cuban X Giants	CIT	23	28-Jun-03		1	1	0	0	1		8.0	14	2	3	1	1	13	8.44	12	7.31
Cuban X Giants	CIT	23	15-Jul-03		1	1	1	1	0		9.0	5	6	0	0	0	0	5.40	0	4.68
Cuban X Giants	CIT	23	25-Jul-03		1	1	1	1	0		9.0	6	8	2	0	0	0	3.97	0	3.44
Cuban X Giants	MIN	23	02-Aug-03		1	1	0	1	0		9.0	7	0	0	0	1	3	3.77	3	3.35
Cuban X Giants	CIT	23	06-Aug-03		1	1	0	1	0		9.0	12	6	2	0	0	4	3.81	2	3.14
Cuban X Giants	PGT	23	12-Sep-03	1	1	1	0	1	0		9.0	6	5	2	0	0	2	3.54	1	2.77
Cuban X Giants	PGT	23	14-Sep-03	4	1	1	0	1	0		9.0	3	3	2	0	1	1	3.21	0	2.36
Cuban X Giants	PGT	24	18-Sep-03	6	1	1	0	1	0		9.0	7	5	1	0	0	3	3.19	2	2.31
Cuban X Giants	PGT	24	25-Sep-03	7	1	1	1	1	0		9.0	3	7	0	0	0	0	2.86	0	2.05
			1903		**10**	**10**	**3**	**8**	**2**	**.800**	**88.0**	**67**	**47**	**14**	**1**	**3**	**28**	**2.86**	**21**	**2.15**

Team	Opp	Age	Date	DH	GS	CG	SO	W	L	PCT	IP	H	K	BB	WP	HB	RS	RN/9	ER	ERA
Philadelphia Giants	CIT	24	10-Apr-04		1	1	0	1	0		9.0	6	11	3	0	0	3	3.00	2	2.00
Philadelphia Giants	CIT	24	17-Apr-04		1	1	0	0	1		9.0	4	6	6	0	1	3	3.00	2	2.00
Philadelphia Giants	CIT	24	25-Apr-04		1	1	0	0	1		8.0	9	4	1	0	2	6	4.15	4	2.77
Philadelphia Giants	CIT	24	05-May-04		1	1	0	1	0		9.0	11	7	3	0	2	8	5.14	8	4.11
Philadelphia Giants	CIT	24	09-May-04		1	1	1	1	0		9.0	5	7	3	0	0	0	4.09	0	3.27
Philadelphia Giants	CIT	24	12-May-04		1	1	0	0	1		8.0	11	3	3	0	1	8	4.85	5	3.63
Philadelphia Giants	CIT	24	30-May-04	2	1	1	0	0	1		11.0	6	6	1	2	0	4	4.57	2	3.29
Philadelphia Giants	CIT	24	10-Jun-04		1	1	0	1	0		9.0	5	0	0	0	0	1	4.13	1	3.00
Philadelphia Giants	CIT	24	14-Jun-04		1	1	0	1	0		9.0	5	0	1	0	0	2	3.89	2	2.89
Philadelphia Giants	CIT	24	19-Jun-04		1	1	1	1	0		9.0	7	5	2	0	0	0	3.50	0	2.60
Philadelphia Giants	CIT	24	25-Jun-04		1	1	0	1	0		9.0	5	2	0	0	0	1	3.27	1	2.45
Philadelphia Giants	CIT	24	26-Jun-04		1	1	0	0	1		8.0	8	5	2	0	0	5	3.45	3	2.52
Philadelphia Giants	CIT	24	30-Jun-04		1	1	0	1	0		9.0	5	0	1	0	0	2	3.34	1	2.41
Philadelphia Giants	CIT	24	04-Jul-04	1	1	1	0	0	0		10.0	8	7	2	0	0	2	3.21	1	2.29
Philadelphia Giants	CIT	24	07-Jul-04		1	1	1	1	0		8.0	0	0	0	0	0	0	3.02	0	2.15
Philadelphia Giants	CIT	24	11-Jul-04	2	1	1	0	1	0		7.0	4	8	1	0	0	1	2.94	1	2.11
Philadelphia Giants	CIT	24	15-Jul-04		1	1	0	1	0		9.0	8	6	2	1	0	3	2.94	3	2.16
Philadelphia Giants	CIT	24	17-Jul-04		0	0	0	0	0		5.3	2	5	0	0	0	1	2.90	0	2.09
Philadelphia Giants	CIT	24	21-Jul-04	2	1	1	0	0	0		7.0	7	3	0	0	0	4	2.99	3	2.16
Philadelphia Giants	CIT	24	25-Jul-04		1	1	1	1	0		9.0	0	17	4	0	0	0	2.84	0	2.05
Philadelphia Giants	CIT	24	01-Aug-04		1	1	0	1	0		9.0	9	0	2	0	0	2	2.79	1	2.00
Philadelphia Giants	CIT	24	03-Aug-04		0	0	0	0	0		4.3	5	6	0	0	0	0	2.73	0	1.95
Philadelphia Giants	CIT	24	05-Aug-04		0	0	0	0	0		1.0	0	2	2	0	0	0	2.71	0	1.94
Philadelphia Giants	CIT	24	06-Aug-04		1	1	0	0	1		9.0	8	6	3	0	1	1	2.64	0	1.85
Philadelphia Giants	CIT	24	10-Aug-04		1	1	0	1	0		9.0	6	3	4	0	0	2	2.61	2	1.86
Philadelphia Giants	CIT	24	14-Aug-04		1	1	1	1	0		9.0	7	7	1	1	0	0	2.50	0	1.78
Philadelphia Giants	CIT	24	20-Aug-04		1	1	0	0	1		8.0	9	6	3	2	0	4	2.57	4	1.88
Philadelphia Giants	CIT	24	23-Aug-04		1	1	0	0	1		10.0	6	8	1	0	0	1	2.50	1	1.83
Philadelphia Giants	CIT	24	25-Aug-04		0	0	0	0	0		0.3	0	1	0	0	0	0	2.49	0	1.83
Philadelphia Giants	CIT	24	31-Aug-04	2	1	1	0	1	0		9.0	8	6	2	0	0	6	2.63	4	1.91
Philadelphia Giants	CXG	24	01-Sep-04	1	1	1	0	1	0		9.0	7	18	5	0	0	4	2.67	3	1.95
Philadelphia Giants	CXG	24	03-Sep-04	3	1	1	0	1	0		9.0	3	6	1	0	3	2	2.65	2	1.95
Philadelphia Giants	CIT	24	10-Sep-04		1	1	0	1	0		9.0	1	0	3	0	1	0	2.56	0	1.89
Philadelphia Giants	CIT	24	16-Sep-04		1	1	1	1	0		9.0	2	9	0	0	0	0	2.48	0	1.83
Philadelphia Giants	ALC	25	27-Sep-04		1	1	0	1	0		9.0	5	14	2	0	1	3	2.49	2	1.83
			1904		**31**	**31**	**6**	**21**	**8**	**.724**	**285.0**	**192**	**194**	**64**	**6**	**12**	**79**	**2.49**	**58**	**1.83**
Philadelphia Giants	CIT	25	01-Apr-05		0	0	0	0	0		2.0	1	0	0	0	0	2	9.00	2	9.00
Philadelphia Giants	MIN	25	08-Apr-05		1	1	0	1	0		7.0	9	2	2	0	0	4	6.00	3	5.00
Philadelphia Giants	CIT	25	22-Apr-05		1	1	0	1	0		9.0	3	9	2	0	0	1	3.50	0	2.50
Philadelphia Giants	CIT	25	30-Apr-05		0	0	0	1	0		4.3	8	1	2	0	0	8	6.04	5	4.03
Philadelphia Giants	CIT	25	14-May-05		1	1	0	1	0		11.0	4	8	1	0	0	3	4.86	3	3.51

Team	Opp	Age	Date	DH	GS	CG	SO	W	L	PCT	IP	H	K	BB	WP	HB	RS	RN/9	ER	ERA
Philadelphia Giants	CIT	25	17-May-05		1	1	0	1	0		9.0	4	5	5	0	0	3	4.46	1	2.98
Philadelphia Giants	CIT	25	20-May-05		1	1	0	0	1		8.0	5	2	5	0	1	4	4.47	1	2.68
Philadelphia Giants	CIT	25	22-May-05		1	1	1	1	0		9.0	5	5	0	0	0	0	3.79	0	2.28
Philadelphia Giants	CIT	25	02-Jun-05		1	1	0	1	0		9.0	5	3	4	0	0	3	3.69	1	2.11
Philadelphia Giants	CIT	25	06-Jun-05		1	1	0	1	0		9.0	7	3	2	0	3	3	3.61	1	1.98
Philadelphia Giants	CIT	25	22-Jun-05		1	1	0	1	0		6.0	3	6	3	1	0	1	3.46	0	1.84
Philadelphia Giants	CIT	25	25-Jun-05		1	1	0	1	0		9.0	0	4	3	0	0	0	3.12	0	1.66
Philadelphia Giants	CIT	25	28-Jun-05		1	1	0	1	0		9.0	9	5	1	0	0	3	3.11	3	1.78
Philadelphia Giants	CIT	25	01-Jul-05		1	1	0	1	0		9.0	5	8	2	1	0	1	2.94	0	1.63
Philadelphia Giants	CIT	25	04-Jul-05	2	1	1	0	1	0		9.0	8	4	6	0	0	2	2.87	2	1.66
Philadelphia Giants	CIT	25	07-Jul-05		1	1	0	1	0		9.0	6	2	1	0	0	2	2.81	1	1.61
Philadelphia Giants	CIT	25	11-Jul-05		1	1	1	1	0		9.0	2	0	0	0	0	0	2.62	0	1.51
Philadelphia Giants	CIT	25	16-Jul-05		1	1	0	0	1		8.0	4	4	1	0	2	2	2.60	1	1.49
Philadelphia Giants	BRG	25	20-Jul-05		1	1	0	0	0		13.0	3	9	1	0	0	2	2.50	1	1.42
Philadelphia Giants	CIT	25	24-Jul-05		1	1	0	1	0		5.0	9	4	2	0	0	3	2.59	2	1.49
Philadelphia Giants	CIT	25	27-Jul-05		1	1	0	1	0		9.0	5	5	2	1	0	2	2.56	1	1.46
Philadelphia Giants	CIT	25	02-Aug-05		1	1	0	1	0		9.0	6	2	2	0	0	4	2.63	3	1.54
Philadelphia Giants	CIT	25	11-Aug-05		1	1	0	1	0		9.0	13	5	3	0	0	4	2.70	3	1.61
Philadelphia Giants	CIT	25	14-Aug-05		1	1	0	1	0		11.0	5	0	3	0	2	3	2.68	3	1.65
Philadelphia Giants	CIT	25	22-Aug-05		1	1	1	1	0		9.0	0	5	2	0	0	0	2.57	0	1.58
Philadelphia Giants	CIT	25	26-Aug-05		1	1	0	1	0		9.0	2	8	0	0	0	2	2.54	1	1.56
Philadelphia Giants	CIT	25	29-Aug-05		1	1	0	0	0		14.0	7	0	4	0	0	4	2.55	2	1.54
Philadelphia Giants	BRG	25	07-Sep-05		1	1	0	1	0		9.0	6	1	2	2	0	1	2.49	0	1.49
Philadelphia Giants	CIT	25	12-Sep-05		1	1	1	1	0		9.0	3	7	0	0	0	0	2.40	0	1.43
Philadelphia Giants	BRG	25	15-Sep-05	2	1	1	0	1	0		10.0	10	0	0	0	0	6	2.51	3	1.48
Philadelphia Giants	CIT	26	18-Sep-05		1	1	0	1	0		9.0	1	0	2	0	0	1	2.46	1	1.46
Philadelphia Giants	CIT	26	24-Sep-05		0	0	0	1	0		5.3	6	6	0	0	0	0	2.42	0	1.44
Philadelphia Giants	CIT	26	30-Sep-05		1	1	0	0	1		8.0	3	2	3	0	1	3	2.44	2	1.46
Cuban X Giants	ALC	26	22-Oct-05		1	1	0	1	0		9.0	8	3	0	0	0	6	2.55	1	1.45
Cuban X Giants	ALC	26	08-Nov-05		1	1	0	0	1		9.0	5	5	1	0	0	4	2.60	1	1.43
			1905		**32**	**32**	**4**	**28**	**4**	**.875**	**301.7**	**180**	**133**	**67**	**5**	**9**	**87**	**2.60**	**48**	**1.43**
Philadelphia Giants	CIT	26	01-Apr-06		1	0	0	0	1		3.7	5	3	4	0	0	8	19.64	4	9.82
Philadelphia Giants	CIT	26	19-Apr-06		1	1	0	0	1		11.0	17	8	1	0	0	5	7.98	3	4.30
Philadelphia Giants	CIT	26	11-May-06		1	1	0	1	0		9.0	6	3	0	0	0	3	6.08	2	3.42
Philadelphia Giants	LLG	26	20-May-06		1	1	0	1	0		9.0	3	5	0	0	0	1	4.68	1	2.76
Philadelphia Giants	BRG	26	31-May-06		1	1	1	0	0		10.0	8	5	1	0	0	0	3.59	0	2.11
Philadelphia Giants	BRG	26	04-Jun-06		1	1	0	1	0		9.0	10	1	2	0	0	4	3.66	2	2.09
Philadelphia Giants	CIT	26	10-Jun-06		1	1	0	1	0		9.0	7	5	0	0	0	1	3.26	1	1.93
Philadelphia Giants	CIT	26	22-Jun-06		1	1	1	1	0		9.0	4	5	0	0	0	0	2.84	0	1.68
Philadelphia Giants	CIT	26	30-Jun-06	1	1	1	0	1	0		9.0	3	2	5	0	0	5	3.09	2	1.72
Philadelphia Giants	CIT	26	18-Jul-06		1	1	0	1	0		10.0	9	7	1	0	0	2	2.94	2	1.73

Team	Opp	Age	Date	DH	GS	CG	SO	W	L	PCT	IP	H	K	BB	WP	HB	RS	RN/9	ER	ERA
Philadelphia Giants	CIT	26	04-Aug-06		1	1	0	1	0		9.0	6	8	2	0	0	3	2.95	2	1.75
Philadelphia Giants	CIT	26	14-Aug-06	2	1	1	0	1	0		9.0	6	2	0	0	0	1	2.78	1	1.69
Philadelphia Giants	CIT	26	23-Aug-06		1	1	0	1	0		9.0	6	4	1	0	0	3	2.80	2	1.71
Philadelphia Giants	CXG	26	03-Sep-06	1	1	1	0	1	0		9.0	10	9	0	0	0	2	2.74	1	1.66
			1906		**14**	**13**	**2**	**11**	**2**	**.846**	**124.7**	**100**	**67**	**17**	**0**	**0**	**38**	**2.74**	**23**	**1.66**
Chicago Leland Giants	CIT	27	28-Apr-07		1	1	0	1	0		9.0	13	6	1	0	0	5	5.00	4	4.00
Chicago Leland Giants	CIT	27	19-May-07		1	1	1	1	0		9.0	4	9	1	0	0	0	2.50	0	2.00
Chicago Leland Giants	CIT	27	30-May-07	2	1	1	0	1	0		13.0	8	17	5	0	0	3	2.32	3	2.03
Chicago Leland Giants	CIT	27	09-Jun-07		1	1	0	1	0		9.0	3	3	0	0	0	1	2.03	0	1.58
Chicago Leland Giants	CIT	27	16-Jun-07		1	1	0	1	0		9.0	2	0	0	0	0	1	1.84	1	1.47
Chicago Leland Giants	CIT	27	22-Jun-07		1	1	0	1	0		9.0	8	7	2	0	0	4	2.17	2	1.55
Chicago Leland Giants	CIT	27	04-Jul-07	2	1	1	0	0	1		8.0	8	3	1	0	0	7	2.86	3	1.77
Chicago Leland Giants	CIT	27	07-Jul-07		1	1	0	1	0		9.0	4	7	1	0	0	5	3.12	3	1.92
Chicago Leland Giants	CIT	27	20-Jul-07		1	1	0	0	1		12.7	11	11	3	0	0	5	3.18	4	2.05
Chicago Leland Giants	ABC	27	27-Jul-07	2	1	1	0	1	0		9.0	7	1	0	0	0	1	2.98	1	1.96
Chicago Leland Giants	CIT	27	04-Aug-07		1	1	0	1	0		9.0	2	3	0	0	0	1	2.81	0	1.79
Chicago Leland Giants	CIT	27	06-Aug-07		1	1	0	1	0		9.0	7	4	2	0	1	2	2.75	2	1.81
Chicago Leland Giants	CIT	27	08-Aug-07		1	1	1	1	0		9.0	5	5	0	0	0	0	2.55	0	1.67
Chicago Leland Giants	CIT	27	10-Aug-07		1	0	0	0	1		8.7	7	7	0	0	0	3	2.58	2	1.70
Chicago Leland Giants	CIT	27	17-Aug-07		1	1	1	1	0		9.0	5	8	2	0	0	0	2.42	0	1.59
Chicago Leland Giants	ABC	27	21-Aug-07		1	1	0	1	0		9.0	10	3	1	0	0	4	2.51	2	1.62
Chicago Leland Giants	CIT	27	24-Aug-07		1	1	0	1	0		9.0	3	5	1	0	0	4	2.60	1	1.58
Chicago Leland Giants	CIT	27	27-Aug-07		1	1	0	1	0		9.0	3	5	1	0	1	1	2.51	0	1.50
Chicago Leland Giants	CIT	27	30-Aug-07		1	1	0	1	0		9.0	8	4	3	0	0	4	2.59	3	1.57
Chicago Leland Giants	CIT	27	15-Sep-07		1	1	1	1	0		9.0	0	7	3	0	0	0	2.46	0	1.50
Chicago Leland Giants	CIT	28	22-Sep-07		1	1	0	1	0		9.0	0	7	3	0	0	0	2.35	0	1.43
St. Paul Colored Gophers	CIT	28	23-Sep-07		1	1	0	1	0		9.0	5	10	4	1	0	3	2.38	0	1.37
Chicago Leland Giants	MIN	28	05-Oct-07		1	0	0	0	0		0.7	0	0	0	0	0	0	2.37	0	1.36
Chicago Leland Giants	CIT	28	13-Oct-07		1	1	0	1	0		7.0	3	4	0	0	0	2	2.38	2	1.40
			1907		**24**	**22**	**4**	**20**	**3**	**.870**	**212.0**	**126**	**136**	**34**	**1**	**2**	**56**	**2.38**	**33**	**1.40**
Chicago Leland Giants	CIT	28	18-Apr-08		0	0	0	1	0		4.0	4	3	1	0	0	2	4.50	1	2.25
Chicago Leland Giants	CIT	28	03-May-08		1	1	0	1	0		9.0	3	9	0	0	0	1	2.08	1	1.38
Chicago Leland Giants	CIT	28	10-May-08		1	1	1	1	0		9.0	5	6	1	0	0	0	1.23	0	0.82
Chicago Leland Giants	CIT	28	17-May-08		1	1	1	1	0		9.0	3	6	1	0	0	0	0.87	0	0.58
Chicago Leland Giants	CIT	28	24-May-08		1	1	1	1	0		9.0	2	11	2	0	0	0	0.68	0	0.45
Chicago Leland Giants	CIT	28	06-Jun-08		0	0	0	0	0		2.0	0	2	0	0	0	0	0.64	0	0.43
Chicago Leland Giants	CIT	28	07-Jun-08		1	1	0	1	0		9.0	4	4	1	0	0	1	0.71	0	0.35
Chicago Leland Giants	CIT	28	20-Jun-08		1	1	1	1	0		9.0	3	6	2	0	0	0	0.60	0	0.30
Chicago Leland Giants	CIT	28	21-Jun-08		0	0	0	1	0		4.7	2	3	0	0	0	0	0.56	0	0.28
Chicago Leland Giants	CIT	28	27-Jun-08		1	1	0	0	1		9.0	3	1	0	0	0	3	0.86	2	0.49
Chicago Leland Giants	CIT	28	04-Jul-08	1	1	1	0	1	0		9.0	6	8	0	0	0	1	0.87	0	0.44

Team	Opp	Age	Date	DH	GS	CG	SO	W	L	PCT	IP	H	K	BB	WP	HB	RS	RN/9	ER	ERA
Chicago Leland Giants	CIT	28	09-Jul-08		1	1	0	1	0		9.0	5	3	0	0	0	2	0.98	1	0.49
Chicago Leland Giants	CBG	28	12-Jul-08		1	1	0	1	0		9.0	11	1	3	0	0	6	1.43	4	0.80
Chicago Leland Giants	CIT	28	19-Jul-08		0	0	0	1	0		9.0	2	8	1	0	0	0	1.31	0	0.74
Chicago Leland Giants	CIT	28	26-Jul-08		1	1	0	1	0		9.0	9	10	1	0	0	3	1.44	2	0.83
Chicago Leland Giants	PGT	28	02-Aug-08	4	1	1	0	1	0		9.0	5	5	1	0	0	1	1.41	0	0.78
Chicago Leland Giants	PGT	28	06-Aug-08	5	1	1	0	0	1		9.0	12	2	3	0	0	8	1.84	5	1.05
Chicago Leland Giants	CIT	28	09-Aug-08	2	1	1	0	0	1		8.0	2	5	7	0	0	4	1.99	3	1.18
Chicago Leland Giants	CIT	28	14-Aug-08		1	1	1	1	0		9.0	2	4	0	0	1	0	1.87	0	1.11
Chicago Leland Giants	CIT	28	23-Aug-08		0	0	0	0	1		1.3	0	0	0	0	0	1	1.92	0	1.10
St. Paul Colored Gophers	CIT	28	28-Aug-08		1	1	1	1	0		9.0	0	6	2	0	1	0	1.81	0	1.04
Chicago Leland Giants	CIT	28	30-Aug-08		1	1	0	0	1		9.0	9	6	1	0	0	4	1.92	3	1.14
Chicago Leland Giants	CIT	28	07-Sep-08		1	1	0	0	1		8.3	9	8	1	0	0	2	1.94	1	1.14
Chicago Leland Giants	CIT	29	19-Sep-08		1	1	0	1	0		9.0	4	6	2	0	0	5	2.08	1	1.13
Chicago Leland Giants	MIN	29	22-Sep-08		0	0	0	0	0		5.0	3	3	3	0	0	2	2.12	1	1.15
Chicago Leland Giants	CIT	29	04-Oct-08		1	0	0	0	0		4.0	2	2	1	0	0	0	2.08	0	1.13
			1908		**20**	**19**	**6**	**17**	**6**	**.739**	**199.3**	**110**	**128**	**34**	**0**	**2**	**46**	**2.08**	**25**	**1.13**
Chicago Leland Giants	CIT	29	11-Apr-09		1	0	0	1	0		6.0	5	6	1	0	0	3	4.50	1	1.50
Chicago Leland Giants	BBG	29	18-Apr-09	2	1	0	0	1	0		8.7	6	6	1	0	0	2	3.07	1	1.23
Chicago Leland Giants	CIT	29	06-May-09		1	1	0	1	0		9.0	4	9	4	0	0	1	2.28	0	0.76
Chicago Leland Giants	CIT	29	16-May-09		1	1	0	1	0		9.0	6	9	4	0	0	1	1.93	0	0.55
Chicago Leland Giants	LOC	29	27-May-09		1	1	0	1	0		9.0	5	7	1	0	0	2	1.94	1	0.65
Chicago Leland Giants	CIT	29	30-May-09		1	1	0	1	0		9.0	6	3	1	0	0	1	1.78	1	0.71
Chicago Leland Giants	CIT	29	31-May-09	2	1	0	0	0	1		0.0	1	0	0	0	0	1	1.95	1	0.89
Chicago Leland Giants	CIT	29	06-Jun-09		1	1	0	1	0		9.0	4	1	4	0	0	1	1.81	1	0.91
Chicago Leland Giants	CIT	29	13-Jun-09	1	1	1	1	1	0		9.0	3	6	3	0	0	0	1.57	0	0.79
Chicago Leland Giants	MIN	29	18-Jun-09		1	1	1	1	0		9.0	5	3	0	0	0	0	1.39	0	0.70
Chicago Leland Giants	CIT	29	19-Jun-09		1	1	1	1	0		9.0	3	4	1	0	0	0	1.25	0	0.62
Chicago Leland Giants	MIN	29	26-Jun-09		1	1	1	1	0		9.0	5	5	0	0	0	0	1.13	0	0.56
Chicago Leland Giants	CSS	29	29-Jun-09		1	1	1	1	0		9.0	6	7	2	0	0	0	1.03	0	0.52
Chicago Leland Giants	CSS	29	01-Jul-09		1	1	1	1	0		9.0	5	4	2	0	1	0	0.95	0	0.48
Chicago Leland Giants	CIT	29	03-Jul-09	1	1	1	0	0	1		8.0	14	4	0	0	1	5	1.26	4	0.74
Chicago Leland Giants	CIT	29	05-Jul-09	2	1	1	0	1	0		9.0	4	6	2	0	0	2	1.31	1	0.76
Chicago Leland Giants	MIN	29	11-Jul-09	1	1	1	0	1	0		9.0	6	5	2	0	0	2	1.35	1	0.77
Chicago Leland Giants	CIT	29	11-Jul-09	2	1	1	0	0	1		9.0	11	4	3	0	0	9	1.82	4	0.97
Chicago Leland Giants	MIN	30	21-Oct-09		1	1	0	0	1		9.0	13	2	1	0	1	6	2.05	4	1.14
			1909		**19**	**16**	**6**	**15**	**4**	**.789**	**157.7**	**112**	**91**	**32**	**0**	**3**	**36**	**2.05**	**20**	**1.14**
Chicago Leland Giants	BRG	30	25-Jan-10		1	1	1	1	0		9.0	3	4	0	0	0	0	0.00	0	0.00
Chicago Leland Giants	BRG	30	04-Mar-10		1	1	1	1	0		9.0	1	4	0	0	0	0	0.00	0	0.00
Chicago Leland Giants	KCK	30	08-May-10		1	1	0	1	0		9.0	6	6	1	0	0	2	0.67	1	0.33
Chicago Leland Giants	CIT	30	15-May-10	1	1	1	0	1	0		9.0	7	8	1	0	0	2	1.00	1	0.50
Chicago Leland Giants	STC	30	22-May-10		1	1	0	1	0		9.0	5	4	1	0	0	1	1.00	0	0.40

Team	Opp	Age	Date	DH	GS	CG	SO	W	L	PCT	IP	H	K	BB	WP	HB	RS	RN/9	ER	ERA
Chicago Leland Giants	CIT	30	29-May-10	1	1	1	0	1	0		9.0	7	5	2	0	0	3	1.33	2	0.67
Chicago Leland Giants	CIT	30	30-May-10	1	1	1	0	1	0		9.0	12	2	2	0	0	8	2.29	3	1.00
Chicago Leland Giants	CIT	30	11-Jun-10		1	1	0	0	1		8.0	9	6	0	0	0	3	2.41	2	1.14
Chicago Leland Giants	CIT	30	12-Jun-10	1	1	1	0	0	1		8.0	9	6	2	0	0	3	2.51	2	1.25
Chicago Leland Giants	CIT	30	18-Jun-10	1	1	0	0	1	0		8.7	5	8	2	0	0	2	2.46	1	1.23
Chicago Leland Giants	SPD	30	20-Jun-10		1	1	0	1	0		9.0	6	5	0	0	0	2	2.42	2	1.30
Chicago Leland Giants	CIT	30	24-Jun-10	1	1	0	0	1	0		7.0	8	7	1	0	0	2	2.43	1	1.30
Chicago Leland Giants	CIT	30	04-Jul-10	2	0	0	0	1	0		4.0	4	3	1	0	0	0	2.34	0	1.25
Chicago Leland Giants	CIT	30	16-Jul-10		1	1	0	1	0		9.0	11	5	1	0	0	3	2.39	2	1.31
Chicago Leland Giants	STC	30	21-Jul-10		1	1	0	1	0		11.0	4	7	1	0	0	1	2.26	0	1.20
Chicago Leland Giants	STC	30	28-Jul-10		1	1	0	0	0		11.0	14	4	2	0	0	4	2.34	3	1.30
Chicago Leland Giants	CIT	30	31-Jul-10	2	1	1	0	1	0		9.0	9	6	1	0	0	1	2.26	0	1.22
Chicago Leland Giants	CIT	30	04-Aug-10		1	1	0	1	0		9.0	12	3	0	0	0	4	2.36	3	1.32
Chicago Leland Giants	CIT	30	26-Aug-10		1	1	0	1	0		9.0	6	4	2	0	0	4	2.44	2	1.36
Chicago Leland Giants	CIT	30	09-Sep-10	1	1	1	1	1	0		9.0	3	8	0	0	0	0	2.32	0	1.29
Chicago Leland Giants	CIT	31	04-Oct-10		1	1	1	1	0		9.0	3	4	0	0	0	0	2.21	0	1.23
			1910		**20**	**18**	**4**	**18**	**2**	**.900**	**183.7**	**144**	**109**	**20**	**0**	**0**	**45**	**2.21**	**25**	**1.23**
Chicago American Giants	CIT	31	28-May-11	2	1	0	0	0	1		3.0	5	5	0	0	0	3	9.00	2	6.00
Chicago American Giants	CSS	31	30-May-11	1	0	0	0	0	0		5.3	2	5	0	0	0	0	3.24	0	2.16
Chicago American Giants	CSS	31	31-May-11		1	0	0	0	0		6.0	7	4	2	0	0	3	3.77	2	2.51
Chicago American Giants	CIT	31	04-Jun-11		0	0	0	0	0		4.0	4	3	1	0	0	4	4.91	3	3.44
Chicago American Giants	CSS	31	15-Jun-11		1	1	0	1	0		9.0	9	2	2	0	0	3	4.28	2	2.96
Chicago American Giants	CIT	31	28-Jun-11		1	1	0	0	1		9.0	16	10	3	0	0	8	5.20	1	2.48
Chicago American Giants	COG	31	03-Jul-11		0	0	0	0	0		6.3	3	3	2	0	0	3	5.06	3	2.74
Chicago American Giants	COG	31	04-Jul-11	1	0	0	0	0	0		4.3	4	4	0	0	0	1	4.79	0	2.49
Chicago American Giants	CIT	31	08-Jul-11		0	0	0	0	0		4.3	5	4	1	0	0	5	5.26	3	2.81
Chicago American Giants	CIT	31	15-Jul-11		1	0	0	0	0		5.7	9	3	1	0	0	6	5.68	4	3.16
Chicago American Giants	CSS	31	15-Aug-11		1	1	0	0	1		9.0	6	6	2	0	0	4	5.45	4	3.27
Chicago American Giants	CSS	31	29-Aug-11		1	1	0	0	1		8.0	5	4	2	0	0	1	4.99	1	3.04
Chicago American Giants	BRG	31	10-Sep-11	1	0	0	0	1	0		7.0	10	4	1	0	0	2	4.78	2	3.00
Chicago American Giants	KCK	31	16-Sep-11		1	0	0	0	0		3.7	2	3	0	0	0	2	4.78	1	2.98
Chicago American Giants	COG	32	08-Oct-11		1	1	0	0	1		9.0	11	2	3	0	0	7	5.00	5	3.17
			1911		**9**	**5**	**0**	**2**	**5**	**.286**	**93.7**	**98**	**62**	**20**	**0**	**0**	**52**	**5.00**	**33**	**3.17**
Chicago American Giants	CIT	32	28-Apr-12		1	1	0	1	0		9.0	5	6	0	0	0	2	2.00	2	2.00
Chicago American Giants	BRG	32	21-May-12		1	1	0	1	0		9.0	8	2	0	0	0	1	1.50	0	1.00
Chicago American Giants	FLP	32	16-Jun-12		1	1	0	1	0		9.0	7	4	2	0	0	5	2.67	4	2.00
Chicago American Giants	SLG	32	20-Jun-12		0	0	0	0	0		1.0	4	0	1	0	0	4	3.86	3	2.89
Chicago American Giants	CSS	32	02-Jul-12		0	0	0	1	0		3.3	2	2	0	0	0	1	3.73	1	2.87
Chicago American Giants	SPD	32	29-Jul-12		1	1	0	1	0		9.0	5	7	1	0	0	1	3.12	0	2.23
Chicago American Giants	CSS	32	06-Aug-12		1	1	0	1	0		9.0	8	5	2	0	0	4	3.28	3	2.37
Chicago American Giants	CSS	32	11-Aug-12		1	1	0	0	0		12.0	11	7	2	0	0	2	2.93	1	2.05

Team	Opp	Age	Date	DH	GS	CG	SO	W	L	PCT	IP	H	K	BB	WP	HB	RS	RN/9	ER	ERA
Chicago American Giants	CSS	32	15-Aug-12		1	1	0	0	1		9.0	6	6	2	0	0	4	3.07	3	2.18
Chicago American Giants	COG	32	08-Sep-12		1	1	0	1	0		9.0	9	5	4	0	0	4	3.18	3	2.27
Chicago American Giants	CIT	33	22-Oct-12		1	0	0	1	0		5.0	4	4	0	0	0	0	2.99	0	2.13
Chicago American Giants	CIT	33	15-Nov-12		1	1	0	0	1		9.0	9	0	4	0	0	3	2.99	1	2.03
Chicago American Giants	CIT	33	24-Nov-12		1	0	0	0	1		2.0	7	1	1	0	0	6	3.49	5	2.45
Chicago American Giants	CIT	33	20-Dec-12		1	1	0	0	1		8.0	7	1	6	0	0	5	3.66	3	2.53
			1912		**12**	**10**	**0**	**8**	**4**	**.667**	**103.3**	**92**	**50**	**25**	**0**	**0**	**42**	**3.66**	**29**	**2.53**
Joe Green's All-Stars	HAS	33	06-May-13		1	1	0	0	1		9.0	8	5	8	0	0	6	6.00	3	3.00
Chicago American Giants	CIT	33	30-May-13	2	1	1	0	1	0		9.0	5	6	0	0	0	2	4.00	1	2.00
Chicago American Giants	FLP	33	03-Jun-13		1	1	0	1	0		10.0	7	6	2	0	0	3	3.54	2	1.93
Chicago American Giants	CSS	33	17-Jun-13		1	0	0	1	0		5.0	6	4	2	0	0	6	4.64	2	2.18
Chicago American Giants	BRG	33	11-Jul-13		1	0	0	0	0		5.0	5	4	2	0	0	4	4.97	3	2.61
Chicago American Giants	SLG	33	31-Aug-13		1	1	0	1	0		9.0	12	5	2	0	0	6	5.17	5	3.06
Chicago American Giants	SPD	33	08-Sep-13		1	1	0	1	0		11.0	7	3	3	0	0	3	4.66	1	2.64
Chicago American Giants	COG	33	14-Sep-13		1	1	0	0	1		9.0	14	5	4	0	0	9	5.24	7	3.22
Chicago American Giants	MIN	34	12-Oct-13		1	1	0	1	0		9.0	8	9	4	0	0	3	4.97	2	3.08
			1913		**9**	**7**	**0**	**6**	**2**	**.750**	**76.0**	**72**	**47**	**27**	**0**	**0**	**42**	**4.97**	**26**	**3.08**
Chicago American Giants	MIN	34	25-Mar-14		1	0	0	0	0		6.0	6	2	1	0	0	4	6.00	3	4.50
Chicago American Giants	CIT	34	10-Apr-14	2	1	1	0	0	1		9.0	7	6	1	0	0	3	4.20	2	3.00
Chicago American Giants	CIT	34	16-Apr-14		1	1	0	1	0		9.0	3	6	1	0	0	1	3.00	0	1.88
Chicago American Giants	CIT	34	03-May-14		1	1	0	1	0		9.0	7	5	2	0	0	6	3.82	6	3.00
Chicago American Giants	CSS	34	25-May-14		0	0	0	0	1		5.0	7	0	1	0	0	4	4.26	3	3.32
Chicago American Giants	CSS	34	28-May-14		1	1	1	1	0		9.0	1	5	0	0	0	0	3.45	0	2.68
Chicago American Giants	ABC	34	01-Jun-14		1	1	1	1	0		9.0	3	7	0	0	0	0	2.89	0	2.25
Chicago American Giants	CIT	34	07-Jun-14		1	1	0	1	0		9.0	8	4	0	0	0	4	3.05	4	2.49
Chicago American Giants	ABC	34	18-Jun-14		1	1	1	1	0		9.0	1	3	1	0	0	0	2.68	0	2.19
Chicago American Giants	FLP	34	29-Jun-14		1	1	0	1	0		9.0	6	5	4	0	0	1	2.49	0	1.95
Chicago American Giants	CSS	34	05-Jul-14		1	0	0	1	0		7.0	7	2	0	0	0	3	2.60	3	2.10
Chicago American Giants	CIT	34	18-Jul-14		1	1	1	1	0		9.0	6	6	0	0	0	0	2.36	0	1.91
Chicago American Giants	ABC	34	29-Jul-14		1	0	0	0	1		5.0	6	4	3	0	0	4	2.60	4	2.16
Louisville White Sox	CIT	34	02-Aug-14		1	0	0	1	0		6.0	9	6	2	0	0	3	2.70	3	2.29
Chicago American Giants	CSS	34	15-Aug-14		1	1	0	0	1		9.0	9	2	3	0	0	5	2.87	2	2.27
Chicago American Giants	ABC	34	25-Aug-14		1	1	0	1	0		9.0	10	3	3	0	0	6	3.09	6	2.53
Chicago American Giants	ABC	34	27-Aug-14		1	1	0	0	1		9.0	10	6	2	0	0	4	3.15	3	2.56
Chicago American Giants	BRG	34	02-Sep-14	4	1	1	0	1	0		9.0	8	5	1	0	0	2	3.08	2	2.53
Chicago American Giants	ABC	35	22-Sep-14		1	1	0	0	1		8.0	8	6	3	0	0	7	3.33	6	2.75
			1914		**18**	**14**	**4**	**12**	**6**	**.667**	**154.0**	**122**	**83**	**28**	**0**	**0**	**57**	**3.33**	**47**	**2.75**
Chicago American Giants	CIT	35	14-Mar-15		1	0	0	1	0		5.0	4	3	2	0	0	3	5.40	2	3.60
Chicago American Giants	MIN	35	09-Apr-15		1	0	0	0	0		6.0	2	2	2	0	0	0	2.45	0	1.64
Chicago American Giants	CIT	35	16-May-15		1	0	0	1	0		6.0	5	2	4	0	0	2	2.65	2	2.12
Chicago American Giants	CIT	35	13-Jun-15	1	1	1	0	1	0		9.0	3	6	1	0	0	2	2.42	2	2.08

Team	Opp	Age	Date	DH	GS	CG	SO	W	L	PCT	IP	H	K	BB	WP	HB	RS	RN/9	ER	ERA
Chicago American Giants	LWS	35	16-Jun-15		1	1	0	1	0		9.0	6	3	2	0	0	1	2.06	1	1.80
Chicago American Giants	ABC	35	20-Jun-15		1	1	0	1	0		9.0	3	3	4	0	0	1	1.84	1	1.64
Chicago American Giants	CSS	35	04-Jul-15		1	1	0	0	1		9.0	10	4	2	0	0	4	2.21	4	2.04
Chicago American Giants	CSS	35	11-Jul-15	2	1	0	0	0	0		1.0	3	0	0	0	0	2	2.50	2	2.33
Chicago American Giants	ABC	35	19-Jul-15		0	0	0	0	0		5.0	3	4	1	0	0	1	2.44	1	2.29
Chicago American Giants	LCS	35	09-Aug-15	6	1	1	0	0	1		9.0	10	2	3	0	0	11	3.57	8	3.04
Chicago American Giants	CSS	35	02-Sep-15		1	0	0	0	0		2.0	4	4	1	0	0	3	3.86	2	3.21
			1915		**10**	**5**	**0**	**5**	**2**	**.714**	**70.0**	**53**	**33**	**22**	**0**	**0**	**30**	**3.86**	**25**	**3.21**
Chicago American Giants	MIN	36	03-Apr-16		1	0	0	0	1		7.7	4	3	3	0	0	8	9.39	6	7.04
Chicago American Giants	CIT	36	14-May-16		1	0	0	0	0		4.0	2	4	1	0	0	1	6.94	0	4.63
Chicago American Giants	SLG	36	13-Jul-16		1	1	0	1	0		9.0	9	5	6	0	0	3	5.23	1	3.05
Chicago American Giants	CSS	36	22-Aug-16		1	1	0	0	1		9.0	8	3	3	0	0	3	4.55	2	2.73
			1916		**4**	**2**	**0**	**1**	**2**	**.333**	**29.7**	**23**	**15**	**13**	**0**	**0**	**15**	**4.55**	**9**	**2.73**
Chicago American Giants	CIT	37	09-Jun-17		0	0	0	0	0		2.0	0	2	1	0	0	0	0.00	0	0.00
Chicago American Giants	CSW	37	02-Jul-17		1	1	0	0	1		9.0	9	0	7	0	0	7	5.73	7	5.73
Chicago American Giants	JBC	37	27-Jul-17		1	1	0	1	0		9.0	4	5	2	0	0	2	4.05	2	4.05
Chicago American Giants	CIT	37	31-Jul-17		1	1	0	1	0		9.0	8	5	1	0	0	2	3.41	2	3.41
			1917		**3**	**3**	**0**	**2**	**1**	**.667**	**29.0**	**21**	**12**	**11**	**0**	**0**	**11**	**3.41**	**11**	**3.41**
Chicago American Giants	BAG	38	04-Aug-18		0	0	0	0	0		4.0	3	2	0	0	0	0	0.00	0	0.00
			1918		**0**	**0**	**0**	**0**	**0**	**.000**	**4.0**	**3**	**2**	**0**	**0**	**0**	**0**	**0.00**	**0**	**0.00**
Rube Foster's Totals	**286 Games**				**259**	**231**	**45**	**191**	**60**	**.761**	**2323.7**	**1645**	**1364**	**454**	**14**	**39**	**724**	**2.80**	**469**	**1.82**

Legend

ABC — Indianapolis ABC's
ALC — All Cubans
BLA — Brooklyn All-Stars
BAG — Bacharach Giants
BRG — Brooklyn Royal Giants
CBG — Cuban Giants
CCG — Chicago Columbia Giants
CIT — City team
COG — Chicago Giants
CSS — Cuban Stars
CSW — Cuban Stars (West)
CXG — Cuban X-Giants
FLP — French Lick (IN) Plutos
HAS — Pete Hill's All-Stars
JBC — Jewell's ABCs
KCK — Kansas City (KS) Giants
LCS — Lincoln Stars
LIN — Lincoln Giants
LLG — Leland Giants
LWS — Louisville White Sox
MIN — Minor League team
PGT — Philadelphia Giants
SLG — St. Louis Giants
SPD — West Baden (IN) Sprudels
SPG — St. Paul Colored Gophers
STC — Stars of Cuba
WMG — Wilmington Giants

Daily Batting Records

Position(s)	Team	Opp	League	Age	Date	DH	AB	R	H	D	T	HR	RB	W	SB	SAC	E	Avg	Slug.
p	Waco (TX) Yellow Jackets	CIT	INT	19	11-Aug-99		4	1	1	1	0	0	1	0	0	0	0	0.250	0.500
					1899	1	**4**	**1**	**1**	**1**	**0**	**0**	**1**	**0**	**0**	**0**	**0**	**0.250**	**0.500**
p	Chicago Union Giants	CIT	INT	22	11-May-02		5	1	1	1	0	0	1	1	0	0	0	0.200	0.400
p	Chicago Union Giants	CIT	INT	22	22-Jun-02		5	1	1	1	0	0	1	0	0	0	0	0.200	0.400
p	Chicago Union Giants	CCG	WS	22	27-Jul-02	1	5	0	0	0	0	0	0	1	0	0	0	0.133	0.267
1b	Chicago Union Giants	CIT	INT	22	30-Jul-02		5	1	3	0	0	0	0	0	0	0	0	0.250	0.350

Position(s)	Team	Opp	League	Age	Date	DH	AB	R	H	D	T	HR	RB	W	SB	SAC	E	Avg	Slug.
cf	Chicago Union Giants	CCG	WS	22	03-Aug-02	2	6	2	2	0	0	0	2	0	0	0	0	0.269	0.346
p	Chicago Union Giants	CCG	WS	22	03-Aug-02	3	4	0	1	0	0	0	0	0	0	0	0	0.267	0.333
p	Otsego Michigan	CIT	INT	22	07-Aug-02		4	1	2	1	0	0	0	0	1	0	0	0.294	0.382
rf	Otsego Michigan	CIT	INT	22	14-Aug-02		4	2	2	0	0	1	1	0	0	0	0	0.316	0.474
	Otsego Michigan	CIT	INT	22	15-Aug-02		5	0	1	0	0	0	0	0	0	0	0	0.302	0.442
p	Otsego Michigan	CIT	INT	22	16-Aug-02		4	1	0	0	0	0	0	0	0	0	0	0.277	0.404
p	Otsego Michigan	CIT	INT	22	22-Aug-02		5	1	2	0	0	0	0	0	1	0	0	0.288	0.404
p	Otsego Michigan	CIT	INT	22	25-Aug-02		3	0	1	0	0	0	0	0	0	0	0	0.291	0.400
p	Otsego Michigan	CIT	INT	22	17-Sep-02		3	1	2	1	0	0	2	0	0	0	0	0.310	0.431
					1902	**13**	**58**	**11**	**18**	**4**	**0**	**1**	**7**	**2**	**2**	**0**	**0**	**0.310**	**0.431**
rf	Cuban X Giants	MIN	EXH	23	24-Jun-03		4	0	1	0	0	0	0	0	0	0	0	0.250	0.250
p	Cuban X Giants	MIN	EXH	23	25-Jun-03		4	0	0	0	0	0	0	0	0	0	0	0.125	0.125
rf	Cuban X Giants	CIT	INT	23	27-Jun-03		5	1	2	0	0	0	1	1	2	0	0	0.231	0.231
p	Cuban X Giants	CIT	INT	23	28-Jun-03		3	0	1	1	0	0	0	1	0	0	0	0.250	0.313
rf	Cuban X Giants	CIT	INT	23	01-Jul-03		5	1	2	0	0	0	2	0	0	0	0	0.286	0.333
cf	Cuban X Giants	MIN	EXH	23	16-Jul-03		4	0	1	0	0	0	0	0	0	0	0	0.280	0.320
p	Cuban X Giants	CIT	INT	23	25-Jul-03		4	0	0	0	0	0	0	0	0	0	0	0.241	0.276
lf	Cuban X Giants	CIT	INT	23	28-Jul-03		3	1	0	0	0	0	0	1	0	0	0	0.219	0.250
cf	Cuban X Giants	CIT	INT	23	03-Aug-03			0	0	0	0	0	0	1	0	0	0	0.219	0.250
p	Cuban X Giants	CIT	INT	23	06-Aug-03		4	1	1	0	0	0	1	0	0	0	0	0.222	0.250
1b	Cuban X Giants	CIT	INT	23	24-Aug-03		4	0	0	0	0	0	0	0	0	0	0	0.200	0.225
1b	Cuban X Giants	CIT	INT	23	03-Sep-03		4	0	1	0	0	0	0	0	2	0	0	0.205	0.227
ph	Cuban X Giants	CIT	INT	23	05-Sep-03	1	1	0	0	0	0	0	0	0	0	0	0	0.200	0.222
rf	Cuban X Giants	CIT	INT	23	05-Sep-03		2	0	0	0	0	0	0	0	0	0	0	0.200	0.222
p	Cuban X Giants	PGT	WS	23	12-Sep-03	1	5	0	2	1	0	0	2	0	0	0	0	0.220	0.260
p	Cuban X Giants	PGT	WS	23	14-Sep-03	4	5	0	0	0	0	0	0	0	0	0	1	0.200	0.236
ph	Cuban X Giants	PGT	WS	23	15-Sep-03	5	1	0	0	0	0	0	0	0	0	0	0	0.196	0.232
p	Cuban X Giants	PGT	WS	24	18-Sep-03	6	6	3	3	0	1	0	1	0	0	0	0	0.226	0.290
cf	Cuban X Giants	CIT	INT	24	19-Sep-03		2	1	1	0	0	0	1	0	1	0	0	0.234	0.297
1b	Cuban X Giants	CIT	INT	24	24-Sep-03		4	0	0	0	0	0	0	0	0	0	1	0.221	0.279
p	Cuban X Giants	PGT	WS	24	25-Sep-03	7	4	0	1	0	0	0	0	0	0	0	0	0.222	0.278
					1903	**21**	**72**	**8**	**16**	**2**	**1**	**0**	**8**	**4**	**5**	**0**	**2**	**0.222**	**0.278**
lf	Philadelphia Giants	CIT	INT	24	03-Apr-04		4	0	1	1	0	0	1	0	0	0	0	0.250	0.500
p	Philadelphia Giants	CIT	INT	24	10-Apr-04		5	0	3	0	0	0	2	0	0	0	0	0.444	0.556
cf	Philadelphia Giants	CIT	INT	24	16-Apr-04		5	1	1	0	0	0	1	2	3	0	0	0.357	0.429
p	Philadelphia Giants	CIT	INT	24	17-Apr-04		4	0	0	0	0	0	0	1	0	0	0	0.278	0.333
rf	Philadelphia Giants	CIT	INT	24	23-Apr-04		4	0	1	0	0	0	0	0	0	0	0	0.273	0.318
cf	Philadelphia Giants	CIT	INT	24	24-Apr-04		5	2	2	0	0	0	2	0	1	0	0	0.296	0.333
p	Philadelphia Giants	CIT	INT	24	25-Apr-04		4	0	1	0	0	0	1	1	0	0	0	0.290	0.323
rf	Philadelphia Giants	CIT	INT	24	01-May-04		4	0	3	1	0	0	0	0	0	0	0	0.343	0.400
cf	Philadelphia Giants	CIT	INT	24	02-May-04		5	0	1	0	0	0	1	1	0	0	0	0.325	0.375

Position(s)	Team	Opp	League	Age	Date	DH	AB	R	H	D	T	HR	RB	W	SB	SAC	E	Avg	Slug.
p	Philadelphia Giants	CIT	INT	24	05-May-04		6	2	2	1	1	0	3	0	0	0	0	0.326	0.435
cf	Philadelphia Giants	CIT	INT	24	07-May-04		5	1	3	1	0	0	3	0	0	0	0	0.353	0.471
1b, cf	Philadelphia Giants	CIT	INT	24	08-May-04		6	1	3	1	0	0	3	0	0	0	2	0.368	0.491
p	Philadelphia Giants	CIT	INT	24	09-May-04		5	1	3	0	1	0	2	0	0	0	0	0.387	0.532
p	Philadelphia Giants	CIT	INT	24	12-May-04		5	3	3	2	0	0	2	0	1	0	0	0.403	0.567
cf	Philadelphia Giants	CIT	INT	24	21-May-04		4	0	0	0	0	0	0	0	0	0	0	0.380	0.535
cf	Philadelphia Giants	CIT	INT	24	22-May-04		5	2	3	1	0	0	3	0	0	0	0	0.395	0.553
p	Philadelphia Giants	CIT	INT	24	30-May-04	2	5	0	2	0	0	0	2	0	0	0	0	0.395	0.543
rf	Philadelphia Giants	CIT	INT	24	05-Jun-04		2	0	1	0	0	0	1	1	0	0	0	0.398	0.542
rf	Philadelphia Giants	CIT	INT	24	06-Jun-04		5	1	0	0	0	0	0	0	0	0	0	0.375	0.511
rf	Philadelphia Giants	CIT	INT	24	08-Jun-04		5	1	0	0	0	0	0	1	0	0	1	0.355	0.484
p	Philadelphia Giants	CIT	INT	24	10-Jun-04		4	0	1	0	0	0	1	0	0	0	0	0.351	0.474
rf	Philadelphia Giants	CIT	INT	24	13-Jun-04		4	0	0	0	0	0	0	1	0	0	0	0.337	0.455
p	Philadelphia Giants	CIT	INT	24	14-Jun-04		5	1	2	0	0	0	2	0	0	0	0	0.340	0.453
rf	Philadelphia Giants	CIT	INT	24	15-Jun-04		4	0	0	0	0	0	0	0	0	0	0	0.327	0.436
rf	Philadelphia Giants	CIT	INT	24	16-Jun-04		6	0	1	0	0	0	1	0	0	0	0	0.319	0.422
rf	Philadelphia Giants	CIT	INT	24	17-Jun-04		4	0	2	0	0	0	2	0	0	0	1	0.325	0.425
p	Philadelphia Giants	CIT	INT	24	19-Jun-04		4	1	1	0	0	0	1	0	0	0	0	0.323	0.419
rf	Philadelphia Giants	CIT	INT	24	23-Jun-04		6	1	1	0	0	0	1	0	0	0	0	0.315	0.408
rf	Philadelphia Giants	CIT	INT	24	24-Jun-04		4	0	1	0	0	0	1	0	0	0	0	0.313	0.403
p	Philadelphia Giants	CIT	INT	24	25-Jun-04		4	1	2	0	0	0	2	1	0	0	1	0.319	0.406
rf	Philadelphia Giants	CIT	INT	24	27-Jun-04		6	0	1	0	0	0	1	0	0	0	0	0.313	0.396
p	Philadelphia Giants	CIT	INT	24	30-Jun-04		5	1	4	0	0	0	3	0	0	0	0	0.329	0.409
p	Philadelphia Giants	CIT	INT	24	04-Jul-04	1	4	1	2	0	0	0	0	0	0	0	0	0.333	0.412
rf	Philadelphia Giants	CIT	INT	24	05-Jul-04		4	1	1	0	0	0	1	0	0	0	0	0.331	0.408
p	Philadelphia Giants	CIT	INT	24	07-Jul-04	1	4	1	2	0	0	0	2	0	0	0	0	0.335	0.410
rf	Philadelphia Giants	CIT	INT	24	08-Jul-04		4	1	1	1	0	0	2	0	0	0	0	0.333	0.412
rf	Philadelphia Giants	CIT	INT	24	09-Jul-04		4	0	0	0	0	0	0	0	0	0	0	0.325	0.402
rf	Philadelphia Giants	CIT	INT	24	11-Jul-04	1	3	0	0	0	0	0	0	1	0	0	0	0.320	0.395
p	Philadelphia Giants	CIT	INT	24	11-Jul-04	2	3	1	1	0	0	1	2	0	0	0	0	0.320	0.411
rf	Philadelphia Giants	CIT	INT	24	12-Jul-04		3	1	0	0	0	0	0	1	1	0	0	0.315	0.404
p	Philadelphia Giants	CIT	INT	24	15-Jul-04		4	1	3	0	0	0	3	0	0	0	1	0.324	0.412
rf, rp	Philadelphia Giants	CIT	INT	24	17-Jul-04		3	0	0	0	0	0	0	1	0	0	0	0.319	0.405
p	Philadelphia Giants	CIT	INT	24	21-Jul-04	2	4	0	2	0	0	0	2	0	0	0	1	0.323	0.407
rf	Philadelphia Giants	CIT	INT	24	23-Jul-04		4	0	0	0	0	0	0	1	0	0	0	0.316	0.399
p	Philadelphia Giants	CIT	INT	24	25-Jul-04		4	1	3	1	0	0	0	0	0	0	0	0.325	0.411
rf	Philadelphia Giants	CIT	INT	24	26-Jul-04		4	0	0	0	0	0	0	0	0	0	0	0.318	0.403
rf	Philadelphia Giants	CIT	INT	24	27-Jul-04		3	2	0	0	0	0	0	2	0	0	1	0.314	0.397
rf	Philadelphia Giants	CIT	INT	24	28-Jul-04		7	0	1	0	0	0	1	0	0	0	0	0.308	0.389
lf	Philadelphia Giants	CIT	INT	24	30-Jul-04		4	0	3	0	0	0	2	0	0	0	0	0.316	0.395
lf	Philadelphia Giants	CIT	INT	24	31-Jul-04		6	1	1	1	0	0	1	0	1	0	0	0.312	0.394

Position(s)	Team	Opp	League	Age	Date	DH	AB	R	H	D	T	HR	RB	W	SB	SAC	E	Avg	Slug.
p	Philadelphia Giants	CIT	INT	24	01-Aug-04		4	0	1	0	0	0	1	0	1	0	0	0.311	0.391
lf	Philadelphia Giants	CIT	INT	24	02-Aug-04		6	1	2	0	0	1	2	0	0	1	0	0.312	0.403
lf, rf, rp	Philadelphia Giants	CIT	INT	24	03-Aug-04		4	0	1	0	0	0	0	0	0	0	1	0.311	0.400
lf	Philadelphia Giants	CIT	INT	24	04-Aug-04		5	0	0	0	0	0	0	0	0	0	0	0.304	0.392
rf, rp	Philadelphia Giants	CIT	INT	24	05-Aug-04		4	1	2	0	0	1	3	1	0	0	0	0.307	0.406
p	Philadelphia Giants	CIT	INT	24	06-Aug-04		3	0	0	0	0	0	0	1	0	0	0	0.304	0.401
lf	Philadelphia Giants	ALC	PRE	24	08-Aug-04		5	1	1	1	0	0	1	0	0	0	0	0.302	0.401
p	Philadelphia Giants	CIT	INT	24	10-Aug-04		4	0	1	0	1	0	1	0	0	0	1	0.301	0.406
lf	Philadelphia Giants	CIT	INT	24	12-Aug-04		3	0	0	0	0	0	0	2	0	0	0	0.297	0.402
lf	Philadelphia Giants	CIT	INT	24	13-Aug-04		3	0	0	0	0	0	0	1	0	0	0	0.294	0.397
p	Philadelphia Giants	CIT	INT	24	14-Aug-04		3	0	1	0	0	0	1	1	0	0	0	0.294	0.396
lf	Philadelphia Giants	CIT	INT	24	15-Aug-04		4	0	2	0	0	0	2	1	0	0	0	0.297	0.398
lf	Philadelphia Giants	CIT	INT	24	16-Aug-04		4	0	0	0	0	0	0	0	0	0	0	0.293	0.392
lf	Philadelphia Giants	ALC	PRE	24	17-Aug-04		5	1	3	0	0	0	1	0	0	0	1	0.299	0.396
lf	Philadelphia Giants	CIT	INT	24	18-Aug-04		6	1	2	0	0	0	2	0	0	0	0	0.299	0.394
lf	Philadelphia Giants	CIT	INT	24	19-Aug-04		2	0	0	0	0	0	0	1	0	0	0	0.297	0.392
p	Philadelphia Giants	CIT	INT	24	20-Aug-04		4	0	0	0	0	0	0	0	0	0	0	0.293	0.386
lf	Philadelphia Giants	CIT	INT	24	21-Aug-04		4	0	1	0	0	0	1	0	0	0	0	0.293	0.384
lf	Philadelphia Giants	CIT	INT	24	22-Aug-04		5	1	2	0	0	0	2	0	2	0	0	0.294	0.385
p	Philadelphia Giants	CIT	INT	24	23-Aug-04		4	0	0	0	0	0	0	0	0	0	1	0.290	0.380
rf	Philadelphia Giants	CIT	INT	24	24-Aug-04		5	1	2	0	0	1	1	0	0	0	0	0.292	0.390
rp	Philadelphia Giants	CIT	INT	24	25-Aug-04			0	0	0	0	0	0	0	0	0	0	0.292	0.390
rf	Philadelphia Giants	CIT	INT	24	29-Aug-04		6	2	3	0	0	0	2	1	0	0	0	0.296	0.392
rf	Philadelphia Giants	CIT	INT	24	30-Aug-04		4	0	1	0	0	0	0	0	0	0	0	0.296	0.390
p	Philadelphia Giants	CXG	WS	24	01-Sep-04	1	5	1	3	0	1	0	3	0	1	0	0	0.300	0.399
ph	Philadelphia Giants	CXG	WS	24	02-Sep-04	2	1	0	0	0	0	0	0	0	0	0	0	0.299	0.398
p	Philadelphia Giants	CXG	WS	24	03-Sep-04	3	4	1	1	0	0	0	0	0	0	0	0	0.299	0.396
rf	Philadelphia Giants	CIT	INT	24	09-Sep-04		5	2	2	0	2	0	3	1	0	0	1	0.300	0.408
p	Philadelphia Giants	CIT	INT	24	10-Sep-04		5	2	1	0	0	0	1	1	1	0	0	0.299	0.405
rf	Philadelphia Giants	CIT	INT	24	11-Sep-04		5	1	2	0	0	1	3	0	0	0	0	0.300	0.414
rf	Philadelphia Giants	CIT	INT	24	13-Sep-04		3	0	0	0	0	0	0	0	0	0	0	0.298	0.410
p	Philadelphia Giants	CIT	INT	24	16-Sep-04		4	0	1	0	0	0	1	0	0	0	0	0.297	0.409
rf	Philadelphia Giants	CIT	INT	24	17-Sep-04		3	0	1	0	0	0	1	0	1	0	0	0.297	0.408
p	Philadelphia Giants	ALC	PRE	25	27-Sep-04		6	2	2	1	0	0	2	0	0	0	0	0.298	0.409
rf	Philadelphia Giants	CIT	INT	25	08-Oct-04		4	1	1	0	1	0	1	1	0	0	0	0.298	0.413
rf	Philadelphia Giants	CIT	INT	25	16-Oct-04		3	0	0	0	0	0	0	1	0	0	0	0.295	0.410
					1904	**86**	**366**	**50**	**108**	**13**	**7**	**5**	**93**	**28**	**13**	**1**	**13**	**0.295**	**0.410**
rf, rp	Philadelphia Giants	CIT	INT	25	01-Apr-05		4	1	0	0	0	0	0	1	0	0	0	0.000	0.000
rf	Philadelphia Giants	MIN	EXH	25	06-Apr-05		4	0	1	0	0	0	0	0	0	0	0	0.125	0.125
rf	Philadelphia Giants	MIN	EXH	25	07-Apr-05		4	0	0	0	0	0	0	1	0	0	0	0.083	0.083
p	Philadelphia Giants	MIN	EXH	25	08-Apr-05		4	1	2	1	0	0	2	0	1	0	0	0.188	0.250

Position(s)	Team	Opp	League	Age	Date	DH	AB	R	H	D	T	HR	RB	W	SB	SAC	E	Avg	Slug.
lf	Philadelphia Giants	CIT	INT	25	19-Apr-05		5	1	0	0	0	0	0	0	0	0	0	0.143	0.190
c	Philadelphia Giants	CIT	INT	25	20-Apr-05		4	1	3	0	1	0	3	0	0	0	1	0.240	0.360
p	Philadelphia Giants	CIT	INT	25	22-Apr-05		3	0	0	0	0	0	0	1	0	0	0	0.214	0.321
rf	Philadelphia Giants	CIT	INT	25	23-Apr-05		5	0	2	0	0	0	2	1	0	0	0	0.242	0.333
rf	Philadelphia Giants	CIT	INT	25	29-Apr-05		5	0	1	0	0	0	1	0	0	0	0	0.237	0.316
cf, rp	Philadelphia Giants	CIT	INT	25	30-Apr-05		7	1	3	2	0	1	3	0	0	0	0	0.267	0.444
rf	Philadelphia Giants	CIT	INT	25	10-May-05		5	1	1	0	0	0	1	0	1	0	0	0.260	0.420
1b	Philadelphia Giants	CIT	INT	25	11-May-05		5	1	2	0	0	0	3	0	1	0	0	0.273	0.418
rf	Philadelphia Giants	MIN	EXH	25	13-May-05		4	0	0	0	0	0	0	0	0	0	0	0.254	0.390
p	Philadelphia Giants	CIT	INT	25	14-May-05		4	0	1	1	0	0	0	0	0	0	1	0.254	0.397
rf	Philadelphia Giants	CIT	INT	25	15-May-05		5	0	1	0	0	0	0	0	0	0	1	0.250	0.382
rf	Philadelphia Giants	CIT	INT	25	16-May-05		4	0	0	0	0	0	0	0	0	0	0	0.236	0.361
p	Philadelphia Giants	CIT	INT	25	17-May-05		4	0	1	0	0	0	0	0	0	0	1	0.237	0.355
rf	Philadelphia Giants	CIT	INT	25	18-May-05		5	1	0	0	0	0	0	1	0	0	0	0.222	0.333
rf	Philadelphia Giants	CIT	INT	25	19-May-05		6	0	0	0	0	0	0	0	0	0	0	0.207	0.310
p	Philadelphia Giants	CIT	INT	25	20-May-05		3	0	1	0	0	0	1	0	0	0	0	0.211	0.311
rf	Philadelphia Giants	CIT	INT	25	21-May-05		6	3	4	0	0	0	3	0	0	0	1	0.240	0.333
p	Philadelphia Giants	CIT	INT	25	22-May-05		5	1	1	0	0	0	1	0	0	0	1	0.238	0.327
rf	Philadelphia Giants	CIT	INT	25	24-May-05		4	1	2	0	0	0	2	1	2	0	0	0.248	0.333
ph	Philadelphia Giants	CIT	INT	25	26-May-05		1	0	0	0	0	0	0	0	0	0	0	0.245	0.330
p	Philadelphia Giants	CIT	INT	25	02-Jun-05		4	0	1	0	0	0	0	1	0	0	0	0.245	0.327
rf	Philadelphia Giants	CIT	INT	25	03-Jun-05		5	1	1	1	0	0	1	0	1	0	0	0.243	0.330
rf	Philadelphia Giants	CIT	INT	25	04-Jun-05		7	3	4	2	2	0	3	0	0	0	0	0.262	0.393
p	Philadelphia Giants	CIT	INT	25	06-Jun-05		5	1	1	0	0	0	1	0	0	0	0	0.260	0.386
rf	Philadelphia Giants	CIT	INT	25	10-Jun-05		4	1	1	1	0	0	1	0	0	0	0	0.260	0.389
rf	Philadelphia Giants	CIT	INT	25	16-Jun-05		4	0	1	0	0	0	1	0	0	0	0	0.259	0.385
rf, ph	Philadelphia Giants	CIT	INT	25	21-Jun-05		1	1	1	0	0	0	1	0	0	0	1	0.265	0.390
p	Philadelphia Giants	CIT	INT	25	22-Jun-05		3	0	2	0	0	0	1	0	0	0	0	0.273	0.396
p	Philadelphia Giants	CIT	INT	25	25-Jun-05		5	2	1	0	0	0	2	1	0	0	0	0.271	0.389
rf	Philadelphia Giants	CIT	INT	25	26-Jun-05		4	0	1	0	0	0	0	0	0	0	1	0.270	0.385
p	Philadelphia Giants	CIT	INT	25	28-Jun-05		5	0	1	0	0	0	0	0	0	0	0	0.268	0.379
rf	Philadelphia Giants	CIT	INT	25	30-Jun-05		4	0	1	0	0	0	1	0	0	0	0	0.268	0.376
p	Philadelphia Giants	CIT	INT	25	01-Jul-05		5	0	0	0	0	0	0	0	0	0	0	0.259	0.364
p	Philadelphia Giants	CIT	INT	25	04-Jul-05	2	5	2	2	0	0	0	1	0	0	0	0	0.263	0.365
rf	Philadelphia Giants	CIT	INT	25	06-Jul-05		6	1	1	0	0	0	1	0	0	0	0	0.260	0.358
p	Philadelphia Giants	CIT	INT	25	07-Jul-05		5	0	3	0	0	0	2	0	0	0	0	0.270	0.365
rf	Philadelphia Giants	CIT	INT	25	09-Jul-05		5	1	2	2	0	0	2	0	0	0	1	0.273	0.377
cf	Philadelphia Giants	CIT	INT	25	10-Jul-05		4	1	2	0	0	0	2	0	0	0	1	0.278	0.380
p	Philadelphia Giants	CIT	INT	25	11-Jul-05		4	0	0	0	0	0	0	0	0	0	0	0.272	0.372
rf	Philadelphia Giants	CIT	INT	25	13-Jul-05		4	0	0	0	0	0	0	1	0	0	0	0.267	0.364
1b	Philadelphia Giants	CIT	INT	25	14-Jul-05		5	1	2	1	0	0	2	0	0	0	0	0.270	0.370

Position(s)	Team	Opp	League	Age	Date	DH	AB	R	H	D	T	HR	RB	W	SB	SAC	E	Avg	Slug.
rf	Philadelphia Giants	CIT	INT	25	15-Jul-05		7	0	5	0	1	0	4	0	0	0	0	0.285	0.391
p	Philadelphia Giants	CIT	INT	25	16-Jul-05		4	0	1	0	0	0	0	0	0	0	1	0.284	0.389
1b	Philadelphia Giants	CIT	INT	25	17-Jul-05		6	0	2	2	0	0	2	1	0	0	2	0.286	0.396
1b	Philadelphia Giants	CIT	INT	25	18-Jul-05		5	2	4	1	0	0	3	0	0	0	2	0.297	0.410
p	Philadelphia Giants	BRG	PRE	25	20-Jul-05		6	0	1	0	0	0	1	0	0	0	0	0.294	0.404
rf	Philadelphia Giants	CIT	INT	25	21-Jul-05		4	1	1	1	0	0	2	1	0	0	0	0.293	0.405
rf	Philadelphia Giants	CIT	INT	25	22-Jul-05		5	1	1	0	0	1	1	0	0	0	1	0.291	0.414
rf	Philadelphia Giants	CIT	INT	25	23-Jul-05		3	1	2	0	0	0	1	0	0	0	0	0.296	0.417
p	Philadelphia Giants	CIT	INT	25	24-Jul-05		3	0	1	0	0	0	1	0	0	0	0	0.296	0.416
rf	Philadelphia Giants	CIT	INT	25	25-Jul-05		6	0	1	0	0	0	0	0	1	0	0	0.293	0.410
p	Philadelphia Giants	CIT	INT	25	27-Jul-05		5	0	1	1	0	0	1	1	0	0	0	0.291	0.409
rf	Philadelphia Giants	CIT	INT	25	28-Jul-05		4	1	1	0	0	1	1	0	0	0	0	0.291	0.419
1b	Philadelphia Giants	CIT	INT	25	31-Jul-05		4	1	1	0	0	0	1	1	0	0	1	0.290	0.416
p	Philadelphia Giants	CIT	INT	25	02-Aug-05		7	4	6	1	0	0	5	0	0	0	0	0.305	0.431
rf	Philadelphia Giants	BRG	PRE	25	03-Aug-05		4	0	2	0	0	0	1	0	1	0	0	0.308	0.432
rf	Philadelphia Giants	CIT	INT	25	04-Aug-05		4	0	0	0	0	0	0	0	0	0	0	0.303	0.426
3b	Philadelphia Giants	CIT	INT	25	10-Aug-05		5	0	0	0	0	0	0	1	0	0	0	0.298	0.418
p	Philadelphia Giants	CIT	INT	25	11-Aug-05		5	0	1	0	0	0	1	0	0	0	0	0.296	0.415
rf	Philadelphia Giants	CIT	INT	25	12-Aug-05		4	1	2	0	0	0	1	0	0	0	0	0.299	0.416
rf	Philadelphia Giants	CIT	INT	25	13-Aug-05		4	1	1	1	0	0	1	0	0	0	0	0.298	0.417
p	Philadelphia Giants	CIT	INT	25	14-Aug-05		5	0	2	1	0	0	1	1	0	0	0	0.300	0.420
rf	Philadelphia Giants	CIT	INT	25	18-Aug-05		6	0	2	0	0	0	1	0	0	0	0	0.301	0.418
cf	Philadelphia Giants	CIT	INT	25	20-Aug-05		4	0	0	0	0	0	0	0	0	0	0	0.297	0.413
p	Philadelphia Giants	CIT	INT	25	22-Aug-05		3	0	0	0	0	0	0	0	0	1	0	0.294	0.409
p	Philadelphia Giants	CIT	INT	25	26-Aug-05		3	0	1	0	0	0	1	0	0	0	0	0.294	0.408
rf	Philadelphia Giants	CIT	INT	25	27-Aug-05		5	1	1	0	0	0	0	0	0	0	0	0.293	0.405
p	Philadelphia Giants	CIT	INT	25	29-Aug-05		6	1	3	0	0	0	1	0	0	0	0	0.297	0.407
rf	Philadelphia Giants	CIT	INT	25	30-Aug-05		7	1	2	0	0	0	1	0	0	0	0	0.296	0.404
rf	Philadelphia Giants	CIT	INT	25	31-Aug-05		4	0	3	0	0	0	2	0	1	0	0	0.302	0.408
p	Philadelphia Giants	BRG	PRE	25	07-Sep-05		4	0	1	0	0	0	1	0	0	0	0	0.301	0.406
p	Philadelphia Giants	CIT	INT	25	12-Sep-05		4	0	1	0	0	0	1	0	0	0	0	0.301	0.405
rf	Philadelphia Giants	CIT	INT	25	13-Sep-05		5	1	3	1	0	0	1	0	0	0	0	0.305	0.410
rf	Philadelphia Giants	BRG	WS	25	16-Sep-05	3	4	0	2	0	0	0	1	1	0	0	0	0.307	0.411
rf	Philadelphia Giants	CIT	INT	25	17-Sep-05		5	0	0	0	0	0	0	0	0	0	0	0.303	0.406
p	Philadelphia Giants	CIT	INT	26	18-Sep-05		4	0	0	0	0	0	0	1	0	0	0	0.299	0.401
rf, rp	Philadelphia Giants	CIT	INT	26	24-Sep-05		4	0	2	1	0	0	2	1	0	0	0	0.302	0.405
cf	Philadelphia Giants	CIT	INT	26	26-Sep-05		4	0	0	0	0	0	0	0	0	0	0	0.298	0.401
p	Philadelphia Giants	CIT	INT	26	27-Sep-05		6	0	1	1	0	0	1	0	0	0	0	0.296	0.399
cf	Philadelphia Giants	CIT	INT	26	28-Sep-05		5	1	1	0	0	0	1	0	0	0	0	0.295	0.397
p	Philadelphia Giants	CIT	INT	26	30-Sep-05		4	0	2	1	0	0	1	0	0	0	1	0.297	0.401
cf	Philadelphia Giants	BRG	PRE	26	01-Oct-05		5	0	1	0	0	0	1	0	1	0	0	0.296	0.398

Position(s)	Team	Opp	League	Age	Date	DH	AB	R	H	D	T	HR	RB	W	SB	SAC	E	Avg	Slug.
rf	Philadelphia Giants	BRG	PRE	26	06-Oct-05		5	0	0	0	0	0	0	0	0	0	0	0.292	0.393
rf	Philadelphia Giants	CIT	INT	26	15-Oct-05		3	0	0	0	0	0	0	0	0	0	0	0.290	0.390
p	Cuban X Giants	ALC	PRE	26	22-Oct-05		5	1	2	0	0	0	1	0	0	0	0	0.291	0.390
p	Cuban X Giants	ALC	PRE	26	08-Nov-05		3	1	0	0	0	0	0	1	0	0	1	0.289	0.387
					1905	**90**	**408**	**48**	**118**	**23**	**4**	**3**	**89**	**19**	**10**	**1**	**19**	**0.289**	**0.387**
p, 1b	Philadelphia Giants	CIT	INT	26	01-Apr-06		5	1	2	2	0	0	2	0	0	0	0	0.400	0.800
rf	Philadelphia Giants	CIT	INT	26	10-Apr-06		5	0	0	0	0	0	0	0	0	0	0	0.200	0.400
p	Philadelphia Giants	CIT	INT	26	19-Apr-06		5	0	2	0	0	0	0	1	1	0	0	0.267	0.400
1b	Philadelphia Giants	CIT	INT	26	20-Apr-06		5	0	1	0	0	0	2	0	0	0	0	0.250	0.350
1b	Philadelphia Giants	CIT	INT	26	24-Apr-06		5	1	2	0	0	0	0	0	0	0	0	0.280	0.360
1b	Philadelphia Giants	MIN	EXH	26	26-Apr-06		6	1	1	0	0	0	1	0	0	0	1	0.258	0.323
rf	Philadelphia Giants	CIT	INT	26	29-Apr-06		5	2	1	0	0	0	1	0	0	0	3	0.250	0.306
rf	Philadelphia Giants	CIT	INT	26	10-May-06		5	0	0	0	0	0	2	1	0	0	1	0.220	0.268
p	Philadelphia Giants	CIT	INT	26	11-May-06		5	1	2	2	0	0	0	0	1	0	0	0.239	0.326
rf	Philadelphia Giants	MIN	EXH	26	13-May-06		4	2	2	1	0	0	2	0	0	0	0	0.260	0.360
1b	Philadelphia Giants	CIT	INT	26	19-May-06		5	1	1	0	0	0	2	0	0	0	0	0.255	0.345
p	Philadelphia Giants	LLG	PRE	26	20-May-06		5	1	1	1	0	0	1	0	0	0	0	0.250	0.350
1b	Philadelphia Giants	CIT	INT	26	27-May-06	1	4	0	0	0	0	0	1	0	0	0	0	0.234	0.328
1b	Philadelphia Giants	CIT	INT	26	27-May-06	2	3	0	0	0	0	0	0	1	1	0	0	0.224	0.313
p	Philadelphia Giants	BRG	PRE	26	31-May-06		4	0	0	0	0	0	0	1	0	0	0	0.211	0.296
rf	Philadelphia Giants	CIT	INT	26	02-Jun-06		6	1	1	0	0	0	0	0	0	0	0	0.208	0.286
rf	Philadelphia Giants	CIT	INT	26	03-Jun-06		5	1	1	0	0	0	0	0	0	0	0	0.207	0.280
p	Philadelphia Giants	BRG	PRE	26	04-Jun-06		6	0	2	0	0	0	1	0	1	1	0	0.216	0.284
rf	Philadelphia Giants	CIT	INT	26	08-Jun-06		4	0	1	0	0	0	1	0	0	0	1	0.217	0.283
rf	Philadelphia Giants	CIT	INT	26	09-Jun-06		3	0	1	0	0	0	0	0	0	0	0	0.221	0.284
p	Philadelphia Giants	CIT	INT	26	10-Jun-06		5	0	0	0	0	0	0	0	0	0	0	0.210	0.270
1b	Philadelphia Giants	CIT	INT	26	15-Jun-06		4	1	2	0	0	0	0	0	0	0	0	0.221	0.279
p	Philadelphia Giants	CIT	INT	26	22-Jun-06		4	0	2	0	0	0	1	0	0	0	1	0.231	0.287
1b	Philadelphia Giants	CSS	PRE	26	29-Jun-06		4	0	1	0	0	0	1	0	0	0	0	0.232	0.286
p	Philadelphia Giants	CIT	INT	26	30-Jun-06	1	4	0	1	0	0	0	1	0	0	0	0	0.233	0.284
rf	Philadelphia Giants	CIT	INT	26	30-Jun-06	2	5	0	2	0	0	0	1	2	1	0	0	0.240	0.289
rf	Philadelphia Giants	CIT	INT	26	10-Jul-06		4	1	1	0	0	0	2	0	0	0	0	0.240	0.288
p	Philadelphia Giants	CIT	INT	26	18-Jul-06		5	0	1	0	0	0	1	0	0	0	0	0.238	0.285
p	Philadelphia Giants	CIT	INT	26	04-Aug-06		4	0	1	0	0	0	0	0	0	0	0	0.239	0.284
rf	Philadelphia Giants	CIT	INT	26	11-Aug-06		6	0	1	0	0	0	1	1	0	0	1	0.236	0.279
rf	Philadelphia Giants	CIT	INT	26	14-Aug-06	1	4	1	3	0	0	0	0	0	0	0	0	0.250	0.292
p	Philadelphia Giants	CIT	INT	26	14-Aug-06	2	7	1	3	0	0	0	1	0	0	0	0	0.258	0.298
1b	Philadelphia Giants	WMG	PRE	26	15-Aug-06		5	1	2	0	0	0	2	0	1	0	0	0.263	0.301
1b, rf	Philadelphia Giants	CXG	PRE	26	18-Aug-06		4	0	1	0	0	0	2	0	0	0	2	0.263	0.300
p	Philadelphia Giants	CIT	INT	26	23-Aug-06		4	1	2	1	0	0	1	0	0	0	0	0.268	0.311
p	Philadelphia Giants	CXG	WS	26	03-Sep-06	1	4	2	2	0	0	0	0	0	0	0	0	0.274	0.315

Position(s)	Team	Opp	League	Age	Date	DH	AB	R	H	D	T	HR	RB	W	SB	SAC	E	Avg	Slug.
rf	Philadelphia Giants	CXG	WS	26	03-Sep-06	2	2	0	1	0	0	0	1	0	0	0	0	0.276	0.318
1b	Philadelphia Giants	MIN	EXH	27	18-Sep-06		4	0	0	0	0	0	0	1	0	0	0	0.270	0.310
1b	Philadelphia Giants	CIT	INT	27	19-Sep-06		5	1	2	0	0	0	1	1	0	0	0	0.274	0.313
rf	Philadelphia Giants	CXG	PRE	27	30-Sep-06	2	2	1	0	0	0	0	0	2	1	0	0	0.271	0.309
1b	Philadelphia Giants	CIT	INT	27	30-Sep-06	3	4	1	0	0	0	0	0	1	1	0	0	0.265	0.303
					1906	**41**	**185**	**23**	**49**	**7**	**0**	**0**	**32**	**12**	**8**	**1**	**10**	**0.265**	**0.303**
p	Chicago Leland Giants	CIT	INT	27	28-Apr-07		4	0	1	0	0	0	1	0	0	0	1	0.250	0.250
p	Chicago Leland Giants	CIT	INT	27	19-May-07		5	0	0	0	0	0	0	0	0	0	0	0.111	0.111
rf	Chicago Leland Giants	CIT	INT	27	25-May-07		5	0	2	0	0	0	1	0	0	0	0	0.214	0.214
rf	Chicago Leland Giants	CIT	INT	27	26-May-07		4	0	0	0	0	0	0	0	0	0	0	0.167	0.167
p	Chicago Leland Giants	CIT	INT	27	30-May-07	2	7	0	1	0	0	0	0	0	0	0	0	0.160	0.160
rf	Chicago Leland Giants	CIT	INT	27	01-Jun-07		5	2	2	0	0	0	0	0	0	0	0	0.200	0.200
rf	Chicago Leland Giants	CIT	INT	27	15-Jun-07		4	0	1	0	0	0	0	0	0	0	0	0.206	0.206
p	Chicago Leland Giants	CIT	INT	27	22-Jun-07		5	1	0	0	0	0	0	0	0	0	1	0.179	0.179
rf	Chicago Leland Giants	CIT	INT	27	23-Jun-07		4	0	0	0	0	0	0	0	0	0	0	0.163	0.163
rf	Chicago Leland Giants	CIT	INT	27	04-Jul-07	1	4	0	1	0	0	0	0	0	0	0	0	0.170	0.170
p	Chicago Leland Giants	CIT	INT	27	04-Jul-07	2	4	0	1	1	0	0	0	0	0	0	1	0.176	0.196
rf	Chicago Leland Giants	CIT	INT	27	06-Jul-07		4	0	0	0	0	0	0	0	0	0	0	0.164	0.182
p	Chicago Leland Giants	CIT	INT	27	07-Jul-07		4	0	1	0	0	0	1	0	0	0	0	0.169	0.186
rf	Chicago Leland Giants	CIT	INT	27	10-Jul-07		4	0	1	0	0	0	1	0	0	0	0	0.175	0.190
rf	Chicago Leland Giants	CIT	INT	27	14-Jul-07		6	0	1	1	0	0	0	0	0	0	1	0.174	0.203
p	Chicago Leland Giants	CIT	INT	27	20-Jul-07		7	1	1	0	0	0	0	0	0	0	0	0.171	0.197
rf	Chicago Leland Giants	CIT	INT	27	21-Jul-07		5	1	0	0	0	0	0	1	0	0	1	0.160	0.185
rf	Chicago Leland Giants	CIT	INT	27	24-Jul-07		5	0	0	0	0	0	0	1	0	0	0	0.151	0.174
rf	Chicago Leland Giants	ABC	PRE	27	27-Jul-07	1	4	0	0	0	0	0	0	0	0	0	0	0.144	0.167
ss	Chicago Leland Giants	ABC	PRE	27	27-Jul-07	2	4	0	1	0	0	0	1	0	0	0	0	0.149	0.170
p	Chicago Leland Giants	CIT	INT	27	04-Aug-07		4	0	2	0	0	0	1	0	0	0	0	0.163	0.184
p	Chicago Leland Giants	CIT	INT	27	06-Aug-07		4	0	1	0	0	0	0	0	1	0	0	0.167	0.186
rf	Chicago Leland Giants	CIT	INT	27	07-Aug-07		3	0	1	0	0	0	1	0	0	1	0	0.171	0.190
p	Chicago Leland Giants	CIT	INT	27	08-Aug-07		3	0	0	0	0	0	0	0	0	0	0	0.167	0.185
p	Chicago Leland Giants	CIT	INT	27	10-Aug-07		4	0	0	0	0	0	0	0	0	0	0	0.161	0.179
p	Chicago Leland Giants	CIT	INT	27	17-Aug-07		5	1	0	0	0	0	0	1	0	0	0	0.154	0.171
p	Chicago Leland Giants	CIT	INT	27	24-Aug-07		6	0	1	1	0	0	1	0	0	0	1	0.154	0.179
rf	Chicago Leland Giants	CIT	INT	27	25-Aug-07		4	0	3	1	0	0	2	0	0	0	0	0.173	0.205
p	Chicago Leland Giants	CIT	INT	27	27-Aug-07		3	1	1	0	0	0	1	0	0	1	1	0.177	0.208
rf	Chicago Leland Giants	CIT	INT	27	28-Aug-07		3	0	1	0	0	0	0	0	0	0	0	0.180	0.211
p	Chicago Leland Giants	CIT	INT	27	30-Aug-07		5	0	1	0	0	0	0	0	0	0	0	0.181	0.210
rf	Chicago Leland Giants	CIT	INT	27	31-Aug-07		4	0	0	0	0	0	0	0	0	0	0	0.176	0.204
rf	Chicago Leland Giants	CIT	INT	27	01-Sep-07		4	1	1	0	0	0	0	0	0	0	0	0.178	0.205
rf	Chicago Leland Giants	CIT	INT	27	02-Sep-07		4	0	0	0	0	0	0	0	0	0	0	0.173	0.200
rf	Chicago Leland Giants	CIT	INT	27	07-Sep-07		4	0	0	0	0	0	0	0	0	0	0	0.169	0.195

Position(s)	Team	Opp	League	Age	Date	DH	AB	R	H	D	T	HR	RB	W	SB	SAC	E	Avg	Slug.
rf	Chicago Leland Giants	CIT	INT	27	14-Sep-07		3	0	0	0	0	0	0	0	0	0	0	0.166	0.191
rf	Chicago Leland Giants	CIT	INT	28	21-Sep-07		5	0	1	0	0	0	0	0	0	0	0	0.167	0.191
p	Chicago Leland Giants	CIT	INT	28	22-Sep-07		3	0	0	0	0	0	0	0	0	0	1	0.164	0.188
p	St. Paul Colored Gophers	CIT	INT	28	23-Sep-07		4	0	1	1	0	0	0	0	0	0	0	0.166	0.195
rf	St. Paul Colored Gophers	CIT	INT	28	24-Sep-07		5	0	0	0	0	0	0	0	0	0	0	0.161	0.190
rf, rp	Chicago Leland Giants	MIN	EXH	28	05-Oct-07		3	0	0	0	0	0	0	0	0	0	0	0.158	0.186
1b	Chicago Leland Giants	CIT	INT	28	12-Oct-07		4	1	0	0	0	0	0	1	0	0	1	0.155	0.182
p	Chicago Leland Giants	CIT	INT	28	13-Oct-07		4	1	1	0	0	0	0	0	0	0	0	0.157	0.184
cf	Chicago Leland Giants	CIT	INT	28	20-Oct-07		4	0	1	0	0	0	0	0	0	0	0	0.159	0.185
					1907	**44**	**189**	**10**	**30**	**5**	**0**	**0**	**11**	**4**	**1**	**2**	**9**	**0.159**	**0.185**
rp	Chicago Leland Giants	CIT	INT	28	18-Apr-08		6	1	2	0	0	0	0	0	0	0	0	0.333	0.333
rf	Chicago Leland Giants	CIT	INT	28	19-Apr-08		4	0	0	0	0	0	0	1	0	0	0	0.200	0.200
p	Chicago Leland Giants	CIT	INT	28	10-May-08		5	1	2	0	0	0	2	0	0	0	0	0.267	0.267
p	Chicago Leland Giants	CIT	INT	28	17-May-08		4	0	1	1	0	0	1	0	0	0	0	0.263	0.316
rp	Chicago Leland Giants	CIT	INT	28	06-Jun-08		1	0	1	0	0	0	0	0	0	0	0	0.300	0.350
p	Chicago Leland Giants	CIT	INT	28	09-Jul-08		4	0	0	0	0	0	0	0	0	0	0	0.250	0.292
p	Chicago Leland Giants	CBG	PRE	28	12-Jul-08		5	1	1	0	0	0	1	0	0	0	0	0.241	0.276
rf	Chicago Leland Giants	CIT	INT	28	18-Jul-08		3	1	3	1	0	0	3	0	0	0	0	0.313	0.375
rf, rp	Chicago Leland Giants	CIT	INT	28	19-Jul-08		7	0	4	0	0	0	2	0	0	0	1	0.359	0.410
p	Chicago Leland Giants	CIT	INT	28	26-Jul-08		5	0	1	0	0	0	1	0	0	0	0	0.341	0.386
1b	Chicago Leland Giants	PGT	WS	28	27-Jul-08	1	5	0	1	0	0	0	0	0	0	0	0	0.327	0.367
1b	Chicago Leland Giants	PGT	WS	28	28-Jul-08	2	4	1	0	0	0	0	0	2	0	0	1	0.302	0.340
1b	Chicago Leland Giants	CIT	INT	28	01-Aug-08		5	1	4	0	0	1	4	0	0	0	2	0.345	0.431
p	Chicago Leland Giants	PGT	WS	28	02-Aug-08	4	5	1	1	0	0	0	1	0	0	0	1	0.333	0.413
p	Chicago Leland Giants	PGT	WS	28	06-Aug-08	5	4	0	0	0	0	0	0	1	0	0	1	0.313	0.388
1b	Chicago Leland Giants	CIT	INT	28	08-Aug-08		5	1	2	0	0	0	0	0	0	0	0	0.319	0.389
rf	Chicago Leland Giants	CIT	INT	28	09-Aug-08	1	6	0	1	0	0	0	0	0	0	0	0	0.308	0.372
p	Chicago Leland Giants	CIT	INT	28	09-Aug-08	2	3	0	0	0	0	0	0	1	0	0	0	0.296	0.358
p	Chicago Leland Giants	CIT	INT	28	14-Aug-08		4	0	1	0	0	0	1	0	0	0	0	0.294	0.353
1b	Chicago Leland Giants	CIT	INT	28	15-Aug-08		5	0	1	0	0	0	0	0	0	0	1	0.289	0.344
rp	Chicago Leland Giants	CIT	INT	28	23-Aug-08		0	0	0	0	0	0	0	0	0	0	1	0.289	0.344
p	St. Paul Colored Gophers	CIT	INT	28	28-Aug-08		3	0	1	0	0	0	0	1	0	0	1	0.290	0.344
p	Chicago Leland Giants	CIT	INT	28	30-Aug-08		4	0	0	0	0	0	0	0	0	0	0	0.278	0.330
1b	Chicago Leland Giants	CIT	INT	28	06-Sep-08		6	1	2	0	0	0	1	0	0	0	1	0.282	0.330
p	Chicago Leland Giants	CIT	INT	28	07-Sep-08		4	0	2	1	0	0	0	0	0	0	0	0.290	0.346
p	Chicago Leland Giants	CIT	INT	29	19-Sep-08		4	0	3	0	0	0	2	0	0	0	1	0.306	0.360
rp	Chicago Leland Giants	MIN	EXH	29	22-Sep-08		2	0	1	0	0	0	0	0	0	0	0	0.310	0.363
p	Chicago Leland Giants	CIT	INT	29	04-Oct-08		1	0	1	0	0	0	1	0	0	0	0	0.316	0.368
					1908	**28**	**114**	**9**	**36**	**3**	**0**	**1**	**20**	**6**	**0**	**0**	**10**	**0.316**	**0.368**
p	Chicago Leland Giants	CIT	INT	29	16-May-09		5	1	1	0	1	0	1	1	0	0	2	0.200	0.600
p	Chicago Leland Giants	CIT	INT	29	30-May-09		4	0	0	0	0	0	0	0	0	0	0	0.111	0.333

Position(s)	Team	Opp	League	Age	Date	DH	AB	R	H	D	T	HR	RB	W	SB	SAC	E	Avg	Slug.
rp	Chicago Leland Giants	CIT	INT	29	31-May-09	2	0	0	0	0	0	0	0	0	0	0	0	0.111	0.333
p	Chicago Leland Giants	CIT	INT	29	06-Jun-09		5	1	1	0	0	0	0	1	0	0	0	0.143	0.286
p	Chicago Leland Giants	CIT	INT	29	13-Jun-09	1	4	0	0	0	0	0	0	0	0	0	0	0.111	0.222
p	Chicago Leland Giants	MIN	EXH	29	26-Jun-09		4	1	1	0	0	0	1	0	0	0	1	0.136	0.227
p	Chicago Leland Giants	CSS	PRE	29	29-Jun-09		4	0	2	0	0	0	2	0	0	0	0	0.192	0.269
rf	Chicago Leland Giants	CSS	PRE	29	30-Jun-09		4	0	0	0	0	0	0	0	0	0	0	0.167	0.233
p	Chicago Leland Giants	CSS	PRE	29	01-Jul-09		4	0	0	0	0	0	0	0	0	0	0	0.147	0.206
p	Chicago Leland Giants	CIT	INT	29	03-Jul-09	1	3	0	0	0	0	0	0	0	0	0	0	0.135	0.189
rf	Chicago Leland Giants	CIT	INT	29	04-Jul-09	1	3	1	1	0	0	0	0	0	0	0	1	0.150	0.200
1b	Chicago Leland Giants	CIT	INT	29	04-Jul-09	2	2	0	0	0	0	0	0	1	0	0	0	0.143	0.190
p	Chicago Leland Giants	CIT	INT	29	05-Jul-09	2	6	1	2	0	0	0	2	0	0	0	1	0.167	0.208
1b	Chicago Leland Giants	CSS	PRE	29	10-Jul-09		4	0	2	1	0	0	1	0	0	0	1	0.192	0.250
1b	Chicago Leland Giants	CSS	PRE	29	12-Jul-09		1	1	1	1	0	0	0	0	0	0	0	0.208	0.283
p	Chicago Leland Giants	MIN	EXH	30	21-Oct-09		4	0	1	0	0	0	0	0	0	0	0	0.211	0.281
					1909	**16**	**57**	**6**	**12**	**2**	**1**	**0**	**7**	**3**	**0**	**0**	**6**	**0.211**	**0.281**
p	Chicago Leland Giants	CIT	INT	30	15-May-10	1	4	2	2	0	0	0	1	0	0	0	2	0.500	0.500
p	Chicago Leland Giants	STC	PRE	30	22-May-10		4	0	0	0	0	0	0	0	0	0	0	0.250	0.250
p	Chicago Leland Giants	CIT	INT	30	30-May-10	1	5	1	2	0	0	0	1	0	0	0	1	0.308	0.308
p	Chicago Leland Giants	CIT	INT	30	30-May-10	2	5	1	2	0	0	0	2	0	0	0	1	0.333	0.333
p	Chicago Leland Giants	CIT	INT	30	11-Jun-10		4	0	0	0	0	0	0	0	0	0	0	0.273	0.273
p	Chicago Leland Giants	SPD	PRE	30	20-Jun-10		3	0	1	0	0	0	0	1	0	0	0	0.280	0.280
ph	Chicago Leland Giants	SPD	PRE	30	21-Jun-10		1	0	0	0	0	0	0	0	0	0	0	0.269	0.269
rp	Chicago Leland Giants	CIT	INT	30	04-Jul-10	2	2	0	0	0	0	0	0	0	0	0	0	0.250	0.250
p	Chicago Leland Giants	CIT	INT	30	16-Jul-10		5	1	1	1	0	0	1	0	0	0	0	0.242	0.273
p	Chicago Leland Giants	STC	PRE	30	21-Jul-10		5	0	1	0	0	0	0	0	0	0	0	0.237	0.263
p	Chicago Leland Giants	STC	PRE	30	28-Jul-10		4	0	0	0	0	0	0	1	0	0	0	0.214	0.238
p	Chicago Leland Giants	CIT	INT	30	31-Jul-10	2	5	0	0	0	0	0	0	0	0	0	0	0.191	0.213
p	Chicago Leland Giants	CIT	INT	30	04-Aug-10		5	1	1	0	0	0	0	0	0	0	0	0.192	0.212
					1910	**13**	**52**	**6**	**10**	**1**	**0**	**0**	**5**	**2**	**0**	**0**	**4**	**0.192**	**0.212**
1b	Chicago American Giants	CIT	INT	31	07-May-11		4	0	2	0	0	0	0	0	0	0	1	0.500	0.500
1b	Chicago American Giants	CIT	INT	31	14-May-11		4	0	3	0	0	0	2	0	0	0	2	0.625	0.625
p	Chicago American Giants	CIT	INT	31	28-May-11	2	1	0	0	0	0	0	0	0	0	0	1	0.556	0.556
p	Chicago American Giants	CSS	PRE	31	31-May-11		3	0	2	0	0	0	1	0	0	0	0	0.583	0.583
rf, rp	Chicago American Giants	CIT	INT	31	04-Jun-11		4	1	1	1	0	0	0	0	0	0	1	0.500	0.563
p	Chicago American Giants	CSS	PRE	31	15-Jun-11		4	0	1	0	0	0	0	0	0	0	1	0.450	0.500
p	Chicago American Giants	CIT	INT	31	28-Jun-11		3	0	1	0	0	0	0	0	0	0	0	0.435	0.478
rp	Chicago American Giants	COG	PRE	31	03-Jul-11		2	1	1	0	0	0	1	0	0	0	0	0.440	0.480
rp	Chicago American Giants	COG	PRE	31	04-Jul-11	1	1	0	0	0	0	0	0	0	0	0	0	0.423	0.462
rp	Chicago American Giants	CIT	INT	31	08-Jul-11		3	1	3	0	0	0	3	0	0	0	0	0.483	0.517
p	Chicago American Giants	CIT	INT	31	15-Jul-11		3	0	1	0	0	0	1	0	0	0	1	0.469	0.500
p	Chicago American Giants	CSS	PRE	31	29-Aug-11		3	0	0	0	0	0	0	1	0	0	1	0.429	0.457

Position(s)	Team	Opp	League	Age	Date	DH	AB	R	H	D	T	HR	RB	W	SB	SAC	E	Avg	Slug.
ph	Chicago American Giants	LIN	PRE	31	04-Sep-11	1	1	0	0	0	0	0	0	0	0	0	0	0.417	0.444
rp	Chicago American Giants	BRG	PRE	31	10-Sep-11	1	3	0	1	0	0	0	0	0	0	0	0	0.410	0.436
p	Chicago American Giants	KCK	PRE	31	16-Sep-11		1	0	1	0	0	0	0	0	0	0	0	0.425	0.450
p	Chicago American Giants	COG	PRE	32	08-Oct-11		5	0	0	0	0	0	0	0	0	0	0	0.378	0.400
					1911	**16**	**45**	**3**	**17**	**1**	**0**	**0**	**8**	**1**	**0**	**0**	**8**	**0.378**	**0.400**
p	Chicago American Giants	BRG	PRE	32	21-May-12		4	0	1	0	0	0	0	0	0	0	0	0.250	0.250
p	Chicago American Giants	FLP	PRE	32	16-Jun-12		5	0	1	1	0	0	1	0	0	0	0	0.222	0.333
ph	Chicago American Giants	SLG	PRE	32	19-Jun-12		1	0	0	0	0	0	0	0	0	0	0	0.200	0.300
rp	Chicago American Giants	SLG	PRE	32	20-Jun-12		1	0	1	0	0	0	0	0	0	0	0	0.273	0.364
ph	Chicago American Giants	SLG	PRE	32	21-Jun-12		1	0	0	0	0	0	0	0	0	0	0	0.250	0.333
rp	Chicago American Giants	CSS	PRE	32	02-Jul-12		1	0	1	0	0	0	1	0	0	0	0	0.308	0.385
1b	Chicago American Giants	SLG	PRE	32	21-Jul-12		3	0	0	0	0	0	0	1	0	0	0	0.250	0.313
1b	Chicago American Giants	SLG	PRE	32	23-Jul-12		3	0	0	0	0	0	0	0	0	0	0	0.211	0.263
1b	Chicago American Giants	SLG	PRE	32	24-Jul-12		4	0	1	0	0	0	2	0	0	0	0	0.217	0.261
1b	Chicago American Giants	SPD	PRE	32	28-Jul-12		4	0	2	1	0	0	1	0	0	0	0	0.259	0.333
p	Chicago American Giants	SPD	PRE	32	29-Jul-12		5	0	0	0	0	0	0	0	0	0	0	0.219	0.281
p	Chicago American Giants	CSS	PRE	32	11-Aug-12		5	0	0	0	0	0	0	0	0	0	0	0.189	0.243
1b	Chicago American Giants	CIT	INT	32	25-Aug-12		4	0	0	0	0	0	0	0	0	0	3	0.171	0.220
p	Chicago American Giants	COG	PRE	32	08-Sep-12		4	1	1	0	0	0	0	0	0	0	0	0.178	0.222
ph	Chicago American Giants	CIT	INT	33	08-Nov-12		1	0	0	0	0	0	0	0	0	0	0	0.174	0.217
p	Chicago American Giants	CIT	INT	33	15-Nov-12		3	0	0	0	0	0	0	0	0	0	1	0.163	0.204
p	Chicago American Giants	CIT	INT	33	24-Nov-12		1	0	1	0	0	0	1	0	0	0	0	0.180	0.220
ph	Chicago American Giants	CIT	INT	33	01-Dec-12		1	0	0	0	0	0	0	0	0	0	0	0.176	0.216
p	Chicago American Giants	CIT	INT	33	20-Dec-12		3	0	1	1	0	0	1	0	0	0	0	0.185	0.241
					1912	**19**	**54**	**1**	**10**	**3**	**0**	**0**	**7**	**1**	**0**	**0**	**4**	**0.185**	**0.241**
p	Chicago American Giants	SLG	PRE	33	31-Aug-13		4	1	1	0	0	0	0	0	0	0	0	0.250	0.250
p	Chicago American Giants	SPD	PRE	33	08-Sep-13		4	0	1	0	0	0	0	0	0	0	2	0.250	0.250
p	Chicago American Giants	COG	PRE	33	14-Sep-13		5	0	0	0	0	0	0	0	0	0	0	0.154	0.154
p	Chicago American Giants	MIN	EXH	34	12-Oct-13		5	0	1	0	0	0	0	0	0	0	0	0.167	0.167
					1913	**4**	**18**	**1**	**3**	**0**	**0**	**0**	**0**	**0**	**0**	**0**	**2**	**0.167**	**0.167**
p	Chicago American Giants	MIN	EXH	34	25-Mar-14		2	0	0	0	0	0	0	0	0	1	0	0.000	0.000
p	Chicago American Giants	CIT	INT	34	03-May-14		5	0	0	0	0	0	0	0	0	0	0	0.000	0.000
rp	Chicago American Giants	CSS	PRE	34	25-May-14		2	0	0	0	0	0	0	0	0	0	1	0.000	0.000
p	Chicago American Giants	CSS	PRE	34	28-May-14		4	0	0	0	0	0	0	0	0	0	0	0.000	0.000
p	Chicago American Giants	CIT	INT	34	07-Jun-14		4	0	1	0	0	0	0	0	0	0	0	0.059	0.059
1b	Chicago American Giants	ABC	PRE	34	17-Jun-14		5	3	3	0	0	2	5	0	0	0	0	0.182	0.455
p	Chicago American Giants	ABC	PRE	34	18-Jun-14		3	0	2	0	0	0	1	1	1	0	1	0.240	0.480
p	Chicago American Giants	FLP	PRE	34	29-Jun-14		4	1	1	0	0	0	1	0	0	0	1	0.241	0.448
p	Chicago American Giants	CSS	PRE	34	05-Jul-14		3	0	0	0	0	0	0	0	0	0	0	0.219	0.406
pr	Louisville White Sox	BLA	PRE	34	26-Jul-14		0	0	0	0	0	0	0	0	0	0	0	0.219	0.406
p	Chicago American Giants	ABC	PRE	34	29-Jul-14		2	0	2	0	0	0	0	0	0	0	1	0.265	0.441

Position(s)	Team	Opp	League	Age	Date	DH	AB	R	H	D	T	HR	RB	W	SB	SAC	E	Avg	Slug.
p	Louisville White Sox	CIT	INT	34	02-Aug-14		2	0	0	0	0	0	0	0	0	0	0	0.250	0.417
p	Chicago American Giants	CSS	PRE	34	15-Aug-14		5	0	1	0	0	0	0	0	0	0	1	0.244	0.390
p	Chicago American Giants	ABC	PRE	34	25-Aug-14		4	1	3	1	0	0	3	0	0	0	1	0.289	0.444
1b	Chicago American Giants	ABC	PRE	35	20-Sep-14		5	2	3	0	0	0	3	0	0	0	0	0.320	0.460
1b	Chicago American Giants	ABC	PRE	35	21-Sep-14		5	1	1	0	0	0	0	0	0	0	0	0.309	0.436
p	Chicago American Giants	ABC	PRE	35	22-Sep-14		5	1	1	0	0	0	1	0	0	0	0	0.300	0.417
					1914	**17**	**60**	**9**	**18**	**1**	**0**	**2**	**14**	**1**	**1**	**1**	**6**	**0.300**	**0.417**
p	Chicago American Giants	MIN	EXH	35	09-Apr-15		2	0	0	0	0	0	0	0	0	0	0	0.000	0.000
p	Chicago American Giants	CIT	INT	35	16-May-15		2	1	0	0	0	0	0	1	0	0	0	0.000	0.000
1b	Chicago American Giants	CIT	INT	35	31-May-15	1	4	0	1	0	0	0	1	0	0	0	0	0.125	0.125
p	Chicago American Giants	LWS	PRE	35	16-Jun-15		4	1	2	0	0	0	1	0	0	0	0	0.250	0.250
p	Chicago American Giants	ABC	PRE	35	20-Jun-15		5	1	1	0	0	0	0	0	0	0	0	0.235	0.235
1b	Chicago American Giants	ABC	PRE	35	23-Jun-15		3	0	0	0	0	0	0	0	0	0	1	0.200	0.200
p	Chicago American Giants	CSS	PRE	35	04-Jul-15		3	1	0	0	0	0	0	1	0	0	0	0.174	0.174
p	Chicago American Giants	CSS	PRE	35	11-Jul-15	2	1	0	1	0	0	0	0	0	0	0	0	0.208	0.208
ph	Chicago American Giants	ABC	PRE	35	18-Jul-15		1	0	1	0	0	0	0	0	0	0	0	0.240	0.240
1b	Chicago American Giants	ABC	PRE	35	22-Jul-15		6	1	2	1	0	0	1	0	0	0	3	0.258	0.290
p	Chicago American Giants	LCS	WS	35	09-Aug-15	6	5	0	1	0	0	0	0	0	0	0	0	0.250	0.278
p	Chicago American Giants	CSS	PRE	35	02-Sep-15		1	0	0	0	0	0	0	0	0	0	0	0.243	0.270
					1915	**12**	**37**	**5**	**9**	**1**	**0**	**0**	**3**	**2**	**0**	**0**	**4**	**0.243**	**0.270**
p	Chicago American Giants	CIT	INT	36	14-May-16		2	0	0	0	0	0	0	0	0	0	0	0.000	0.000
p	Chicago American Giants	SLG	PRE	36	13-Jul-16		5	0	0	0	0	0	0	0	0	0	0	0.000	0.000
p	Chicago American Giants	CSS	PRE	36	22-Aug-16		4	0	0	0	0	0	0	0	0	0	0	0.000	0.000
					1916	**3**	**11**	**0**	**0**	**0**	**0**	**0**	**0**	**0**	**0**	**0**	**0**	**0.000**	**0.000**
1b	Chicago American Giants	CSW	PRE	37	29-May-17		4	0	2	0	0	0	2	0	0	0	0	0.500	0.500
1b, rp	Chicago American Giants	CIT	INT	37	09-Jun-17		4	0	2	0	0	0	3	0	0	0	0	0.500	0.500
1b	Pop Lloyd All-Stars	HAS	PRE	37	29-Jun-17		3	0	0	0	0	0	0	1	0	0	0	0.364	0.364
p	Chicago American Giants	CSW	PRE	37	02-Jul-17		4	0	0	0	0	0	0	1	0	0	0	0.267	0.267
1b	Chicago American Giants	CSW	PRE	37	03-Jul-17		4	0	0	0	0	0	0	0	0	0	0	0.211	0.211
1b	Pop Lloyd All-Stars	HAS	PRE	37	06-Jul-17		3	0	0	0	0	0	0	1	0	0	0	0.182	0.182
p	Chicago American Giants	JBC	PRE	37	27-Jul-17		4	0	0	0	0	0	0	0	0	0	0	0.154	0.154
					1917	**7**	**26**	**0**	**4**	**0**	**0**	**0**	**5**	**3**	**0**	**0**	**0**	**0.154**	**0.154**
Rube Foster's Totals		**431 Games**					**1756**	**191**	**459**	**67**	**13**	**12**	**310**	**88**	**40**	**6**	**97**	**0.261**	**0.335**

Legend

ABC — Indianapolis ABC's
ALC — All Cubans
BLA — Brooklyn All-Stars
BAG — Bacharach Giants
BRG — Brooklyn Royal Giants
CBG — Cuban Giants
CCG — Chicago Columbia Giants
CIT — City team
COG — Chicago Giants
CSS — Cuban Stars
CSW — Cuban Stars (West)
CXG — Cuban X-Giants
FLP — French Lick (IN) Plutos
HAS — Pete Hill's All-Stars
JBC — Jewell's ABCs
KCK — Kansas City (KS) Giants
LCS — Lincoln Stars
LIN — Lincoln Giants
LLG — Leland Giants
LWS — Louisville White Sox
MIN — Minor League team
PGT — Philadelphia Giants
SLG — St. Louis Giants
SPD — West Baden (IN) Sprudels
SPG — St. Paul Colored Gophers
STC — Stars of Cuba
WMG — Wilmington Giants

*Cuban Pitching Statistics**

Year	Team	W	L	Pct.
1903	Cuban X-Giants	2	3	.400
1905	Cuban X-Giants	2	2	.500
1907	Fe	10	5 (a)	.667
1908	Habana	8	5	.615
1910	Leland Giants	1	1	.500
1912	Fe	0	0 (b)	.000
1916	San Francisco	0	1	.000
		23	17	.575

(a) Foster was the league leader in Complete Games (15) and Wins (10).
(b) Foster pitched in two games with no decisions.
*Jorge S. Figueredo, *Who's Who in Cuban Baseball, 1878–1961* (Jefferson, NC: McFarland, 2003), 365. Jorge S. Figueredo, *Cuban Baseball: A Statistical History, 1878–1961*(Jefferson, NC: McFarland, 2003), 48, 60, 66, 67, 69, 73, 88, 89, 99, 117, 121, 136, 139.

D: Foster as Manager

Chicago American Giants—Official League Standings Under Foster's Management

Year	Lg.	TG	Won	Lost	Pct	Finish	Manager
1920	NNL	45	32	13	.711	1	Rube Foster
1921	NNL	64	42	22	.656	1	Rube Foster
1922	NNL	59	36	23	.610	1	Rube Foster
1923	NNL	70	41	29	.586	2T	Rube Foster
1924	NNL	73	49	24	.671	2	Rube Foster
1925	NNL	94	54	40	.574	4	Rube Foster
1926	NNL	52	39	13	.750		Rube Foster
8–28–26	NNL	28	18	10	.643		Dave Malarcher
1926 Total		80	57	23	.713	2	
CAG TOTALS		485	311	174	.641		
Foster's Totals		457	293	164	.641		

*Managerial Career in Cuba**

Start Date	Finish Date	Team	W	L	Pct.	Finished
12/4/1915	3/26/1916	San Francisco	5	16	.238	3rd place (c)
12/2/1920	2/14/1921	Bacharach	4	26	.133	3rd place
			9	42	.176	

(c) Foster took over the team from manager Manuel Martinez, after a 1–21 W/L start, restocking the team with American Giants players. They finished with six wins and 37 losses (.140).

Comparison of Foster's managerial records against those "selected as managers" into the National Baseball Hall of Fame.

Manager	TG	W	L	Pct.
Joe McCarthy	3487	2125	1333	.615
Frank Selee	2180	1284	862	.598
John McGraw	4769	2763	1948	.586
Al Lopez	2425	1410	1004	.584
Earl Weaver	2541	1480	1060	.583
Harry Wright	2145	1225	885	.581
Walter Alston	3658	2040	1613	.558
Sparky Anderson	4030	2194	1834	.545
Leo Durocher	3739	2008	1709	.540

Manager	TG	W	L	Pct.
Whitey Herzog	2409	1281	1125	.532
Ned Hanlon	2530	1313	1164	.530
Bill McKechnie	3647	1896	1723	.524
Dick Williams	3023	1571	1451	.520
Casey Stengel	3766	1905	1842	.508
Wilbert Robinson	2819	1399	1398	.500

Teammates who became managers:

1. Oscar Charleston — HOFer
2. Pete Duncan
3. Willie Foster — HOFer
4. Sam Crawford
5. Bill Gatewood
6. Joe Green
7. Pete Hill — HOFer
8. Bruce Petway
9. Chappie Johnson
10. Grant "Home Run" Johnson
11. Pop Lloyd — HOFer
12. Dick Lundy
13. Dan McClellan
14. Jose Mendez — HOFer
15. Louis Santop — HOFer
16. Ben Taylor — HOFer
17. Dizzy Dismukes
18. Wise Johnson
19. Bunny Downs
20. Cristobal Torriente — HOFer
21. Sol White — HOFer
22. Smokey Joe Williams — HOFer
23. Jude Gans

Foster's Managerial successors for Chicago teams only:

- David Malarcher, 1926–28 Chicago American Giants
  - Jim Brown, 1929–30 Chicago American Giants
    - *Willie Foster, 1930 Chicago American Giants*
      - Sam Crawford, 1931 Chicago American Giants
  - Candy Jim Taylor, 1937–39, 1941–42, 1945–47 Chicago American Giants
    - *Wilson Redus, 1940 Chicago American Giants*
    - *Ted "Double Duty" Radcliffe, 1943 Chicago American Giants*
    - *Larry Brown, 1943 Chicago American Giants*
    - *Elwood "Bingo" DeMoss, 1944 Chicago American Giants*
    - *Quincy Trouppe, 1948 Chicago American Giants*
      - Winfield Welch, 1949, 1951 Chicago American Giants
        - *Double Duty Radcliffe, 1950 Chicago American Giants*
        - *Paul Hardy, 1952 Chicago American Giants*

Unlike most athletes of his day, Candy Jim Taylor habitually gnawed on candy instead of a little Red Man. Next to Rube Foster, Taylor was perhaps black baseball's most colorful and winningest manager. Although his older brother C.I. Taylor had an adversarial relationship with Rube, they exhibited professional civility on the field (NoirTech Research).

E: Foster's Teammates in the Hall of Fame

Cuban X Giants
1903 Sol White, 1b

Philadelphia Giants
1904 Pete Hill, of — Sol White, 1b
1905 Pete Hill, of — Sol White, 1b
1906 Pete Hill, of — Sol White, mgr

Leland Giants
1907 Pete Hill, of
1908 Pete Hill, of
1909 Pete Hill, of
1910 Pete Hill, of — Pop Lloyd, ss

Chicago American Giants
1911 Pete Hill, of
1912 Pete Hill, of
1913 Pete Hill, of — Ben Taylor, 1b — Smokey Joe Williams, p
1914 Pete Hill, of — Pop Lloyd, ss — Smokey Joe Williams, p
1915 Pete Hill, of — Pop Lloyd, ss — Louis Santop, c
1916 Pete Hill, of — Pop Lloyd, ss
1917 Pete Hill, of — Pop Lloyd, ss
1918 Pete Hill, of — Cristobal Torriente, of — Jose Mendez, p — Oscar Charleston, of (4)
1919 Cristobal Torriente, of — Oscar Charleston, of
1920 Cristobal Torriente, of
1921 Cristobal Torriente, of
1922 Cristobal Torriente, of
1923 Cristobal Torriente, of — Willie Foster, p
1924 Cristobal Torriente, of — Willie Foster, p
1925 Cristobal Torriente, of — Willie Foster, p
1926 Willie Foster, p

F: Foster Baseball Collectibles

Cards

1974 Laughlin Old Time Black Stars—#35
1980 SSPC Hall of Fame—#175
1981 Perez Steele Hall of Fame Cards, Series 6—#174
1981 National Baseball Hall of Fame Plaque card
1983 Conlon's 1933 Negro League All-Stars—#55
1984 O'Connell and Son Ink—#139
1986 Negro League Fritsch—#18
1987 Negro League Phil Dixon Postcard—#25
1988 Conlon's Negro League Stars—#1
1988 Negro League Duquesne University—#1
1990 Stars of the Negro Leagues—#16
1991 Conlin—The Sporting News—#138
1991 Pomegranate Black Ball Postcard Book—#27
1992 Remembering the Negro Leagues—#7
1994 Ted Williams Card Set—#105
1994 Upper Deck: The American Epic—#31
1995 Negro League San Francisco Examiner Tribute—#11
1997 Sammie Haynes' Negro League Playing Cards—#SJKO
1999 Greg Stokesberry's Bobblehead statute
2001 Fleer Greats of the Game—#111
2001 Fleer Stitches in Time—#20
2001 What Could Have Been—Topps 50 Years—#WCB5
2004 Black Ball II—The Negro Baseball Leagues—#4
2005 Helmar Negro Leaguers—#9
2010 Tri-Star OBAK—Game Changers—#28
2010 United Postal Service, Rube Foster se-tenant stamp, 44 cent.

July 15, 2010 United States Postal Service (USPS) Honors Andrew Foster

The two se-tenant stamps feature a scene painted by award-winning artist Kadir Nelson of Los Angeles, California.

Along with the dual 44 cent stamp, USPS also offered a host of other related Foster memorabilia:

- Negro Leagues Baseball Giclée Print
- Negro Leagues Baseball "Safe at Home!" Giclée Print
- Negro Leagues Baseball Framed Art (both stamps)

- Negro Leagues Baseball "Safe at Home!" Framed Art
- Negro Leagues Cultural Diary Page
- Special Edition We Are the Ship: The Story of Negro Leagues Baseball
- Negro Leagues Baseball Commemorative Folio

Although the action scene is supposed to be generic and non-identifiable, players, teams, uniforms, stadium and city, it is taking place in 1924, according to Louis Plummer of PhotoAssist. Shown above is the painting of the se-tenant stamp prior to its approval by the USPS (courtesy artist Kadir Nelson).

G: Death Certificate and Medical Analysis

Foster's death certificate listed the cause of death as "General Paralysis of the Insane." In volume 14, on page 609, of the 1911 *Encyclopædia Britannica*, this disease is said to be characterized by symptoms of progressive degeneration of the central nervous system, and is invariably fatal. The disease is essentially the result of toxemia or poisoning, and acquired or inherited syphilitic infection is an important predisposing factor. A history of syphilitic infection occurs in 70 to 90 percent of the patients affected.

The view in 1911 was that the disease is a bacterial invasion to which syphilis, alcoholism, excessive mental and physical strain, and a too exclusively nitrogenous diet, only act as predisposing causes. Further examination reveals the onset of general paralysis is slow and gradual, and the earliest symptoms may be either physical or mental. The disease may commence either in the brain itself or the spinal cord may be primarily the seat of lesion, the brain becoming affected secondarily.

Early physical symptoms generally affect motor skills. The patient loses energy, readily becomes tired and the capacity for finely coordinated motor acts, such as shuffling playing cards, is impaired. Transient attacks of partial paralysis of a hand, arm, leg or one side of the body, or the speech center are not uncommon. Or the symptoms may be purely mental, as in Foster's case, and affect one's moral sense and the faculty of self-control. Foster was known to become irritable, burst into violent passions over minor chaffs, and exhibit changes in character and habits, as reported by player-tenant George Sweatt.

The disease impairs the memory, making Foster's decisions facile. The disease can also cause wild attacks of sudden excitement, following upon a period of restlessness and sleeplessness. Speech can be slurred and the facial muscles lose their tone, giving the face a flattened expression. Other symptoms, according to the *Britannica*, include impaired muscular power, and a straddling gait. Additionally, the encyclopedia says the duration of the disease is from 18 months to three years, but has been known to persist for seven. Foster was institutionalized in 1926 and died in 1930.

Today, the disease is called neurosyphilis, known as an infection of the brain or spinal cord. It is considered a life-threatening complication of syphilis. There are four different forms of neurosyphilis: (1) asymptomatic, (2) meningovascular, (3) tabes dorsalis and (4) general paresis, which is an impairment of mental function caused by damage to the brain. General paresis usually begins about 15–20 years after the syphilis infection.

Syphilis infections can be passed through sexual contact with an infected person, but may also be transmitted by non-sexual contact. Bejel, or endemic syphilis, is transmitted by non-sexual contact in communities living under poor hygiene conditions, or acquired by an unborn fetus through an infected mother. It may never be known how Rube Foster acquired this disease that resulted in his early passing from the national game.

H: Draft Card and 1880 Census

1880 Census

Line 29 on this census page shows the household members of the McKinny family living in Winchester, Fayette County, Texas, about 18 miles Northwest of La Grange.

Listed with their respective ages are:

[7-396.]

Received Sep. 1, '80, C.

Page No. 27
Supervisor's Dist. No. 5
Enumeration Dist. No. 57

Note A.—The Census Year begins June 1, 1879, and ends May 31, 1880.
Note B.—All persons will be included in the Enumeration who were living on the 1st day of June, 1880. No others will. Children BORN SINCE June 1, 1880, will be OMITTED. Members of Families who have DIED SINCE June 1, 1880, will be INCLUDED.
Note C.—Questions Nos. 13, 14, 22 and 23 are not to be asked in respect to persons under 10 years of age.

72

SCHEDULE I.—Inhabitants in ______, in the County of Fayette, State of Texas, enumerated by me on the 10 day of June, 1880.

W.H. Thomas, Enumerator.

Line	Dwelling No.	Family No.	Name	Color	Sex	Age	Month born (if within Census year)	Relationship to head	Single	Married	Widowed	Occupation	Cannot read	Cannot write	Place of birth	Father's birthplace	Mother's birthplace
1	231	233	— Ann	W	F	16		daughter	/			at Home			Ala	N.C.	N.C.
2			Miller, M.	W	M	24			/			Farm labor			Ala		
3	232	236	Bain, Mike	W	M	35				/		Farmer			Ireland	Ireland	Ireland
4			— Eliza	W	F	23		wife		/					Ala		
5			— Mary	W	F	4		daughter							Texas	Ireland	Texas
6			— Jennie	W	F	2		daughter							Texas	Ireland	Texas
7			Robinson, Berry	B	M	14			/			Farm labor			Texas		
8	233	237	Williams, Moses	B	M	60				/		Farm labor	/	/	N.C.		
9			— Allie	B	F	40		wife		/		Keeping House	/	/	N.C.		
10			— Susie	B	F	25		daughter	/			works on Farm	/	/	Texas	N.C.	N.C.
11			— John	B	M	9		g-son							Texas		Texas
12			— Kate	B	F	5		g-daughter							Texas		Texas
13			— Ada	B	F	3		g-daughter							Texas		Texas
14			— Kittie	B	F	10/12	Aug	g-daughter							Texas		Texas
15	234	238	Mason, Parish	B	M	25			/			Farm labor	/	/	S.C.		
16	235	239	Lee, Margaret	B	F	38					/	Farm labor			La		
17			— Salina	B	F	13		daughter	/			works on Farm			Texas		La
18			— Ophelia	B	F	10		daughter	/			at Home			Texas		La
19			— Tibby	B	F	8		daughter							Texas		La
20			— Lizzie	B	F	4		daughter							Texas		La
21	236	240	Lewis, Geo	B	M	35				/		Farmer			Ark		
22			— Mary	B	F	28		wife		/		Keeping House	/	/	Texas		
23			— John	B	M	7		Son							Texas	Ark	Texas
24			— Emma	B	F	5		daughter							Texas	Ark	Texas
25			— Sallie	B	F	3		daughter							Texas	Ark	Texas
26			— Jxx	B	F	1		daughter							Texas	Ark	Texas
27			Bridgewater, Milt	B	M	24			/			Farm labor			Texas		
28	237	241	Miller, J. M.	W	M	46			/			Farmer			Ky	Va	Va
29	238	242	McKenny, J. L.T.	W	M	57					/	Farmer			Alabama	N.C.	N.C.
30			— Edgar	W	M	16			/			Attending School			Arkansas	Alabama	N.C.
31			Foster, Andy	B	M	29				/		Farmer			Miss	Ala	Ala
32			— Eveline	B	F	24		wife		/		Keeping Home			Miss		
33			— Willie	B	M	5		Son							Texas	Miss	Miss
34			— Gertrude	B	F	4		daughter							Texas	Miss	Miss
35			— Christina	B	F	2		daughter							Texas	Miss	Miss
36			— Bishop	B	M	3/12	Feb	Son							Texas	Miss	Miss
37			Brown, Ruth	B	F	29		Servant			/	Farm labor	/	/	Miss		
38			— Lulu	B	F	3									Texas		Miss
39			— Augusta	B	F	3/12	Feb								Texas		Miss
40			Gates, Sampson	B	M	16		Servant	/			Farm labor	/	/	Texas		
41			Williams, Rich.	B	M	21		Servant	/			Farm labor	/	/	Texas		
42	239	243	Dunson, Wm	B	M	35				/		Farm labor			Ala		
43			— Annie	B	F	30		wife		/					Ala		
44			— Alice	B	F	8		daughter							Texas	Ala	Ala
45			— Lawrence	B	F	7		daughter							Texas	Ala	Ala
46			— Dixon	B	M	3		Son							Texas	Ala	Ala
47	240	244	Moses, Jim	B	M	28				/		Farm labor	/	/	Ala		
48			— Becky	B	F	24		wife		/		Keeping House	/	/	Ala		
49	241	245	Dunson, Robt	B	M	29				/			/	/	Ala	Ga	S.C.
50			— Alice	B	F	25		wife		/			/	/	Texas		

Note D.—In making entries in columns 9, 10, 11, 12, 18 to 23, an affirmative mark only will be used—thus /, except in the case of divorced persons, column 11, when the letter "D" is to be used.
Note E.—Question No. 12 will only be asked in cases where an affirmative answer has been given either to question 10 or to question 11.
Note F.—Question No. 14 will only be asked in cases when a gainful occupation has been reported in column 13.
Note G.—In column 7 an abbreviation in the name of the month may be used, as Jan., Apr., Dec.

J.L.T. McKinny 57
Edgar McKinny 16
Andy [Andrew] Foster 29
Eveline [Evaline] Foster 24
Willie Foster 5
Gertrude Foster 4
Christina Foster 2
Bishop (or Rube) Foster 8 months
Ruth Brown 29
Lulu Brown 3

REGISTRATION CARD

SERIAL NUMBER 2321 ORDER NUMBER 190

1 Andrew Rube Foster
(First name) (Middle name) (Last name)

2 PERMANENT HOME ADDRESS:
3242 Vernon Ave Chicago
(No.) (Street or R. F. D. No.) (City or town) (County) (State)

Age in Years 3 38 | Date of Birth 4 Sept 17 1879
(Month) (Day) (Year)

RACE

White	Negro	Oriental	Indian: Citizen	Indian: Noncitizen
5	6 ✓	7	8	9

U. S. CITIZEN: Native Born	Naturalized	Citizen by Father's Naturalization Before Registrant's Majority	ALIEN: Declarant	Non-declarant
10 ✓	11	12	13	14

15
If not a citizen of the U. S., of what nation are you a citizen or subject?

PRESENT OCCUPATION 16 Baseball player owner
EMPLOYER'S NAME 17 J.M. Schorling

18 PLACE OF EMPLOYMENT OR BUSINESS:
39th & Princeton —
(No.) (Street or R. F. D. No.) (City or town) (County) (State)

NEAREST RELATIVE
Name 19 Mrs Sarah Foster
Address 20 3242 Vernon Ave
(No.) (Street or R. F. D. No.) (City or town) (County) (State)

I AFFIRM THAT I HAVE VERIFIED ABOVE ANSWERS AND THAT THEY ARE TRUE

P. M. G. O.
FORM No. 1 (Red) Andrew Rube Foster
(Registrant's signature or mark) (OVER)

2842

Augusta Brown	3 months
Sampson Gates	16
Kelly Williams	21

It is thought that Bishop may have been a nickname, considered his father was a Reverend, or perhaps a middle name to avoid the confusion of having two Andy or Andrews in the same home.

The unincorporated town of Winchester was along the tracks of the Texas and New Orleans Railroad, and when a second railroad (The San Antonio and Arkansas Pass) came

12-1-3-G REGISTRAR'S REPORT

DESCRIPTION OF REGISTRANT

HEIGHT			BUILD			COLOR OF EYES	COLOR OF HAIR
Tall	Medium	Short	Slender	Medium	Stout		
21 5-9	22	23	24	25	26 ✓	27 Brown	28 Black

29 Has person lost arm, leg, hand, eye, or is he obviously physically disqualified? (Specify.)

30 I certify that my answers are true; that the person registered has read or has had read to him his own answers; that I have witnessed his signature or mark, and that all of his answers of which I have knowledge are true, except as follows:

Hattie Lois Todd
(Signature of Registrar)

Date of Registration Sept 12-1918

LOCAL BOARD FOR
DIVISION No. 3
3103 INDIANA AVE.
CHICAGO, ILLINOIS

(STAMP OF LOCAL BOARD)

2842

(The stamp of the Local Board having jurisdiction of the area in which the registrant has his permanent home shall be placed in this box.)

(OVER)

through in 1888, the town financially benefited with hotels, saloons, rooming houses, blacksmiths, wheelwrights, barbers and seven mercantile stores. Current population is 50. The Fayette County courthouse had no record of Rube's birth. According to Oscar Charleston biographer Geri Strecker, the Fosters were sharecroppers for J.L.T. McKinny, who owned more than 200 acres. Land deed records suggest they lived on the southeastern side of Winchester, the corner closest to LaGrange. The McKinny land was part of the "Rabb Mill Grant" of 22,000 acres granted to William Rabb (1770–1831), a Pennsylvanian who helped Stephen F. Austin (known as the Father of Texas and thus the naming of the Capital city) to explore the area in 1819. Rabb moved to Fayette County in 1821 and built a grist mill in exchange for the lands. As more settlers came to the area, Rabb sold off portions of his land, much of which was covered by pine forests. As farmers cleared the acres, they began planting cotton. This is the crop that brought McKinny to Winchester, about 85 miles southwest of Calvert. McKinny was a widower with one son, Edgar, who was 16 years old in 1880. With only one son, he hired Andrew Foster, Sr., along with five other persons listed-living on the McKinny property to manage the farm and work the crops. The 1900 census show the Foster family living in Calvert, Texas, the most common place listed as Rube Foster's birthplace. Rube may have refrained from claiming he was from La Grange, which is infamously known as the "Chicken Ranch" or brothel. La Grange is the setting of *The Best Little Whorehouse in Texas*, a 1982 movie about the Chicken Ranch. A possible association with La Grange's Chicken Ranch in his youth may have subsequently led to his death from syphilis in 1930.

Map link to Winchester, La Grange and Calvert, Texas. *http://www.mapquest.com/mq/9-CF4r*

*Documents courtesy Tim Rives from the National Archives, Bannister Branch, Kansas City, Missouri.

I: Court Documents from the Leland Lawsuit

In 1906, the *Chicago Broad Ax* ran this resume of the central figure in the Frank Leland lawsuit, under the heading **"Lawyer, Orator, Ex-Journalist and Property Holder."**

> "Col. Beauregard F. Moseley is so well known throughout Chicago that he needs no introduction to the thousands of readers of *The Broad Ax*; he came into this world in the State of Georgia. He received his education in the public schools of his native State where he afterwards taught. After severing his connection with the schools he entered politics holding several positions of trust under the national government at New Orleans.
>
> "In the course of time, Col Moseley decided to cast his lot in the northern section of the country and he removed with his family to Montreal, Canada, but it was too cold that far north for his warm southern blood and early in the 90s he came to this city to reside.
>
> "Soon after settling in Chicago, The Chicago Republic, a lusty journalistic youngster, made its appearance with the hustling Colonel at its helm. The journalistic craft was piloted fearlessly and successfully until 1896 when the field of journalism was forsaken for the more lucrative practice of law.
>
> "Since his admission to the bar in 1896, he has been a hard student of the law. His law offices [at] 6258 South Halsted Street are filled with law books, and it is safe to say that he has more clients among white persons than any other Afro-American lawyer in Chicago.
>
> "By strict attention to business and ever watchful of their interest of his clients he has met with phenomenal success in the world of law.

"He knows how to look out for number one and the result of being endowed with sufficient wisdom to do this he resides with his interesting family in a nice home of their own at 6248 Sangamon St.

"He is a member of the Appomattox Club, and at all times he is in demand as an orator."—*Chicago Broad Ax*, 29 December 1906.

State of Illinois
Circuit Court of Cook County
Leland Giants Base Ball and Amusement Association
Vs.
Frank Leland's Chicago Giants Base Ball Club, Frank C. Leland, Major R.R. Jackson, A.H. Garrett, Nathan Harris and the Chicago City League.
Gen. No. 296934 Term No. 8218

The answer of Frank Leland's Chicago Giants Base Ball Club, Frank C. Leland, R.R. Jackson, A.H. Garrett and Nathan Harris, defendants to the above named complainants bill of complaint as amended.

These defendants new and at all times hereafter first saving and reserving unto itself and themselves all and all manner of benefit of advantage to the manifold errors and uncertainties in said bill and amended bill contained. And these defendants pray the same advantage of this answer as though they had specially demurred thereto; and these defendants say that in and by said bill and amended bill the said complainant has not setup or shown any cause of action or any reason why this Honorable Court should in any wise take jurisdiction of this cause or grant unto the said complainant the relief prayed for in said amended bill. And these defendants say that said bill as amended is without equity on its face; and these defendants pray the same advantage as though they had set the matter up by special demurrer.

And these defendants for answer to said amended bill of complaint, or so much thereof, as it is advised that it is material or necessary for them to make answer unto answering say; that the defendant Company and A.H. Garrett have no knowledge as to whether in the Spring of 1907, Frank C. Leland went to Beauregard F. Moseley and desired of him assistance for the purpose of raising money to keep any baseball organization in existence, therefore it neither admits or denies the same, but calls for strict proof thereof.

This defendant, the Frank Leland Chicago Giants Base Ball Club answering says that it has no knowledge in relation to the allegations in said bill as amended contained in regard to the incorporation of said complaint and the taking over of the business name "Leland Giants" and good will of Frank C. Leland, as set forth in said bill as amended and it therefore calls for strict proof of the same.

This defendant, the Frank Leland Chicago Giants Base Ball Club, says that it has no knowledge as to whether the Lelands Giants Base Ball Association by bill of sale or otherwise transferred to the complainant, as alleged in said complainant's amended bill various personal property, and the name and good will of the Leland Giants, and it calls for strict proof thereof.

These defendants say that on the 2nd day of November 1909, the defendant Company herein was duly incorporated under the laws of this State under the name "The Frank Leland's Chicago Giants Base Ball Club" and as such begun playing in 1910, games of base ball with other base ball clubs—And as a base ball club was advertised and sought to advertise itself and be known as the Chicago Giants Base Ball Club of Chicago Giants; that none of these defendants in any wise or in any way or manner intend wish or desire to advertise or it out to the public or to have anyone understand, call or know said defendant club as the "Leland Giants"—And these defendants now here state and declare that they have no desire or intention to themselves, or anyone of them print, publish, or advertise, or to have anyone of them print, publish or advertise the said defendant Base Ball Club as the "Leland Giants" but these defendants wish and intend to be known to the public as the "Chicago Giants"—And these defendants say that they also wish and desire to have the base ball public know that said Chicago Giants are under the management of Frank C. Leland, because of his reputation as a base ball club manager—But these defendants expressly state and wish it understood by all, that they are the "Leland Giants" Base Ball Club; nor is said defendant club herein known by that name—and these defendants say that they have not in the past, nor do they intend in the future, to make prominent or feature the first two words, to wit; "Frank Leland" of said Base Ball club's name; but to intend as feature and make prominent the name "Chicago Giants"—And that said Club is managed and was gotten together by Frank C. Leland, and that he is directing their play and games.

These defendants say that Frank C. Leland, together with R.R. Jackson, are engaged in the active management of said base ball club that said Frank C. Leland, was during the years 1887, 1888 and 1889, a base ball player; that during the years 1896, 1897, 1898, 1899, 1900, 1901, 1902, 1903, 1904, 1905, 1906,

1907, 1908 and 1909, he was actively engaged in managing base ball clubs, and is known throughout this city of Chicago, and in many States of this Union as a successful manager of base ball clubs—That said Frank C. Leland has managed in Chicago, base ball clubs known as "Chicago Union Giants," "Chicago Unions," and as a manager has deservedly acquired a reputation for his success in getting together and combing in a base ball club some of the very best base ball players of color in these United States.

These defendants and each of them further answering deny that the said Frank C. Leland and the Chicago Base Ball League as the Chicago League, or anyone of these defendants or anyone for them, are about to issue a base ball schedule announcing the "line up" of teams in the places and where and when they will play upon the City Circuit, giving the teams new managed by the said Frank C. Leland and his defendant, Frank C. Leland's Chicago Giants "line up" under the name of and title "Leland Giants."

These defendants further answering say, that the defendant company has never been known by the name of "Leland Giants"; that it never has at any time claimed or pretended to be the "Leland Giants." These defendants say that the base ball schedule to be issued of the City League games will not name nor mention this defendant's base ball club as the "Leland Giants," but it is the intention of these defendants to have its name placed upon the said schedule as the "Chicago Giants."

These defendants say, that the letter heads upon which correspondence is had upon which letters are written in relation to the base ball business of the defendant base ball club are an exact duplicate of the letter head hereunto annexed to this answer, and marks "A" and made apart of this answer.

These defendants say that the defendant company uses and has used no other letter head since the date of its incorporation.

These defendants annexes [sic] hereunto an envelope and mark the same "B" and make it a part of this answer, and say that in regard thereto that it is the only envelope containing any advertising or a matter that the defendant company now uses in connection with its business; and these defendant says that they have no intention whatever of in any wise using or undertaking to use the name "Leland Giants."

These defendants say that news of and concerning the games played by said base ball clubs are not sent out under the name of the "Leland Giants" but as the "Chicago Giants" and these defendants annex to this answer clippings from the *Chicago Daily Tribune* of April 16th, 1910, and the *Inter-Ocean* of April 18th, 1910 and mark the same "C" and make the same a part thereof; And defendants say that this is the way news of its games are reported and sent out.

These defendants annex hereto and mark the same "I" and make said exhibit "I" a part of this answer, one of the bills advertising games of base ball—And these defendants say that this is the way games of the defendant Company are advertised.

These defendants deny all and all manner of unlawful combing and confederating charged against it in said bill as amended.

These defendants deny that they are advertising itself and its players as the "Leland Giants."

And these defendants deny that it or they or anyone for it or them is writing or at any time has written letters to owners of base ball teams, Clubs and parks, or to anyone announcing that it is the owner of the "Leland Giants," or that it or they has or have in any way advertised or sought to have the public or anyone know believe or understate that this defendant was in reality the "Leland Giants" owned and operated by the said complainant, but on the contrary, this defendant says that it and they has and have given the widest possible publicity to the fact that it was the "Chicago Giants Base Ball Club."

These defendants annex hereto and mark the same exhibits "D"- "E"—"F" -"G"—and "H," and make the same a part of this answer and say that the said exhibits are true and correct duplicates of the advertising matter used by it and them.

These defendants deny that the said complain is entitled to the relief prayed for and pray to be dismissed with its and their reasonable cost in this behalf most wrongfully sustained.

Signed by:

E.H. Morris and W.L. Houston, solicitors for the defendants.

Document was undated.

State of Illinois, County of Cook
Circuit Court of Cook County
Leland Giants Base Ball & Amusement Association
Vs.
Frank Leland's Chicago Giants Base Ball Club, A. Corp., Frank C. Leland, Major R.R. Jackson, A.H. Garrett, Nathan Harris and Chicago City League, A Corp.

Your orator, the Leland Giants Base Ball & Amusement Association, a corporation, by B.F. Moseley, its secretary and treasurer, of Chicago, Cook County, Illinois, respectfully shows unto your Honor that early in the spring of 1907 Frank C. Leland, then the owner of a base ball team, which had been playing base ball in and around Chicago for the past two years previous under the name and title of the Leland Giants, came to B.F. Moseley, secretary and treasurer of the Leland Giants Base Ball & Amusement Association, complainants herein, and requested that said B.F. Moseley assist him in keeping his team, the Leland Giants, in existence, asking for financial assistance, and after stating to said Moseley the fact that he was indebted to A.G. Spalding & Bros., for uniforms and base ball supplies; to one John Schorling, or lessee of the grounds upon which the Leland Giants, then owned by the said Frank C. Leland, played ball, for money advanced for the season previous, and to W.J. Winterburn, printer, for posters and printed matter, and of his inability to raise money to keep his team together, and that he would do anything that was reasonable for the purpose of raising money to keep the team active as a base ball club.

Whereupon the said Moseley suggested that a corporation be formed, and that the same, when formed, take over the business, name and good will of the said Frank C. Leland, trading and operating as the Leland Giants, which was agreed to, and later done by the appointment upon proper application to the Secretary of State by Willis V. Jefferson, F.C. Leland and B.F. Moseley, as commissioners, to open books for the subscription to the capital stock of the Leland Giants Base Ball Club, which books, in accordance with said license issued by the Secretary of State, were duly opened by the said commissioners and subscriptions taken, where upon the commissioners acting for the intended corporation received from Frank C. Leland, under date of April 13, 1907, a Bill of Sale for and in consideration of the sum of Five Hundred Dollars ($500.00) conveying all the following goods, chattels and property, to-wit: Twelve bats, five hundred cushions, two mitts, three mufflers, one thousand tickets, contract of use and occupancy of club park with John Schorling, name and good will of the Leland Giants Base Ball Club, all contracts with players, and every right appertaining thereto belong, from the said Frank C. Leland, wherein he vouches himself to be the true and lawful owner, with good right and lawful authority to dispose of the same, and that he would for himself and heirs, executors and administrators and assigns against the lawful claims and demands of all and every person or persons whomsoever.

This bill of sale was, upon the formation of the association, the Leland Giants Base Ball Association, approved and accepted by the stock holders, and stock issued to the amount of Five Hundred Dollars ($500.00) to the said Frank C. Leland in payment therefore, and was filed for record in the Recorder's Office June 3rd, 1907, as document no. 4045555, and recorded in book 9600 of records, page 362.

The said Leland Giants Base Ball Association being duly organized in compliance with the laws of the State of Illinois, the Secretary of State issued to it a charter under the date of April 20, 1907, as document No. 4045554, and recorded in the book 156 of corporation records, page 353, and therefore employed Andrew Foster, James Booker, George Wright, Nathan Harris, Harry Moore, Danger Talbert, William Norman, Walter Ball, Robert Winston and others, being the best colored talent of its kind procurable at an expense of One Thousand Dollars ($1,000.00) per month or more, assumed the lease of John Schorling of Auburn Park, elected officers, Major R.R. Jackson, President; J.H. Bolden, First Vice President; W.V. Jefferson, Second Vice-President; B.F. Moseley, Secretary & Treasurer; Frank C. Leland, Manager and Andrew Foster, Captain and Team Manager, and began operating by advertising throughout the summer and fall of 1907, ending the season without a defeat in a single series of games played — winning 103 — 32 being shutouts, and losing 1, and firming establishing their title "The World's Colored Champions" under the name of the Leland Giants.

Upon the uniform of each player was printed the words "Leland Giants." All contracts with reference to the team were known and referred to by the words "Leland Giants." Upon the literature used by the association was in large letters "L G" over the words "World's Colored Champions, Leland Giants."

In the fall of 1907, the stock holders became convinced that the capital of the corporation, Leland Giants Base Ball Association, Twenty-Five Hundred Dollars ($2,500.00) was too small, and became desirous of increasing its capital stock. It paid off all of the obligations and authorized by regular vote of its stock holders and directors and sale of all its assets, to wit: All and singular the rights, privileges, powers, franchises, patents, royalties, grants and immunities, and all property, real and personal, and mixed, agreement, all debts due of whatsoever kind, and the name and good will of the Leland Giants Base Ball Association to the Leland Giants Base Ball & Amusement Association, the complainant herein, which bill of sale was duly executed by R. R. Jackson, President, and attested in the presence of B.F. Moseley, Secretary and Treasurer, and filed of record December 4th, 1907, as document No. 4133218, and recorded in book 8424 of records, page 597, and received in addition thereto the bill of sale from Frank C. Leland to the Leland Giants Base Ball Association and an agreement of Frank C. Leland with the commissioners licensed by the Secretary of State to open books, and receive subscriptions to the capital stock of the Leland Giants Base Ball Association. Said stock holders to receive and distribute from the Leland Giants Base Ball & Amusement Association Fifty-five thousand dollars ($55,000.00) worth of stock among the stockholders of the Leland Giants Base Ball Association, according to their holdings and share therein, and the Leland Giants Base Ball & Amusement Association was duly organized after a license had been issued to Frank C. Leland, J.H. Bolden, W.V. Jefferson, Andrew Foster, and B.F. Moseley, as commissioners, by the Secretary of State to open books of subscriptions to the capital stock of the Leland Giants Base Ball & Amusement Association, and a charter therefore on the 6th of March, 1908, was issued and filed of record in Cook County on March 17th, 1908, as document No. 4173234, and recorded in book 143 of corporation records, page 129. The officers elected for the years 1908 were Frank C. Leland, President and Booking Agent, R.R. Jackson, First Vice-President, W.V. Jefferson, Second Vice-President, B.F. Moseley, Secretary and Treasurer, J.H. Bolden, Rink Manager and Andrew Foster, Manager and Captain. Said Association operated its team under the name of "Leland Giants" and as such entered the Chicago Base Ball League, and played not only the games in the league, but throughout the country under the name of "Leland Giants," winning the pennant in the Chicago City League as the Champions of that organization. On September 20th, 1909, Frank C. Leland was discharged as Booking Agent by reason of his activity in forming another club to compete with the Leland Giants, and Andrew Foster was appointed in his stead.

But now so it is may I please your honor that the said Frank Leland's Chicago Giants Base Ball Club, A Corp., Frank C. Leland, Major R.R. Jackson, A.H. Garrett, Nathan Harris and Chicago City League, a Corp., are combining and confederating together with diverse persona at present unknown to your orator, whose names when discovered your orator prays he may be a liberty to insert herein with apt words that charge them as party defendants hereto, and contriving how to wrong and injure your orator in the premises, they, the said Frank Leland's Chicago Giants Base Ball Club, a Corp., Frank C. Leland, Major R.R. Jackson. A.H. Garrett, Nathan Harris, and Chicago City League, a Corp., are advertising the fact that they have the Leland Giants for the year 1910, and the said defendants, Frank C. Leland, R.R. Jackson and A.H. Garrett have organized a corporation known as Frank Leland's Chicago Giants Base Ball Club, and by themselves, individually and through such corporation and with the Chicago City League, are stating upon their literature that the said Frank C. Leland had organized and managed the said Leland Giants, and caused envelopes to be printed with an inscription thereon "Leland's Chicago Giants Base Ball Club," and have written letters to the owners of the base ball clubs through the city and country announcing that they were the owners of the Leland Giants, and giving the line-up of such players as Walter Ball, Harry Moore, Danger Talbert, Nathan Harris, George Wright, Robert Winston and William Norman, most of said players being under contract to the complaint as herein, and the said letters and advertising matter that signed by Frank C. Leland, and intending and conveying the idea that he and his players were and are the "Leland Giants," which is a fraud upon the rights of the complainant, Leland Giants Base Ball & Amusement Association, and a deception and deceit upon the public, and the said Frank C. Leland is now about to commence the playing of base ball under the advertised name of "Leland's Giants," all which acts, doings and pretenses of the said defends are contrary to equity and good conscience, and tending to the manifest wrong and injury of your orator in the premises.

In TENDER CONSIDERATION WHEREOF, and forasmuch as your orator is wholly remediless in the premises at and by the strict rules of the Common Law, and cannot have adequate relief except in a court of equity where matters of this nature are properly cognizable and relievable.

To the end, therefore, that the said defendants, Frank Leland's Chicago Giants Base Ball Club, Frank C. Leland, Major R.R. Jackson, A.H. Garrett, Nathan Harris, and Chicago City League, a Corp., if they can show why your orator should not have the relief herein prayed, and that they may full, true, director and perfect answer make (but not under oath, answer under oath being hereby expressly waived) to all and singular the matters and things therein contained, and that in the mean time the said defendants, Frank Leland's Chicago Giants Base Ball Club, Frank C. Leland, Major R.R. Jackson, A.H. Garrett, Nathan Harris, and Chicago City League, a Corp., their counsel, solicitors, officers, agents or servants, may be restrained by an injunction of this Honorable Court from advertising or using the name of "Frank C. Leland" or "Leland Giants" in connection with the game of base ball, and that upon a final hearing of this cause such injunction may be made perpetual, and

May it please your Honor to grant unto your orator the writ of summons in chancery issuing out of his honorable Court directed to the Sheriff of the said County of Cook, commanding him that he summon Frank Leland's Chicago Giants Base Ball Club, Frank C. Leland, Major R.R. Jackson, A.R. Garrett, Nathan Harris and Chicago City League, to be and appear before his Honorable Court then and there to stand to, abide and perform such order, direction and decree therein as to your Honor shall seem meet, according to equity and good conscience, and

Your orator will ever pray,

Signed by Beauregard F. Moseley, Secretary & Treasurer

State of Illinois
Cook County
Gen. No. 296934 Term No. 8218

B.F. Moseley being first duty sworn on oath deposes and says that he is secretary and treasurer of the Leland Giants Base Ball and Amusement Association, a corporation, and as such is authorized to sign the above bill of complaint, and make affidavit thereto; that he has read the foregoing bill of complaint, and knows the contents thereof; that the same is true of his own knowledge, except as to the matters and things therein stated to be on information and belief, and that as to the those matters and things, he believes it to be true.

Signed Beauregard Moseley.

Subscribed and sworn to, before me, this 19th day of March , A.D. 1910.

Signed Agnes Murphy, Notary Public.

Chancery Summons
Melville T. McGavin, Solicitor
State of Illinois
County of Cook
Gen. No. 296934 Term No. 8218

This cause having come on to be heard upon the bill of complaint herein, the answer of the defendant thereto, the replication of the complainant to such answer and the proofs taken in this cause and the testimony introduced and heard in open court, and court having heretofore rendered a decretal order in said cause, and the court having heard counsel and being fully advised in the promises and on consideration thereof, IT IS ORDERED, ADJUDGED AND DECREED by the court that hereafter neither the defendants nor any person or persons, Firm or corporation acting for the defendants or the defendants for themselves, shall use the name "Leland" in connection with the baseball Club now known as the Frank Leland's Chicago Giants Base Ball Club, or shall in any way use the name "Leland" in connection therewith and that the defendants pay the cost herein.

Signed O.M. Walker, Judge.

We command you that you summon: Frank Leland's Chicago Giants Base Ball Club (a corporation) Frank C. Leland, Major R.R. Jackson, A.H. Garrett, Nathan Harris and Chicago City League, a corporation

If they shall be found in your County, personally to be and appear before the Circuit Court of Cook County, on the first day of the term thereof, to be holden at the Court House in the City of Chicago in said Cook County, on the third Monday of April A.D., 1910, to answer unto

Leland Giants Base Ball & Amusement Association, a corporation

In its certain Bill of Complaint filled in said Court, on the Chancery side thereof.

And have you then and there this writ with an endorsement thereon, in what manner you shall have executed the same.

Witness, Joseph E. Bidwell, Jr., Clerk of our said Court, and the seal thereof, at Chicago, in said County, this 21st day of March, A.D. 1910.

Signed Joseph E. Bidwell, Jr., Clerk.

State of Illinois, County of Cook
Circuit Court of Cook County
Leland Giants Base Ball & Amusement Association
Vs.
Frank Leland's Chicago Giants Base Ball Club
Gen. No. 296934 Term No. 8218

Amended bill of complaint filed by complainants in the above entitled cause by leave of court first had and obtained.

Humbly complaining unto your Honor, your orator, the Leland Giants Base Ball & Amusement Association, a corporation, doing business in the State of Illinois by virtue of the laws of said Cook County, Illinois, respectfully shows unto your Honor that your orator is a going concern, and is the owner of the base ball team known as the Leland Giants, and that said team is now on the road playing base ball.

Your orator further shows unto your Honor that the said Moseley suggested that a corporation be formed, and that the same when formed take over the business name, Leland Giants, and good will of Frank C. Leland, trading and operating as the Leland Giants, which was agreed to, and later done by appointment upon proper application to the secretary of state by Willis V. Jefferson, Frank C. Leland, Beauregard F. Moseley as commissioners, to open books for the subscription to the capital stock of the Leland Giants Base Ball Club, which books in accordance with said license issued by the secretary of state were duly opened by the said commissioners, and subscriptions taken, whereupon the commissioners acting for the intended corporation received from Frank C. Leland under date of April 13th, 1907, a bill of sale conveying all goods and chattels, to-wit, twelve bats, five hundred cushions, two mitts, three mufflers, one thousand tickets, contract and use and occupancy of club park with John Schorling name and good will of the Leland Giants Base Ball Club, and all contracts with players and every right pertaining thereto belonging for the sum of Five Hundred Dollars ($500.00).

Your orator further shows unto your Honor that the said Frank C. Leland in said bill of sale vouched himself to be the true and lawful owner with good right and lawful authority to dispose of the same, and that he, for himself and heirs and executors and administrators would warrant and defend the said goods, chattels and property to the said parties of the second part, its heirs, executors, administrators and assigns against the lawful claims and demands of all and every person and person whomsoever.

Your orator further represents unto your Honor that this bill of sale was upon the formation of the Leland Giants Base Ball Association approved and accepted by the stockholders and stock was issued to the amount of Five Hundred Dollars ($500.00) to the said Frank C. Leland in payment therefore, and was filed for record in the Recorder's Office June 3rd, 1907, as document number 4045555, and recorded in book 9600 of records page 362.

Your orator further represents that the said Leland Giants Base Ball Association being duly organized in compliance with the laws of the State of Illinois, the Secretary of State issued to it the charter under date of April 20th, 1907, which charter was duly filed for record in Cook County, June 3rd, 1907, as document number 4045555, and recorded in book 156 of Corporation Records, page 353, and thereafter employed Andrew Foster, James Booker, George Wright, Nathan Harris, Harry Moore, Danger Talbert, William Norman, Walter Ball, Robert Winston and others as ball players at an expense of several thousand dollars, and assumed the lease with John Schorling of Auburn Park entered into by him with Frank C. Leland, elected officers, as follows: Major R.R. Jackson, President; John H. Bolden, First Vice-President; Willis V. Jefferson, Second Vice-President; Beauregard F. Moseley, Secretary and Treasurer, Frank C. Leland, Manager and Andrew Foster, captain and team manager, and began operating by advertising throughout Chicago and Illinois the name "Leland Giants" The Champion Colored Base Ball Team of the World, and played exhibition games, throughout the summer and fall of 1907, ending the season with a defeat in a single series of games played, winning 103 games— 32 games being shutouts, and losing one, and firmly establishing their title "The World's Champions" under the name of the "Leland Giants." Upon the uniform of each player was printed the words "Leland Giants." All contracts with reference to the team were known and referred to by the words "Leland Giants." Upon the literature used by the association was in large letters "L G" over the words "World's Colored Champions, Leland Giants, and as such the team was known throughout the country.

Your orator further represents and shows unto your Honor that in the fall of 1907, the stockholders of the Leland Giants Base Ball Association became convinced that its capital, Two Thousand Five Hundred Dollars ($2,500.00) was too small, and became desirous of increasing its capital stock. By regular vote of the stockholders its Board of Directors was authorized to pay off all its existing obligations, and to sell all of its assets, to-wit: All and singular the rights, privileges, powers, franchises, patents, royalties, grants, immunities and all property, real, personal and mixed, agreements, all debts due of whatever kind, and the name and good will of the "Leland Giants" to the Leland Giants Base Ball & Amusement Association, the complainants herein, which was subsequently done, and which bill of sale was duly executed by R.R. Jackson, President, and attested in the presence of Beauregard F. Moseley, Secretary & Treasurer, and file of record December 14th, 1907, as document number 4133218, and recorded in book 8424 of records, page 597, and thereupon your orator received in addition to said bill of sale, the bill of sale from Frank C. Leland to the Leland Giants Base Ball Association, and the records of Leland

Giants Base Ball Association, wherein said company have authorized the directors to act as trustee for the stockholders to receive and distribute from the Leland Giants Base Ball & Amusement Association, Fifty-Five Thousand Dollars ($55,000.00) worth of stock among the stockholders of the Leland Giants Base Ball Association, according to their holdings and share therein.

Your orator, the Leland Giants Base Ball & Amusement Association, was duly organized by virtue of a license issued by the secretary of state to Frank C. Leland, John H. Bolden, Willis V. Jefferson, Andrew Foster and Beauregard F. Moseley, as commissioners, to open books of subscription to the capital stock of your orator, and a charter on the 6th day of March, A.D., 1908, was issued by the said secretary of state to your orator, and filed of record in Cook County on March 17th, 1908, as document number 4173234, and recorded in book 143 of Corporation Records, page 129.

Your orator further shows unto your Honor that the officers elected for the year 1908 were Frank C. Leland, President and Booking Agent; R.R. Jackson, First Vice-President, Willis V. Jefferson, Second Vice-President, Beauregard F. Moseley, Secretary & Treasurer, John H. Bolden, Rink Manager and Andrew Foster, Manager & Captain.

Your orator further shows unto your Honor that it began operating its base ball team under the name Leland Giants, which name it had purchased from the Leland Giants Base Ball Association, which at a prior date purchased it from Frank C. Leland, one of the defendants herein, and under the name of Leland Giants your orator secured a place in the Chicago Base Ball League, and played exhibition games in said league and throughout the country under the name and style of Leland Giants; that said team was composed of thirteen or fourteen men at salaries ranging in monthly sums from One Hundred Dollars ($100.00) to One Hundred and Fifty Dollars ($150.00), or more, per month; that it caused each individual member of said team to wear uniforms upon the breast of which were the words "Leland Giants" and that in said uniforms and under said name your orator won the pennant in the Chicago City League as the champions of that organization, and that it was able by reason of its prowess as a base ball team to secure and play dates or a series of games with the National League Club, to-wit: The Cubs, and that it now has money invested in said name "Leland Giants" to a large amount; that its stationery and uniforms are placarded with said name, and that your orator has expended more than One Thousand Dollars ($1,000) in the past year in advertising said name, and that it has used, and is now using said name as a trademark, and that wherever the said name is used by your orator it is the means of securing a large attendance in an exhibition of base ball given by it, and it is a source of revenue and profit amounting to more than Thirty Thousand Dollars ($30,000.00) yearly.

Your orator further represents unto your Honor that on or about the 20th day of September, A.D., 1909, Frank C. Leland, then your orator's President was discharged as Booking Agent by reason of his activity in promoting another club to compete with your orator and that your orator was compelled to and did appoint Andrew Foster his successor, and that since that appointment of the said Andrew Foster, the said Andrew Foster has made engagements with various base ball clubs throughout the country and in the City of Chicago to play exhibition games of base ball during the year 1910, and is now with your orator's teams, the Leland Giants, engaged in playing games so arranged by him as a representative of your orator with various base ball teams in the country, and that it has cost your orator a large sum of money in uniforming and furnishing transportation to the members of its team, the Leland Giants, now under the direction of its representative, Andrew Foster, and traveling from town to town to play exhibition games of ball for the benefit and the interests of you orator.

Your orator further shows unto your Honor that said team is expected to return to the City of Chicago in the month of May, 1910, and play exhibition games of base ball at its own grounds 69th and Green Streets in the City of Chicago, that said grounds have been secured by your orator at a great cost of more than Three Thousand Dollars ($3,000.00); that upon the top of the grand stand has been erected a large sign upon which is printed in large bold letters "Home of the Leland Giants, City Champions," and on the west wing of said grand stand the words "Home of the Leland Giants," and on the east side of said grounds, and upon the fence enclosing same in two or more places the words "Leland Giants"; that contracts have been let for advertising with the newspapers, advertising the Leland Giants, and that your orator is now, and has been the recipient of money and profits accruing to it from the use of said team under said name, and that it would be injured to a great extent if others are permitted to use said name "Leland Giants" as a name for a base ball club, or in conjunction with a club of base ball players.

Your orator further shows unto your Honor that the said Frank C. Leland has no interest in the Leland Giants Base Ball & Amusement Association, or in its team, the Leland Giants, and that all representations to that effect are false, untrue and a libel and slander upon the rights of the complainant herein.

Your orator further represents that the said Frank C. Leland, and the Chicago Base Ball League as the Chicago League are now about to issue a Base ball schedule announcing the lineup of teams in the places where and when they will play upon the city circuit, giving the team now managed by the said Frank C. Leland, and the defendant, Frank Leland's Chicago Giants' lineup under the name and title of "Leland Giants" and that if such schedule is used it will be injurious to your orator, as it will be the impossible to recall such schedule when once issued and distributed, which your orator states is now about to be done by the said defendants to the great injury and ruin of your orator, except the same is restrained by the injunction of this Court, and if the said injunction is not issued without notice such injury will ensue, because your orator is informed, and so states the facts to be that upon any notice to them of your orator's intention to get an injunction restraining the use of the words "Leland Giants" said defendants will distribute at once said schedules.

Your orator further represents that the said Chicago Base Ball League and the said Frank C. Leland have no means or money other than that which the latter receives from his salary and the former from a percentage of the gate receipts of games played by the teams in its association.

But now so it is may it please your Honor that the said Frank C. Leland doing business as Frank Leland's Chicago Giants Base Ball Club, Frank C. Leland, Major R.R. Jackson, A.H. Garrett, Nathan Harris and the Chicago City League, a corporation, are combining and confederating together with diverse other persons at present unknown to your orator, whose names when discovered your orator prays it may be at liberty to insert herein with apt words that charge them as party defendants hereto, and contriving how to wrong and injury your orator in the premises; that the said Frank C. Leland, doing business as Frank Leland's Chicago Giants Base Ball Club, Frank C. Leland, Major R.R. Jackson, A.H. Garrett, Nathan Harris and the Chicago City League, a corporation, are advertising that a club of base ball players, which they claim to own and operate are the Leland Giants for the 1910, and are now advertising a tem or club of base ball players under the name of "Leland Giants" and have and are now writing letters to the owners of base ball teams, clubs and parks throughout the city and country announcing that they are the owners of the Leland Giants, and giving in their lineup such players as have been discharged by your orator, who were members of its club under the name "Leland Giants" last year for the sole purpose of conveying the idea to the public that their team is in reality the Leland Giants owned and operated by your orator, which representations are false, untrue and a fraud upon the rights of the complainant, your orator, the Leland Giants Base Ball & Amusement Associations, and a deception and deceit upon the public, and is resulting in much injury to your orator in this that the public is led to believe that your orator is playing exhibition games of base ball at one place, when it is really playing at another place; that games are being lost by the team owned and operated by the defendants there in before named under the name of Leland Giants, and as such has a tendency and effect of lowering and lessening the popularity and decreasing the attendance at games played by your orator's team, the Leland Giants, and thereby reducing considerably the receipts and profits which your orator is entitled to received by reason of the article of perfection to which it has brought its team under the name, title and description of the Leland Giants.

Your orator further represents that the said Frank C. Leland is wholly insolvent; that he was recently filed a schedule showing that he possessed practically nothing except this wearing apparel, and a salary received from this employment and that the injury he is perpetrating upon your orator is almost irreparable, and is continuous, and will be until the said Frank C. Leland and his confederates named herein are enjoyed by the writ of injunction from this Honorable Court restraining them from the use of said name, Leland Giants.

Your orator further shows unto your Honor that the consideration paid to the said Frank C. Leland for the use of the name Leland Giants was a valuable one, and that the said Frank C. Leland is now using the name to the detriment of your orator, all of which acts and doing and pretenses of the said Frank C. Leland and the defendants are contrary to equity and good conscience and tending to the manifest wrong and injury of your orator in the premises.

IN TENDER CONSIDERATION WHEREOF, and forasmuch as your orator is wholly remediless in the premises at and by the strict rules of Common Law, and cannot have adequate relief in the premises, except in a court of equity, where matters of this nature are properly cognizable and relievable.

To the end, therefore, that the said defendants, Frank Leland's Chicago Giants Base Ball Club, Frank C. Leland, Major R.R. Jackson, A.H. Garrett, Nathan Harris and the Chicago City League, a corp., may, if they can, show why your orator should not have the relief herein prayed and that they may full, true, direct and perfect answer make (but not under oath, answer under oath being hereby expressly waived) to all and singular the matters and things herein contained, and that in the mean time the said defendants, Frank Leland's Chicago Giants Base Ball Club, Frank C. Leland, Major R.R. Jackson, A.H. Garrett, Nathan Harris and the Chicago City League, a corporation, their counsel, solicitors, officers, agents or servants, may be restrained by an injunction of this Honorable Court from advertising or using the name of "Frank C. Leland" or "Leland Giants" in connection with the game of base ball, and that upon a final hearing of this cause such injunction may be made perpetual, and

That your orator may have such other and further relief in the premises as the nature of this case may require, and to your Honor shall see meet, according to equity and good conscience.

May it please your Honor to grant unto your orator the people's writ of injunction, issuing out of and under the seal of his Honorable Court, to be directed to the said Frank Leland's Chicago Giants Base Ball Club, Frank C. Leland, Major R.R. Jackson, A.H. Garrett, Nathan Harris and the Chicago City League, a corp., their counselors, attorneys, solicitors, officers, agents and servants, therein commanding them and each of them absolutely to desist and refrain from advertising or using the name of "Frank C. Leland" or the "Leland Giants" in connection with the game of base ball.

May it please your Honor to grant unto your orator the writ of summons in chancery issuing out of and under the seal of this Honorable Court, directed to the Sheriff of the said County of Cook, commanding him that he summon Frank Leland's Chicago Giants Base Ball Club, Frank C. Leland, Major R.R. Jackson, A.H. Garrett, Nathan Harris and the Chicago City League, to be and appear before this Honorable Court, then and there to stand to, abide and perform such order, direction and decree therein, as to your Honor shall seem meet, according to equity and good conscience, and

Your orator will ever pray.

Signed: Beauregard F. Moseley

Beauregard F. Moseley being duly sworn on oath deposes and says that he is secretary and treasurer of the Leland Giants Base Ball & Amusement Association, and as such, has authority to sign its name.

Affiant further says that he has read the foregoing bill and knows the contents thereof; that the same is true of his own knowledge, except as to the matters and things therein stated to be upon information and belief, and, as to those matters and things it is true.

Affiant further states the except an injunction issue herein as prayed for in said bill without notice the complainant will sustain irreparable injury in this— that the defendants, or some of them will issue a schedule using the name and distributing the same broadcast over the country, and further affiant, sayeth not.

Signed Beauregard F. Moseley

Subscribed and sworn to before me this 12th day of April, 1910

Agnes Murphy, Notary Public.

State of Illinois
County of Cook
Gen. No. 296934
Term No. 8218

A.H. Garrett, being first duly sworn deposes and says that he has read the foregoing answer and knows the contents thereof, and that the matters and things therein contained are true as therein set forth. Affiant further says that he is the Treasurer of the defendant making the above and foregoing answer. Affiant further says that Frank C. Leland and R.R. Jackson are respectively President and Secretary of the defendant making this answer, and that they the said Frank C. Leland and R.R. Jackson are out of the city, somewhere in the State of Louisiana with the defendant Base Ball team; and that each of them has been continuously out of the State of Illinois since April 8, 1910.

Signed, A.H. Garrett

Subscribed and sworn to before me this 18th day of April, A.D. 1910.

Louis B. Anderson, notary public.

Notes

Introduction

1. http://www.just-quotes.com/scott_fitzgerald_quotes.html
2. "Rollo Says... (column), *Pittsburgh Courier*, 11 October 1924."
3. The 1900 U.S. Census lists Foster as a day laborer, living in Calvert, Texas. Also noted in the 8 December 1912 edition of the *San Jose Mercury News*, Foster "spent his youth picking boll weevils off cotton. "
4. *San Antonio Daily Light*, 12 August 1899
5. Ibid.
6. *San Antonio Daily Light*, 14 August 1899.
7. *The Half-Century Magazine*, May 1919, 8.
8. Ibid.
9. *Fort Worth Morning Register*, 23 July 1901.
10. *Fort Worth Morning Register*, 4 August 1901.
11. *San Jose Mercury News*, 8 December 1912.
12. *Fort Worth Morning Register*, 4 July 1901.
13. *Otsego Union*, 31 July 1902.
14. *Otsego Union*, 7 August 1902.
15. *Otsego Union*, 14 August 1902.
16. "Dave Wyatt's 'Base Ball,'" *Indianapolis Freeman*, 10 March 1917, 7.
17. Email from Mr. Ryan Wieber, August 13, 2010.
18. *Otsego Union*, 14 August 1902.
19. Ibid.
20. Ibid.
21. *Otsego Union*, 21 August 1902.
22. *Otsego Union*, 24 September 1902.
23. *Chicago Daily Tribune*, 14 June 1910.
24. Leland thought to rename the Union Giants when W.S. Peters returned to the game in 1904 and incorporated a team in Springfield, Illinois, under the old name of Union Giants. In the process the Intercity Baseball Association ruled that league teams were forbidden to play against Peters' new club. *Chicago Daily Tribune*, 7 June 1904.

1st Inning

1. *New York Evening World*, 26 June 1903.
2. *Trenton Evening News*, 23 June 1903.
3. *New York Sun*, 8 February 1902.
4. *Philadelphia Item*, 17 April 1904.
5. *Jersey City Evening Journal*, 10 May 1907.
6. *Denver Daily News*, 29 April 1888.
7. Ibid.
8. When Sol White published his classic book in 1907, he picked Rube Foster to write a section on the science of pitching. Of equal importance was his selection of Grant "Home Run" Johnson to write his formula for successful hitting, entitled: "Art and Science of Hitting." By way of Findlay, Ohio, Johnson played five seasons in Cuba, 1907–12. In 156 island games, he got 175 hits in 549 at bats, with 11 doubles, eight triples and four home runs, for a .319 batting average. He led the Cuban Winter League in hits twice, becoming the first American to win a batting title in 1912 with a .410 average. When Foster re-organized the Leland Giants in 1910, he brought along Grant Johnson to play second base with Pop Lloyd at shortstop. That season they lost only six games in 129 contests. The following year, 1911, the double play duo of Johnson and Lloyd joined Lou Santop, Spot Poles, Smokey Joe Williams and Cannonball Dick Redding with the Lincoln Giants of New York. The Lincoln Giants won the unofficial World Colored Baseball title in 1912 and 1913. Teammate Arthur W. Hardy remembered Johnson as "One of those natural hitters." Hardy vocalized, "Oh man, he laid on it! He laid on it! The pitchers then overpowered the batters, like [Smokey Joe] Williams and [Cannonball Dick] Redding. They just threw the ball by you. Very few threw the change of pace. But Home Run Johnson would hit any and everything." Johnson later served as manager for the Lincoln Stars and the Brooklyn Royal Giants. During his fade years, he played with Pittsburgh Giants, Buffalo Colored Giants and the Pittsburgh Colored Stars at age 44.
9. The *Chicago Tribune* of March 24, 1901, reported that "Indian ball player secured by McGraw for Baltimore club." The paper noted, "At first Muggsey [McGraw] thought he was a Negro, and was about to tell him to move on when he noticed his straight, black hair. He walked over and took a look at him then asked him if he wasn't an

Indian. Tokie said he wasn't anything else, and he would show 'them guys' how to play ball if he only had a chance, so Mug told him to come on." On May 19, 1901, the *Washington Post,* under the banner of "McGraw Wants His Indian," wrote, "Charlie Grant, captain and second baseman of the Columbia Giants who was signed by McGraw of the Baltimore team early this season as an Indian, under the name of Tokohama, has been ordered to report to Baltimore at Boston on Monday." Currently, no evidence has been found of Grant playing for the Baltimore Orioles.

10. "Alligator Bag: Spoiled a Promising Career in Major League Baseball," *Washington African-American,* 17 September 1938.
11. *Chicago Daily Tribune*, 12 September 1904.
12. *Philadelphia Item*, 1 September 1904.
13. Ibid.
14. *Chicago Daily Tribune*, 12 September 1904.
15. *Chicago Daily Tribune*, 8 May 1905.
16. *Philadelphia Item*, 12 May 1905.
17. As the heavyweight boxing champion of the world, Jack Johnson completely destroyed the white supremacy myth with his body-and-mind dominance of white contenders. As champion, his "uppity" image was more recognizable then Frederick Douglass, W.E.B. DuBois, B.T. Washington, Bert Williams, Noble & Sissle, William Monroe Trotter, Ma Rainey, Jimmy Winkfield, Maggie Lena Walker, Mary Bethune, Bob Marshall, Paul Laurence Dunbar, Alain Locke, W.C. Handy, Claude McKay and other successfully prominent African Americans of the period. The "Galvestonian Gabber" defied conventional Jim Crowism with a belligerent attitude before there was a "Louisville Lip"; coupled with an extravagant life style of fur coats, expensive horseless buggies, gold karat teeth, studded shirts, and cufflinks with bling, defined his signature bravado. The self-promoter's reckless obsession with white women and quick marriages did not bode well with the current political climate of segregated America, as the nation's most visible black athlete. His flamboyant persona gave Americans, black and white, a suggestion of what may come by mixing of the races. The heavyweight champion of the world had become the heavyweight paperweight of racial progressions. In ranking popularity, or the ridicule barometer of public opinion, he surpassed black politicians, activists, entertainers, and writers of his day. A major figure in sports in general and the world globally, Jack Johnson was arguably the most profound image of blackness in white America's eyes.
18. Holway, John B. "Rube Foster: Father of Black Game," *The Sporting News,* 8 August 1981.
19. *Indianapolis Freeman*, 14 September 1907.
20. Robert Charles Cottrell. *The Best Pitcher in Baseball: The Life of Rube Foster, Negro League Giant (*New York. New York University Press,), 20.
21. *Harrisburg Telegraph*, 19 September 1905.
22. *Chicago Height Star*, 2 April 1908.
23. *Philadelphia Item*, 16 April 1906.
24. *The Half-Century Magazine*, May 1919, 8.
25. *New York Age*, 6 September 1906.
26. *Philadelphia Item*, 18 November 1906.
27. W. Rollo Wilson, "Thru the Eyes," *Pittsburgh Courier*, 20 January 1944.

2nd Inning

1. *Fort Worth Morning Register*, 24 February 1907.
2. *Englewood* (IL) *Times*, 19 July 1907.
3. *Indianapolis Freeman,* 8 October 1910.
4. *Englewood* (IL) *Times*, 9 August 1907.
5. *Indianapolis Freeman*, 8 October 1910.
6. When Joe Gans won his world lightweight boxing title in 1902, he became the first American-born black world title holder in any sport. Gans was famously known for his 42-round title defense in Goldfield, Nevada, against Oscar Nelson in 1906. Few boxing historians make note that future heavyweight champion Jack Johnson selected Gans as his trainer for the hyped 1910 "Great White Hope" fight with James Jeffries in Reno, Nevada. Gans is one of ten fighters to score more than 100 knockouts professionally.
7. "Rube Foster in Star Roll: Pitches No Hit, No Run Game," *Indianapolis Freeman*, 28 September 1907.
8. Byron E. Clarke, "Some Queer Catchers," *Duluth News-Tribune*, 8 August 1907.
9. Tom Simon, ed., "*Deadball Stars of the National League*" (Washington, D.C.: Brassey's, 2004).
10. *Indianapolis Freeman*, 7 September 1907.
11. *Indianapolis Freeman*, 14 September 1907.
12. *Chicago Daily Tribune*, 28 August 1907.
13. *Indianapolis Freeman*, 7 September 1907.
14. *Celebrate the Century: A Collection of Commemorative Stamps* (Richmond, VA: Time-Life Books, 1998–2000), 21.
15. *Indianapolis Freeman*, 7 September 1907.
16. Tom Cowan and Jack Maguire, *Timelines of African American History: 500 Years of Black Achievement* (New York: Roundtable Press/Perigee Books, 1994).
17. *Chicago Daily Tribune*, 28 August 1907.
18. Ibid.
19. Ibid.
20. The Fifteenth Amendment (1870) was the third of the Reconstruction amendments. This amendment prohibited states and the federal government from using a citizen's ethnicity or previous status as a slave as a voting

qualification. By providing people of color the right to vote, the amendment granted them citizenship, basically overturning the Supreme Court decision in the Dred Scott case of 1857, which ruled that because slaves were not citizens, they could not sue in courts.

21. *Indianapolis Freeman*, 21 September 1907.
22. *Indianapolis Freeman*, 12 October 1907.
23. *Chicago Broad Ax*, 16 May 1908.
24. *Chicago Broad Ax*, 12 October 1907.
25. *Englewood* (IL) *Times*, 5 June 1908.
26. *Indianapolis Freeman*, 27 June 1908.
27. Ibid.
28. *Chicago Daily Tribune*, 8 August 1908.
29. *Suburban Economist*, 5 June 1908.
30. *Chicago Daily Tribune*, 4 June 1908.
31. *Detroit Free Press*, 8 August 1908.
32. *Indianapolis Freeman*, 1 August 1908.
33. *Englewood* (IL) *Times*, 21 May 1909.
34. *Indianapolis Freeman*, 15 May 1909.
35. *Indianapolis Freeman*, 12 June 1909.
36. *Chicago Daily Tribune*, 13 July 1909.
37. *Indianapolis Freeman*, 19 June 1909.
38. *Chicago Daily Tribune*, 19 October 1909.
39. Todd Peterson, "Can You Hear the Noise?" *Baseball Research Journal 36*, Society for American Baseball Research.
40. *Chicago Daily News*, 19 June 1909.
41. *Hibbing Daily Tribune*, 16 July 1910.
42. "Gopher-Leland Series," *Twin City Star*, 21 July 1910.
43. "Independents," *Minneapolis Tribune*, 18 July 1909.
44. "Gopher-Leland Series," *Twin City Star*, 21 July 1910.
45. In 1962, the *Chicago Defender* reported that 84-year old Joe Green's leg was amputated as a result of the injury suffered in 1909. He would die a week later in Cook County Hospital, which was built on the former property of the Chicago Cubs, West Side Grounds. After the 1909 season, Green joined the Chicago Giants and became manager in 1921. He was known for his comedy routines on the diamond and considered an excellent manager.
46. *Chicago Daily Tribune*, 22 October 1909.
47. *Chicago Daily Tribune*, 19 October 1909.
48. *Chicago Defender*, 21 August 1948.
49. *Chicago Defender*, 27 January 1965.
50. *Chicago Daily Tribune*, 23 October 1909.
51. Ibid.
52. *Chicago Defender*, 27 January 1965.
53. *Chicago Defender*, 21 August 1948.
54. John B. Holway, "Rube Foster: Father of Black Game," *The Sporting News*, 8 August 1981.
55. *The Half-Century Magazine*, March 1919, 8.
56. *Chicago Defender*, 31 July 1909.

3rd Inning

1. The Pekin Theatre was called by Dempsey Travis "the formal cradle of Negro drama in the United States," and considered one of the first northern venues to feature jazz musical performances. Owned by noted gambler Robert T. Motts, the Pekin Theatre billed itself as "Home of the Colored Race." The legacy of the Pekin, as the race's first modern theatre, was so expansive that venues all over the country caught the "Pekin fever" by taking on the name of Chicago's most famous race house. It was also here where black patrons could see film of Jack Johnson's fights. Davarian L. Baldwin, *Chicago's New Negroes: Modernity, the Great Migration, and Black Urban Life* (Chapel Hill: University of North Carolina Press, 2007, 47, 100,111.
2. *Chicago Broad Ax*, 13 June 1908.
3. Advertisement, *Chicago Broad Ax*, 13 June 1908.
4. *Chicago Broad Ax*, 6 June 1908.
5. *Chicago Broad Ax*, 16 January 1909.
6. *Chicago Broad Ax*, 23 April 1910.
7. This case brief was written (January 13, 2010) by attorney Branden Gregory of the Williams & Morris, LLC, law firm, at 1509 Washington Avenue, Ste. 660 in Saint Louis, MO 63103.
8. *Indianapolis Freeman*, 4 February 1911.
9. *New York Times*, 6 October 1913.
10. *New York Times*, 17 September 1910, reports, "Rube Foster's Leland Giants, a strong colored aggregation, will make their first appearance in this city tomorrow in a double-header against the Stamford team and the [All-Star] Manhattans at Olympic Field. The Giants claim to have won thirty-five straight games up to the time they left Chicago last week." The *Times* also reports that the Giants have won 101 out of 104 games this season, and Foster will pitch both games of the double-header for the Giants.
11. *Chicago Daily Tribune*, 12 June 1910.

12. *Chicago Defender*, 27 August 1910.
13. *Chicago Daily Tribune*, 6 June 1910.
14. *Chicago Defender*, "In the Wake of the News," 17 December 1930. Park owner W.C. "Bill" Niesen wrote, "Rube Foster, former colored baseball player and manager is dead. To me, Rube was an honorable gentleman and a great and true sportsman. He was one of the greatest baseball pitchers and managers I ever have known. Foster and [Jose] Mendez, I believe, were the equal of any white pitchers of their day. As a manager, Rube was one of the best."
15. *Palm Beach Daily News*, 26 January 1910.
16. *Chicago Broad Ax*, 12 March 1910.
17. *Chicago Broad Ax*, 16 April 1910.
18. *Chicago Broad Ax*, 28 May 1910.
19. *Chicago Broad Ax,* 4 June 1910.
20. *Chicago Defender*, 28 May 1910.
21. *Indianapolis Freeman*, 8 October 1910.
22. Ibid.
23. Indianapolis Freeman, 10 September 1910.
24. Chicago Defender, 4 January 1941.
25. Chicago Daily Tribune, 11 March 1911.
26. Chicago Defender, 4 January 1941.
27. Dave Zirin, "The Hidden History of Muhammad Ali." *International Socialist Review.* Issue 33, January–February 2004.
28. Chicago Defender, 13 August 1910.
29. "Unforgivable Blackness: The Rise and Fall of Jack Johnson" by Florentine Films and PBS, 2004.
30. *Chicago Defender*, 6 August 1910.
31. *Chicago Daily Tribune*, 15 April 1910.
32. *Chicago Daily News*, 29 November 1910.
33. *Indianapolis Freeman,* 4 February 1911.
34. *New York Times*, 4 December 1910.
35. *New York Times*, 18 December 1910.
36. *Chicago Broad Ax*, 26 November 1910.
37. *Chicago Broad Ax*, 31 December 1910.

4th Inning

1. "John Schorling, Former Ball Park Owner, Dies at 74," *Chicago Defender*, 30 March 1940.
2. *Chicago Daily Tribune*, 9 May 1911.
3. *Fort Wayne Sentinel*, 1 October 1912.
4. *Los Angeles Times*, 18 October 1912.
5. *Los Angeles Times*, 30 October, 1912.
6. *Los Angeles Times*, 9 November 1912.
7. *Chicago Defender*, 29 August 1942. The no-hitter occurred on June 6, 1921.
8. *Albany* (GA) *Herald*, 30 June 1926. The no-hitter occurred on June 29, 1926.
9. *San Diego Union*, 7 December 1912.
10. *San Diego Union*, 9 December 1912.
11. *San Diego Union*, 12 December 1912.
12. *San Diego Union*, 9 February 1913.
13. *San Diego Union*, 23 March 1913.
14. *Chicago Defender*, 10 May 1913.
15. William F. McNeil, in *The California Winter League: America's First Integrated Professional Baseball League*, on page 42 quotes the *Chicago Defender*: "Never before in the history of baseball have a colored team accomplished what the American Giants under the leadership and management of Andrew (Rube) Foster, have accomplished on their present trip on the Pacific Coast. They have won the highest praise from the fans and citizens everywhere they have played; not only for their high-class baseball playing, but also for their gentlemanly conduct on the ball field." McNeil adds, on page 13, that Foster brought the first Negro team to California to compete in the 1910–11 winter league.
16. "American Giants Won Pennant in the Winter League of the Coast," *Grand Forks Daily Herald*, 31 December 1912.
17. "Rube Foster Loses $600 Ring, *The Lake County Times*, 19 July 1917.
18. "Rube Foster Has Won 23 Straight," *Duluth News Tribune*, 19 September 1914.
19. *Indianapolis Freeman*, 18 July 1914.

5th Inning

1. The Federal League, founded in 1912, lasted two years as a major league, 1914–1915. The eight-team league was represented by Chicago, St. Louis, Pittsburgh, Brooklyn, Baltimore, Buffalo, Indianapolis, and Kansas City. Some of the prominent Major League players who joined the Federal League and later became Hall of Famers included Bill McKechnie, Chief Bender, Mordecai Brown, Eddie Plank, Edd Roush and Joe Tinker. Brown and Tinker played at times with the Chicago Whales. During the 1914–15 off-season, the Federal League owners filed an antitrust lawsuit

against the American and National Leagues. Future Commissioner Judge Kenesaw Mountain Landis presided over the case but refused to rule on it. Unable to sustain capital funding, teams folded, as the lawsuit dragged though the court system and was never resolved.

2. *Chicago Defender*, 9 October 1915.
3. *Chicago Defender*, 20 November 1915.
4. *Chicago Defender*, 11 December 1915.
5. *Chicago Defender*, 29 April 1916.

6th Inning

1. Author's interview, St. Louis, MO, Webb's home, 17 February 1990.
2. Author's interview, St. Louis, MO, James Bell's home, 17 February 1990.
3. John B. Holway, *Voices from the Great Black Baseball Leagues* (New York: Dodd, Mead Company, 1975) 70.
4. John B. Holway, *Voices from the Great Black Baseball Leagues* (New York: Dodd, Mead Company, 1975) 39.
5. Ibid.
6. Author's interview, St. Louis, MO, James Bell's home, 17 February 1990.
7. John B. Holway, *Black Diamonds: Life in the Negro Leagues from the Men Who Lived It.* (Westport, CT: Meckler Books, 1989), 39.
8. John B. Holway, *Voices from the Great Black Baseball Leagues* (New York: Dodd, Mead Company, 1975), 169.
9. John B. Holway, *Voices from the Great Black Baseball Leagues,* (New York: Dodd, Mead Company, 1975), 70.
10. Charles E. Whitehead, *A Man and His Diamonds: The Story of Rube Foster.* (New York: Vantage Press, 1980), 139.
11. John B. Holway, "Rube Foster: Father of Black Game," *The Sporting News,* 8 August 1981.
12. John B. Holway, *Voices from the Great Black Baseball Leagues* (New York: Dodd, Mead Company, 1975), 107.
13. *Chicago Defender*, 2 November 1918.
14. *Chicago Defender*, 12 October 1918.
15. *Chicago Defender*, 2 November 1918.
16. *Chicago Defender*, 2 August 1919.

7th Inning

1. *Fort Wayne News Sentinel*, 25 August 1920.
2. State of Illinois decree to dissolve the Negro National League of Professional Baseball Clubs, signed by M.S. Szymczak, on June 5, 1929, a clerk of the Superior Court. File number #49074.
3. Davarian L. Baldwin, *Chicago's New Negroes: Modernity, the Great Migration, and Black Urban Life* (Chapel Hill: University of North Carolina Press, 2007), 211.

8th Inning

1. *Chicago Defender*, 17 November 1923.
2. *Chicago Defender*, 24 November 1923.
3. Ibid.
4. Department of Labor, Consumer Price Index, Bureau of Labor Statistics.
5. Wanted poster issued by the New York City Police Department, July 25, 1925, stating "Wanted for Murder." Brown had killed Benjamin Adair, a man, in a barroom fight over some cocaine, on April 28, 1925. He played under the alias "Lefty Wilson" for Gilkerson's Union Giants of Spring Valley, Illinois, and other town teams in like the Bertha Minnesota Fishermen, the Sioux City Iowa Kary Alls Club, and the Little Falls Minnesota Independents. He was last seen in 1930 and his passing is unrecorded.
6. *Chicago Defender*, 20 February 1915.
7. Larry Lester. *Baseball's First Colored World Series: The 1924 Meeting of the Hilldale Giants and Kansas City Monarchs* (Jefferson, NC: McFarland, 2006), 33.
8. John B. Holway, "Rube Foster: Father of Black Game," *The Sporting News,* 8 August 1981
9. Charles E. Whitehead, *A Man and His Diamonds: The Story of Rube Foster* (New York: Vantage Press, 1980), 139.
10. Ibid.
11. *Pittsburgh Courier*, 3 January 1925.
12. Ibid.
13. *Philadelphia Tribune,* 10 January 1925.
14. *Chicago Defender*, 31 January 1925.
15. *Philadelphia Tribune*, 14 February 1925.
16. Ibid.

9th Inning

1. The *Philadelphia Tribune* of June 6, 1925 reports Mrs. Eubanks's first name as Alfreda, and that Foster's unconscious body was found at 9 am (not 10am), in (not near) the bathtub.

2. "Roundy Says," from the *Wisconsin State Journal*, 7 July 1938, reported Foster was born in La Grange, Texas. However, the 1880 census shows young Foster living in Winchester (about 18 miles NW of La Grange) with parents.

3. Trimble was reported to have been committed to a mental institution by his brother in the *Chicago Defender*, 7 August 1948, page 10.

4. There have been references to a lawsuit between the Foster family and John Schorling. In 1928, when Schorling sold the American Giants to florist William E. Trimble, while Andrew Foster was in the mental institution, it was reported that Sarah Foster contested the sale of the team, claiming her husband had part ownership. The author was not able to locate any legal filings involving the two parties. A search by archivist Jeanie Child on May 18, 1995, from the Office of the Circuit Court Clerk of Cook County, yielded no legal documents regarding these allegations.

5. *Sepia*, 24 July 1955.

Extra Innings

1. *Pittsburgh Courier*, 7 December 1930.
2. *Pittsburgh Courier*, 3 January 1931.
3. *Pittsburgh Courier*, 10 January 1931.
4. Letter from James P. Finley, Fort Huachuca Museum Director, dated 19 October 1996.
5. Cornelius C. Smith, Jr., *Fort Huachuca: The Story of a Frontier Post* (Washington, D.C.: Department of the Army, 1978).
6. *Pittsburgh Courier*, 7 August 1943.
7. Ibid.
8. Fort Huachuca was established on March 3, 1877, by Captain Samuel Marmaduke Whitside. Whitside had found the mouth of the Huachuca Canyon, where mountains formed a natural barrier to attacks from marauding Apaches. There was plenty of tall grass (for the horses), lots of cool water, timber for construction and an abundance of wild game to supplement the soldiers' usual diet of beans and hardtack (saltless, hard crackers). Ethel Jackson Price, *Fort Huachuca* (Charleston, SC: Arcadia, 2004), 8.
9. A.S. Doc Young, "What About Rube?" *Los Angeles Sentinel,* 9 September 1976.
10. A.S. Doc Young, "Oh, Happy Day!" *Los Angeles Sentinel*, 19 March 1981.

Bibliography

Newspapers and Magazines

Albany (GA) Herald
Albert Lea (MN) Evening Tribune
Anaconda (MT) Standard
Appleton (WI) Post-Crescent
Baltimore Afro-American
Benton Harbor (MI) Daily Palladium
Big Spring (TX) Daily Herald
Boston Daily Globe
Brookshire (TX) Eagle
Brownsville (TX) Daily Herald
Capital Times (Madison, WI)
Carthage (TX) Panola Watchman
Cedar Rapids (IA) Evening Gazette
Charleston (WV) Gazette
Chicago Broad Ax
Chicago Daily Tribune
Chicago Defender
Chicago Heights Star
Chicago Inter-Ocean
Commerce (TX) Journal
Cumberland (MD) Evening
Daily Globe (Ironwood, MI)
Danville (VA) Bee
Decatur (IL) Daily Review
Denver Daily News
Des Moines (IA) Daily News
Detroit Free Press
Duluth News-Tribune
Englewood (IL) Economist
Englewood Times
Evening Independent (Massillon, OH)
Fitchburg (MA) Daily Sentinel
Fort Wayne (IN) Journal-Gazette
Fort Wayne (IN) News-Sentinel
Fort Wayne (IN) Sentinel
Fort Worth (TX) Morning Register
Fresno (CA) Bee
Galveston (TX) Daily News
Grand Folks Daily Herald
Half-Century Magazine
Hartford (CN) Courant
Hibbing Daily Tribune
Indianapolis Freeman
Indianapolis Star
Janesville (WI) Daily Gazette
Jersey City (NJ) Evening Journal
Kansas City (MO) Call
Kansas City (MO) Globe-Journal
Kingsport (TN) Times
Kokomo (IN) Tribune
LaCrosse (WI) Tribune
Lake County Times
Laredo (TX) Times
Letherbridger (Alberta, Canada) Herald
Lima (OH) News
Logansport (IN) Pharos-Reporter
Lowell (MA) Sun
Mansfield (OH) News
Mexia (TX) Evening Ledger
Minneapolis Tribune
New Castle (PA) News
New York Evening World
New York Sun
New York Times
New York Tribune
Oakland (CA) Tribune
Oelwein (IA) Daily Register
Ogden (UT) Standard-Examiner
Oshkosh (WI) Daily Northwestern
Otsego (MI) Union
Philadelphia Evening Item
Piqua (OH) Daily Call
Pittsburgh Courier
Pittsburg Post
Racine (WI) Daily Journal
Reno (NV) Evening Gazette
San Antonio (TX) Daily Light
San Antonio (TX) Express
San Antonio (TX) Light
San Jose Mercury News
Seguin (TX) Post Gazette Enterprise
Sepia Publications
Star Publications (Chicago, IL)
Suburbanite Economist (Chicago, IL)
Syracuse (NY) Herald
Trenton (NJ) Evening Times
Tucson (AZ) Daily Citizen
Twin City Star
Victoria (TX) Daily Advocate
Washington Post
Weimar (TX) Daily Tribune
Weimar (TX) Mercury
Williamsport (PA) Daily Gazette & Bulletin

Books, Articles, Entries, Chapters

Brennan, Gerald E. "*Foster, Andrew 'Rube'*." In *Biographical Dictionary of American Sports, Baseball*, David L. Porter, ed. (Westport, CT: Greenwood Press, 2000); 489–491.

Cottrell, Robert Charles. *The Best Pitcher in Baseball: The Life of Rube Foster, Negro League Giant*. New York: New York University Press, 2001.

Malloy, Jerry. "Rube Foster and Black Baseball in Chicago." *Baseball in Chicago*, Chicago Regional Chapter of SABR, 1986; 24–27.

Peterson, Robert. "Men Who Changed Baseball." *Boy's Life* 72, August 1972; 14–17.

Reilly, Edward J. "Foster, Andrew 'Rube'." In *Baseball: An Encyclopedia of Popular Culture*. Santa Barbara, CA: ABC-CLIO, 2000; 105.

Toole, Andrew O. "Now Is the Time: Rube Foster." In *The Best Man Plays: Major League Baseball and the Black Athlete, 1901–2002*. Jefferson, NC: McFarland & Company, Inc., Publishers, 2003; 7–24.

Whitehead, Charles E. *A Man and His Diamonds*. New York: Vantage Press, 1980.

Young, Frank. "Rube Foster — The Master Mind of Baseball." *Abbott's Monthly*, November 1930; 42–49, 93.

Index

Abbreviations RF and AG stand for Rube Foster and American Giants. Page numbers for Notes contain both chapter and note identifiers (e.g., 244n5:1 indicates page 244, chapter 5, note 1). Page numbers in ***bold italics*** indicate photographs, sketches, caricatures, and newspaper advertisements.